£1.30

Buying a property
IRELAND

Nguides

Contents

08
Letting Your Property 261

09
References 275

Index 303
Colour Touring Maps
end of guide

Author's Acknowledgements

Cathy Gerrard would like to say 'Thanks to all my family (Mide for planning advice, Peter for historical perspective, Esther for research, Ailbhe for proofreading and lots of discussion, Mena for architectural consultancy, Joy and John for long-distance support), to Monica and Kate for being two corners of the Dublin-Biot-Rome 'Buying a Property' support network and to Frank for keeping me calm and well-fed in the midst of huge upheaval for him. Thanks also to Rupert Wheeler at Navigator Guides for commisioning the book and to all the people who contributed their experiences of moving to Ireland.'

About the authors

Cathy Gerrard was born in Dublin, brought up in Co. Tipperary and has lived in Hungary, Italy and New York. She has worked as a language teacher, as director of a language school and as a writer for an e-learning company. She now works as a freelance writer and editor. She has renovated a house in Dublin – dealing with renegade builders, discovering an unusual 18th-century roof and becoming an expert on regulations for listed buildings were just part of the process. She's now in the midst of getting planning permission for another project, and these experiences underpin much of this book.

Joseph McArdle is a member of both the Irish and English Bars. He has practised commercial law in Ireland, worked in London, Nigeria, Kenya and Brussels, and for the past ten years has been a legal consultant to newly independent countries in Eastern Europe, Central Asia, the Balkans and the Caucasus.

Conceived and produced for Cadogan Guides by **Navigator Guides Ltd**, The Old Post Office, Swanton Novers, Melton Constable, Norfolk, NR24 2AJ
info@navigatorguides.com
www.navigatorguides.com

Cadogan Guides
Network House
1 Ariel Way
London W12 7SL
info@cadoganguides.co.uk
www.cadoganguides.com

The Globe Pequot Press
246 Goose Lane, PO Box 480, Guilford, Connecticut 06437–0480

Cover design: Sarah Rianhard-Gardner
Cover and photo essay photographs © Tim Mitchell
Editor: Susannah Wight
Proofreader: Mary Sheridan
Indexing: Isobel McLean

Printed in Italy by Legoprint

A catalogue record for this book is available from the British Library
ISBN 1-86011-160-2

The author and publishers have made every effort to ensure the accuracy of the information in this book at the time of going to press. However, they cannot accept any responsibility for any loss, injury or inconvenience resulting from the use of information contained in this guide.

Please help us to keep this guide up to date. We have done our best to ensure that the information in it is correct at the time of going to press. But places are constantly changing, and rules and regulations fluctuate. We would be delighted to receive any comments concerning existing entries or omissions. Authors of the best letters will receive a copy of the Cadogan Guide of their choice.

Introduction

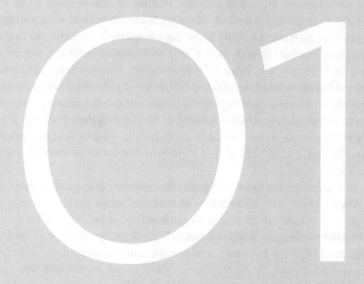

You may be thinking of buying a property in Ireland because your company is moving you to work there; you may have decided to set up a business and start a new life; or you may be buying a flat because sterling is so strong against the euro that it seems a wise investment. You may know everything there is to know about the country, the culture and the process of buying property, or perhaps nothing at all. There are as many reasons to buy a home here as there are individuals wanting to buy. This book aims to be a practical handbook to the nitty-gritty of buying a home, from selecting an area and a house, through financial and legal requirements and potential pitfalls, down to the nuances of which telephone supplier to choose. It also tries to give a sense of some of the intangible things that draw people to Ireland, with profiles of the regions and some information about the history and local architecture. This will help you to get an idea of the place and what might have happened in the cottage, bungalow or Georgian country house that you plan to buy, who lived there and why the building is the way it is.

Throughout the book you'll find personal anecdotes from people who have taken the plunge and committed to Ireland in the most tangible way possible – by buying property. Some have set up businesses, some are retirees, some are bringing up children. Some have found the whole process easy, others less straightforward. Some bought years ago, others more recently. We hope that these people's stories will help you to learn from their experiences and to anticipate potential hitches – or simply to be entertained.

First Steps and Reasons for Buying introduces you to Ireland and runs though the reasons people choose to buy property in Ireland; it also has information on residency, visas and permits. **Profiles of the Regions** gives an overview of each county in Ireland, including Northern Ireland, with average house prices in each county or city. **Selecting a Property** introduces you to the Irish property market, as well as the pros and cons of restoring property, building from scratch and buying for investment. The two legal chapters, **Making the Purchase** and **Financial Implications**, explain everything you need to know about the process of buying the property, from the tax implications to how to bid at auction. Finally, **Settling In** and **Letting your Property** give you a wealth of information about living in Ireland – taxes, schools, shops, food and driving, and how to ensure an income from your property if it is a second home.

Note: In any guidebook like this, things will inevitably change after publication. Always check any information given here before making decisions based on it. This book concentrates on the Republic of Ireland – but it gives relevant information on **Northern Ireland**, particularly where this differs from Britain. There are full profiles of the six counties and information on politics and education. When Northern Ireland is not mentioned, you can assume that the situation is similar to that in Britain.

First Steps and Reasons for Buying

02

A Note about the Use of Irish in the Text

When giving Irish and English terms, the Irish word is placed first and the English translation in brackets afterwards when the Irish term is the most commonly used – for example, Dáil (Parliament) and Gaeltacht (Irish-speaking area). However, occasionally the English term is used more frequently and in this case the English comes first with the Irish in brackets – for example, the Constitution of Ireland (Bunreacht na hÉireann). Where the word is difficult to pronounce, suggested pronunciation is given in brackets.

This book aims to help you buy a house in Ireland and is structured to help you with all the practicalities – where to buy, how to make the purchase, tax implications and so on. But before you embark on your voyage you'll need to ask yourself some questions about your motivations. The lure of Ireland may be emotional, it may be romantic, it may be pre-eminently practical or perhaps triggered by a sense of something lacking where you live now. This chapter first explores the reasons people come to Ireland to live and the reasons for buying property in the country; the second part of the chapter gives basic information about visas, permits, taxes and other paperwork.

Why Ireland?

It is striking how difficult most people find it to explain why they want to live in Ireland. 'We just love it here,' is the most common reply to the query. There are probably as many reasons for moving to Ireland as there are immigrants, but some themes recur. Some attractions have brought people here for decades – the landscape, the people and the myriad connections between Britain and Ireland – and there are also newer motivations: a changing Ireland that offers more ways of making a living, more routes and cheaper air fares between the two countries as well as a booming property market that has meant windfall gains for many house-buyers.

Landscape and the Pace of Life

Landscape may be one of the biggest draws. Every guide book will tell you how much variety is packed into Ireland, but you may not really believe it until you've travelled around the country and marvelled at how this tiny island fits so much into so little space. A couple of hours' drive, from the Clare coast to inland Tipperary, for example, will take you from rocky coasts and long sandy strands through dramatically different landscapes – tiny stony fields, wide open bogs, rolling mountains, rich farmland and majestic trees. Ireland still has one of the lowest population densities in Europe and you can find many completely unspoilt regions.

Weather is another draw, if not in the generally accepted sense. Light and air feel different in Ireland. People don't come for bright sunshine and warmth but they do come for the colours – clear water-washed blues, pewter greys and a million different greens – and the huge skies. In the west the sky can change every few minutes, from great white mushroomy clouds with sun glinting from behind them to clouds ringed with purple and gold as the sun sets and every shade of blue and grey in between. On a fine day Ireland is one of the best places in the world to be.

One of the most common clichés about Ireland is that things move slowly, but it is also absolutely true. Outside the cities life does move at a slower pace. It is genuinely possible to get away from everything and, perhaps, to start over again, if that's what you want to do.

The People

The friendliness of the Irish is legendary. Without falling into cliché, the Irish are open, courteous and genuinely interested in you. You will be struck by the friendliness with which the Irish treat strangers. In the country people will always salute you as you pass, be it on foot, by bicycle or in a car. Grizzled old farmers will tip their caps, motorists will raise a finger from the wheel and children will wave enthusiastically from roadside farms. People will strike up conversations at bus stops, on trains and in the pub. The Irish do not approve of reticence; you are expected to recount your life story and especially your views on the place. 'How are you getting on?' is a common query. For although a new confidence has arrived with the affluence of the 1990s, Ireland is always curious to know what other people think of her, and anxious not to be found wanting.

Cultural and Economic Links between Britain and Ireland

Ireland and Britain, despite a turbulent history, have many cultural similarities and economic links. Many of those planning a move to Ireland have direct family connections. The writer Pete McCarthy wrote a whole book, *McCarthy's Bar*, about looking for a sense of belonging in Ireland despite being born and brought up in Britain. (The book isn't all about inner musings and identity; it is also a very funny account of his travels around the island.) Ireland is the UK's fifth largest export market and the UK is Ireland's largest market. Many Irish people have lived in Britain and feel more at home there than in other European countries; statistics show that 5 per cent of Ireland's population currently lives in London. The 2002 Census in the Irish Republic showed that 2.7 per cent of the Republic's population holds UK citizenship (many of these are Irish nationals who lived and worked in the UK at some point) and that 6.4 per cent of the population was born in the UK (including Northern Ireland). In total, including Irish citizens returning to Ireland, immigration from the UK into Ireland over the last 4 years has reached almost 120,000 people, increasing the Republic's population by a massive 3 per cent.

The crossovers extend to the media and other areas. Irish consumers have easy access to UK television, radio and newspapers, and share many British tastes in food, drink and fashion. Irish plays are performed to packed houses in Britain and British soaps are avidly followed in Ireland. More than half of Ireland's soccer team is British-born, and Manchester United is passionately followed across the country – most famously by Bertie Ahern, the Taoiseach (pronounced Tee-shock) or Prime Minister. Indeed, Manchester United's captain, Roy Keane, is from Cork.

Today, now that the poverty that led so many to emigrate has been eradicated and Ireland stands confidently on the world stage, many Irish people focus on the more positive aspects of their relationship with Britain. Sport is one area where the shift in attitudes is clear. There was a time when Ireland would automatically support whoever was playing against the English. Now this attitude is changing – during the 2003 Rugby World Cup many Irish people, sometimes without really acknowledging it, hoped that the Brits would win.

Quite simply, moving to Ireland means that you are not going that far away – it is quite different from making a decision to move to France, Spain or perhaps Florida. Conversely, the very familiarity of the place might lull you into thinking that it is more like the UK than it really is.

A Changing Ireland

Ireland has gone through enormous change very quickly and is asking what from the past it should keep and what it should discard. A theme that comes up again and again is that of two Irelands existing side by side. One is the Ireland of the Celtic Tiger – big cars and bigger wallets. In this Ireland you find American style brunch complete with Bloody Marys, every imaginable variety of latte, designer clothes, sunglasses and babies. This Ireland is confident, savvy, forward-looking and energetic. Some might say that it is materialistic, losing touch with the comforts and certainties of the past; others say it is casting off the shackles of the past and looking to the future. Then there is another Ireland, where a pub owner won't have any idea what an espresso is, where old women cross themselves passing a church, where old men wear ancient caps shiny with decades of use and hold their coats together with twine, and where the only vegetables you'll find are carrots and cabbages.

This, of course, is far too simplistic. We could add another 40 Irelands in between – that of the immigrant Chinese person working in a newsagent, of the Dutch organic farmer selling sausages in a Saturday farmers' market, of the American computer engineer whose children are growing up Irish. I could list as

The Celtic Tiger

It's gone, officially as of 7 November 2001. But what was it, and why do Irish people refer to it all the time? Simply put, the term refers to the 10 years from 1990 or thereabouts up until 2001 when the Irish economy expanded exponentially and parts of the country were utterly transformed.

Dublin became one of the most popular weekend destinations in Europe, a brand new cultural quarter was planned and built, a new financial district was created, unemployment fell to negligible levels, emigration, a staple of the Irish experience, almost died away, while immigration reached record levels. Property prices in the capital quadrupled and then doubled again, thousands of new restaurants opened, and all changed utterly.

At the same time corruption scandals revealed that much of the development was eased on its way by the proffering, and acceptance, of substantial amounts of cash in brown envelopes to various elected representatives who then salted away their gains in illegal offshore bank accounts. Tribunals investigating planning irregularities are still ongoing and fresh revelations are still occurring.

The reasons for the Tiger's leap forward are disputed: some put it all down to EU funds, others to a 10 per cent (now 12.5 per cent) corporate tax rate that encouraged thousands of American technology firms to set up their European operations in Ireland, and others to the young, motivated and highly educated population. The reason is probably a mixture of all the above, with a certain amount of self-fulfilling prophecy thrown into the mix. As the economy grew and reports circulated about the miraculous growth levels, thousands of former emigrants returned from abroad to start new lives in Ireland, injecting fresh dynamism into the economy.

many as there are individuals. The basic point is that homogeneity, once such a feature of Irish life, is disappearing. If you plan to live here permanently you will probably see even more changes. For example, new waves of immigration are likely to change the face of Ireland; anyone visiting a maternity hospital cannot but be struck by the numbers of babies being born to foreign parents. Similarly, the parents of children going to primary school (particularly in the cities) will also notice the newly multicultural nature of the classes. For new immigrants most of this will be positive. People moving here even 10 or 15 years ago had to be prepared to give up lots of things: the latest films, good wine and food, and eating out. Today all this is completely changing – art house cinemas are opening up in small towns, a small army of artisan producers and organic farmers are ensuring that food is improving beyond all recognition, and ethnic restaurants are springing up across the country. The bright economic outlook also means that it is becoming easier to find work or to set up a business if you plan to move permanently (see **Settling In**, 'Working and Employment' and 'Starting Your Own Business', pp.224–9 and pp.229–32).

Other Things to Consider

Visitors to a country don't always see the whole picture, and indeed they don't need to. Even those who have lived here for a while find that they are always learning something new about the place and its people, and that is exactly as it should be. But if you are planning to live here you may find that some of the characteristics that delighted you as a visitor – the laid-back attitudes and the relaxed approach to timekeeping – may infuriate you as a house renovator. For example, the Irish don't like to disappoint, and the Italian concept of the *bella figura* or looking good also applies to the Irish. Tradesmen (and they'll always be men) will promise you the world, but when the work is started all kinds of problems crop up and the final result may take a little or considerably longer than you expected.

If you left Ireland a long time ago and are thinking of returning, you will find that many of the old certainties – especially the role of the Church (*see* **Settling In**, 'Religion', pp.256–7) – are being eroded. Nearly 40 per cent of the Republic's population is under 25 (*see* box, below), and these young citizens see things differently. Births outside wedlock are common, women are having children later and later and religion plays a minor role in many people's lives.

Some aspects of the Irish character may also take you back. Picture perfect villages like Adare outside Limerick are not common. The Irish can be untidy, and don't have a strong aesthetic sense. You may come across old mattresses, fridges and other household junk – even cars and farm equipment – dumped in forests or mountainous areas. Many farms are surrounded by rusting machinery, mud and the remains of plastic feedsacks. The famed friendliness of the Irish may seem different to you as a resident rather than a visitor. Being friendly and actually making friends are two somewhat different things. People may be very affable and charming but they may not go out of their way to invite you to their houses and start long-term friendships. This is probably the case in most countries, but new arrivals to Ireland often comment on the detachment of the Irish once they have moved, compared with their initial effusive welcome.

In common with most small countries Ireland likes to think of itself as exceptional. The cultural commentator Fintan O'Toole points out that it is generally held that Irish monks saved civilisation during the Dark Ages; the Irish were

Ireland's Population by Age Group, April 2002

Age	Total	% of total
0–14	827,400	21
15–24	641,500	17
25–44	1,180,300	30
45+	1,268,000	32
Total	3,917,200	100

Names, Names, Names...

What's the difference between Eire, the Republic of Ireland and the 26 counties? Or indeed between the North of Ireland, Northern Ireland and the six counties? What about Ulster? It's confusing even to the Irish, so here is an overview.

From independence in 1922 until the enactment of the constitution, the state was known as Saorstat Éireann or the Irish Free State. The 1937 Constitution of Ireland (Bunreacht na hÉireann) states that 'The name of the State is Eire, or in the English language, Ireland.' Today British media tends to use the term Eire or Southern Ireland. Irish media refers to the Republic or just Ireland.

Within Northern Ireland, Unionists often use the term Ulster. Nationalists prefer to use the North of Ireland. Extreme republicans use the term Six Counties. Northern Ireland is the official name and the one used most widely across the communities. Ulster is the name for one of Ireland's ancient provinces, with six counties in Northern Ireland and three in the Republic.

While we are on the subject, look out for name changes, the English spent a long time anglicising Irish placenames, often with woeful results. After independence the Irish put a considerable amount of effort into doing the same thing, so, for example, the village of Edgeworthstown in County Westmeath reverted to its ancient Irish name of Mostrim for a while, before the villagers petitioned to have the English one back. Diverse spellings are also not uncommon – Roosky on the Shannon, depending on which direction you approach it, is variously signposted as Roosky, Rooskie, Rusky and Rúscaí.

more devout than anyone else in Europe; the Irish struggle for freedom inspired small nations across the world; the Irish sense of fun is unmatched; Ireland's great leap forward during the Celtic Tiger years was unsurpassed anywhere else; and the Irish football team can (if circumstances are right) beat anyone into a cocked hat. You might find this charming or exasperating but it is certainly something that you will hear quite a lot of – especially if you like to stay in the pub until late.

Why Buy?

You may know that you want to spend more time in Ireland but you may not be sure about whether to buy or not. The reasons for buying a property abroad can be divided into two intertwined strands – one is predominantly rational and reasonable, the other is often romantic and impractical.

Let's look at the practical reasons first. First is the simple fact that Ireland is much cheaper than many areas of Britain for property:

- Average house prices in the Greater London area are now more than £250,000. This is considerably more than the average house price in Ireland (approximately €245,000 in mid 2004) and if house-hunters look in less fashionable locations they can improve on this considerably.

• Sterling remains strong against the euro. Although the euro has appreciated against sterling it has been very stable since June 2003. Many economists believe that sterling has found its niche and is unlikely to fluctuate further.

• Irish interest rates are at historic lows, making mortgages exceptionally affordable.

• House prices in Ireland are still rising but this means that purchasing a property here is likely to be a good investment: you are unlikely to lose anything and you'll probably gain considerably over time.

• You don't have to pay property taxes, water taxes and other expenses associated with owning property in Britain. Overall the cost of living in Ireland is lower, and retirees find that benefits outstrip those in Britain.

The second set of reasons for buying are more nebulous and perhaps less logical. Many people remember idyllic childhood summers, others imagine a whole new life away from the stresses of the city, while others want their children to grow up in the countryside and attend a small village school. Some plan to have a second home and retire there at a later stage. All these people feel that buying a home will give them more than the simple possession of a deed of ownership. The purchase will commit them to the country and its people and demonstrate that they plan to stay. They also have something in common with the Irish, who consider property ownership essential and make enormous sacrifices to own their own houses. If buying makes sense emotionally you will probably manage to make it add up economically. Many people eventually buy whether it makes perfect economic sense or not. So, go ahead and buy, but do make sure you are as well informed as possible.

Your choice of location will depend on your circumstances and your finances – whether you wish to live and work, own a holiday home, or simply invest in a property that will appreciate over time. In fact deciding where to buy is probably as multifaceted as the reasons you decided to come. Parts of Ireland have traditionally been home to many visitors – Killarney was the first real tourist destination, and seaside resorts like Clifden have been popular for holiday homes since the last century. In many of Ireland's most charming villages – Rosses Point in Sligo, Roundstone in Galway or Castletownshend in Cork – prices rival those of the cities. Some remote and formerly less fashionable places such as Leitrim and Roscommon have become more popular as prices rise elsewhere. Many house-hunters want to escape urban areas – therefore the focus of this book is on more rural areas, while giving an overview of life and costs in the cities. **Profiles of the Regions**, pp.23–64, gives information on all the counties of Ireland with average property prices.

Case Study: Culture Shock

Sean and Sophie decided to make the move to Limerick in 1999. Sean's mother had been Irish, and the family remembered many enjoyable holidays in the west. Despite being very positive about the move in the beginning, Manchester-born Sophie found the change harder than she had expected. 'I think it was a kind of culture shock,' she recalls. 'Being on holidays is very different from living somewhere. The kids settled in almost immediately, and seemed to have a ready-made circle of friends in their new schools. Sean's new colleagues were very kind, but I think I began to despair of ever getting used to it.' The family had bought an old house needing restoration, and Sophie also found it difficult to come to terms with what she calls 'the Irish sense of time'. 'Neighbours recommended very good builders and workmen, but I found it hard to deal with them initially. They'd say they would call at 11, and not arrive till 2. Or they'd agree to arrive on Thursday, and I'd be waiting in all day for them.' In one instance, the plumber did arrive on Thursday, but it was Thursday two weeks later! 'The lovely relaxed side to Irish life does have its drawbacks,' says Sophie, 'and until I learned how to deal with it, it drove me demented. I think it is all about understanding that there are different ways of doing things. I wouldn't go back now, but I do have to say that during the first year there were times I was quite ready to get the next plane home.'

Living in Ireland

Many people buy property simply because they want to live in Ireland. This section briefly reviews some of the employment opportunities and retirement possibilities open to you. Each section is dealt with in more detail in **Settling In**.

Since joining the European Union in 1973 the Irish economy has changed radically – from one based on agriculture and traditional manufacturing to one reliant on high-tech commerce and the service sector. Ireland is the world's largest exporter of software, and a major centre for the pharmaceutical and biotech industries. The huge growth of the economy in the 1990s has slowed a little but growth is estimated to continue at about 5 per cent a year up to 2010.

Income taxes are slightly higher in Ireland than in Britain but the cost of living is a little lower and the cost of property is often significantly less, so it balances out in the long run. Casual work is very easy to come by; you will find jobs advertised in local newspapers, through agencies and often simply through advertisements in shops and other noticeboards. If you are planning to look for more professional or career jobs it may take a little longer, especially since the job market has slowed since the heady days of the late 1990s when people with the right skills could name their price. It is best to start planning before you arrive, and in some cases before you buy. Research your area thoroughly before moving to see if there is a market for your particular skills. Qualifications gained in the UK are generally valid in Ireland. If you are unsure, there are associations for most professions and you can contact them to find out more about the market for your skills and the validity of your qualifications. There's more information about the employment market in **Settling In**, pp.224–32.

Starting a Business

Changes in society, eating habits and a new-found affluence means that many new opportunities are springing up. Health-food shops, restaurants, crafts, organic farming and bed and breakfast businesses are all areas where foreigners have been conspicuously successful, but British people have set up all kinds of other businesses from aircraft-leasing to software companies. If you have an original idea or if you already have experience in setting up a similar business in Britain, do investigate what support is available. The Irish government actively promotes small businesses and will give you a great deal of help at the onset if you can produce a properly thought out business plan or feasibility study. If you are setting up a business there are hundreds of other things you'll need to know, from business planning to company and employment law. Many of these are outlined in more detail in **Settling In**, pp.229–32. One thing to consider is that the home market in Ireland is very small – make sure that there is an adequate market for your product and that you are aware of the implications (currency fluctuations, duties and so on) if you decide to export a product.

Self-employment

Self-employment covers anything from farming to composing. If you plan to be self-employed you have to ask yourself many of the questions someone looking for work needs to ask. Is there a market for your skills? Can you work alone without a team and colleagues? Ireland offers tax-free status to artists (*see* box 'The Artist's Exemption', p.229). Writers like Frederick Forsyth have taken up residence to avail themselves of this tax break and it can mean a substantial saving if you do make your living from making art. As teleworking becomes more common many people find that they can live in remote areas and work productively with a far lower cost of living. One British couple works on ESL textbooks from the centre of Tipperary; others work as translators; and many people make a good living doing jobs as varied as web design (Ireland is also the software localisation capital of Europe) and violin-making from home.

Farming and Land Prices

Ireland is traditionally an agricultural country and farming is still a major employer (about 7 per cent of the workforce are farmers or directly involved with agribusiness). Land has always been an emotional subject in a country where so many emigrated or died because their holdings could not support them. Many of the old feelings about the land linger on. Irish farmers are noto-riously reluctant to sell land, so remarkably little agricultural land comes on to the market and a huge amount of farmland is rented. This also means that Irish farms are small – the average farm size is 30 hectares.

Since Ireland joined the EU in 1973, money has been poured into farming from EU structural funds – the idea being that, eventually, Irish farmers would be in a position to survive on their own. Precisely the opposite has happened. Most Irish farmers are dependent on subsidies and would be unable to survive without them; it is estimated that 75 per cent of Irish farm incomes come from direct payments. New Common Agricultural Policy (CAP) reforms that decouple grants from the product (milk, meat and grain) and pay them to single farms instead are likely to change farming radically.

Demographics also play a part: Irish farmers are getting older, more and more are being forced into part-time farming to survive (33 per cent of farmers combine farming with another job) and the younger generation tends to look away from the land for careers.

If you are interested in farming you will need to become familiar with the alphabet soup of EU acronyms (try starting with REPS – the Rural Environment Protection Scheme – which provides a substantial income for many farmers). Predicted growth areas include organic farming and forestry. The market for organic food in Ireland is expected to quadruple over the next four years and many new immigrants have started organic and sustainable businesses (although a two-year conversion period is required before a farm is given organic status; see **www.irishorganic.ie**). Government targets for forestry are 17 per cent of total land cover by 2030 (the figure is currently about 9 per cent countrywide). During the 1990s over 12,000 farmers planted 250,000 hectares of forestry, prompted by generous grants, particularly for broadleaf planting.

The Irish *Farmer's Journal* (**www.farmersjournal.ie**) published comparative land prices in February 2004 (reproduced below) and is a good resource for information on farming. **Teagasc** (**www.teagasc.ie**), the Irish agriculture and food development authority, is also an excellent resource.

Comparative Agricultural Land Prices (from *Farmer's Journal*)

Country	To Buy	To Rent
Republic of Ireland	€5,000–9,000 per acre for drystock farms; €7,500–15,000+ per acre for dairy farms	€100–160 per acre for grazing (more in some areas) and €150–200+ per acre for tillage with milk quota attached
Northern Ireland	Good quality land in north Co. Down averages €6,500 (£4,500) per acre; good quality land in north Antrim is €10,000–14,500 per acre	€145 per acre (£100 per acre) for grazing and tillage ground in north Co. Down; north Co. Antrim costs more at €200–230 (£140–160) per acre

Educating and Raising Children in Ireland

Ireland is famous for the quality of its educational system. The curriculum at primary and secondary level is national and is very structured, so students are liable to be studying the same thing at more or less the same time. Participation rates are very high: 90 per cent of all Irish children go to secondary school and 35 per cent of school-leavers go on to third-level education. The system in the North of Ireland is similar to that in Britain but it has generally better achievement rates. There is much more information on the education system in **Settling In**, pp.232–8.

Families with children will find it very easy to fit into the community and children are generally welcome everywhere, even in pubs, although a new law means that, officially, under-18s shouldn't be in pubs after 9pm. However, although Ireland is a wonderful place to bring up children, the government does not make it very easy for both parents of a small child (or children) to work.

Case Study: Greenwich to Nenagh

Dennis and Rae Croft retired to Ireland three years ago from southeast London. Dennis used to work for the Fire Brigade as an engineer and Rae was a primary school teacher. They bought a newly built house in an estate outside Nenagh in County Tipperary and a small flat in London with the proceeds from the sale of their Greenwich house. 'To be honest we were staggered by how much it sold for, prices in that area had shot up,' says Rae. They may have been lucky with the sale but in many ways they are poster children for how to do the move. They did everything right – rented for 12 months to try it out, didn't buy in a fashionable and expensive part of the country and, most importantly, worked very hard to carve out a niche for themselves in the community. 'We knew that people wouldn't come to us, we did have to work at it,' Dennis points out. 'We joined everything going, and we went to everything we were invited to.' Now Rae is secretary of the local history society, Dennis is the project development officer for the refurbishing of the local hall and both are busy in their local active retirement group and environmental organisations. They both emphasise that life in Ireland is infinitely better than their lives in London. 'The pace of life in Ireland is relaxed; we've got lots of time to enjoy life, garden and do all the things we're interested in doing,' says Rae. Dennis does notice differences in the systems – builders were slow to finish the house; everything tends to be done by word of mouth so misunderstandings can occur; local services are underprovided. 'Then again I paid out lots in council tax and water rates in London; the only tax I pay here is for the television licence, but it does mean that services aren't as good, or as plentiful.' The only thing they miss? Dennis draws a blank, but for Rae it is good supermarkets. Their advice for would-be immigrant retirees? Don't expect things to be the same, and do make an effort to get involved.

Crèches are often oversubscribed (particularly in the cities), there are no tax-free allowances for childcare costs, and flexible working arrangements depend on the company. Nonetheless many people have moved to Ireland from the UK specifically to give their children an excellent education and a freedom that they feel is no longer possible in Britain.

Retiring to Ireland

More and more people, with and without Irish links, are choosing to retire to Ireland. One newspaper article described Ireland as a kind of east-Atlantic Florida for British grandparents, and although this is overstating it somewhat, not least because the weather can't hope to compete with Florida, many British retirees find life in Ireland very pleasant. Older people are generally respected and seem to fit into communities and establish routines easily. Ireland offers a huge range of activities that retirees are particularly well positioned to take full advantage of. Among them are golfing, fishing, gardening, walking and horseracing. Another advantage is that Ireland is not very far away – many retirees travel back to the UK to visit family and friends several times a year.

As a retiree you might be better off in Ireland than in the UK. People aged over 70 in Ireland automatically qualify for a free TV licence, a medical card, a free telephone connection, an electricity (or gas) allowance and free public transport (in fact the free transport kicks in when you reach 66) regardless of means. The basic state pension is £77.45 (€110) in the UK compared with the €154 non-contributory pension in Ireland. You can transfer many of your UK benefits and pensions to Ireland, but not all. For more details *see* **Settling In**, 'Retirement and Pensions', pp.244–7.

Visas and Permits

Ireland does not have very complicated bureaucratic procedures. Citizens of the following countries do not need a visa to enter Ireland: Andorra, Argentina, Australia, Austria, Bahamas, Barbados, Belgium, Botswana, Brazil, Brunei, Canada, Chile, Costa Rica, Croatia, Cyprus, Czech Republic, Denmark, El Salvador, Estonia, Finland, France, Germany, Greece, Grenada, Guatemala, Holy See, Honduras, Hong Kong, Hungary, Iceland, Israel, Italy, Jamaica, Japan, Korea (Republic of), Latvia, Lesotho, Liechtenstein, Lithuania, Luxembourg, Malawi, Malaysia, Malta, Mexico, Monaco, Nauru, Netherlands, New Zealand, Nicaragua, Norway, Panama, Paraguay, Poland, Portugal, San Marino, Singapore, Slovenia, South Africa, Spain, Swaziland, Sweden, Switzerland, Tonga, Trinidad and Tobago, UK and colonies, Uruguay, USA, Venezuela, Western Samoa, Zimbabwe.

Citizens of other countries should apply to their local Irish embassy or consulate for a visa. Citizens of countries outside the EU can generally remain in

> ### EU Accession Countries
> The accession countries are Cyprus, Czech Republic, Estonia, Hungary, Latvia, Lithuania, Malta, Poland, Slovakia and Slovenia. From 1 May 2004 these accession state nationals no longer require work permits to work in Ireland. Although people from the accession states can work, they do not have all the rights of an Irish citizen for three years. Social welfare benefits, for example, are likely to be lower. The legislation governing this is still being drafted.

Ireland for up to 90 days before applying for leave to remain or a residence permit. EU law allows any national of an EU or EEA member state (the EEA comprises the European Union, Norway, Iceland and Liechtenstein) to work in another member state without a visa or work permit. As a UK national you have all the rights of EU membership and in addition you have the right to vote in Irish parliamentary elections (elections to the Dáil). This is because Irish citizens can vote in British parliamentary elections (see box 'Voting Rights', p.19). You can travel between Ireland and Britain without a passport but you do need a recognised form of photo ID. Driving licences, student cards, national ID cards and work ID are all accepted.

If you are not from within the EU you don't have an automatic right to work in Ireland. However, Ireland distinguishes between non-EU nationals who wish to work and those who simply wish to reside in Ireland. If you want to work you must obtain a work permit and this can be quite difficult. If you wish to live here or stay for a period longer than the statutory three months you merely need to satisfy the authorities that you have sufficient funds to support yourself in Ireland and that you don't intend to seek work. You can then apply for a residence permit (see 'Residence Permits', p.19).

Work Permits

There are two types of work permit. One is a standard work permit issued for a maximum of one year. Only employers can apply for this and they must show that they have tried to recruit within Ireland before taking on a non-EU national. The majority of these work permits are for low-skilled jobs – catering, construction and so on – and around 50,000 were issued in 2003.

Fast-track and Working Visas

There are also a limited number of so called fast-track visas for professionals from non-EU countries with job offers from employers in Ireland. These visas are only for professionals in areas with serious skills shortages. Again, only the employer can apply for these visas – not the employees. The areas are:

- information and computing technologies professionals
- information and computing technologies technicians
- architects, including architectural technicians and technologists
- construction engineers, including engineering technicians
- quantity surveyors
- building surveyors
- town planners
- registered nurses

This type of visa is far more attractive than the standard work permit as they can be issued for up to two years at a time and applicants can bring their spouse and children with them. The official name for this visa is an expedited working visa or a work authorisation.

Canadians, Australians and New Zealanders between the ages of 18 and 30 are eligible for a 12-month working holiday visa. You can get more information about this from the Department of Foreign Affairs in Dublin (**http://foreign affairs.gov.ie**); the criteria and place to apply differ slightly for each country.

It is important to note that if you entered the country on a 90-day visitor's visa, and you are then offered work and decide to stay on, you will not be issued a work permit. This is to prevent people coming in on a tourist visa and looking for work. You need to leave the country and then apply for the work permit (through your employer) in the usual way. People who have been granted refugee status, asylum-seekers who have temporary leave to remain in the state on humanitarian grounds and postgraduate students coming here to carry out related work do not usually need work permits. You are also exempt if you are an employee posted on an intra-corporate transfer or secondment, for a maximum period of four years, to a company in Ireland (provided the group has operations in more than one country).

Irish Residency

You can own property in Ireland without being resident for tax purposes. As a UK citizen you don't need to establish residency in Ireland and you have the right to live here without a permit. However, you may need to understand some of the more legalistic terminology for tax reasons.

You are liable for Irish tax on your worldwide income earned in any given tax year if you are **resident**, **ordinarily resident** or **domiciled** in Ireland for tax purposes. Below is a brief summary of these terms; see **Financial Implications**, pp.174–95, for more information on residence, taxation and the tax implications of moving to Ireland.

> ## Buying Property as a Non-national
>
> As a non-national you can buy a house or land in Ireland provided the amount of land is less than 2 hectares (around 5 acres). If the piece of land is more than 5 acres and lies outside a town or city you need special consent to purchase. This stipulation was put in place in 1965 to ensure that non-nationals did not buy agricultural land and in practice is rarely implemented. Once you've been resident in Ireland for over seven years you are exempt from these regulations.

Ireland has a **double taxation agreement** with the UK and other countries worldwide (*see* **References**, p.291, for a list). The agreement ensures that you don't pay tax in both countries by either exempting the income from tax in one of the countries or allowing a credit in one country for the tax paid in the other country on the same income. The table 'Liability to Irish Tax' on p.177 gives an indication of your liability for Irish tax under Irish domestic law. Note that the provisions of a double taxation agreement might change some of these depending on your circumstances and income.

It would be wise to consult a lawyer if you have extensive assets that you wish to bring into Ireland. Otherwise, the only thing that you might need to consider is when to sell your residence in Britain – if this is your primary residence you are not liable to capital gains tax on the sale, but if you become resident in Ireland and later sell your house and remit the proceeds of the sale to Ireland you might find yourself liable for capital gains tax in Ireland.

The Irish **Revenue Commissioners** (**www.revenue.ie**) publish helpful leaflets on moving to Ireland and tax liability.

Resident

Your residence status for the purpose of calculating Irish tax is established by the number of days you spend in Ireland during the tax year (in Ireland this coincides with the calendar year and runs from January to December).

You are considered resident in Ireland if you spend 183 days or more in Ireland during that tax year. If you spend 280 days or more in Ireland over a period of two consecutive tax years you are regarded as resident in Ireland for the second tax year. You can elect to be resident in Ireland for tax purposes without spending the full 183 days here, but if you do so you cannot rescind this election at a later stage.

Ordinarily Resident

This refers to your pattern of residence over a period of years. If you are resident in Ireland for three tax years (for example, you spend more than 183 days in Ireland per year) you are considered ordinarily resident from the beginning of the fourth tax year. You stop being ordinarily resident if you are non-resident for three years in a row. If you are ordinarily resident you are generally liable for Irish tax even if you have not spent time in Ireland during a particular year.

Domicile

Domicile is a legal concept that means residence in a particular country with the intention of residing permanently in that country. Everybody acquires a domicile of origin at birth. If you were born in the UK that is your domicile unless you formally elect to change it.

Residence Permits

The residence permit situation is slightly hazy. Officially any EU national seeking to live and work in Ireland needs a residence permit. In practice almost none does so. The tacit situation appears to be that if you want a residence permit you can have one but nobody will ask you for it for work or any other purpose. Non-EU citizens wishing to remain in Ireland must apply for a residence permit within three months of entering the country. They will need a work permit or evidence of income to get this (but note that if you entered the country on a tourist visa you will need to leave before being granted a work permit). You apply at the Alien Registration Office or the local Garda station for your permit.

Irish Citizenship

What Irish Citizenship Involves

Being an Irish citizen means that you are legally an Irish national and a citizen of the European Union. The Irish constitution guarantees you certain rights and privileges as an Irish citizen; these include equality before the law, freedom of expression, freedom to travel, religious liberty and various other fundamental rights. You also have the right to carry an Irish passport, to travel abroad and to live and work anywhere in the EU or EEA. With citizenship come duties and

---

Voting Rights

Only Irish citizens can vote in presidential elections or referenda (held to make changes to the Irish constitution). All UK citizens living in Ireland and registered to vote can vote in elections to the Dáil (Irish Parliament). This is because Irish citizens can vote in British parliamentary elections. Anyone resident in the country can vote in local elections (they will have an L after their name in the electoral register). *See* **Settling In**, 'Irish Politics', pp.253–6, for more on politics and voting in Ireland.

responsibilities. These include observing the rule of law in Ireland and carrying out jury duty if asked to do so. Holding Irish citizenship means that you can vote in all Irish elections and referenda: presidential, to the Dáil (Irish Parliament), to the European parliament, for local government and in any referenda. Irish citizens are entitled to Irish passports, so Irish citizens and Irish passport-holders are synonymous.

Who is Entitled to Irish Citizenship?

Irish citizenship is obtained in three ways: through birth or descent; through marriage to an Irish citizen; or through naturalisation.

Citizenship through Birth

Irish passports are granted immediately on the basis of *jus sanguinis* – citizenship based on ancestry. Anyone born within the Republic of Ireland after 1921 and until May 2004 is entitled to Irish citizenship, regardless of parental nationality. The Citizenship Referendum held in May 2004 has changed the rules. Now only people with one or more parents who are Irish citizens is entitled to Irish citizenship. Anyone born outside Ireland to an Irish parent or grandparent is also entitled to an Irish passport. To obtain your passport you need to register as a foreign birth. To do this you need your long form civil birth certificate, your parents' marriage certificate and the long form birth certificate of the Irish parent. If you are applying on the basis of a grandparent you must supply their marriage and birth certificates. If your parents or grandparents were born in the North of Ireland before 1921 they are considered Irish by birth. If you are applying from a country outside Ireland you need to get the passport forms from the Irish embassy or consulate in that country. Passport application forms (PAS1 if you are already living in Ireland; PAS2 if you are from England, Scotland or Wales; PAS3 if you are from Northern Ireland; PAS4 for anywhere else in the world) can be obtained from the nearest Irish embassy or consulate.

If you are:

- **A, born in the island of Ireland, you are entitled to Irish citizenship or you are an Irish citizen provided one or more of your parents is an Irish citizen.**

- **B, the child of A, born outside the island of Ireland, you are an Irish citizen.**

- **C, the child of B and a grandchild of A, born outside the island of Ireland, then you are entitled to Irish citizenship, but you must first register in the foreign births register.**

- **D, a child of C and a great-grandchild of A, born outside the island of Ireland, then you are entitled to Irish citizenship by having your birth registered in the foreign births register, but only if your parent C had registered by the time of your birth.**

Citizenship through Marriage

You can also apply for citizenship if you are married to an Irish citizen. The government has recently made some changes to the laws governing citizenship through marriage and temporary rules apply until 2005. If you married your spouse before 30 November 2002 you can simply make a declaration of post-nuptial citizenship providing you have been married for at least three years, and this will give your spouse full Irish citizenship. You can't make a post-nuptial declaration of citizenship if you married after 30 November 2002 or if your spouse did not become an Irish citizen until after 30 November 2002. If you married before 30 November 2002, the latest date for making a post-nuptial declaration of citizenship is 29 November 2005. You should note that you can only make a post-nuptial declaration of citizenship if your current marriage is valid under Irish law. It is valid if your first husband or wife died, or if your divorce would be recognised under Irish law. If you are not sure of the validity of your marriage under the law in Ireland you should consult an Irish lawyer to check.

From 30 November 2005 it will no longer be possible to become an Irish citizen by simply lodging a post-nuptial declaration. Instead, you need to apply to the Department of Justice for a certificate of naturalisation based on marriage to an Irish citizen. This will be subject to a number of conditions, including residence in Ireland.

Citizenship through Naturalisation

Once you've lived in the country for five years continuously you can apply for citizenship through naturalisation. This is granted only at the 'absolute discretion' of the Minister for Justice. The criteria for this are that you are resident in the state and are over 18. You must have been resident in the state for one year immediately before the application for naturalisation and in the eight years preceding this have had a total reckonable residence of four years in the state (see 'Irish Residency', p.17–19, for more on residency). The Minister must be satisfied of your good character – and will ask the Garda Síochána (Ireland's national police) to provide a report – and be sure of your intention to live in Ireland following naturalisation. You must also make a declaration of fidelity to the nation and loyalty to the state before a judge. The documents you will require are:

- a passport
- registration certificate (from the Garda Síochána)
- a birth certificate (certified translation required if not in English)
- a statement from the Revenue Commissioners that all taxes due have been paid
- proofs of financial status (bank statements or similar)
- evidence of having sworn loyalty to the state in court

> **An Essential Resource**
> One of the most useful websites for aspiring immigrants is the government
> website **www.oasis.gov.ie**, developed to give anyone living in Ireland detailed
> information about all their social and civil rights. It has an extensive section on
> moving to Ireland, with links to all the relevant government departments and
> information about everything from importing a car to choosing a school.

Once the Minister grants you naturalisation you pay a fee of €634.87 (this is
less if you are the spouse, widow or widower of a naturalised Irish citizen, or a
minor, and costs nothing if you are a refugee).

Dual Nationality

The Irish government has no difficulty with your holding dual citizenship but
advises you to ensure that your home government also has no objection. If you
are a US citizen you are supposed to use your US passport when entering or
leaving the States. Note also that Irish citizenship does not automatically
excuse you from certain duties such as military service in the other country
where you hold citizenship.

For all queries about citizenship, contact the Citizenship Section of the
Department of Justice, Equality and Law Reform at 13–14 Burgh Quay, Dublin 2,
t (within Ireland) LoCall 1890 551500 (*helpline 10–12.30pm Tues and Thurs*);
t (from outside Ireland): (01) 616 7700 (*helpline as above*); **info@justice.ie**.

Administrative Departments

The **Republic of Ireland** consists of three provinces and part of the fourth
province (Ulster), which are divided into 26 counties. The majority of them were
laid out by English settlers and have remained largely unchanged since then.
The provinces are far more ancient divisions but they are not administrative
regions and do not claim people's allegiances (except when it comes to sport –
Gaelic football and hurling championships are organised first within and then
between the provinces). For administrative purposes the country is divided into
29 county councils and five city authorities. Most of them are tied to the counties or cities (County Tipperary is divided in two and County Dublin in four). Each
region has a directly elected council, which is responsible for many of the issues
of local government – including planning, water, sewerage and so on. *See*
References, pp.282–6, for a complete list of councils.

Northern Ireland consists of six counties. These were administrative divisions
up until 1973, when Northern Ireland was divided into 26 administrative units
called districts. Each district elects a council, which manages local government
for the area.

Profiles of the Regions

A Note about Prices

The prices given in this chapter are based on the permanent TSB/ESRI House Price Index published in January 2004, a survey carried out by the *Sunday Times* in January 2004 and the University of Ulster/Bank of Ireland *Quarterly House Price Index* published in September 2003. Prices in the Republic are given in euro, and in Northern Ireland in sterling.

This section should help you begin to narrow down where you want to live. If you have already decided exactly where you plan to go, this chapter will help you compare and contrast prices and amenities in different areas of the country. Don't be absolutist when it comes to choosing a location – if you just stick to one county you may miss out on something very similar just over the county border, so keep an eye on the map as you read about each region. What mainly distinguishes each county is its landscape and history; you will not find enormous cultural differences between regions, the exception being Ulster – although Dubliners or Corkonians might vociferously disagree. The biggest differences are probably between urban and rural areas. Once you've settled in and spent some time in the country you'll certainly start to notice the subtleties.

The country is divided into four provinces – Leinster, Munster, Connacht and Ulster – which in turn comprise 32 counties, each of which is briefly described here. Some counties are interesting for their history, others for their land-scape, others for literature, others for where they fit into modern Ireland. All escape simple categorisation. Somewhere generally dismissed as boggy and boring may have exactly the combination of solitude, walking and water that you're looking for, so do take this as a jumping-off point and read further if you like the sound of a place. Remember if you are doing further research on a region that the tourism authority divides the country up slightly differently – the mid-west region includes Clare, Limerick and North Tipperary and the southwest region is Cork and Kerry, for example.

The profile of each county described below includes a rough idea of property prices in the region. There is more detail on exactly what you can get for different price brackets in **Selecting a Property**.

Leinster

Leinster stretches from the border with Ulster just above Dundalk all the way down Ireland's eastern coast to Carnsore Point in Wexford. Its open, flat shoreline has encouraged invaders down the centuries from Norsemen to Cromwell. Contrary to popular belief, the Romans landed here too, although they seem to have decided that this misty island didn't have much to offer and didn't take things further. However, they did give Ireland a name – Hibernia, or 'Land of Winter'. The next arrivals – the Vikings, or Norsemen – did stay (perhaps bad weather didn't bother them as much or, more likely, by that stage there were hundreds of rich monasteries to raid). Dublin and Waterford are both Viking towns. Later the Normans invaded towards the end of the 12th century.

In Norman times Dublin and a fluctuating hinterland was known as the Pale. This term was first used in 1495 to denote the area of Ireland under English rule but you'll still hear it used occasionally, either in a self-deprecating way by those living within it or in a disparaging way by those living outside. There are many ruined Anglo-Norman tower houses in Leinster. These are generally simple constructions as this area was subdued quickly, reducing the need for defensive dwellings. More elaborate and later tower houses are found all over Munster and Connacht. Fertile land and proximity to the seat of power in Dublin Castle means that Leinster is also dotted with big houses and estates; Castletown and Russborough are the largest.

This is one of the richest provinces of Ireland and the most populated, with over two million people. It is dominated by Dublin, with a population of over one million. The hills of Wicklow to the south of Dublin have discouraged growth in that direction but the fertile flat plains of Kildare and Meath are being slowly colonised by urban sprawl. Statisticians are usually sober reporters and choose their words carefully, but the senior statistician for the 2002 Census described the movement of people from Dublin into the commuter belt (including counties Longford, Westmeath and Laois) as 'unprecedented' and 'incredible'. A simple rule of thumb is that the closer you are to Dublin, the higher property prices are likely to be. If the region is on a transport route out of the city it is likely also to have lured commuters. If you go just a few miles off the beaten track prices will drop a little, but for bargains you need to go quite a bit further afield. In addition to County Dublin, Leinster contains 10 other counties: Louth, the smallest and most northerly; rich Meath, ancient seat of the High Kings of Ireland; Longford; the midland counties of Westmeath, Offaly and Laois; the horse-breeding county of Kildare; mountainous Wicklow; the rich farmland of Kilkenny and Carlow; and the maritime county of Wexford.

Dublin

Dublin city and county are practically synonymous. Dublin is a low-lying city set on the River Liffey looking out over the wide sweep of Dublin Bay, with the Wicklow Mountains to the south. Dublin overwhelms the rest of Ireland; it is by far the largest city in the country, with over one million people – 30 per cent of the population of Ireland. Despite this the city is an intimate place and the centre is easy to explore on foot. Dublin is above all a Georgian city; the broad streets and squares lined with tall brick houses typical of the centre were laid out in the early 18th century. It is also a friendly and cosmopolitan city where

Victorian Dublin

Although most people think Georgian when they think of Dublin's architecture, the Victorian era left a legacy of suburbs. Inner suburbs like Rathmines, Drumcondra, Glasnevin and Clontarf all expanded during the 19th century, partly because of new tramways (sadly all removed in the 1960s and now being replaced at enormous expense) and partly because the growing middle classes thought that the suburbs were healthier than the city. While many of the great ascendancy town houses in the city slowly became tenements, spacious brick middle-class houses were built. These suburbs remain some of the most sought-after areas in the city. Incidentally, the Victorians also left a huge number of pubs with wonderful ornate brass, mahogany and marble interiors. Many of the old Victorian pub interiors were pulled out in the 1990s but some fine examples remain, particularly the Stag's Head in Dame Court and Ryans of Parkgate Street.

people from all over the world have settled, albeit without the racial mix of London, and some of the newcomers have found settling in difficult – particularly African immigrants in inner-city areas.

In the past Dublin tended to be described in terms of pubs, grand Georgian buildings, literature and its famed sociability. All of these are still present but the defining characteristic of the city today is change. The city has completely altered in the last 10 years – becoming sleeker, more confident and, unfortunately, more expensive. Two completely new city centre districts have been created: Temple Bar – an artistic and bohemian quarter – and the Financial Services Centre (known as the IFSC) – where brand new apartments, offices, shops, restaurants and pubs followed the opening of an international banking centre in 1987. Property prices have rocketed – by 244 per cent since 1996 – and Dublin is becoming less and less affordable: house prices now average €326,000 and it is almost impossible to find anything for less than €200,000. The equity built up in the homes of many Dubliners means that they can afford second homes along the coast and in the west so house prices there are also affected by the city.

As prices are so high and most people moving to Ireland don't tend to buy in Dublin there is no detailed introduction to the city here but *see* **References**, 'Further Reading', p.290, for lots of suggestions of books to read if you want to learn more about this captivating city.

Louth

Louth is the smallest of all 32 counties, covering only 317 square miles and with a population of just over 100,000. It is also on the northern boundary of the Republic, seen traditionally as guarding the gateway to Ulster. The 'gap of the north' was a historic pass into south Armagh. During the Troubles, Louth was generally regarded as something of a backwater, but now it is located on an important strategic corridor between Dublin and Belfast, with the M1 motorway slicing through it.

Most of Louth is undulating farmland except for the spectacular mountainous **Cooley peninsula**. Here Queen Maeve and Cuchulain battled over the brown bull of Cooley recounted in the ancient Irish tale 'Táin Bó Cuailnge' ('The Cattle Raid of Cooley'). This is an almost untouched region and is exquisitely beautiful. You can find cottages and farmhouses at a reasonable price since southern buyers have tended look west or south rather than north for second homes. **Carlingford** is particularly delightful, a tiny medieval village right on the sea with some good restaurants, unusual for a place its size.

Louth has always been a border county so many fortified tower houses and castles still remain. You will also find prehistoric monuments and the ruins of great religious settlements – Mellifont Abbey and Monasterboice. The southern part of the county has always been rich agricultural land so Louth has a particularly wide selection of rural buildings from the 18th and 19th centuries; if you are particularly interested in restoring a farmhouse or outbuilding this may be the place for you. Dublin commuters have begun to slip over the border basing themselves all around **Drogheda** and up as far as **Ardee**, so prices here are on the rise. **Dundalk** is the county town, placed firmly on the map when Bill Clinton delivered a speech from there during his Irish visit in 2000.

Average prices in Louth are around €200,000.

Meath

Meath lacks wild mountains and spectacular scenery. Instead it has some of the richest pastureland in Ireland, flanked by the lazily rolling river **Boyne**. Meath is also a place of ancient kingdoms and land that has been cultivated since the dawn of prehistory. Here the whole history of Ireland is written in miniature; every age and every invasion has left its mark. The first farmers cultivated land here and built great tombs for their dead 2000 years before Christ. The graves Knowth, Dowth and Newgrange (the best-preserved passage grave in Europe) lie in a bend of the river Boyne. Later the pagan Kings of Tara (Ard Rí) were crowned on the **Hill of Tara**, giving Meath the name Royal Meath. Saint Patrick lit a huge Easter bonfire on the hill of Slane in AD 433 as a challenge to the pagan King of Ireland. This pascal fire now marks the takeover of Christianity. *The Book of Kells*, one of Ireland's greatest illuminated books, now held by the Library of Trinity College in Dublin, was made in the monastery of **Kells**. This was once a European centre for learning but is now a ruin in a quiet village. When the Anglo-Normans arrived in the 13th century they left many fortified tower houses across the landscape; St John's Castle in **Trim** is the largest castle in Ireland. The Battle of the Boyne was fought here, where William of Orange defeated King James II. The victory is still celebrated by Unionists in much of the North, if largely forgotten in its own county. Later still, once revolt had died down, many ascendancy houses were built here, ringed by elegant walled parklands and huge beech trees.

Today Meath is in an awkward position. It is so close to Dublin that its suburbs have engulfed much of the southern part of the county and city mores have swamped its previously rural ethos. Dubious publicity comes from a radio skit, featuring Navan Man and his sidekick the Drunken Politician, which lampoons the new Ireland. Despite the influx of commuters and suburban developments Meath remains rural in parts but you won't find property bargains anywhere.

Average house prices here reflect its position with second-hand houses at €240,000 and new houses at €250,000.

Longford

Longford is a quintessential midland county, bordered by the Shannon on its western side and full of lakes and boggy land, although to the south the land becomes flatter and richer. Some think that this area is rather bleak, others that it has yet to be discovered. Advantages of the area include wonderful coarse fishing, some pretty villages (especially **Ardagh**), the Royal Canal, some very attractive farmland to the south, and relatively low property prices. The entire county comes under the Rural Renewal Scheme, which gives tax rebates on rental income for investors and on income tax for owner-occupiers.

If bream, rudd, perch and pike don't set you alight, you may be interested in the county's literary connections: the poet and playwright Oliver Goldsmith, the novelist Maria Edgeworth and the poet Pádraic Colum were all born here. Maria Edgeworth came from a large and eccentric family. Her father was an inventor, scientist, educationalist, pioneering landlord, writer and politician. Among other things he invented wind-driven carriages, a turnip-cutter and a veloci-pede, a precursor to the bicycle. Edgeworthstown, the family's estate village, is now called Mostrim. The national routes N4 and N5 converge here, so many people pass though on their way elsewhere.

Average house prices are €180,000.

Westmeath

Another midland county, this was originally part of County Meath and the Anglo-Norman Pale until 1541, when Gaelic lords reclaimed it. Ruined tower houses and Norman mottes across the county are witness to its past as a disputed area. Some lovely Georgian estates still dot the county; chief among them are the Palladian Belvedere House and Gothic Tullynally Castle; their estate villages Tyrellspass and Castlepollard, respectively, are charming.

If you are looking for real countryside, with old-fashioned hedgerows and a low-key way of life, Westmeath has lots to offer. The county is mainly grassland, with the **Esker Riada**, a long, narrow, sandy hill left behind after the Ice Age, winding across its centre, and quite a lot of raised bog in between. A little hill in the heart of Westmeath is said to be the centre of Ireland, **Uisneach Hill** or 'navel of Ireland'. Here you will find a stone that marks where the four ancient provinces of Ireland meet, although their borders have moved somewhat in the intervening time.

Westmeath has four lakes, one of which, **Derravaragh**, was where the three children of King Lir, turned into swans by their jealous stepmother, spent three hundred years of the nine hundred they spent as swans. **Lough Ree**, the middle of the Shannon lakes, borders Westmeath to the west with the town of **Athlone** straddling the Roscommon border just below. It has always been a border town, situated between the provinces of Leinster and Connacht on a ford on the river Shannon. Now Athlone is a thriving market town and a hub for road and rail. Houses in its hinterland and on Lough Ree are very much in demand.

The county town is **Mullingar**. Like so many Irish towns, Mullingar has evolved from a grey, austere and rather forbidding town to a lively, colourful and increasingly cosmopolitan place. Property prices in its environs have been rising as it has become a satellite town for Dublin and a regional hub – the population rose by a startling 47 per cent in the last census (it is now 8,833). **Lough Sheelin** on the border with Cavan and Meath is becoming a fashionable spot for weekend homes, so prices are rising accordingly, but other parts of the county towards Longford and Roscommon are still quite reasonable. The new M6 motorway will pass through Westmeath so there is a growing interest in the towns and villages along its path.

Average house prices here are €196,000.

Offaly and Laois

Like Westmeath, both these counties were once part of the Pale but the Anglo-Normans couldn't gain a firm foothold and retreated back to the area nearer Dublin. In the 16th century the counties were finally subdued and were the first in Ireland to be 'planted' or colonised by Tudor settlers. The Parsons family (the Earls of Rosse, still living in Birr Castle) took over from the Gaelic O'Carrolls of Ely. Laois was known as Queen's County and Offaly as King's County after Mary Tudor and her consort Philip of Spain, right up until 1922 when the Irish Free State was established.

The enormous **Bog of Allen** covers most of Offaly and overlaps into neighbouring Kildare. To the southeast of Offaly, overlapping with north Laois, are the **Slieve Bloom Mountains**, a National Nature Reserve. Although they are not very high they offer wonderful views over the surrounding flat fields, rivers and bogs. If you take the Slieve Bloom Way up through the hills you find woods, heathery uplands, waterfalls and beautiful valleys. Property here is very much off the beaten path and therefore reasonably cheap. Further east, villages like

Edenderry and the town of **Portarlington** on the borders of County Kildare are within the Dublin commuter ambit and have new developments springing up around them.

If you like the slower pace of life in the midlands and aren't set on sea and wild mountainous scenery, property in Offaly or Laois might be for you. **Birr**, for example, on the Tipperary border, is not well known but is a charming town. Its wide streets are lined with classically proportioned Georgian houses, any one of which would sell for millions in Dublin. It has good pubs and restaurants, is surrounded by tranquil farmland, and is within easy reach of Dublin, Lough Derg and, a little further west, the coast. **Tullamore** is a garrison town that only developed in the 19th century. A catastrophic fire caused by a hot air balloon destroyed much of the thatched roofed town in 1785 and is responsible for its present-day layout with wide streets and some Georgian architecture. The Grand Canal flows through the town and once connected it to Dublin. It has been identified as a regional hub in the government's National Spatial Strategy to balance development in the regions. **Portlaoise** (pronounced Port-leash) is best known for its high security prison but is expanding as Dublin commuters fan out from the Greater Dublin area. Further south, **Abbeyleix** in Laois is a very pretty town with tree-lined streets, unusual for many midland Irish towns. It is likely that as Dublin grows this region will become better known and more popular making investment here a canny choice.

Average prices in both Offaly and Laois are around €180,000, but near the border with Kildare they tend to be higher.

Kildare

The inland county of Kildare is famous as a sporting, racing and hunting region. Bordering Dublin, it is situated on the edge of the central plain. The county's main features are flat, open grasslands, perfect for tillage and horses, large tracts of raised bog to the west and the river Liffey, coiling through the eastern half – all interspersed with trees and gentle rolling hills. Kildare is traversed by arterial roads leading out of Dublin (Kildare town has just been bypassed removing a notorious bottleneck) and as a result is growing faster than any other county in Ireland with the exception of Meath. The 2002 Census showed it was just five people short of the Strategic Planning Guideline target of 164,000 for 2006, demonstrating all too starkly that many of the attempts to regulate runaway growth in the Dublin region are failing. Its population grew by 21.5 per cent from 1996 to 2002, mainly in the areas nearest to Dublin; towns like **Naas**, **Newbridge** and **Kildare** itself grew by over 30 per cent and the village of **Kilcock** almost doubled in size. Many other towns and villages in north Kildare have become dormitory Dublin towns, although resident computer companies such as Intel and Hewlett Packard are partly responsible for the rapid expansion of towns like **Leixlip** and **Celbridge**.

One of the best-known features of Kildare is the **Curragh** – 5,000 acres of open grassland. The word means racecourse and Ireland's best-known flat racing takes place here. Apparently the limestone underlying the plain builds strong horses' bones and this county is the centre of the Irish bloodstock industry. Before a motorway cut across it you could see horses and jockeys exercising as you drove through. Today you have to go off the main road to see them, but they are still there.

There are many fine houses and estates in Kildare. The Earls of Kildare, known as the Geraldines, once the most powerful family in Ireland, had their seat in Carton House, designed by Richard Cassels. Wealth and proximity to Dublin make this an expensive county for property. This is not a place to track down derelict country houses – they are all renovated, with outhouses converted into housing for staff, and wooden stud-fencing enclosing fields full of valuable thoroughbred horses. The most southern part of the county, down towards Carlow, is quieter and if you want to be close to Dublin city in lovely green country you might like to look here.

Average house prices are over €260,000 although houses in towns are less.

Case Study: Surprises

You don't always get what you expect when you buy a house. Sometimes it is an unpleasant surprise and sometimes, happily, it is an extremely pleasant one. Peter Hamilton, originally from Oxford, moved to Ireland in the early 1990s, initially just planning to have a look around but, like so many others, ending up staying, finding love and a stone-built cottage on an acre of land in County Kildare. But he didn't realise that that was what it was until some time after he'd bought it. 'It was amazing,' explains the IT specialist, musician and passionate gardener. 'It was a funny little house that had been extended twice, creating two almost completely separate parts. That suited us perfectly since my mother was coming to live with us and needed a self-contained flat. The whole house was covered in pebbledash on the outside and inside was all dry-lined walls. Even the surveyor thought it was a block-built house from the fifties, and it wasn't until we tried to change one of the back windows into a door that we discovered a stone wall and realised that the cottage was far older than we'd thought.'

Living in this country spot yet only 45 minutes from the city by train (Peter used to keep his bicycle at the train station in Dublin and cycle to work at a software company in the city) has been idyllic, but Peter is now getting itchy feet – partly because he now works freelance and can work from anywhere and partly because he's beginning to hanker after a more undulating landscape. 'The countryside around is absolutely flat. I even built earth features in the garden but we couldn't go that high, the neighbours would have complained,' he laughs. He's in a good position to make a move; having bought in 1996, Peter and his partner have watched the value of their house more than triple in seven years.

The K Club

Ireland's most exclusive club, the Kildare Hotel and Country Club (known as the K Club), is an immaculately restored Georgian estate with a five-star hotel, two 18-hole golf courses designed by Arnold Palmer and 20 super-exclusive holiday homes. Some of the state's top business figures own homes at the K Club and there was considerable excitement when rumours circulated that former US president Bill Clinton was about to join their ranks. Alas, the rumours were unfounded – Bill may have been thinking about it but he's a man with a reputation for changing his mind.

If you are passionate about golf, can get though the stringent approval process and can come up with around €1 million this might be for you. The price looks a little more reasonable when you consider that 50-year memberships of the club have been selling for something in excess of €225,000. And if you need another selling point, the Ryder Cup will be held here in 2006.

Wicklow

There are many sides to Wicklow, birthplace of the Liffey River, James Joyce's Anna Livia Plurabelle. One is the Wicklow of picture-postcard villages like **Enniskerry** and **Ashford** – long, white, sandy beaches lined with holiday homes, millionaire estates and mellow landscapes of glens and rivers. This is the county called the Garden of Ireland. The other side is desolate and isolated, featuring dark lakes, upland bogs and spectacular mountains with their lower slopes covered with oak and beech woods and the newer arrival, conifer forests that spill over sections of the mountains like ink.

Even though the mountains look low from the city, once you are out among them you find a different world. For some reason Irish mountains seem bigger than their prosaic measurements in feet or metres. Daphne Pochin-Mould flew over Ireland in a small plane in the 1960s to photograph the landscape and noted how the little hills behave with all the savagery of high mountains and fierce winds roar down the valleys. The poet J.M. Synge, who was born here, wrote of the 'mists rolling down the bog'. Much of this area is the **Wicklow Mountains National Park**, which covers 49,420 acres – most of upland Wicklow – and is home to grouse and the occasional red deer. The films *Excalibur* and *Braveheart* were both shot here, which gives you some idea of the grandeur of the place.

When you are high up on the military road, built by the British in 1800 to flush out the rebels who took refuge in the hills, you feel a very long way from the city. Despite this the county is close to Dublin, so close that the narrow roads leading down from the mountains are clogged with traffic early in the morning and late at night, and property has reached Dublin prices and beyond in many cases.

The average price of a new house in the north of the county is almost €400,000 and second-hand houses are just a little less at €362,000. South Wicklow and the town of Arklow are quite a bit less at around €230,000, making averages for the whole county around €288,000.

Kilkenny

Kilkenny is an undulating county bordered by gentle hills. Most of the county consists of the river valleys of the Barrow, the Nore and the Suir. The land is fertile and well cultivated, reminding some of England. Perhaps this is because it was politically stable for much of its history, unlike many other counties. Kilkenny was originally a monastic settlement. The town was named after a 6th-century monk St Canice and the 13th-century St Canice's Cathedral is the second-largest cathedral in Ireland. Later it became a seat of Anglo-Norman power, at one point challenging Dublin for the title of most important city in Ireland. Here the Normans intermingled with the native Irish, so much so that in 1366 the Statutes of Kilkenny were passed. These aimed to preserve the Englishness of the Anglo-Normans by excluding Irish influences.

Norman colonists were required to use the English language, law and customs. Marriage and fosterage between the two groups was banned, as was Irish dress. The statutes did not have lasting influence as the Anglo-Normans (later known as the Old English to distinguish them from the Tudors and Stuarts or New English who arrived later) became, in a well-known phrase, 'more Irish than the Irish themselves'. Today many British people have moved to the county, drawn by the landscape, proximity to Dublin and reasonable property prices.

Kilkenny is not only one of Ireland's most interesting and historical towns, it is also one of its most attractive. The city (it is really only town size with a population of 8,594 but holds on fiercely to its city status granted in 1609 by James I) is characterised by many beautifully restored medieval buildings and winding, cobbled streets. It is the national centre for craft and design, so many potters, woodworkers, jewellery makers and other craftspeople live in or near the city. It has one of Ireland's best arts festivals and the Cat Laughs comedy festival. The city has been designated a regional hub as part of the National Spatial Strategy Plan. It is only 75 miles (123km) to Dublin and is also easy to get to by train since it is on the main Dublin–Waterford line.

Outside Kilkenny, places like **Goresbridge**, **Thomastown**, **Bennetsbridge** and **Inistioge** (an incredibly picturesque village with lovely limetrees and a ten-span 18th-century bridge over the river Nore) are all attractive places to settle. However, property prices in Kilkenny have been shooting up and larger country houses with some land are particularly in demand.

New houses cost €210–258,000 and second-hand ones around €285,00.

Carlow

Carlow, shaped like an inverted triangle, is the second-smallest county in Ireland, covering 346 square miles and with a population of 45,845. The valley of the river Barrow forms the border with neighbour and rival Kilkenny, and the Blackstairs mountains rise to the south. It is a quiet county with few grand houses and features unspoilt countryside, hedgerows and trees in abundance. Like its neighbour Kilkenny, Carlow offers much to those attracted to old-fashioned farming landscapes and a quiet pace of life, but the urban areas are changing rapidly. **Carlow town** is uneasily positioned between an ambitious plan that positions it as a 'model town for sustainable living in the 21st century' and an influx of people from Dublin that has seen the population of the town soar by almost a third in the last five years, from 17,000 in 1998 to 22,000 in 2002. Dubliners see it as a good alternative to Dublin, with prices being up to a third less than they are in the city and a relatively quick 52-mile commuting journey. Carlow is also home to three of Ireland's national walking routes: the **South Leinster Way**, the **Wicklow Way** and the **Barrow Way**, which links with the Slieve Margy Way in Laois. And you'll find the largest dolmen in Ireland here, too, the 100-ton **Browne's Hill Dolmen**.

Average house prices in Carlow are about €200,000.

Wexford

This county lies at the southern tip of Ireland's east coast and is known for warm, sunny weather, sandy beaches, birds, opera and strawberries. This may sound like an odd combination but Wexford is indeed home to one of Ireland's most interesting arts festivals – the Wexford Opera Festival, every year in October. One of its aims has always been to perform lesser-known operas and rediscover works that have slipped out of the repertoire. The town of **Enniscorthy**, in the heart of strawberry-growing country, holds its own strawberry festival every year in July. Incidentally, one of the former owners of Enniscorthy's castle, Sir Henry Wallop, gave the word 'wallop' to the English language because of beatings he gave his workers when they displeased him.

The sea defines Wexford – flat lowlands with low granite hills to the north and a flat coastline with sand dunes leading on to some wonderful beaches. Traditionally the county has been prosperous. It was known as the Model County, since it is neater and tidier than much of the rest of Ireland; its towns – Wexford, **Enniscorthy**, **Gorey** and **Rosslare** – are comfortable and middle-class and its farms are well kept. Some of the most intensive tillage farming in the country takes place here, with harvests of wheat, barley and sugar beet.

Wexford itself is a delightful town. Much of it still conforms to the medieval street plan, with narrow, winding streets and a working fishing port, although centuries of silting in the harbour means that its commercial activities have

> ### Bird Life in Wexford
> Along Wexford's flat coast are several protected nature reserves filled with birds. The most famous of these is called the North Slobs and here migratory Greenland white-fronted geese arrive in huge numbers each winter. The tiny uninhabited Saltee Islands just off the village of Kilmore Quay are a cacophonous home for puffins, guillemots, thousands of other sea birds and a colony of grey seals.

moved to the port of Rosslare. **Rosslare** is where ferries arrive from France and Wales and is therefore many visitors' first glimpse of Ireland. Anecdotally, the sun shines here a little more than in other places and statistics show that there is a little less rain than in other parts of Ireland. Although you shouldn't expect Mediterranean-style summers, children will find the wide, sandy beaches a joy in almost any weather.

Wexford is a peaceful county and many Irish families still take their summer holidays near Wexford's beaches – Curracloe and Rosslare Strand. But Wexford had a tumultuous past. It was first invaded by the Norsemen who founded the town of Wexford. Next, the Normans arrived in 1169, invading Wexford before spreading out all over Ireland. They have left a dense legacy of tower houses and abbeys. Wexford was the centre of the 1798 rebellion against the English by the United Irishmen who were eventually routed at Vinegar Hill just above Enniscorthy. Today the invaders are Dublin commuters. The N11 runs down the east coast bringing workers from as far as Wexford to Dublin, roughly a two-hour drive. 70 per cent of the population of Gorey commutes to the city. This inevitably means that house prices here have soared in the last 10 years. Many houses are second homes; the generation that holidayed here in the 1960s and 1970s has returned to buy holiday homes, and property prices all along the coastline reflects the demand. Inland prices drop somewhat – you can find attractive houses with distant sea views and beaches a 20-minute drive away for much less than on the coast.

Average prices here are €189,000.

Munster

Munster offers a little bit of everything – the fertile plains of Tipperary; Kerry's steep craggy mountains and Cork's more gentle sloping ones, with farmland running up their sides; the incredibly luxurious vegetation of Valentia in Kerry; and the barren Dingle peninsula. There is rich farming land in South Cork and Tipperary, while the apparently desolate and rocky Burren region hides a wealth of wild flowers and unusual plants. All this in only six counties: Waterford, Cork, Kerry, Limerick, Tipperary and Clare. Cork is admittedly Ireland's largest county and its capital, Ireland's second city. Waterford and Limerick are also major urban centres. Limerick is a thriving technological and university centre and its commuters have spread out along the Shannon up as far as Killaloe, driving up prices for lakeside or riverside properties. Getting there is getting easier as budget airlines expand their schedules into Cork and Kerry airports.

Munster is full of abbeys, castles and ancient sites. Here you will find ringforts, stone circles, Norman towers and watch towers along the coast, many large estate houses and smaller gentlemen's residences. Here too you will find some of the largest new houses in Ireland, symbols of prosperity and progress for some, blots on the landscape for others. As with Dublin, property prices rise the closer you get to the cities but the brightly painted coastal villages in West Cork also command high prices. If you are looking for property anywhere along Munster's coast, remember that a sea view or even the smell of the ocean will increase prices by up to 50 per cent. Look inland if you want a bargain.

Waterford

Around the corner from Wexford, although barely touching it, is County Waterford. Like Wexford, **Waterford city** was founded by the Norsemen who used it as a base for raids deep into the surrounding countryside. Later the Normans arrived, capturing the city after a three-day siege in 1170. In Norman times Waterford became one of the most prosperous cities in Ireland. Medieval shipbuilding and the wool trade with Flanders in Belgium brought riches to the city and its hinterland. It remained the second city of Ireland throughout the 16th century and after. Despite stagnation for much of the 19th century, and almost no population growth for much of the 20th century, Waterford city (population 44,564) retains a proud sense of self, an attractive provincial Georgian centre and a prosperous hinterland, somewhat marred by ugly suburbs and industrial estates. The city is the main commercial centre of the southeast, with a busy working port which can accommodate large modern ships. It is also famous for crystal.

Waterford, like so many other Irish counties, offers a wide variety of landscapes – the Monavullagh and Comeragh mountains in the centre with many peaks above 2,000ft, the wooded valley of the river Blackwater, fertile farmland and the low-lying coast with little fishing villages, low cliffs and wide, sandy beaches. **Dunmore East** is probably the most fashionable and the prettiest of Waterford's villages. It is surrounded by little red sandstone cliffs and pleasant coves for swimming. Houses here are very much in demand, especially since planning controls have ensured that the village has retained its character. Along the coast the resort town of **Tramore** is where many Irish people have second homes, but many feel that the town has been spoiled with attractions such as 'Splashworld', a huge water-sports centre with pools and chutes. Between Waterford and Cork the coastline becomes much more indented. Property tends to be comparatively expensive in this coastal region; commuters to both cities set up home here and there are many holiday homes as well.

Inland, the **Blackwater valley** has many large, elegant Georgian houses. You will also find many big houses along the **Slaney** and **Suir valleys**. The towns of **Cappoquin**, **Stradbally** and **Annestown** are favourites for people looking for property in the upper price echelons. The **Nire valley** in the Comeragh Mountains is a wonderful rural retreat, with heathery walks, reasonably priced cottages and farmhouses and views of mountains, little rivers and woodlands. The village of Ballymacarberry is a jumping off point for this area.

Average prices in Waterford are €202,000.

Cork

It is hard to summarise Cork. It is the largest county in Ireland and one that manages the difficult feat of being attractive to tourists while remaining a good place to live. It is called the 'rebel county' and, although it was not dramatically more rebellious than many other places, the name pinpoints an enduring theme. Cork feels itself to be different, kookier perhaps, with a sardonic wit and an all-encompassing confidence that no other Irish city or county can hold a candle to it.

The population of the county is almost half a million, with over 150,000 in the city of Cork and its suburbs. Starting from the border with Waterford East, Cork is known for food, crafts and a soft landscape with large fields, black and white Friesian cattle, huge trees and the long stone walls of old estates. **Youghal** (pronounced Yawl) on the coast is a walled seaside town where Sir Walter Raleigh allegedly planted the first Irish potato in 1588. Less than 200 years later it had become the staple diet of an enormous peasantry and when the crop failed disaster ensued. To the south is affluent farmland.

Inland, market towns like **Michelstown**, **Kanturk**, **Fermoy**, **Mallow** and **Macroom** are all surrounded by enchanting green countryside. Farming is the main activity but you can find cottages and farmhouses without land here for far less than in the coastal areas. Steeplechasing was invented here when two gentlemen challenged each other to a cross-country race from Buttevant to Doneraile, guided by the steeple of Doneraile church. This is still good country for horses, and further north the Duhallow Foxhounds are one of the oldest hunts in Ireland, founded in 1745.

Cork, the second city of the Irish republic, sits in a huge natural bay. This is an intimate place; people feel at home here quickly. Perhaps that's because it doesn't have imposing buildings or grand squares. Instead it has narrow winding streets, solid red-brick houses and countless church spires. It is a good city to walk in: streets run up and down hills, sometimes turning into stairs; bridges crisscross the river Lee; and quays run along the water, giving the whole place a bright, airy feel. The city centre is jam-packed into a central island with two tributaries of the Lee on either side.

This has always been a wealthy city. Its leading families were called the merchant princes of Cork. Rather like Dublin, the city is divided by the river; to the south the city is more middle-class and affluent; to the north there are more working-class estates and a grittier feel. It is a university town, a city renowned for its wit, a centre for the arts (it will be Europe's Capital of Culture in 2005), a modern city with pharmaceutical, brewing and computer industries among others, and a place where, if you are looking for city life within a stone's throw of the country, you might decide to settle. It doesn't come cheap though. Prices are still below those of Dublin but have been climbing steadily for the last five years. If you look a little outside the city you will find that commuters are your main competitors for property along the coast. In towns like **Cobh**, where emigrants once set sail for America on rickety sailing ships, people now settle, working in the area or travelling into Cork city.

Cork also has a certain amount of glamour that isn't found elsewhere. Further down the coast the port of **Kinsale** is twinned with Antibes in the south of France. And, yes, there are sleek yachts, beautiful people and really good food. You're unlikely to be fooled though – although temperatures in the winter are roughly the same as the south of France summer is a tad cooler. This hasn't deterred a sizeable number of UK commuters, however, attracted by the high quality of education, the beautiful location and, most importantly, the proximity of Cork airport. This means that larger and more exclusive properties are far and few between. Long-term rentals are also common around Kinsale.

To the west along the coast lie a string of vibrant, brightly painted towns and villages: **Courtmacsherry**, **Clonakilty**, **Rosscarbery**, **Skibbereen**, **Baltimore**, **Schull** and **Glengarriff**. It was along this coast, just off Bantry, that the French attempted to land in 1798 but were driven back by storms. Now it is home to some of Ireland's largest expatriate communities. They have come from Britain, from other parts of Europe and from further afield looking for alternative lifestyles, a place to retire, a place to sail, a place to bring up children or simply a place to relax. As with all the most popular locations there are good reasons for people flocking here. The mild, damp climate creates extraordinarily lush growth. Fields are richly green, gardens flourish and warrens of tiny country lanes are hemmed with dense fuchsia hedges. The wilder, harsher scenery of the west of Ireland can make visitors feel almost intimidated; here you feel welcome. Everyone moving here is looking for the same thing: a lovely traditional cottage or farmhouse with a view of the sea. Such is the demand for tumbledown dwellings that there are hardly any left, and purpose-built holiday villages are beginning to appear. As usual, stepping inland a few miles will bring prices down.

One thing to be wary of in this area is the ownership of land and title deeds. If you plan to buy, make sure an independent solicitor confirms that what is on

Case Study: A Vernacular Architect

Bena Stutchbury came to Union Hall in west Cork every year when she was growing up in London. 'Ireland was the garden of Eden for me,' she says. It is an apt description for this part of west Cork, all lush green with a sapphire sea and a remote dreamy quality. She made a permanent move to west Cork 12 years ago when her own children were born.

On making the move she initially worked as an assistant to her architect father – 'theoretically he had retired to Ireland but architects never retire, someone is always asking for a little dog kennel design or a kitchen extension,' she says. When he died in 1994, leaving unfinished projects, she carried on his work, initially with a local architect and later branching out on her own. Now she carries out an eclectic range of tasks for people moving to west Cork – finding houses, designing new ones, extending them and giving advice and support to newcomers. Her signature is careful restoration; she scavenges in salvage yards, reinstates old doors and fireplaces and does extensive research into original mortars and finishes. Her most famous client is probably Jeremy Irons. She spent six years working on his castle in Roaringwater Bay (*see* box 'Pink Castles and Statuettes', p.117, for the story of the restoration).

Bena thinks that many English people moving to Ireland hanker after their own childhoods. 'In Ireland children can come home across the fields, there's no need for a curfew, and they have real freedom of a kind they can't have in England any more,' she says. Ironically, her own teenage boys – who have lived in Ireland for most of their lives – look to England nostalgically. 'I dreamt about west Cork as a child; they are always asking when are we going to London.'

Now Bena is working on plans to restore a disused mill near Rosscarbery for her own family. This isn't a picturesque old stone watermill; it is a solid, concrete extension to the original mill. It was only added in the 1920s when the mill swapped from waterpower to a diesel engine. 'It's cheaper than a site,' Bena says, and points out that there is a wonderful river running along the bottom of her garden and that when the work is done she'll have a four-storey house in a place she loves. Bena's advice to house-hunters is always to go for more space. 'Don't think that you are being clever by buying something on half an acre; privacy is the new thing, so make sure you have a couple of acres around you. At the very least it'll stop anyone building on top of you.'

sale is what can be sold. Families passed property down; fields were swapped; accuracy in mapping was not a strong point; titles weren't confirmed; and now that the land is actually worth something legal title can be a nightmare. The further west you go from Cork City the more problematic the deeds can be.

The furthest point west in Cork, shared with neighbouring Kerry, is the **Beara peninsula**. This is a completely different place from lush, west Cork and verdant Glengarriff; it is far wilder and feels more remote. In fact it has much more in common with Kerry than with the rest of Cork.

Eating Well in Cork

The old clichés die hard, and you can still find soggy cabbage and limp pink bacon in far too many places, but all over Ireland a real food revolution has been quietly going on. It is not yet in the league of France or Italy, but it is getting there. And Cork is one of the best places to be a foodie. Most of the little towns along the coast and many inland have farmers' markets once a week, where you'll find a range of stalls with locally produced food, much of it organic. Think wild salmon oak smoked to a traditional recipe, handmade cheeses, organic pork and all kinds of artisan produce. The grandfather (or mother) of them all is the English Market in Cork. Unlike the upstarts along the coast, delightful though they may be, this venerable market dates from a charter of James I in 1610. The present building dates from 1786. Inside is the kind of market you expect in Europe, but not in Ireland. It is filled with stalls selling everything imaginable: fish with an extraordinary range of shapes, fins and iridescent colours; conventional and organic vegetables; home-made terrines and pâtés; speciality teas and coffees; cheeses... The food writer Tamsin Day-Lewis says that the most remarkable thing about the English Market is its regionality. It is intrinsically of Cork: although you'll find everything from Sardinian olive oil to Greek baklava, you'll also find crubeens (pig's feet) and buttered eggs. These were traditionally coated with butter to keep them fresh for up to a year. And here, too, you will find the national dish of Cork – tripe and drisheen. Not for the faint-hearted, this is blood pudding cooked in milk and served with tripe and onions. An Bord Bia (the Irish Food Board) publishes a list of farmers' markets countrywide at **www.bordbia.ie/consumers/farmersmarkets.html**.

Average prices in the city of Cork are €240,000; outside they drop to €218,000. Be warned that price inflation in the city was 22 per cent in 2003 and this probably won't slow down in 2004 and beyond.

Kerry

This is where the playwright J.M. Synge was driven to ask 'why is anyone left in Dublin, or London, or Paris, when it would be better, one would think, to live in a tent or hut with this magnificent sea and sky, and to breathe this wonderful air, which is like wine in one's teeth'. And Kerry is indeed extraordinarily beautiful, almost intoxicatingly so. Its narrow, twisty roads reveal wonderful vistas of sea, sky and mountains, primeval forests of oak and yew, mirror-calm lakes, subtropical gardens and tiny islands where communities of medieval monks lived solitary and contemplative lives. The people of the place also have a reputation for friendliness and goodwill, tempered with acerbic wit. All of this comes at a price – long lines of tour buses lumbering around the winding roads of the Iveragh peninsula, tacky tourist shops and ugly bungalows stretching out from the towns.

Perhaps this is because tourism has been part of Kerry's landscape for a very long time. Killarney was one of Ireland's first resort towns, and the newly opened railway brought thousands of people to marvel at the beauty of the lakes and mountains around. Tennyson came in 1848 and described how the 'long light shakes across the lakes'. Queen Victoria came too: a gap in the mountains called Ladies' View marks where she picnicked with her ladies-in-waiting. So the busloads of check-capped American tourists are in exalted company. If you decide to stay and settle you can, with a little work, avoid the most crowded spots – especially Killarney and its environs.

Kerry is where you really see the Gulf Stream at work. There is practically no frost in winter, so along the coast and in any sheltered place you'll find luxurious and lush vegetation. Although the higher slopes of the mountains are bare and austere, beneath them gardens like Derreen near Kenmare and Glanleam on Valentia Island are crammed with palm trees, tree ferns and other tropical plants. The flip side of this is a changeable climate: mist can roll up from the sea or down from the hills very quickly and rain falls often. However, sunshine breaks out just as often and the clouds are often as spectacular as the mountains.

The county consists of two rugged peninsulas jutting out into the Atlantic and a low-lying northern region, which has more in common with Limerick than with the spectacular scenery of the southern part. Coming from County Cork you first encounter the Kerry side of the **Beara peninsula**. **Kenmare** is the main town here, sited on the long inlet of the Kenmare River (a sea inlet not a river at all) where, if you are lucky, you might glimpse porpoises and dolphins. Kenmare is full of life, and people, some of them tourists but many resident all year round. *Forbes Fortune* magazine once named Kenmare as one of the top 20 places to retire to in the world. Local estate agents say that they still get enquiries about the article five years on.

A bit further along is the **Iveragh peninsula**, with Ireland's most spectacular mountains, the **Macgillycuddy Reeks**. Normans never really settled here – Gaelic clans held the area until well after Tudor invasions of the Beara and Dingle peninsulas. Later some Catholic familes held on to their lands and religion through the penal times. One of these was that of Daniel O'Connell, known as the Liberator, who fought long and hard – though always refraining from physical violence – for Catholic Emancipation. The N70 winds its way around the peninsula but is better known as the **Ring of Kerry**. Here every house has a spectacular view and a price tag to match. Another smaller ring links **Caherciveen** with **Waterville**; here there are fewer coaches in summer and a more rural feel. Just off the coast are the rocky **Skellig islands**, now home to countless sea birds but once the site of the most western monastic settlement in Europe. **Valentia Island** is famous for its microclimate. The harbour area is sheltered from the Atlantic gales and poppies and primulas flourish. Here property on the coast is always at a premium, higher up with views almost as much again. High up in the mountains property is cheaper, especially abandoned and dilapidated cottages, but the downside is that you will be a long way from villages and other people.

The town of **Killarney** is teeming with tourists in the summer and has lots of leprechaun-and-harp-type souvenir shops. It is also a popular place to settle and there's a shortage of new houses on its outskirts. You might prefer the **Dingle peninsula** – Irish-speaking, rockier, wilder, more austere and more isolated, although tourism is what maintains the town and people of **Dingle** these days. There was a large increase in the price of property in this area in 2003. Little towns and villages like **Castlegregory** and **Ventry** attract surfers and many foreigners looking for an alternative life. Beyond Dingle the county flattens out and the scenery becomes greener as farmland takes over. Property here is considerably cheaper and the whole area has more in common with Limerick.

Average prices in the whole of Kerry are €192,000.

Limerick

Most of Limerick is quiet, farming land and lacks spectacular scenery. It is a county that people tend to pass though on their way to Kerry, Clare and Cork. Limerick city has a bit of a chip on its shoulder, mainly because it was immortalised in Frank McCourt's best-selling childhood memoir *Angela's Ashes* as the gloomiest, dampest, most miserable place imaginable. Before him the novelist Kate O'Brien characterised **Limerick** as a city of commerce, narrow, conventional and rigidly Catholic. Of late, long-running family feuds have been in the news with faked kidnappings, accusations, beatings and murder. Add to that a town centre that has not developed very gracefully and perhaps you might agree that Limerick has something to be petulant about. But this is not the full story; indeed, it is only a tiny portion of it. Prosperity brought by new industry, technology parks, the runaway success of its university and the rapid expansion of the city means that a new spirit is abroad and it has become a happier place. Many of the villages nearby are expanding rapidly as commuters are sprawling out from the city into Clare and Tipperary. The main reason for this is government incentives for businesses and development in the Shannon Development Zone centred on Limerick and Shannon in County Clare.

Another interesting Limerick titbit is that it is the centre of rugby in Ireland. Unlike Dublin, where the game is concentrated in middle-class schools and their alumni, in Limerick the game is a traditional working-class sport that everyone is passionate about, whatever their background or allegiance. The style of play has something in common with the city – tough and uncompromising. Outside the city you'll find some very attractive towns and villages and some lovely scenery. The village of **Adare** is one of the few that can genuinely be called picturesque.

Average house prices in Limerick are €199,000; country areas are cheaper.

Tipperary

Everyone knows of Tipperary – the First World War song with its chorus 'it's a long way...' has percolated into the consciousness of half the world – but few people know what the large county is really like. It is divided into North and South Ridings with separate administrations, the only county in Ireland to be so divided. It is also the only landlocked county in Munster. To make up for this it has the largest of the Shannon lakes, **Lough Derg** to the west. Around the borders of the county, mountains encircle rich pasture land; **Slievnamon**, known as a fairy mountain, to the southeast; the **Knockmealdowns** to the south; the **Galtys** and **Silvermines** to the southwest; and the Arras above Lough Derg. Here you will find some of the landscapes most typical of Ireland's central plain – dark green hedges bushy with trees enclosing vivid green fields, with an occasional golden or brown square creating a chequered, patchwork effect.

To the south the county has much in common with Cork; the fertile valley of the **Golden Vale** is a centre for dairying and is so called because of the rich butter that is produced here. There are many comfortable farmhouses around and a large number of middle-sized 18th- and 19th-century houses, many with some land still attached. If your interests are horses and hunting this area might suit you. Tipperary is excellent hunting country with two hunts, the Ormond and the North Tipperary; it is also good horse-breeding country with many stud farms, particularly in the south.

North Tipperary offers several regions that feel quite different. To the north where the Shannon borders County Galway, it is flat and smallish farms dot a country that is quite off the beaten track. Go up into the mountains behind **Nenagh** and it again feels remote, with some lovely views over the Tipperary plain to compensate. Both regions are places where you might find a cheapish property. But the lakeside region is different again with lovely rolling hills, big trees and spectacular views of water and the mountains in Clare. Demand from Limerick commuters means that the southern end of the lake is built up as far as the village of **Newtown** (the primary school here has one of the best views in Ireland). All along the lakeside drive sites with lake views are at a premium. Popular villages for second homes are **Terryglass** and **Dromineer**; if you sail or are interested in messing about in boats without having to cope with the vagaries of the Atlantic this may be a very good spot to set up home.

Some auctioneers see this region as a challenger to more established areas like west Cork and Connemara, mainly because it is simple to get to, with easy access to Shannon airport and continual upgrades on the route from Dublin. Despite this, even though so many of the key roads are being upgraded, often with EU structural funds, the ever-increasing traffic sometimes makes the whole enterprise seem rather futile – no sooner is a road upgraded than a new bottleneck pops up a few miles further on.

Community before Commuting

Cloughjordan is one of the many Irish country towns that has not changed much in the last 30 years or so. Remote isn't really the right word for it, as it is only two hours' drive to Dublin and there is a train station in the village, but it isn't really on the map. Few tourists come here, so the wide main street hasn't been enlivened with brightly coloured houses. Some buildings are abandoned and boarded up as many residents have chosen to build their new houses outside the village boundaries. But this is where a diverse group, whose members are linked mainly by a passionate desire to escape the rat race, plans to build Ireland's first ever eco-village. Their primary aim is to create a community of people living in harmony with the local community and the surrounding landscape but they also hope to rejuvenate the surrounding community and provide a blueprint for co-operative developments elsewhere in Ireland.

The members of the group are not quite what you'd expect: shareholders include architects, retirees, journalists and engineers, and their business model has been applauded by *Business and Finance* magazine and the *Sunday Times*. The founders are following in the footsteps of several other groups who created their own rural utopian communities in Ireland. The Moravians, a Protestant sect, founded the model village of Gracehill in Armagh, and the Palatines, German refugees from the Rhineland, founded several villages in County Limerick. Although both groups were active in the 18th century, their aims are not that different from the modern day eco-villagers, who wish to create a community where they can live in accordance with their beliefs.

The modern-day group of idealists plans to build a hundred houses together with an organic farm, orchards, community gardens and community buildings on the 70-acre site just outside Cloughjordan in Tipperary. Houses will be built ecologically with natural materials sourced from the area, using solar power for energy needs. Any waste will go into special wetlands with plants that can cleanse waste water. But this is an outward-looking community: a wireless broadband Internet network will allow members to telework and keep in contact with the wider world. So far the group has an option on the site and is in the process of consulting with the local community and applying for planning permission for the first tranche of houses. If all goes according to plan, the quiet village of Cloughjordan will find itself well and truly on the map in 2004. And, this being Ireland, the Limetree Pub will be a key element of the new village, although unlike other Irish pubs each householder will own a share.

If this kind of enterprise is what you are looking for, or if you fancy owning a bit of your local, check out their website **www.thevillage.ie** or request information from **info@thevillage.ie**.

Average house prices in Tipperary are low at €179,000, but around Lough Derg they are at west Cork or Connemara levels – over €200,000 for even smallish cottages.

Clare

Clare is a rather odd mix, with some of Ireland's most popular tourist spots as well as some lovely remote areas. Every American tour bus stops at Bunratty Castle before detouring to the Cliffs of Moher en route to Galway, and Lahinch is a popular seaside resort town. But much of the county, thankfully, has completely avoided mass tourism, although the seaside resorts and spas of Clare were among Ireland's first tourist attractions. Victorian tourists came by train to take the waters at Lisdoonvarna and Clifden and to marvel at the cliffs. Today archaeology and botany bring many people here, as do walking and fishing. It is also one of the best places in Ireland to hear traditional music centred around the village of Doolin.

This is a county bounded by water: the Atlantic to the west, with boats to the **Aran Islands** from **Doolin**; the winding **Shannon Estuary** to the south; and the river itself and its largest lake, **Lough Derg**, to the east. **Shannon airport** gives easy access to the whole region; nowhere is more than an hour's drive away so this area might be a good choice for someone who'd like to be able to get back and forth easily. In inland Clare the western shores of Lough Derg are nothing like as built up as the eastern side, possibly because it is much further to get to from Dublin or perhaps because the land is hilly and poor. The little village of **Mountshannon** is popular because of its wonderful lake views, but around Limerick new dormitory towns and thousands of one-off homes have sprung up. Commuters flood into the city from Shannon, built to house workers in the new airport of Shannon, opened in 1959. The airport introduced Irish coffee and duty-free shopping to the world. **Ennis** is the county capital and is an attractive town with narrow streets and bright shop fronts; it is a country place, though, and feels a little way from the sea. **Killaloe**, on the lake, linked to its twin Ballina in Tipperary by a long bridge with 13 arches, is a very attractive town with some lovely houses along the water, in demand for Dublin and Limerick commuters.

The most attractive part of Clare is in and around **the Burren**. Like Connemara, this is not a clearly delineated region but covers about 100 square miles. Doolin on the Atlantic, Kilfenora a little inland and Gort in Galway mark its borders.

Information Age Town

Visitors to the rather sleepy town of Ennis might be surprised to hear that it was a testing ground for the much vaunted information society. On 24 September 1997 Ennis was selected from 46 other Irish towns to become Ireland's Information Age Town. Over the next five years €15 million was spent on saturating the town with 21st-century communications technology. The main aim was to see how people came to terms with such technology. You'll instantly see that the town's website is a step above the average rural site, and the people of the town, right across generations, use e-mail and the Internet as a matter of course.

The Burren Region: Stones in Every Fertile Place

The Burren – *boireann* means 'place of rocks' – is a karst limestone region covering about 100 square miles of northwest Clare. A typical karst region consists of huge sheets of flat, pale limestone rock, broken up into terraces and crisscrossed by joints. Limestone weathers in a particular way: acidic rainwater etches away the rock to create deep clefts, called grykes, and the limestone slabs, clints. Under this clint and gryke landscape lies an even weirder underworld, caves filled with stalactites and stalagmites and long subterranean passageways. One of Cromwell's surveyors famously said that here there was not enough water to drown a man, nor enough earth to bury a man, nor a tree to hang him. But he was mistaken; it appears bare but close up the blueish-grey recesses in the rock hide dense vegetation – a bizarre juxtaposition of Alpine, Arctic and Mediterranean plants. The limestone retains heat, so more delicate plants can survive winter frosts and the cracks protect the plants from salty winds. The rarer plants include names like bloody cranesbill, hoary rockrose, shrubby cinquefoil, mountain avens and spring gentian. This combination of fertility and barrenness (cattle can graze on the hills all year round) is what gives the Burren its particular quality.

Everywhere in Ireland you'll find subtle demarcations between villages and towns. Here, for example, Limerick buyers tend to purchase second homes in **Lahinch**, five miles from Liscannor (famous for slate, many houses have floors made of the dark grey flagstones pitted with tiny fossils). In **Liscannor** itself you find lots of well-heeled Dublin professionals who have also bought property all along the stretch of coast up to Ballyvaughan and as far as Kinvarra in Galway. Many Europeans and some British people have settled in the region. Househunters here who are not set on a sea view could concentrate on some of the less-known inland areas. The coastal region is still less expensive than Galway just a few miles up the coast, although demand is creeping downwards and the shorter journey from Dublin makes it popular with second homebuyers.

The average price for new and second-hand houses here is €186,000 but you won't find much under €200,000 in the more popular holiday locations like Liscannor, Bell Harbour and Ballyvaughan.

Connacht

Connacht (sometimes spelt Connaught) is the smallest province of Ireland. It includes Galway, Mayo, Sligo, Leitrim and Roscommon, and is bounded by the Atlantic on one side and the Shannon River for much of its eastern flank. Its main towns are Galway and Sligo. It often regarded as the most 'Irish' of areas, not least because the main Irish-speaking area, the Gaeltacht, is here, but also because it has represented Ireland in films, tourist literature and on a million postcards. Going to the west is still for many Irish people a journey of escape. It is a place that epitomises a life apart from that of the city and the modern world. This romantic idea of the west comes partly from the view of the Gaelic revivalists in the 1900s that this part of Ireland retained integrity and the old customs and traditions while the rest of the country became contaminated with modernity. The film *Into the West* captures some of this idea with its tale of two boys travelling west across Ireland from their constrained life in a Dublin high-rise to a mythic region of mystery and magic. This area can feel truly magical, perhaps because of a particular quality of the light, but it has a sad and at times desperate history.

The land was so barren and the region so distant that the province, together with County Clare, was not part of the confiscations that followed the wars of the 17th century. As a result people flooded into the area and until the late 19th century it was the most populous part of Ireland. It was also desperately poor, so the potato famine of the 1840s struck here with particular force. All over Connacht you can see the remains of deserted villages abandoned after the famine.

The sea is still the main influence on the province – the Atlantic pummels the coast, trees are almost doubled over, permanently fixed into crouched silhouettes by the continual wind from the west, rain and squalls sweep in often and mists come down quickly. Edith Somerville memorably described the Twelve Pins in Galway as 'elephants shrouded in muslin'. But when the sun comes out it is a startlingly beautiful place; shafts of sunlight pick out distant lakes shimmering in the hills and the whole coast is filled with glittering light contrasting with the dark blues and purples of the mountains. And not all of Connacht is wild sea and mountain; inland much of the province is farmland and heathery hills with a calm low-key quality.

The Gaeltacht

Gaeltacht means Irish-speaking area (its reverse, less often heard, is Galltacht, district where Irish is not spoken). The first task of the Free State Government following independence was to establish the borders of the Irish-speaking areas (you'll find that most Irish people call the language Irish rather than Gaelic). These are mainly along the western seaboard and Donegal although there is a tiny Irish-speaking enclave in Ring in Waterford. Today Gaeltacht areas are shrinking and many of their inhabitants use English in daily life.

Údarás na Gaeltachta (the Gaeltacht Authority) is the state development agency for Irish-speaking areas and aims to promote the use of Irish as a daily means of communication for those living in the Gaeltacht. TG4 (originally called Telefís na Gaelige – Irish television) has been one of the success stories, broadcast mainly in Irish but with English subtitles. Its fresh and dynamic programming has, after an initial lull, lured viewers from the more mainstream stations. *See also* **Settling In**, 'The Irish Language', pp.208–209.

> ## Case Study: A Novelist in Roundstone
>
> Sadie Browne always wanted to live in Ireland but finances, a journalistic career in London and a family meant that it was always impossible. She and her late husband bought a dilapidated house in Roundstone in 1968 and for over 20 years she spent as much time as she could there. 'As soon as the school year finished, we'd be straight into the car, on to the ferry and driving across to Connemara,' she remembers. Finally, in 1990, a miracle happened: she sold a novel and got a substantial advance. 'Immediately I paid off the mortgage and moved to Ireland permanently and I've been perfectly happy ever since!' she declares.
>
> Sadie remembers the days when it was hard to find a tomato in the village shop – now it stocks balsamic vinegar. But although she has seen many things change – far more houses built and far more visitors arriving – she thinks that a lot of things are still the same. 'Connemara people are still the loveliest in Ireland; I've seen children grow up and known generations of families. In London, you might know people for years, but you never meet their parents or their brothers and sisters; here you are friends with everyone and you know everyone,' she says. What does she miss? She reflects, 'It seems silly to quibble when you have wonderful fresh salmon and fish but what I do miss, I think it is the only thing, is having ethnic food delivered to the door.' Most would agree it is a small price to pay for having the Atlantic on your doorstep and the wonderful scenery of Connemara all round.

Galway

Galway is the second largest county in Ireland and one with two distinctly opposing faces. The western side is Connemara, facing the ocean with a wild and grand landscape of mountains, lakes, bogs and deep sea inlets, including Ireland's only fjord, Killary Harbour. The massive Lough Corrib chops the county in half and the eastern region is flat farmland dotted with tiny lakes, stone-walled farms and ruined tower houses. **Galway City**, sited at the mouth of Galway Bay looking out to the Aran Islands, links the two. This is a small city (population 65,000) but one that has always been cosmopolitan, with traces of Spanish influence and a strong seafaring tradition that saw merchants travelling to the West Indies. It continues to have a lively cultural life; the weird and wonderful puppets of Macnas Street Theatre feature in many photographs of the town and the Galway Arts Festival is Ireland's biggest. It also has an early music festival, a literary festival and, for those more interested in eating and drinking, the Galway Oyster festival.

Galway always had a reputation for being laid-back and happy-go-lucky. Despite or perhaps because of this, Galway has become Ireland's fastest-growing city. Grants from the European Union have triggered growth and there has been much international investment from high-tech companies. It is also a university town, and students from University College Galway (UCG), National

University of Ireland Galway (NUIG) and the Galway-Mayo Institute of Technology (GMIT) give the place even more energy. Tourism is also a big revenue source and in the summer the city and the Aran Islands are filled with visitors. The result of all this growth is that villages in Galway's hinterland such as **Spiddal**, **Oranmore** and **Clarinbridge** have become commuter towns and ribbon development beyond **Salthill** has spoiled the wildness of some of the coast. The national Irish-language television station is based in Spiddal and the village has been transformed over the last decade. Spiddal also marks the start of the Gaeltacht or Irish-speaking area (*see* box 'The Gaeltacht', p.47) and you'll notice that the road signs become Irish-only as you drive into the coastal region.

The area generally considered most typical of the west is the mountainous area of **Connemara**. This is an area of the mind and is not delineated by clear borders, but is roughly the western part of Galway between Lough Corrib and the Atlantic with Killary Harbour to the north. Here are the purplish mountains, the dark blue lakes, the heather and the mountain sheep of archetypal western Ireland captured by artists such as Paul Henry (who in fact worked mainly in Achill in County Mayo). Connemara is one of Ireland's most sought-after holiday home locations and is one of the few places that attracts visitors all year round. There is a substantial expatriate population in Connemara, many of them British. An Indian maharajah once owned Ballynahinch Castle, now a country house hotel. The attraction is hard to quantify; part of it is to do with the quintessential 'Irishness' of the area, part perhaps to do with the openness and friendliness of the people and the spectacular scenery. Many houses are holiday homes; an early evening drive during the week will reveal many unlit houses.

East Galway is quite different with flatter more fertile land. This is the place to look for reasonably priced country homes and cottages.

Sites with planning permission anywhere along the coast sell for up to €100,000. The average cost of houses in the whole county is €240,000. However, in the most popular areas, Roundstone, Clifden and Ballyconneelly, prices can be considerably higher. Auctioneers in Galway confirm that people will wait for years to find the right house in this region. In compensation you can still find something inhabitable for under €150,000 (albeit in need of some work) in parts of East Galway.

Mayo

Boggy to the north, mountainous to the south, with hundreds of sandy beaches and lakes full of fish, Mayo is further north than Galway and far more isolated. It is a big county; over two thousand square miles in area but with a population of only 117,000. The interior of the county is one of Ireland's most unspoilt and much of it still looks as it might have a hundred years ago – empty, with bare mountains and open, treeless expanses of purple bog. The only differences are Sitka fir plantations on some of the hills and the occasional new house. The Mullet peninsula is one of the least populated areas of Europe, allowing wild geese, storm petrels and other birds to live in great profusion on its boggy land. People still speak Irish here, on **Achill Island** and around Belmullet. Mayo also has a wealth of prehistoric remains – Neolithic tombs, dolmens and the Céide Fields Stone Age settlement. Perhaps this is because man has not disturbed the landscape too much. In fact, Mayo county council is the only one in Ireland to have an in-house archaeological unit employing 16 archaeologists to deal with the thousands of antiquities in the area.

Fishing is big business in Mayo, for trout and salmon on the River Moy and game fishing on lakes Mask, Conn and Cullen. Pilgrims come here too. Ireland's holy mountain, **Croagh Patrick**, dominates its corner of Mayo, towering over **Clew Bay**, and Westport with the Marian Shrine of **Knock** is another draw. Here St Patrick cleared Ireland of snakes; the more prosaic reason for their absence is that they, along with moles, didn't make it over before the land bridge joining Ireland with Britain sank beneath the Irish Sea.

Near the border with Galway Lord Sligo named the mountains overlooking Killary Harbour **Delphi** for their resemblance to the site of the Greek oracle; further north is lovely, hilly country with views of island-studded Clew Bay and the **Nephin Beg** mountain range. To the east is **Lough Mask** and just above it green **Lough Carra**; a chalk bottom gives it its vivid colour. As in most remote areas people have abandoned houses in the hills and shifted to the sea and to the outskirts of the towns, leaving the landscape beautiful and empty. The

The Céide Fields

In the most westerly part of Europe a Neolithic settlement was slowly submerged under a thick layer of blanket bog and lay completely undisturbed for over 5,000 years. The site contains hundreds of interlinked Stone Age farms. Parallel walls, over a mile long, run inland from the coast, and dividing walls break up the land into plots big enough to sustain an extended family – usually between 5 and 17 acres. Excavation only began in 1969 although the fields were first discovered in the 1930s. Today some of the walls have been excavated but many still lie beneath the bog. White poles dot the landscape, indicating the patterns of settlement beneath.

One of the most interesting things is the order and organisation revealed. Neolithic man does not seem to have been a haphazard farmer. The layout of the farms looks similar to the rundale system in use in Ireland up until the 19th century. Long rectangular fields ran out from a settlement like the petals of a daisy and each family farmed several plots that were periodically redistributed. Beyond the cultivated area lay a communal grazing area called the outfield. Even the houses are similar to the traditional Irish cottage, with indoor hearths and thatched roofs. Perhaps the ancient landscape did not look that different from the long-established Irish one so familiar across the west.

The Islands of Mayo

Off the coast of Mayo are hundreds of islands, some home only to a few sea-gulls and perhaps the ruins of a hermit's retreat, others with tiny populations eking out a living from small farming, fishing and, increasingly, tourism.

Achill Island is the biggest, with a population of 3,000. Perhaps it is not strictly an island, though, since it is linked to the mainland by a land bridge. This is probably the most touristy part of Mayo and you'll find several purpose-built holiday villages dotted around its coast. Despite this it is incredibly beautiful, with huge cliffs and deserted uplands.

Clew Bay is littered with tiny uninhabited islands. Each one is the top of a submerged drumlin, part of a belt that extends inland and across the country. Further out is Clare Island with a population of 140 people. They have been approached with an unusual proposal; a businessman wants them to grow wildflower seeds for sale all over the world via the Internet. The island is an ideal spot for the project: flowers with alluring names like creeping cinquefoil, slender speedwell, sea sandworth, and birdsfoot trefoil flourish here. So far the response has been enthusiastic as the islanders realise that their future depends on looking beyond traditional occupations.

Other islands include Inisturk, also full of wild flowers and with a population of about 90, and the uninhabited island of Caher, with the remains of an ancient monastic settlement. Occasionally an island comes up for sale, so if you are looking for your own Irish island this might be the spot.

Leenane to Louisburgh road passes though dramatic mountain landscapes and many think it the most beautiful road in Ireland.

Depopulation of the interior means that most of the population of Mayo hugs the coast, with the exception of **Castlebar**, the county town, which has experienced huge growth. The most built-up areas are around Westport and the holiday centre of **Newport**. **Westport** is an elegant planned Georgian town. Thackeray spent some time here, noting that the traveller ought to be thankful, first to nature for the position and aspect of the town, and secondly to Lord Sligo, who laid it out. In fact it was the architect James Wyatt who did the hard work, albeit at the behest of Lord Sligo; his tree-lined Mall is still a feature of the town. Westport has been a resort town for some time and as a result well-off Dublin visitors have driven property prices up all around. Many Mayo residents also choose to live here and commute to Castlebar, 12 miles or so inland, and some even commute to Galway down the coast. **Ballina** on the river Moy is another prosperous town set in green farmland stretching up along the valley.

Despite its isolation Mayo does have an international airport. The tangled tale about how this came to be involves apparitions of the Virgin Mary, determined parish priests and religious tourism and is too long to recount here. But Knock airport now serves Dublin, Birmingham, London and Manchester and is the gateway to all of the northwest of Ireland.

Mayo is so large that it is difficult to give prices for the whole county. Averages are around €180,000 but that includes the bustling towns of Castlebar and Ballina as well as popular holiday home destinations like Westport and Achill Island. In very remote areas you might find cottages for half that or less.

Sligo

Sligo is renowned for its beauty and its artists and poets, particularly the brothers William and Jack Butler Yeats. W.B. Yeats called Sligo 'the land of heart's desire'. There is something special about a landscape that has been eulogised in poetry and the numbers of people who visit the Lake Isle of Innisfree are testimony to this. It is almost as if the poet has put into words what people feel but cannot say when faced with such landscapes. Add to that long, sandy beaches, oddities like Edwardian seaweed baths, a special quality to the light and lots of peaceful villages and towns and you may have found one of the most appealing places in Ireland to live. But lots of other people think that too, so property prices, especially on the coast or near to Sligo town, are high. South away from the coast, around Tobercurry, prices drop.

The sea gave Sligo its prosperity. Its name, 'the place of shells', comes from the rich supply of shellfish found in the Garavogue river estuary. This ensured that it was widely settled during prehistoric times. The county has more pre-Christian

Lissadell House

One of the biggest Sligo property stories of 2003 was the sale of Lissadell House in Sligo. This was the home of the Gore-Booth sisters, Eva and Constance, friends of W.B. Yeats; he stayed there often and wrote a famous poem commemorating the sisters.

Constance married a Polish count and became Countess Markiewicz. She had a turbulent nationalist and feminist career fighting in the 1916 rising and was the first woman to be elected to Westminster (where she refused to take her seat) and subsequently to the first Irish parliament, Dáil Eireann. In 2003 Sir Jocelyn Gore-Booth decided that he could no longer maintain the house and put it on the market. It was suggested that the state should buy it but eventually the government refused, citing a restoration cost of over €28 million. The subsequent controversy unearthed many divergent views on the legacy of the big house, the occasional commentator feeling that such a house represented the worst of British colonisation and should be torn down, others that it should be preserved and turned into a museum of Irish women. Eventually the house was bought for €3.5 million by two Dublin barristers who plan to use it as a family home. But the auction of its contents revealed just how much interest there was in the house – all kinds of household items including wooden toilet seats, children's toys and kitchen linen went for far more than their reserve prices.

monuments and sites than any other place in Ireland. Later, fishing and trade maintained Sligo's status as the pre-eminent town of the region, although agriculture is the primary activity in the county. Although the landscapes here are as beautiful as those of Kerry and Donegal, tourism came late and as a result the countryside is much less populated. (The county has a population of only 58,118.)

Sligo town today is a colourful place with a reputation for the arts, traditional music and a lively nightlife. Here you will find a sizeable hospital, an institute of technology that brings thousands of students to the town, a flourishing arts centre, the Model Arts and Niland Gallery, the Hawk's Well Theatre, lots of bars and restaurants, smart Victorian streets and houses, and a substantial number of residents from outside the county. The town's main downside is probably the appalling traffic partly caused by a complex one-way system but also reflecting its status as the largest town in the northwest. Statistics also show that it is one of the most affluent towns in Ireland (outside the major cities). This means that there is quite a discrepancy between prices in the town (averages are about €220,000) and prices outside (rural areas average only €145,000). This does not include the very popular coastal strip. Houses along the Sligo–Strandhill road, for example, are very expensive. Sligo's attractiveness as a place to settle has leached out into the surrounding counties, Western Leitrim and Northern Roscommon, mainly because of lower prices there.

Leitrim

Leitrim is a small county, only 46 miles long with a maximum breadth of 18 miles and a toe dipping into the sea at Donegal Bay. Packed into this small area is a little bit of everything: glens and mountains to the north, pleasant farming country, hundreds of lakes, small tussocky hills and the River Shannon to the south. It feels gentler and more approachable than the wildness of Galway and Mayo. Lough Allen, the first of the Shannon lakes, almost bisects the county, and the Shannon–Erne Waterway, Europe's longest inland navigable waterway, stretches through the county. In fact the amount of water in the county leads people to say that land here is sold by the gallon rather than by the acre.

As in so many other rural counties the population of Leitrim has declined radically over the past 150 years, and Leitrim has the dubious distinction of being the only county to have had continuous population decline – from over 155,000 in 1841 to just over 25,000 in 2002. This means that property in the region is reasonably priced and in the last five or six years Leitrim has had something of a renaissance, with artists, organic farmers and others seeking a peaceful rural lifestyle settling there. The north of Leitrim has become the centre of an unofficial green box with many eco-tourist projects based at the Organic Centre in **Rossinver**. Visual Leitrim and the Leitrim Design House promote the work of local artists and craftspeople and the little village of **Manorhamilton** has a

Case Study: Bags of Good Hope

In 1998 textile designer Angela Hope and her partner Martin lived in Bristol and worked as a marketing director and the manager of Waterstone's Bristol branch, respectively. Today the couple are based outside Manorhamilton in Leitrim where Angela makes exquisite handbags and Martin has a business making decking. How did they change their lives and find themselves in Leitrim? Their Irish saga began in 1999 when Angela bought a derelict cottage overlooking Killala Bay in Mayo for €30,000. 'We planned to renovate it and use it as a holiday home occasionally,' she explains, but after a few months the lure of Ireland took hold. 'One day I came home and said to Martin that I wanted to live there,' she says. After remarkably little deliberation the two threw up their jobs in Britain and moved to Mayo, without much money and with no jobs. The leap of faith paid off: Martin found work doing carpentry and landscaping and Angela did some freelance marketing work.

But Mayo is very remote and much of Martin's work turned out to be based around Sligo. After a year or so they decided to move. Angela was drawn to the north Leitrim area (even though she hadn't realised its reputation for the arts) and they found a turn-of-the-century cottage just two miles from Manorhamilton in mid 2002. 'But it took a lot of finding,' says Angela, 'over a year.' Angela's advice to house-hunters is to decide on the area that interests them and develop a relationship with local auctioneers. 'The Internet is useful, but it doesn't have all the properties that are available. Local estate agents have lots of English people looking for houses and they won't take you seriously unless you are there in person – you need to visit frequently.'

For Angela the best thing about Leitrim is the mix of cultures: lots of Irish people, of course, but also English, Hungarians and Germans. She also found that there was a local network of artists and craftspeople that she could link into. Once she'd decided to set up her own business the county enterprise board was incredibly supportive, giving her a small grant to renovate her studio and helping with contacts and business plans. Within a year she was inundated with orders for her colourful bags and the name Angela Hope is becoming known in Irish craft circles (**www.angelahope.com**).

Sculptors' Centre. This village is sited at the meeting of four river valleys; driving down to the village you get wonderful views of woods and mountains. From here you are just a few miles from Sligo Town and the sea. Leitrim is also one of the counties singled out under the Rural Renewal Scheme for the Upper Shannon region. (*See* **Selecting a Property**, 'Choosing a Location', p.81, for more on this scheme.)

To the south, **Carrick-on-Shannon** is the county town, set on the river Shannon, which meanders across the plain. There are 41 lakes within six miles of the town so fishing is one of the most popular activities here. This is also where people begin boating holidays, taking lake cruisers down the Shannon. From here you can go up the Boyle river to Lough Key, down the Shannon towards Lough Ree or Lough Derg, or up to Lough Allen and on through the Ballinamore–Ballyconnell Canal to Lough Erne. Properties on the river are particularly popular and often have their own jetties, allowing you to go boating or fishing from your front door (although the little known Irish midge can be a pest for lake-dwellers).

Average property prices in Leitrim are among the lowest in the country at €180,000. Although house price growth is less than in other counties, it is still substantial at 10 per cent in 2003.

Roscommon

Roscommon is the only county in Connacht without a coast, and as a result it has quite a different character from the rest of the province. Bordered by the Shannon all along its eastern flank, it is rather isolated. Bogs and poor land dominate the east on the river and to the west on the border with Galway, but the centre is good farming land. Peaceful, drowsy, small-town Ireland still reigns, where the main topics of conversation are livestock prices and local gossip. Property is still fairly cheap here, but a decision to move here will depend on what kind of lifestyle you are looking for: if it is the simple life, with few other expatriates, in fact few visitors at all, it may suit you down to the ground; if not, perhaps somewhere more lively might suit you better. Roscommon has a large number of ruined big houses built by planters in the 17th century: Clonalis, Mount Plunkett near Athlone, Mount Talbot and Glinsk Castle. Stokestown Park House has been painstakingly restored and is well worth a visit, particularly since it juxtaposes a picture of ascendancy life with a moving museum about the Great Famine. Roscommon is also rich in prehistoric monuments.

Its county town is **Roscommon** with a population of only 1,630. People tend to look to the towns of Longford, Athlone, Ballinasloe and Sligo so there is no definite centre. Although Roscommon cannot be called an exciting place, nonetheless the landscape, scattered with lakes and small farms and traversed by almost deserted country roads, is lovely in its own quiet way. To the north, where Roscommon borders Sligo and Leitrim, the scenery becomes more spectacular with woods and hills rising to the **Curlew Mountains**. **Boyle**, between Lough Key and Lough Gara, is an attractive place with some Georgian houses and a ruined Cistercian abbey just outside the town on the banks of the River Boyle. Alas this means that property prices are on the rise as more Dubliners look for holiday homes here.

Roscommon, in common with Mayo and Monaghan, showed price increases of 20 per cent in 2003. Average house prices are about €186,000.

Ulster and Northern Ireland

Ulster is the least known of Ireland's provinces. The tourist board pleads, a little wistfully, 'you'll never know until you go'. Of late more tourists have ventured over the border. Very few people without personal or professional links settle here although many northerners who left during the Troubles are returning (*see* 'The Troubles', below). The ancient province of Ulster consisted of nine counties. Six of these – Antrim, Down, Armagh, Tyrone, Fermanagh and Londonderry – are part of the British Isles. Three – Donegal, Cavan and Monaghan – are part of the Irish Republic. The border dates from 1921 when the British government concluded the Anglo-Irish treaty with the representatives of the new Irish state. Unionists refused to join the fledgling Free State and the six counties remained part of Britain.

There are many differences between Ulster and the rest of the island and the reasons behind them complex. Landscape, history and culture all play a part. The very distinctive hummocky and hilly countryside that runs across Ireland from Strangford Lough in the northeast to Donegal Bay in the northwest is difficult to traverse and has 'been a barrier to communication and a cultural divide since prehistoric times'. Originally Ulster was culturally similar to the rest of the island – Catholic and Gaelic – but this changed in the 17th century. The Ulster plantation began in 1608 when 200,000 English and Scottish settlers flooded the province. The land was planted by small farmers and other artisans rather than scattered landlords as in the rest of the island.

The scale and the social variation of the plantation created viable communities that have survived to this day, making most of Ulster very different in ethnic makeup from the rest of Ireland. Dissent between the majority community of Protestants and Presbyterians and the Catholic minority has led to great strife and violence; it is to be hoped that this is now over. Ulster was also the only part of Ireland to be heavily industrialised. The south on the other hand was always

The Troubles

The Troubles is the term used to refer to the period of violent sectarian conflict in Northern Ireland. During the Troubles more than 3,000 people were killed, most of them civilians. They began with the Civil Rights marches in the late 1960s and are generally considered to have ended with the IRA ceasefire in 1997 and the 1998 Good Friday Agreement. The Good Friday Agreement is a settlement designed to create a political framework based on 'parity of esteem' rather than the previous divisive system of majority rule. The Agreement respects the right of each political tradition to remain part of the United Kingdom or to work towards joining the Irish Republic. It would be impossible to summarise or explain the troubled past of Northern Ireland in a guidebook such as this but there are suggestions for more detailed delving into the subject in **References**, 'Further Reading', p.290.

predominantly rural with the occasional tiny pockets of industry near the main cities. However, despite this industrial past, Ulster now reminds some people of England in the 1950s: quiet, undeveloped and sleepy. Property in the three southern counties costs rather less than in the Republic generally but the rate of increase is very high, as much as 20 per cent in some cases. In Northern Ireland prices are considerably less, on average £105,779, and many investors from the Republic have bought property there (especially in Belfast).

In 2002 the population in Ulster was 1,931,838; in Northern Ireland it was 1,685,267. Belfast and its environs contain about 45 per cent of the population of the six counties (source: the 2002 Population Census).

Donegal

Donegal is famous for its wild and beautiful scenery and its remoteness. The sea creates its most characteristic landscapes: the wide sweep of Donegal Bay, the high sea cliffs around the Slieve League peninsula, the deep inlet of Lough Swilly and hundreds of islands dotted along the deeply indented coast, over 200 miles long. All kinds of different rocks – limestone, granite and quartzite – underlie Donegal, and it is this that creates so much variety in the scenery. Inland, Donegal has rivers and boggy mountains and is one of the most sparsely populated regions in Ireland. People in this area survived by doing a little bit of everything: their tiny farms had a patch devoted to potatoes, another to oats and the last field to a cow or two, which would be moved up the mountains in the summer. Money came in from immigrants to America, but the mainstay of most families was seasonal migration to work on the potato fields of Scotland. This sort of migration differed from the rest of Ireland, where peasants tended to stay put or emigrate permanently, and it accounts for some of the differences between Donegal and Ulster, and the south. The county retains many links to Scotland, particularly to Glasgow.

Because the county was almost cut off from the rest of the Republic by the border with the north of Ireland, the Irish government placed particular emphasis on encouraging development in the region and many multinational factories were set up in predominantly rural communities. Despite this investment public transport is still poor; there are no trains and instead a medley of private bus companies provide transport within the region. Only 20 per cent of the population (137,383) lives in towns, making Donegal one of the most rural counties in Ireland; nonetheless, the towns, particularly **Letterkenny**, are booming. One-third of the county is deemed to be Irish-speaking and the Donegal Gaeltacht is the largest in the Republic.

Donegal is traditionally where urban northerners from Belfast and other towns come on holiday. Formerly they lived in caravans, but now, with new prosperity north and south, holiday home developments are springing up along the coast. It is estimated that 50 per cent of new homes on Donegal are holiday homes. **Port na Blagh** and **Dunfanaghy** are where there has been most development but much of the coast is now lined with bungalows. This is where you'll see urban sprawl, more than in other counties – some villages consist of little more than a shop, a pub and a few houses but have miles of bungalows lining the roads to either side.

If you are looking for somewhere really off the beaten track the **Inishowen peninsula** seems to have been bypassed by many tourists and is one of the most unspoilt and beautiful areas in Ireland. It is almost encircled by **Lough Swilly** to the west and **Lough Foyle** to the east. Its coast is hemmed with beaches backed by cliffs and spectacular inland mountains.

Donegal is consistently Ireland's cheapest place to buy property. Average house prices are around €170, 000 but if you go inland or to a more remote area even this can drop considerably.

Cavan

Cavan is drumlin country. Hundreds of little rounded hills dot the landscape, left behind as the glaciers retreated at the end of the Ice Age. Between the hills and woods are countless little lakes. The official name for this topography is a 'basket of eggs' landscape. To the west the land rises and the river Shannon has its source a few miles short of the border. Just under 60,000 people live here, concentrated in the main towns of **Cavan**, **Cootehill** and **Bailieborough**. Cavan has a reputation for sleepiness and quietness. This is probably because it is not on the way to anywhere. The advantage of this is that it is very unspoilt: if you are looking for peace and solitary country walks, lots of water, excellent coarse fishing and unspectacular but pretty countryside this may be the place for you.

Tourists began to rediscover this country when the Ballinamore–Ballyconnell Canal reopened in 1994, and **Lough Sheelin**, straddling the border with Meath and Westmeath, is becoming a popular destination for weekend homes. The Dublin commuter is beginning to show up as well – houses outside Virginia, an attractive town with many pretty cottages, are selling to people who have flexible working hours in the city. There's no train service in this part of the world, though, so that might discourage widespread commuter interest.

Average house prices are between €170,000 and €180,000.

Monaghan

Monaghan is a sparsely populated county (52,000), well known to anglers but with few other tourists. Drumlins dot the countryside. Between the hills lie small fields, narrow roads and sparse hedgerows. This is an unspoiled corner of Ireland, partly because of its border location, but also because not very much happens here. Monaghan has yet another sad story of population decline and economic stasis. Pre-famine it had one of the highest population densities in Ulster. Afterwards the population steadily dropped and stagnation set in, especially when the border divided north from south and Monaghan from the neighbouring counties of Fermanagh, Antrim and Tyrone.

The main towns are **Monaghan, Castleblaney** and **Carrickmacross,** strung out along the N2 which leads on over the border to Tyrone and Derry City. Off the main roads the drumlins break the country up and the roads become labyrinth-like, winding and crisscrossing, ideal for solitary walks, less ideal for getting from A to B. But it is not all fields and farms; an 18th-century linen industry gave the county many classical and Regency buildings and Castleblaney at the head of Lough Muckno has been called the Killarney of the North. Monaghan is also famous for mushroom and chicken production. Celebrity-spotters may already know that Paul McCartney married Heather Mills here in gothic Castle Leslie.

Patrick Kavanagh, one of Ireland's finest poets, was born here in the village of Inniskeen in 1904. Every Irish school-goer knows his ambivalent Monaghan poems, casting doubt on Yeats' vision of the noble peasant and telling of the narrowness of life in this stony grey land but at the same time seeing the 'spirit shocking wonder in a black Ulster hill'. Here too is Annaghmakerrig House, a retreat for writers and artists. If, like them, you are seeking absolute peace and quiet, this county might be for you.

You won't be surprised to hear that very few foreigners buy here and property is still relatively cheap – around €203,000 on average. Like other counties where property is reasonable the percentage increase is far higher than the national average – at around 20 per cent in 2003.

The Six Counties of Northern Ireland

Antrim

Antrim is the most northeastern county of Ulster. Historically it has retained close connections with Scotland from the 14th century, with more Scots settlement in the 16th and 17th centuries. Today most of its population is Presbyterian and Protestant. Antrim is one of the most visited counties in the north of Ireland mainly because of its spectacular coast and natural phenomena such as the **Giant's Causeway**, the only UNESCO World Heritage site in Ireland. It also has some of the best golf courses in Ireland – over 30 of them including the famous Royal Portrush and Portstewart courses spanning the Derry county boundary. Antrim has a large population: about 650,000 people live here, with over half of these in Belfast and its surrounds.

The county is full of variety. The Antrim coast is one of the loveliest in Ireland, with the nine **glens of Antrim** stretching down to the sea. Irish was spoken in the glens up until the middle of the 19th century and this is a region of scattered farms and remote hills. Along the river Bann valley you find good farmland and prosperous market towns like **Balleymoney** and **Ballymena**. The river Bann then flows into **Lough Neagh**, the biggest lake in the British Isles covering 150 square miles of open water and famous for its eels. The land around the lake is rather flat and boggy. Just below the lake is **Belfast**, administrative centre of the six counties and the most important city in Ulster.

The poet Louis MacNeice said that he was 'born in Belfast between the mountains and the gantries' and this is as good a place as any to start describing the city. The mountains are the Antrim Plateau on one side and the Castlereagh and Holywood hills on the other. Squeezed in between them, the city has a long, elongated shape running up the Lagan valley. As for the gantries, Belfast was the only Irish city to be comprehensively industrialised. Ropemaking, linen, engineering and shipbuilding were the engines that drove its development and growth. Belfast is far younger than most Irish cities, indeed than most European cities. In the 17th century it was just a village but it expanded rapidly during the Industrial Revolution, doubling in size several times during the late 19th century – from 20,000 in 1800 to 350,000 by 1900.

Since the 1997 ceasefire and the Good Friday Agreement in 1998 the city has been transformed: unemployment has dropped, multinational investment has been pumped in and new apartments, hotels, concert halls and offices have sprung up. Although the worst of the violence is over, Belfast remains ethnically divided in the traditional working-class areas, which are rigidly separated, sometimes by high fences. But visitors are often surprised to see how closely the two communities are intertwined – a Nationalist estate can directly face a Loyalist one. If you see property advertised at extraordinarily low prices, the chances are that it is in an area known for sectarian violence (most of these are council estates but some are privately owned). Just as during the very worst of the Troubles parts of Belfast were almost unaffected, today most visitors will see little or no evidence of trouble unless they venture into some of the poorest parts of the city. Belfast has a well-deserved reputation for friendliness and the best nightlife on the island.

The quarterly *House Price Index* published by the University of Ulster in partnership with the Bank of Ireland notes that annual house price growth in Belfast has barely kept pace with inflation (2 per cent) while outside the city growth is measured in double digit figures. The conclusion is that, while many people choose to work in the Greater Belfast area it is not the place they want to live. Homebuyers seem to be focusing outside the city and the commuter belt is expanding outwards, in some cases up to 40 miles or more away. This is different from Dublin, where the centre and suburbs are intensely desirable but unaffordable for many. The most exclusive property in the city is around the university area, with the Malone Road fetching the highest prices. Here good quality four- or five-bedroom houses can cost up to £500,000. In the city centre new apartments range from £90,000 to £120,000. Many investors have bought near the Odyssey Project, Northern Ireland's millennium development and

Profiles
of the Regions

Leinster

<< page 24

Leinster is the Republic's most populated region with over two million people, concentrated around energetic and cosmopolitan Dublin. Many ruined Norman castles and large Ascendancy estates bear witness to Leinster's long and turbulent history as the seat of power in Ireland. More recently Dublin's commuters have spread out from Dundalk to the north to Wexford in the southeast, driving property prices up throughout the province. The land here is fertile and flat, except for the Wicklow Mountains, which have halted Dublin's growth eastwards, and the huge bogs of the Central Plain.

1 Wicklow National Park, Co. Wicklow
2 Cat Stone, Co. Westmeath
3 Powerscourt Waterfall, Enniskerry, Co. Wicklow
4 Peat bog, Wicklow

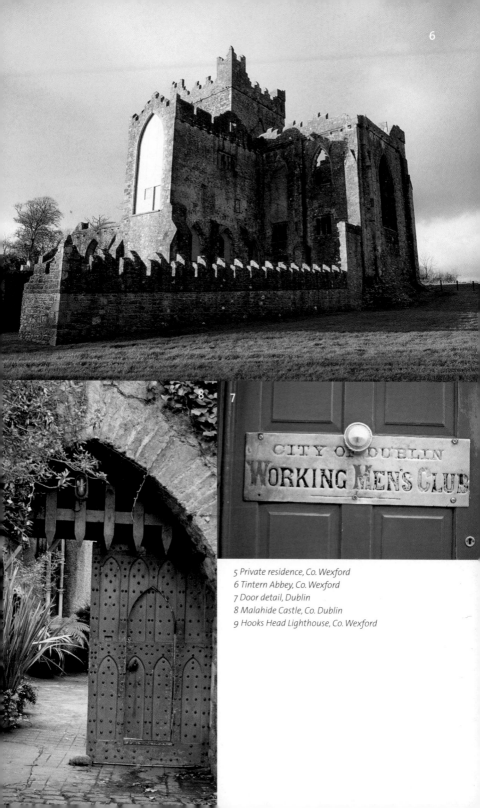

5 Private residence, Co. Wexford
6 Tintern Abbey, Co. Wexford
7 Door detail, Dublin
8 Malahide Castle, Co. Dublin
9 Hooks Head Lighthouse, Co. Wexford

Munster
<< *page 35*

Munster, Ireland's largest province, packs a huge amount into six counties: rich pastureland in Cork, wild mountainous landscapes in Kerry, technological parks around Limerick, the seascapes and bare limestone plateau of Clare, maritime Waterford, and the fertile fields of Tipperary, the only landlocked county in the province. Property, from tumbledown cottages to Georgian estates, is at a premium in West Cork and much of Kerry, but you can still find a bargain in parts of Clare and Tipperary.

1 *Coastline, Rathbury, Co. Cork*
2 *Castle in mist, Co. Tipperary*
3 *Cottage, Co. Cork*
4 *Coastline, Co. Kerry*

5 Staigue Fort, Co. Kerry
6 Cliffs of Moher, Co. Clare
7 Private residence, Co. Clare
8 Sailing, Kinsale harbour, Co. Cork
9 South of Kinsale, Co. Cork
10 Killarney National Park, Co. Kerry

9

10

Connacht
<< page 47

1 Coastline, North Mayo
2 Roonah Quay, Co. Mayo

Connacht is Ireland's most remote region and was once its poorest. Now modern high-tech industries and tourism co-exist with isolated sheep-farmers and fishermen. Most of the country's Irish-speakers live in Connacht's Gaeltacht areas, and Ireland's Irish language television station is based just outside Galway. This lively and colourful town, with a reputation for the arts and a bohemian atmosphere, is the gateway to Connemara, famous for wild landscapes battered by the Atlantic and the spectacular Twelve Pins mountains. This area is one of Ireland's most popular places for holiday homes, and prices from Westport to Clifden reflect this demand. However, elsewhere in Connacht, particularly in the remoter parts of Mayo, prices can halve.

1

2

3

4

8

6

SURFING
is good for you

7

Ulster
<< *page 56*

The ancient province of Ulster is divided
– six counties in Northern Ireland and
three in the Republic. This is still a
relatively unknown and unexplored area,
but for those willing to go a little off the
beaten path it has a huge amount to
offer: spectacular landscapes,
particularly in Donegal and Antrim,
fantastic fishing, and some of the best
golf courses in the country. Today, after
years of strife, a new sense of hope and
possibility is emerging. Belfast is being
regenerated at a tremendous pace – new
arts centres, shopping, houses and
apartments are springing up. The price
of property here is still well below that in
the rest of the country, although
increases are in double-digit figures in
the three counties of the Republic.

1 *Giant's Causeway, Co. Antrim*
2 *White Park Bay, Ballycastle, Co. Antrim*
3 *Fishing boats, Co. Donegal*

2

4 Slieve League Mountains, Co. Donegal
5 Fields, Co. Antrim
6 Glenveagh Castle entrance, Co. Donegal

home to several new apartment blocks. Overall the most expensive location in Northern Ireland is south Belfast, where the average price was just short of £140,000, while north Belfast is the least expensive, with an average of £77,629.

Down

County Down is by reputation the sunniest and breeziest part of Ulster. It also has beautiful mountains, drumlin country (described by C.S. Lewis as 'earth-covered potatoes') and a long sea coast. Down is a cornerstone of Loyalist Ulster. During the 17th and 18th centuries it was planted with Scottish and English settlers and the native Irish shifted to the hilly countryside around the Mourne Mountains. As a result the landscape is orderly, with neat farmhouses and well-tended fields. The north of the county is dominated by Belfast; many commute to work in the city from **Bangor** on the coast and **Lisburn** inland, making much of the countryside suburban in appearance.

The most attractive part of the county lies to the south. **Strangford Lough** is an almost landlocked sea inlet fed though a small channel called the Narrows. The water rushes in with the tide at over eight knots an hour and has scoured out a deep passageway. The eastern side of the lough is called the **Ards peninsula** and many northerners have holiday homes along the coast. Holiday homes around Strangford Lough are popular particularly in pretty towns and villages like **Portaferry** and **Strangford** itself. To the south are the rounded silhouettes of the **Mourne Mountains**, once famed for smugglers. Their uplands are very remote and few roads cross them, making them a haven for walkers. Below the mountains lies the smaller inlet of **Carlingford Lough** marking the border with the Republic.

In north Down property costs more, an average of £125,709, reflecting its proximity to Belfast. Properties in mid and south Down average £107,756 but cottages in popular villages like Portaferry will probably be more.

Armagh

Armagh is the smallest county in Ulster but one that offers varied scenery. The northeast of the county, just below Lough Neagh, is fairly industrial and built up. The city of **Armagh** is associated with St Patrick, and two cathedrals of St Patrick, Catholic and Protestant, face each other from adjoining hills – it was from here that Saint Patrick spread Christianity all over Ireland. During the Troubles sectarian strife was particularly polarised in Armagh. **Portadown** is probably best known for the standoff at Drumcree church every year. This is between the Orange Order wanting to march down the Nationalist Garvaghy Road and the authorities preventing them from doing so. On a brighter note, apples are grown in the northeast around Portadown and this region is known as the Orchard of Ireland. Apple Blossom Sunday is held every year in late May when the orchards are in flower.

The hills and villages of south Armagh are predominantly Catholic and this area gained a reputation for violent republicanism during the Troubles. Today many of the army watch towers have been dismantled, helicopters no longer hover over the fields and the people are beginning to look to a brighter future. The countryside in South Armagh is wilder and more unkempt than the northern parts of the county but has some very attractive parts especially around Slieve Gullion. **Crossmaglen** is famous for traditional music. This region has few tourists and fewer still settle here, which is a shame because parts of the countryside are very beautiful.

Prices here are low – £96,871 on average.

Tyrone

Tyrone is the largest of the northern counties, but is also the least populated and most agricultural region of Ulster. It is known for its inaccessibility, with little public transport in the south of the county. The **Sperrin Mountains** cover much of the north and to the south is farmland with the neat hedges and whitewashed farmhouses typical of this part of Ulster. The poet Seamus Heaney grew up on the edge of the Sperrins and gold has been found in their hills – which is an apt metaphor for the literature that has come out of Northern Ireland, even during the worst of the Troubles. The last Gaelic lords of Ireland, headed by Hugh O'Neill, Earl of Tyrone, fought bitterly against the English but were finally overthrown at the Battle of Kinsale in 1601. Two years later O'Neill surrendered in Tyrone. Following this defeat and the subsequent departure of the Gaelic aristocracy (*see* box 'The Flight of the Earls') the county was planted in 1608 and most of the modern towns date from that time. Much of the county is Scots Presbyterian, although up in the Sperrin Mountains you can still find Catholic descendants of the O'Neill family. The capital of Tyrone is

The Flight of the Earls

On 14 September 1607 a ship sailed out from Lough Swilly in County Donegal carrying the last Gaelic rulers of Ireland to exile in Europe. This departure became known as the 'Flight of the Earls' and resulted from the final defeat of the native Irish headed by Hugh O'Neill, Earl of Tyrone. Historians still debate over whether they intended to return or not, but most agree that this event marks the beginning of English domination over Ireland and thus shaped Irish history over the following four centuries. After the Flight of the Earls the plantation of Ulster began. This was an ambitious programme of colonial settlement designed to quell native unrest and completely change the face of the province by converting the 'rude and barbarous Irish' to 'civility' and Protestantism. Peace only returned at the very end of the 17th century and by this time the people living in the province, their religion, the layout of their towns and their farming practices had all changed utterly.

Omagh, probably best known for the worst individual atrocity of the Troubles, where 29 people were killed by a single bomb.

Again, not many people from outside the county settle here, and property averages £107,281 (this includes the neighbouring county of Fermanagh).

Fermanagh

Fermanagh is quite different from Tyrone, with far more visitors, many of them anglers or boaters. A third of Fermanagh is underwater: **Upper Lough Erne** is a complicated nest of little lakes and **Lower Lough Erne** is a huge boomerang-shaped body of water that can be as dangerous and stormy as the sea in winter. Here you can fish for eel, rudd, roach, bream or pike all year around. The trout season begins in early March and the salmon season in June; both run to the end of September. In prehistoric times the narrow strip of land between the two lakes was the main highway between Ulster and Connacht. Today the town of **Enniskillen** spreads over the former land bridge and marks the boundary of the two lakes. This is a lively town that is recovering from the economic stagnation and violence of the last 30 years. Oscar Wilde and Samuel Beckett were pupils at the Portora Royal School just outside the town. The rest of the county is small farms dotted between the drumlins. The county has never been rich; farming and fishing were the main activities and now tourism is, little by little, becoming an important activity.

As in the rest of Ulster, very few strangers settle here and property costs far less than in the Republic just over the border, with the average house costing £107,281 (this includes the neighbouring county of Tyrone).

Derry (Londonderry)

Derry is a county of rich river valleys, particularly that of the Bann dividing Derry from Antrim and the uplands of the Sperrin Mountains. Its coast has some wonderful beaches. Linen and shirt-making were the industries that made the county prosperous, but during the Troubles parts of Derry were among the most deprived areas in Europe.

Derry itself is a lovely medieval walled city on the river Foyle with steep streets and some attractive houses, although much of the city was bombed during the Troubles, destroying a great deal of its architectural heritage. Like Belfast, Derry is divided ethnically with Nationalists in the Bogside to the west of the city and Unionists to the east in the Waterside. However, unlike Belfast, Derry is predominantly Catholic (71 per cent), and Protestants make up only one-third of the population. Derry itself is something of an anomaly – a mainly Catholic county divided from its natural hinterland in Donegal to the west. Of late, Letterkenny in the Republic has taken over much of its former role, while Derry is the second city of Northern Ireland. After a grim period during the Troubles, epitomised by

Derry/Londonderry: Stroke City

In a city with two communities and three names, what to call the city of Derry/Londonderry has always been a political issue. Catholics call it 'Derry', Protestants 'Londonderry'. The British government tends mostly to stick with 'Londonderry' and the Irish government 'Derry'. The BBC, trying to be even-handed, shifts between the two. Those who wish to be neutral use the rather clumsy Derry/Londonderry (pronounced 'Derry stroke Londonderry'), and those who find the whole thing overly pernickety have shortened this to the simpler Stroke City. Others have decided on the more neutral-sounding Maiden City, supposedly because its defensive walls have never been breached.

the violence of Bloody Sunday where 14 unarmed civil rights protesters died after being fired on by the British Army, today the city is cheerful and optimistic and has managed the difficult feat of genuine power-sharing. It is more alternative than Belfast, with a reputation for the arts and for a unique brand of ironic humour.

House prices in Derry city are among the lowest in Northern Ireland at £88,273, but along the coast, including Coleraine and Limavady, they are £108,225.

Selecting a Property

04

Travelling to Ireland

Ireland is an island, so flying or sailing are your only options. No plans are afoot, unfortunately, to link Ireland to mainland Britain by tunnel. Then again, the island is getting easier to get to as low-cost airlines proliferate. However you intend to travel, you should always shop around for fares and, if possible, plan well ahead. Fares vary widely depending on the season, the day of the week, time of day and your length of stay. If you know exactly what you want, shopping online is really the only way to go; if you aren't very familiar with routes, vendors and what's available a good travel agent can save endless difficulty and money. One-way fares are almost always more expensive than return fares. Travel taxes are built into the price of air and ferry travel.

By Air

Ireland has four international airports and seven regional airports. **Aer Rianta** (**www.aerrianta.aero**; **t** (01) 814936) owns and manages the Republic's three international airports: Dublin, Shannon and Cork. (Knock Airport in Mayo has scheduled flights from Birmingham, Manchester and Glasgow and a few to European destinations but doesn't really deserve to be called an international airport.) If you are planning to commute or to travel to your Irish property regularly, research regional airports and airlines carefully – you may be able to cut a considerable amount of time off your journey by selecting a region near an airport with regular scheduled services. Think laterally as well: the quickest way to get to Donegal might be through Derry airport rather than an airport in the Republic. Aer Arann is expanding rapidly and offers good deals from airports like Galway and Knock to the UK.

Dublin Airport (**www.dublin-airport.com**; **t** (01) 814111), just 13km (8 miles) from the city centre, has undergone extensive upgrading and expansion in the last couple of years. It is by far the biggest airport in the Republic of Ireland with over 15 million people travelling though it each year. Half of this traffic is to the UK and the rest to continental Europe and the USA (there are no direct flights from Dublin to Asia or Australia). Competition on all the Ireland–UK routes has slashed prices and you can get to most British cities for less than €50 return if you choose your departure dates carefully and book in advance. Aer Lingus and Ryanair have been slugging it out over fares and currently are about level. Ryanair still comes up with the lowest fares but flights tend to be at inconvenient times. Aer Lingus certainly offers good value, especially at weekends, and flies directly to more convenient airports (London Heathrow, London Gatwick and Paris Charles De Gaulle rather than London Stansted and Paris Beauvais, for example). British Midland also offers good deals.

Cork Airport (**www.cork-airport.com**; **t** (021) 431 3131) is 6km (4 miles) south of Cork city. The airport recently overtook Shannon as the Republic's second airport. It is currently expanding and new facilities are being installed including a new passenger terminal, a multistorey car park and road infrastructure. Currently the airport offers direct flights to several destinations in the UK, Belgium, France, Germany, the Netherlands and Spain and flights via Dublin and the UK to other destinations. UK traffic is by far the highest – over half the airport's passengers travel to UK destinations.

Shannon Airport (www.shannonairport.com; t (061) 712000) lost much of its traffic when the compulsory Shannon stopover (a regulation stipulating that all incoming and outgoing transatlantic flights had to land in Shannon) was relaxed – a percentage of transatlantic traffic still stops here. It is still the main hub for the western region, though.

Belfast (**www.belfastairport.com; t** (028) 9448 4848) has two airports: **Belfast City Airport (BCA)**, which is about 10 minutes from the city centre, and **Belfast International Airport (BIA)**, about 32km (20 miles) outside the city on the flat land to the east of Lough Neagh. Flights from smaller regional airports in the UK arrive into BCA and scheduled flights with international airlines generally use BIA. Buses transport passengers from both airports to the city centre.

Kerry Airport (www.kerryairport.ie; t (066) 976 4644), 15mins from Killarney, also offers scheduled flights to a limited number of European destinations including Dublin, Stansted and Frankfurt.

Airlines Serving Ireland

From Mainland Britain

- **Aer Arann (www.aerarann.com;** UK **t** 0800 587 2324; IRL **t** 0818 210 210.
- **Aer Lingus (www.aerlingus.com;** UK **t** 0845 084 4444; IRL **t** (01) 886 8844/0818 365 000).
- **bmiBaby (www.bmibaby.com;** UK **t** 0870 264 2229; IRL **t** (01) 435 0011).
- **British Airways (www.britishairways.com;** UK **t** 0870 850 9850; IRL **t** 1800 626 747).
- **British Midland (www.flybmi.com;** UK **t** 0870 607 0555).
- **Eastern Airways (www.easternairways.com;** UK **t** (01626) 80600).
- **easyJet (www.easyjet.com;** UK **t** 0871 750 0100).
- **Flybe (www.flybe.com;** UK **t** 0870 567 6676).
- **Flykeen (www.flykeen.com;** UK **t** 0800 083 7783).
- **Jet2 (www.jet2.com;** UK **t** 0870 737 8282).
- **MyTravelLite (www.mytravellite.com;** UK **t** 0870 156 4564).
- **Ryanair (www.ryanair.com;** UK **t** 0871 246000; IRL **t** 0818 303030).

From Europe

- **Air France (www.airfrance.com;** UK **t** 0845 359 1000; IRL **t** (01) 605 0312).
- **Alitalia (www.alitalia.co.uk;** UK **t** 0870 544 8259; IRL **t** (01) 677 5171).

By Sea

Ferries are probably the cheapest and most convenient way to get to Ireland if you have lots of luggage or furniture to transport, or if you want to bring your car. The main crossings are as follows:

- **Dublin Port and Dun Laoghaire (pronounced Dunleary) are served from Holyhead and Liverpool.**
- **Rosslare Harbour (in County Wexford) is served from Fishguard and Pembroke in Wales and from Roscoff and Cherbourg in France.**
- **Belfast and Larne are served from Cairnryan and Stranraer in Scotland and from Liverpool.**
- **Cork is served by Swansea in Wales and Roscoff in France.**

Travel times can vary considerably depending on whether your ferry is a high-speed one or not. Pricing depends on the size of your car, the number of passengers, the length of stay and, most importantly, the time of year. Peak times can be extremely expensive.

Be careful to go to the right port when leaving Ireland: Dublin Port is near the city centre to the north of the river Liffey. Dun Laoghaire is 11km (7 miles) from the city centre to the south. They should both be signposted but it is easy simply to follow the ferry signs and then find yourself at the wrong port. In winter the Irish Sea can be very stormy and ferries are often cancelled, sometimes for more than a day. If you miss a sailing the staff generally put you on the next one.

Ferry Companies Serving Ireland

From Britain

- **Irish Ferries (www.irishferries.ie;** UK **t** 0870 517 1717; IRL **t** 0818 300400): Holyhead, Wales, to Dublin (3½ hrs, catamaran sailings 2hrs), and Pembroke, Wales, to Rosslare, County Wexford (3½ hrs).
- **Norse Merchant Ferries (www.norsemerchant.com;** UK **t** 0870 600 4321; IRL **t** (01) 819 2999): Liverpool to Dublin (7½ hrs) and Belfast (8½ hrs).
- **P&O Irish Sea (www.poferries.com;** UK **t** 0870 242 4777; IRL **t** (01) 800 409049): Liverpool to Dublin, and Cairnryan, Scotland, to Larne, County Antrim, just outside Belfast (2hrs).
- **SeaCat (www.seacat.co.uk; t** 0870 552 3523; IRL **t** (01) 874 1231): Liverpool to Dublin (4hrs), Heysham and Troon, both in Scotland, to Belfast (4hrs), and Douglas in the Isle of Man to Dublin (4½ hrs).
- **Stena Line (www.stenaline.com;** UK **t** 08705 707070; IRL **t** (01) 204 7777): Holyhead to Dun Laoghaire, Dublin (3½ hrs); Fishguard, Wales, to Rosslare, County Wexford (3½ hrs); and Stranraer, Scotland, to Belfast (3½ hrs, catamaran sailings 1½ hrs).

> ### *Indicative High- and Low-season Prices for Car and Passengers*
> - Holyhead–Dublin (prices in sterling):
>   Car + driver (ferry): £129 off-peak, £174 peak
>   Car + driver (fast): £149 off-peak, £194 peak
> - Fishguard–Rosslare (prices in sterling):
>   Car + driver (ferry): £114 off-peak, £169 peak
>   Car + driver (fast): £129 off-peak, £184 peak
> - Rosslare–Roscoff (prices in euro):
>   Car + 2 adults: €229 off-peak, €569 peak
>   Car + 1 extra adult: €40 off-peak, €50 peak

- **Swansea Cork Ferries** (**www.swansea-cork.ie**; UK **t** (01792) 456116; IRL **t** (021) 427 1166): Swansea, Wales, to Ringaskiddy, County Cork (just outside Cork city) (10hrs, overnight crossing).

From Continental Europe

- **Brittany Ferries** (**www.brittany-ferries.com**; UK **t** 0870 536 0360; IRL **t** (021) 427 7801): connects Roscoff, France, to Cork.

- **Irish Ferries** (**www.irishferries.ie**; UK **t** 0870 517 1717; IRL **t** 0818 300400): from Roscoff and Cherbourg, France.

- **P&O European Ferries** (**www.poferries.com**; UK **t** 0870 242 4777; IRL **t** 1800 409049): Cherbourg, France, to Rosslare.

By Train

Ferries crossing the Irish Sea all link with trains from the major UK cities. You can book a sleeping berth on some of the night trains. You can get combined train/ferry tickets from **National Rail** (**www.nationalrail.co.uk**; UK **t** 0845 748 4950) or from most train stations and booking offices.

By Coach

Several bus companies offer all-in packages from most towns and cities in Ireland to mainland Britain. Be warned that the journey is often not very pleasant and it is long. It is, however, by far the cheapest way to travel (particularly if you are of a stoic disposition and have the ability to sleep anywhere). Smaller bus companies are usually listed in provincial newspapers.

Northern Ireland is served by **Eurolines/National Express** (**www. gobycoach. com**; UK **t** 08705 808080) and **Ulsterbus** in Belfast (**www.translink.co.uk**; **t** (028) 90 666 630).

Travelling around Ireland

Don't be fooled by the quaint postcards showing a solitary car behind a herd of sheep. Ireland is not a traffic-free haven, particularly in the cities. The Irish adore their cars and a culture of cars as personal chariots and social status symbols is omnipresent. Official figures show that a quarter of all car journeys during the morning peak period are of less than a mile – mainly school runs. Nearly half of all journeys within three miles are made by car. As a result urban congestion is truly dreadful and there's quite a bit of congestion in rural areas as well. The reasons for this are understandable. During the boom, Irish people found being well-off for the first time ever intoxicating, and bought new cars in their thousands. Unfortunately infrastructure hasn't caught up yet, and poor planning means that it may take some time. In fact it may take a completely different approach to car ownership to reduce congestion. Public services, too, haven't caught up, but efforts are being made to improve the situation.

By Air

Unfortunately competition on the Ireland–UK routes and subsequent price reductions hasn't affected internal travel as yet. Aer Lingus and Ryanair take you from Dublin to Cork, Galway, Shannon and Belfast but prices are still fairly high. Aer Arann started out as a little island-hopping service from the three Aran Islands to the mainland and is growing extraordinary rapidly. Today it serves several smaller regional airports.

Domestic Airlines
- **Aer Arann (www.aerarann.ie**; IRL **t** 1890 462726; UK **t** 0800 587 2324).
- **Aer Lingus (www.aerlingus.com**; UK **t** 0845 084 4777; IRL **t** (01) 886 8844).
- **Ryanair (www.ryanair.com**; UK **t** 0871 246000; IRL **t** 0818 303030).

King of the Dodgers

Michael O'Leary, the voluble Ryanair boss, has developed his own unique method for avoiding Dublin gridlock. Dublin traffic planners have installed 'quality bus corridors' (QBCs) on some of the most congested routes into the city – buses and taxis are the only vehicles that can legally use the speedy lanes. Last year Mr O'Leary purchased a taxi plate for his top-of-the-range Mercedes and zips into the city, perfectly legally, along the Stillorgan QBC. Reactions among Dubliners varied from indignant rage to begrudging admiration for the quintessential entrepreneur. Jokes have been circulating about getting into a taxi and asking for O'Connell Street but finding yourself dropped at Stephen's Green instead. Jokes and sniping aside, O'Leary hasn't been taken off the roads yet, despite a fine for speeding.

By Road

If you are house-hunting or simply trying to get to more remote parts of the country you need a car – buses and trains won't take to you to where you want to go. There is practically no public transport linking smaller country towns and villages so if you plan to buy in the country you'll find a car is essential.

Main roads in Ireland radiate out from Dublin and are generally known not by letters or numbers but by their eventual destination – the Wexford Road (N11), the Cork Road (N7/N8 branching off to Limerick and Kerry on route), the Galway Road (N6) and the Sligo Road (N4).

So far Ireland boasts only 100 kilometres of motorway, and these do not join up, so don't plan to get from A to B very quickly. Travel times tend to be unpredictable. Leaving Dublin on a Friday evening for any country destination usually guarantees an hour or more spent in congestion hotspots like Fermoy. The AA Road Watch service (broadcast with the news on RTE Radio 1 and 2) highlights traffic jams nationwide. This means that you'll often end up hearing about an overturned truck in Cork or cattle on the road in Wexford before getting information about your destination.

In Ireland all roads are not equal. A road marked on the map as a national primary route can shift from being a dual carriageway to a narrow potholed road more suited to tractors than cars in the course of 50 miles or so. In very rural areas it is a good rule of thumb to accept a local's recommendation of the best route to your destination even if your map shows what appears to be a shorter, more direct option. But do carry a map, as signposts can be far and few between. The Michelin (#923) *Motoring Map of Ireland* is probably the best general map of the country. The *Complete Road Atlas of Ireland* published by the Ordnance Survey is a handy size for use when travelling with lots of extra information. The AA also has a route finder on its website (**www.aaireland.ie/routes/**).

Place names on signposts in the Republic are in both English and Gaelic. The more modern green signs use kilometres and the older white ones use miles. Most Irish people give distances in miles despite Ireland's changeover to metric in 1970. Confusingly, speed limits are always in miles per hour (30mph/48kph in urban areas, 60mph/97kph on main roads and 70mph/113kph on motorways). Although the stereotype of farmers slowly pottering down country boreens (small roads) is still peddled in much Irish tourist literature the country is speeding up, sometimes dangerously so. Speed cameras have been installed on all major roads so be wary, especially when entering a town or village. The Celtic Tiger has filled the roads, particularly in South Dublin, with new Mercedes, BMWs and Range Rovers. The Tiger can also be blamed for serious congestion in many of the main towns. Some – Cork and Sligo are the worst culprits – have installed impenetrable one-way systems. Try a map, but it is best to become a native if you really want to find your way around these towns.

'An 04 Merc'

Irish licence plates carry the year of issue, the county the car is registered in and the number registered. So a car with the plate 03 TN 1223 would be the 1,223rd car to be registered in Tipperary North in 2003. You'll often hear Irish people say 'He drives an 04 Merc.' The tone will be disparaging or admiring, depending on their perspective, or on their own mode of transport. The colourful procession of ancient vehicles once found on Irish roads has been considerably reduced since the introduction of a national car test. Prior to the NCT you could drive your car, and many people did, until it sat down and would go no further (see box 'The National Car Test', p.248, for more information on the NCT).

During the height of the boom a new car with the lowest possible registration number was the ultimate status symbol and people fought to get their names on the registration list to bag an elusive 01 D 1 plate (in practice the first plate in the city goes to the Lord Mayor but the numbers from 2 on go on general release). If you buy a car in Ireland, remember that cars with lower numbers were registered at the start of the year so will carry a whole year more wear and tear than a car with a higher number. And if none of this applies to you, try spotting a car from every county when travelling – especially recommended for children on long journeys.

Despite this, driving in Ireland can be an extraordinary pleasure. The island is crisscrossed by thousands of miles of minor roads. These roads, tiny, winding and almost always completely empty, take you to some of the most spectacular scenery in the country. The poet Louis MacNeice wrote of 'whitewashed walls and fuchsia hedges' and you will still find them all over the west of Ireland (although untrimmed hedgerows of any variety can be dangerous when driving). Other hazards you may encounter on rural roads include tractors with trailers overloaded with teetering bales of hay or straw, stray cattle, appalling surfaces, colossal potholes and, in tourist areas like the Ring of Kerry, the ubiquitous tour bus. Drink-driving can also be a hazard after pub closing time. Social and community life revolves around the pub and in rural areas this inevitably involves travel. The problem endures despite extensive police clampdowns over the last 10 years.

It is also as well to bear in mind that over 40 per cent of drivers on Irish roads have never passed a driving test. Some of these are elderly drivers who benefited from an amnesty in 1979; others are young (and not so young) drivers who 'drive on the provisional'. This means that they have been issued a provisional licence to learn to drive and are supposed to carry a large 'L' plate on their car and be accompanied by a licensed driver. Many people simply renew the licence year after year and never sit a test. This state of affairs is partly the result of a long waiting list for tests but also because people can 'get away with it'.

Most towns operate a disc parking system: buy the disk in a shop or some-times from a roadside machine and display it in your car. Failure to pay the fee will result in a ticket, clamping or, in the worst case, towing. Clamping has enthusiastically been carried out in Dublin since the system was privatised.

Car Hire

Car hire is expensive, particularly during the high season. Off-peak rates are a lot cheaper. Few companies will rent to you if you are under 23 and have had a driving licence for less than two years, and some companies do not rent to people over 70. All the usual suspects operate in Ireland: Avis, Budget, Europcar, Hertz and Thrifty. Local names include Atlas, Dan Dooley, Malone and Murray's. Most operators have offices in the main airports and city centre locations.

Car Hire Companies

- **Atlas Car Rentals (www.atlascarhire.com; t** (01) 844 4859).
- **Avis Rent a Car (www.avis.ie; t** (01) 605 7500).
- **Budget (www.budget.ie; t** (090) 66 27711).
- **Dan Dooley (www.dan-dooley.ie; t** (0625) 3103).
- **Europcar (www.europcar.ie; t** (01) 812 0410).
- **Hertz (www.hertz.ie; t** (01) 676 7476).
- **Malone (www.malonecarrental.co; t** (01) 844 1944).
- **Thrifty (www.thrifty.ie; t** 1800 515800).

By Rail

Trains are operated by **Iarnród Éireann (www.irishrail.ie; t** (01) 703 4070), which translates directly from the Irish as Irish Iron Road. It is a good example of how words for new concepts were invented in Irish and unfortunately also a good indicator of the modernity of the system. Delays are common, and over-crowding, especially at peak travel times, is often a problem. Iarnród Éireann is investing over €1.3 billion into a programme called 'On Track'. The money is earmarked for an impressive list of improvements to the rail service: track improvement, station renovation and reconstruction, new carriages, bridge renewals, level crossing upgrades, safety studies and signalling. Perhaps by the time you move here, glitches and delays will be a thing of the past – but don't count on it. However, not all routes are problematic – the Belfast–Dublin Enterprise express service is exemplary and has been a major factor (along with the new M1 motorway) in many a Dubliner's decision to invest in Belfast prop-erty (it takes two hours). Iarnród Éireann and **Northern Ireland Railways (www.translink.co.uk**; UK **t** (028) 90 899411) jointly operate the service.

All routes radiate out from Dublin, so if you want to get from Killarney to Galway, for example, you have to return to Dublin and then take the Galway

Examples of Train Fares from Dublin

To	Adult Single	Day Return	Monthly Return
Cork	€50	€51.50	€59.50
Belfast	€31	€46	€46
Galway	€25–35	€25–38	€35–38
Kilkenny	€18.50–23.50	€18.50–23.50	€23.50
Killarney	€52.50	€52.50	€62.50
Limerick	€38	€42	€48.50

train. Intercity services run from Dublin's Heuston and Connolly stations to Ballina, Belfast, Cork, Ennis, Galway, Limerick, Rosslare Europort, Sligo, Tralee, Waterford and Westport. Services also run between Rosslare Europort and Limerick, Cork and Tralee, and Cork and Limerick. Campaigners are also trying to get a Western Rail link opened between Sligo and Ennis. Some counties, Donegal and Cavan, for instance, don't have any train service at all.

Fares are comparatively expensive and there are some odd anomalies: a return ticket from Dublin to Nenagh in County Tipperary is €34 but one the other way round is only €21. The idea is that people from the country are subsidised to travel while Dubliners and tourists pay full whack. If you plan to do extensive travelling by train, buy a special **railcard**. These give you unlimited travel for various time periods and offer a considerable saving – check Iarnród Éireann's website for details. The site also has timetables and general information, and is being upgraded to allow online booking.

If you plan to commute from your new home, check train times before committing to the purchase. Although many towns are de facto dormitory towns for Dublin, Iarnród Éireann hasn't in every case realised this, and trains run at times designed for people going to the city for lunch and shopping rather than for people who need to be at their desks before 9am. Taxsaver Commuter Tickets are available – contact Iarnród Éireann for details.

Northern Ireland Railways (NIR) runs rail travel in Northern Ireland. You'll find that the trains are more modern and better maintained than in the Republic.

By Bus and Coach

There is a much more extensive bus network covering the entire country. Buses are always cheaper than the train. Timetabled services are reliable but buses can be infrequent. That said, you can travel by bus between all major towns, but watch out for convoluted connections between buses. **Bus Éireann** (**www.buseireann.ie**; IRL **t** (01) 836 6111) serves the Republic and Ulsterbus; part of **Translink** (**www.translink.co.uk**; UK **t** (02890) 666630) serves Northern Ireland. There are lots of private bus companies as well, which sprang up in the 1990s when Bus Éireann lost the monopoly on coach travel. The biggest of these is probably **J.J. Kavanagh & Sons** of Urlingford, County Kilkenny (**www.**

jjkavanagh.ie; **t** (056) 883 1106), travelling as **Rapid Express Coaches**, but many others operate throughout Ireland – check the local paper for details. If you leave Dublin by bus you'll depart from **Busárus**, one of Ireland's finest modernist buildings, designed by Michael Scott. Although it is a little bedraggled now, a major refurbishment is planned.

In Belfast, Cork, Dublin and Galway buses are the main form of public transport. Dublin has two light-rail systems: the **Dart** (Dublin Area Rapid Transit) service running around the bay from Howth to Bray and the new **Luas** (Irish for speed) service from Sandyford and Tallaght (pronounced Talla), due to start running in 2004. Buses don't adhere rigidly to schedules and you can be kept waiting at off-peak times. Smaller towns rarely have any form of public transport. Occasionally there may be a local bus running into a town in the morning and out again in the afternoon – enquire in local shops or post offices.

By Sea

All Ireland's islands are fairly close to the coast. The largest, Achill Island, is connected to the mainland by a land bridge. The 17 other inhabited islands are reached by ferry; the largest operator is **Aran Island Ferries** (**www.aranislandferries.com**; IRL **t** (091) 561767), which leaves from Galway. Check with the local tourist office for sailing times and frequencies for other islands.

By Bicycle and Moped

Many people cycle around the main cities. This is generally a traffic avoidance measure rather than for pleasure, since drivers are notoriously cavalier towards cyclists and the roads tend to be full of lumps and holes left behind by street excavators putting in everything from cable television to new gas pipes. If you plan to cycle in Dublin, get yourself a dilapidated-looking bike and at least one large, expensive lock, preferably one with a chain inside rather than a U-shaped one. The situation is changing somewhat, as cycle lanes are installed across the city, but it is not like Amsterdam yet, by a very long stretch. If cycling in the countryside, make sure you have lights and reflective clothing at night.

Mopeds are becoming more popular in Dublin as the traffic gets steadily worse, but will probably remain a niche market because of the weather and their cost – there are not many second-hand mopeds on the market.

Climate

It is unlikely you decided to come to Ireland for balmy weather and al fresco dining. Changeable is probably the adjective most often applied to Ireland's weather. In fact some people say that there is no such thing as climate in

Ireland, merely an irregular sequence of weather patterns. But this is over-stating the case somewhat. Yes, the weather in Ireland is unpredictable, and yes, it does rain quite a bit. But it rarely rains solidly for any length of time. Wet, grey days with rain beating ceaselessly against the windows do occur very occasion-ally, but more often you'll have bright sunshine, clouds moving in, a shower, a little more sunshine, a light drizzle and a little mist, another clear patch...and the cycle repeats. So bring raincoats, carry an umbrella and wear layers.

The reason for all this changeability is that Ireland is situated beneath a convergence zone where cold air from the north, warm dry air from Asia and damp air from the Gulf Stream meet. When they meet, they produce low-pressure systems, or depressions, characterised by wet weather followed by periods of hot or cold clear, dry weather. The main influence on Ireland's weather is the Gulf Stream (also known as the North Atlantic Drift). This huge ocean current brings warm water from the Caribbean across the Atlantic and ensures that Ireland's climate is far milder than it should be at its northerly lati-tude. It also ensures that neither winter nor summer has extremes of temperature. The average yearly temperature is about 10°C. This ranges from about 5°C in January, generally the coldest month, to 16°C or so in July and August, although temperatures can reach the late 20s. Sometimes tempera-tures can even reach 30°C for a day or so, which provokes major media coverage and general bemusement.

Spring is generally dry(ish); winter is cold and damp with occasional gales that topple trees and pull slates from roofs; and autumn is generally dry and fresh.

If climate is a consideration for you when deciding where to live, you should know that the rainfall figures are highest in the northwest, west and southwest (up to 3,000mm per annum in mountainous areas compared with 800mm in Dublin). Do remember that just one heavy shower can create a 'wet day' statistic (about one in three for the east coast and one in two for the west). Sunshine is highest in the southeast (hence the tourist board claim: 'the sunny southeast'). Wind speed on the west coast is on average double that on the east coast (some say that, in compensation, the landscape is doubly spectacular).

If you are interested in weather (and if you're thinking about living in Ireland you probably need to be), **Met Éireann**, the Irish Meteorological Service, has statistics going back to the 19th century on its website (**www.met.ie**).

The jury is still out on whether global warming will have a major effect on Ireland's weather; Cassandras warn that the Gulf Stream may be diverted further south and Ireland's climate will end up closer to that of Irkutsk in Russia (on the same line of latitude), while optimists dream of Mediterranean-style sun. One of the driest years on record was 2003 (although heavy rainfall caused landslides and floods in some parts of the country), whereas 2002 was one of the wettest (and mildest), so perhaps all that can be concluded is that some-thing is afoot.

Landscape and Geography

Ireland is generally described as saucer-shaped (on a map it is rather endearingly bear-shaped), the flat, central plain covers much of the centre of the country and mountains ring the edges, except along the east coast where an open, flat coastline stretches from Drogheda to Wexford, punctuated only by the Wicklow Mountains. In total the island has over 2,000 miles of coastline and nowhere is the sea more than 70 miles away. This has had a major effect on its climate – the air all over the country is moist and fresh – and on urban development: early towns all developed in natural harbours and inland settlements developed only where there were navigable rivers to give access.

There are two primary influences on the geography of the island. The first is the underlying rocks. As you might expect, nothing is simple in Ireland and the island has a particularly complex geological history. Limestone underlies the central plain and crops up further west in the Burren and the Aran Islands; the west is mainly quartzite and granite; old red sandstone softens the contours of the southeast; and to the north are carboniferous shales, granite gneisses and black basalts. Secondly, much of the island is shaped by glaciation. When the ice

Natural and Untouched?

Many people coming to Ireland mistakenly believe that the Irish landscape is quintessentially 'natural' and unspoilt. In a shallow sense this is true – there are many areas in Ireland where electricity wires don't crisscross above you, roads are narrow and signs of human habitation few. However, Ireland most emphatically does not have a 'natural' landscape. Humans have shaped it over a long settlement period, so much so that some commentators call it a 'cultural landscape'. To take a simple and recent example, the intense green of Irish grass has become a symbol of the island. Ireland is known as the Emerald Isle and visitors often comment on how vibrant the colour is. Ireland is indeed a green island – the mild, moist climate means that grass can grow almost all year round – but that particularly vivid, luminous green so typical of the countryside is usually the result of artificial fertilisers and has only become a feature of the landscape in the last 20 years. More recently, new EU benefits for farmers who reduce the amount of fertilisers they use on their land means that many fields have reverted to a lighter shade of green.

Other examples include the blanket bogs of the northwest, caused by forest clearances in Neolithic times. Much of the soil in the west, on the Aran Islands and along the Connemara coast, was created over hundreds of years by humans applying seaweed, sand, turf, refuse, animal dung and decayed thatch to the rocky ground to create tiny fields that could support a crop of potatoes. This in turn leads to one of the more poignant signs of the impact of humans on the Irish landscape – the remains of potato ridges in long-deserted fields.

retreated at the end of the last Ice Age, 12,000 years ago, it left a deposit of drift sheets smeared unevenly across the land. Some of the glacial drift is rich, productive soil, as in the farmland of North Cork, Tipperary and Kilkenny. In other places the ice left poorer boggy soils. A band of hummocky land with countless little hills called drumlins and long, sandy ridges called eskers stretches across the top third of the country, physically dividing the province of Ulster from the south. Along the west coast most areas have been stripped of cover and the barren rock is covered with thin soils and countless lakes. Human habitats occupy a narrow coastal strip and the interiors are desolate, if scenic, bogs and mountains.

Since Ireland has a damp climate, lots of low-lying land and sticky soils, drainage tends to be poor. Waterlogging has created some of Ireland's most distinctive landscapes – the bogs. Bogs cover one-sixth of Ireland's surface and form many of its most characteristic landscapes. They have become a symbol of the country, so much so that little sods of peat, known as turf, are sold in many

What are Bogs and How are They Formed?

Bogs are made up of peat. This is a dense acidic waterlogged soil made up of plants that have not fully decomposed. The micro-organisms that cause decay are starved of oxygen, partly because of the acidic environment. Bogs may look similar, especially to the inexpert eye, but there are two different types – 'blanket bog', so called because it covers the terrain thickly, like a blanket, and 'raised bog', so called because of its characteristic domed shape.

Blanket bog is far more extensive than raised bog. It occurs mainly in mountainous areas with high rainfall – all along the west coast with some patches in the centre and on the Wicklow mountains. Although it may appear to be a wholly natural feature it was in fact primarily the result of human intervention. Tree clearance in Neolithic times caused mineral leaching and waterlogging in soils. Slowly plant matter began to build up and even more water was retained. Blanket bog creates a harsh, treeless landscape, which is difficult for people to live in, but is austerely beautiful.

Raised bogs developed from the countless little lakes left behind when the ice sheets retreated at the end of the Ice Age. The lakes filled up with vegetation and the water became more and more acidic, preventing decomposition, and layer upon layer of peat built up. Most raised bogs are very thick – up to 12 metres deep. They are found scattered all across the central lowlands with a few in the north. Bord na Móna (the Turf Board) was set up in 1946 to exploit this seemingly endless natural resource. There was a peat-burning electricity station in Portarlington, County Laois, but it was closed in 1988 as the supply dwindled and conservationist concerns grew.

In the north most raised bogs are conserved as Areas of Special Scientific Interest. In the south some are still being cut commercially for fuel but conservation organisations are campaigning to declare all remaining bogs Special Areas of Conservation and bring a complete end to cutting.

tourist shops. Driving around you will see endless expanses of bog, sometimes with little conical stooks of turf stacked up to dry. In winter you'll smell distinctive, slightly acrid, turf smoke wherever you go. If you buy a large house or a farm, it may still have its own portion of bog, which would have originally provided fuel for the winter. And bogs are mysterious places. Pollen trapped in their layers gives glimpses into ancient landscapes and climates; the enormous horns of the extinct Great Irish Elk have been found in the bog and treasures buried millennia ago have been discovered deep in the black peat – golden torcs and chalices and even a bag filled with butter, perfectly preserved after a thousand years.

Hedgerows of hawthorn, blackthorn, hazel and holly are another distinctive feature of the countryside, and some date back over 200 years. Ireland is one of the least forested countries in Europe, partly because of widespread deforestation in the 19th century, but some pockets of ancient deciduous woodland have survived – for example in Killarney National Park.

The highest mountain is Carrantuohill (1,040 metres/3,414ft) in County Kerry. The longest river (and the longest in the British Isles) is the Shannon (370km/230 miles, including estuary), which flows into the sea in County Limerick. The largest lake (and again the largest in the British Isles) is Lough Neagh (396 square km/153 square miles), bordering counties Armagh, Down, Antrim, Derry and Tyrone in the north of Ireland.

If exploring the Irish landscape in more depth interests you, have a look at the wonderful *Atlas of the Irish Rural Landscape*, edited by F.H.A. Aalen and Kevin Whelan from Cork University Press.

When to Go

House-hunting can be done at any time of the year but spring, summer and autumn, when the light lingers until late in the evening, are probably the best times. Summer can be full of tourists, making accommodation expensive and booked up, so spring would be ideal. As in Britain, many houses come on the market after the winter when they can be shown to best advantage with spring flowers in the garden and foliage at its best, but if you want to see an area in the winter there's no pressing reason why you shouldn't house-hunt then. Check out Irish bank holidays (*see* **References**, p.291) before planning a buying trip.

Choosing a Location

For some people, looking for a new home is addictive – they love the thrill of the chase, scanning the property pages, driving up endless country lanes, trekking through shabby rooms, making lists of pros and cons. This type is almost disappointed when, finally, the perfect property is found, signed, sealed and delivered. Now the really hard work begins, the drudgery of packing, organising bills and setting up home. Others hate the whole performance and only begrudgingly give up time they'd far rather spend elsewhere, doing almost anything else. No matter where you lie in this continuum, the job is easier if you do some preparation.

Try and clarify your priorities. This is particularly important if you are someone who falls in love at first sight. If you are clear about how much renovating an old stone farmhouse will cost, and on whom your neighbours are likely to be in that inner city Georgian mansion, it will make the decision that much easier, and means that you won't get too many surprises. Sit down and make a proper wish list. Then break that into 'must have' and 'nice to have'. Then research and, if you can, visit all the areas that might meet your criteria.

I also can't urge you strongly enough to have a really good look around the area that interests you. The countryside can change radically in a short distance; what looks like flat, boring bog might have a charming little river valley a few miles further on. Ireland is small enough for you to be able to cover an area very thoroughly so take the time to explore. Since Ireland is so small you also stand a good chance of being able to combine several items on your wish list. For example you might be looking for a country location within easy reach of the sea, but you might also want to be near a cultural centre with theatre and the arts – West Leitrim or Sligo might be perfect.

Also consider all of the following. Parts of the countryside are very isolated. How far do you want to be from shops? From a bank? From a hairdresser? From a good coffee, or perhaps from a good martini? Do you want to use public transport? Cost will also be a consideration. If you are looking for a classic Georgian

Living in the Sticks

If you haven't lived in the country before, remember that many rural areas in Ireland are *very* rural. Here's a tongue-in-cheek guide to some of the vocabulary beginning with 's' that you'll become familiar with:

• **sheepdog**: generally black and white; highly intelligent and highly trained animals, the Irish farmer's best friend; spend off-duty hours lying in wait for unwary cyclists – general modus operandi is to race alongside nipping ferociously at tyres and ankles for at least a mile.

• **silage**: fermented grass used to feed cattle; smell is difficult to describe, but pungent.

• **slurry**: unmentionable gunge spread on fields as fertiliser, smells like nothing else on earth; you'll become familiar with it when driving though rural areas.

• **sugar beet**: a member of the beet family used to make granulated sugar, harvested in winter and transported by tractor, leaving all roads near the field a sticky quagmire of mud for much of the winter.

country house but have a restricted budget you might be better off searching in one of the less fashionable areas, Leitrim or Roscommon, for example. If you are determined to be beside the sea, think about whether you want to be lashed by Atlantic storms in the winter on the wild west coast, or if the more sedate east coast might suit you better. Do tourists drive you bananas? If so, towns on the well-trodden tourist trail such as Killarney may not be for you. Or do you plan to set up a B&B business? If so, you'll want to see tourists and lots of them. How far do you want to be from a city? Donegal, exquisite though parts of it are, is a good 4–6 hours' drive from Dublin. If you are planning to buy a holiday home, how accessible is it? Where is the nearest airport? Check out the roads: will the traffic worsen in the mornings or evenings? Otherwise idyllic Wicklow villages may have Dublin commuter traffic flowing though them morning and evening.

If you plan to make a living doing something like running a country house hotel, a craft shop or an organic farm, you should research particularly carefully. Some regions offer grants to people setting up businesses; others may be black holes where countless similar enterprises have collapsed in a relatively short amount of time. Make sure you make a business plan for your first five years. The local county or city enterprise boards offer support, advice and training programmes for small businesses and can give information on grants available (*see* **Settling In**, 'Starting Your Own Business', pp.229–32).

The **Rural Renewal Scheme** (check with the Revenue Commissioners for more information) might reimburse you for some of the outlay on a new home or restoration but bear in mind that the money comes back over years and is payable only against income tax, so if you are not paying Irish income tax you won't be able to make use of the tax breaks. Be aware also that, even though there are no property taxes in Ireland, many counties are now introducing levies on new building. This is partly to pay for services, but is also an easy way to raise revenue in counties where there has been a lot of speculative building.

If investment is your primary aim you are advised not to choose a rural area. Rural properties may provide a good return on investment if you do extensive work on a dilapidated property and then sell, but rental income is likely to be intermittent. In parts of the west, rental houses can lie empty for 10 months of the year (*see* 'Buying to Let', pp.107–108, for more information).

If you are moving with children you will want to find out what the local schools are like (*see also* **Settling In**, 'Education', pp.232–8). If you plan to send them to boarding school in England will they be able to travel back easily? Think also about who you'd like your neighbours to be. In parts of Kerry, Connemara and West Cork you may be surrounded by artists and craftspeople, yoga teachers and cheese-makers, many of them foreign. Or you could find yourself without any neighbours at all if you choose a purpose-built holiday village where many of the houses are second homes. Outside cities your neighbours may be busy professional people who travel long distances to work each day. You could find yourself next to a bachelor farmer and his dog, who will never invite you into his house but will engage you in long conversations over the gate. If this is important to you, see who spends time in the village pubs, linger in the local shops, get chatting to people and see what your potential neighbours are like. The same goes for shopping. What's in the local supermarkets? Can you get what you need and are used to or will you need to stock up elsewhere? (This is what Dublin weekenders are often reprimanded for: bringing weekend supplies from M&S rather than patronising local businesses.)

Location always always counts. **Profiles of the Regions**, pp.23–64, gives a good indication of which areas are most fashionable at present but trends change and if you choose a part of the country that's relatively undiscovered you may get a very sizeable return on your investment some time in the future. In the end only you know exactly what you want – and you probably already know that desire often doesn't coexist with logic. It is true that lots of people have ended up somewhere totally unexpected without planning it at all and been perfectly happy but, then again, there are some who've been disappointed and have ended up selling up and moving on. Try and do your best to avoid this risk by researching really carefully.

Expatriate Communities

British people make up by far the largest number of immigrants to the country: 2.7 per cent of the entire population holds British citizenship and 6.4 per cent was born in the UK or Northern Ireland. Many of these are Irish people born in Britain but a large number are British people who've taken the plunge and moved here for good. They are a mixed bunch: many retirees, people with Irish spouses, people who have come to work and bring up children and a whole spectrum of people looking for an alternative lifestyle. The most recent is Tony Blair's father-in-law, Tony Booth, who has declared himself fed up with Britain and is planning to settle in Sligo. Actors, writers, musicians and film directors make up another group. Many of them are taking advantage of Ireland's tax-free status for artists (see box 'The Artist's Exemption', p.229). West Cork is the only place where you will find what could be called an expatriate community in the generally understood sense of the word. Here a sizeable number of British people have decided to settle, but they don't fit into homogenous categories – some are *very* alternative and others are absolutely conventional and commute to jobs in Britain each week. Connemara, particularly the coastal strip from Galway to Clifden, is also home to a large number of British immigrants. Apart from these hotspots people from the UK are scattered across the country, living in all kinds of houses and doing all kinds of very different things.

The Dutch and the Germans bought a huge amount of Irish property in the 1970s and 1980s and you still find little communities of people who moved here then, with Irish-born children. Anecdotally, the Germans have started to sell up and are now investing in EU candidate Eastern European countries. (Ireland is

shortly to cease being a beneficiary of EU funds and begin to be a net contrib-
utor, a prospect regarded with horror by many of the nation's farmers.) Many
towns have a Chinese family running a local takeaway; now they often also
have Indian families managing an Indian restaurant – some from the UK and
others directly from India or Pakistan. In some parts of the country you'll find
small communities of former asylum-seekers who were housed outside the
main cities as part of the Government's drive to spread arrivals over the
Republic. Dublin particularly has been transformed into a multicultural city very
quickly. The area around Parnell Street has been dubbed Little Africa because of
the number of immigrants living and setting up businesses like Afro-Caribbean
shops. There's also a growing Chinese community.

General Overview of the Housing Market

Ireland is not cheap: you may find the odd bargain but it is more likely to be for
a pint of Guinness and a dozen oysters than for an idyllic thatched cottage overlooking Galway Bay. The Irish are home-owners. They see rent as 'money down
the drain'. They seem to feel truly secure only when they possess the bricks and
mortar surrounding them, no matter how much debt this may entail. Property
is to a large degree an extension of the self – ornate gate posts and grandiose
porches all signify that the person purchasing the property has arrived and is
someone of status. This may be because in the past the Irish experienced
dispossession, and the fear of being homeless lurks somewhere deep in their
psyches. Without delving any further into the historical and psychological
origins for this attitude towards property, the blunt fact remains that as property ownership is so desirable, prices reflect this. Irish people would rather
invest in property than in almost anything else. And if you look at the Dublin
property market over the last 10 years, they have been absolutely right.

The cost of property has been the major downside of the economic boom of
the 1990s, (although a few would say it is been the high point, as some canny
investors now live off rental incomes from properties purchased in the early
1990s). Despite a slowdown at the beginning of the 21st century, property prices
continue to climb: by 18 per cent in 2002 and 13.7 per cent in 2003. The average
price paid for a house nationally in December 2003 was €234,066. This is more
than three times the average price of €75,169 in March 1996. The equivalent
price in October 2002 was €205,898. In Dublin the average price for a house
tipped the €300,000 mark for the first time in October 2003 and has since risen
to €325,000. The exception to all of this is Northern Ireland. In some parts of
Belfast you can buy an entire terrace of artisan cottages for what you'd pay for a
single cottage in Donnybrook, Dublin 4 (around €350,000). However, prices are
moderating somewhat; the rate of growth from June 2003 to June 2004 was
11.4 per cent and this slowdown looks set to continue.

What You Get for €300,000

- **North Dublin**: three-bedroom apartment in Coolock near Dublin Airport.
- **South Dublin**: one-bedroom apartment with balcony in the Wintergarden apartment complex off Pearse Street.
- **Cork City**: three-bedroom semi-detached family house near Douglas.
- **West Cork**: three-bedroom bungalow in the centre of Dunmanway (away from the coast).
- **Galway**: two-bedroom apartment in Knocknacarra (3 miles from city centre).
- **Clare**: a three-bedroom suburban detached house in Ennis.
- **Limerick**: semi-detached four-bedroom surburban family house in Raheen.
- **Kerry**: a semi-detached three-bedroom stone cottage on 2 acres in Waterville.
- **Kilkenny**: three-bedroom stone cottage with old forge in Inistiogue.
- **Wexford**: detached three-bedroom bungalow 25mins from Wexford Town.
- **Belfast**: large four-bedroom redbrick Victorian house with a garden and patio on the Ormeau Road.

Irish Homes

What kind of home are you looking for? This probably depends on your priorities and your budget. Aesthetics might also play a part: will nothing but Georgian do or are you willing to compromise? Before starting the hunt it is a good idea to get a brief overview of the traditions that exist in Ireland and the history that underlies the buildings you are likely to be looking at. One important thing to remember is that for centuries Ireland was desperately poor. As a result it doesn't have the housing stock of other countries. From medieval times until the late 19th century the houses of the poorest were built of mud and thatch and have, in most cases, completely disappeared.

Clochans and Castles

The earliest surviving examples of architecture in Ireland are the beehive-shaped **clochans** built of stone fitted tightly together without mortar (passage tombs could also be considered architecture but here we are tracing the themes leading to houses still found in the countryside). The most famous example is the Gallurus Oratory on the Skellig Islands, an extraordinary boat-shaped building. Around the same period hundreds of **round towers** were built, again of stone.

The Normans built fortified stone **tower houses** in late medieval times. The remains of these can be seen all over Ireland – angular grey blocks in varying states of collapse. (Oddly enough they are almost never cylindrical.) They generally have a tall, slender profile; inside you find spiral staircases leading to living rooms that take up the whole width of the castle, with bedrooms above. Usually they have narrow slit windows and other intriguing features like murder holes above the entrances where boiling pitch or other unpleasant surprises could be dropped on unwanted visitors. Some have been restored as homes (see box 'Pink Castles and Statuettes', p.117, for the story of Jeremy Irons and his castle) but you would need to have substantial resources to undertake doing up a castle. Sometimes you find properties with the original castle beside or attached to its replacement, although they are generally in ruins.

As Ireland and the Gaelic chiefs were gradually subdued by Protestant settlers and the need for strong defences lessened (in the 1600s), these fortified castles were sometimes converted into castellated mansions with formal gardens. Others were replaced with brand new houses. The new Georgian architecture emphasised order, progress and rationality with classical proportions and references to ancient Greece. By the late 18th century the Irish landed class was at the peak of its wealth, power and influence. In County Cork alone the number of big houses leapt from 20 to over 200 by the 1740s.

The Big House

After the Elizabethan conquest the 'big house', home of the Protestant planter, became a feature of the landscape, shaping much of the countryside and settlement around it. They were built in many different architectural styles: Palladian, Gothic Revival and later Victorian. The big house is so called because it towered economically, physically and symbolically above the houses of the cottiers and farmers that encircled it. A demesne, usually accounting for 10 per cent of the whole estate, surrounded most big houses. Within the demesne lay a farm and a walled kitchen garden that allowed the house to be self-sufficient as well as ornamental gardens and lawns, parkland for deer and cattle, woodland for game, and a range of buildings that housed staff and animals. Outside the demesne lay the estate. Hundreds and sometimes thousands of tenants farmed the land and paid the rent that supported the house and its occupants.

Estates ranged in size from 500 acres to huge areas spanning counties. The Marquis Conyngham owned almost 157,000 acres in Meath, Clare and Donegal in the late 19th century. Solid towns like Mallow, Youghal and Charleville in County Cork and Birr in Offaly have many big houses in their hinterlands. At their high point there were probably 4,000 big houses in the country. After the Land Acts of the late 19th century the tenant rent rolls that had supported the big houses were considerably reduced and many landlords were forced to sell or abandon their houses. Many of them were burnt down in the 1920s and others were abandoned over the next 50 years as their Protestant owners moved out of Ireland or simply couldn't manage their upkeep any longer. Elizabeth Bowen probably describes the conflicted situation of the Anglo-Irish best: 'inherited loyalty to England – where their sons went to school and to whom they owed their land and power – pulled them one way; their own latent blood-and-bone "Irishness" the other.' Ironically, in many cases the gate lodges have survived while the big house lies in ruins. Today many of the houses are known for their architecture or for political, historic or literary associations.

Even if you don't plan to buy a big house or if it would be outside your budget, you should try to understand something of their history, since they shaped the estates they stood in and in many cases the landscape and urban settlements around. Big houses have triggered mixed feelings amongst many Irish people but, increasingly, as Ireland turns away from a preoccupation with its colonial past, people now see these houses as a part of the Irish heritage and as monuments to Irish craftsmen rather than simply symbols of oppression and suffering. Today these houses are among the most expensive on the market. Some are lived in by millionaire globe-trotters that may have several homes all over the globe. If you are interested in the subject, read Valerie and Thomas Pakenham's *The Big House in Ireland*, which gives a picture of life in ascendancy houses, and *The Lost Houses of Ireland*, which shows poignant archival photographs and drawings of houses that have disappeared.

Vernacular Housing

These big houses were generally built in a formal style by the privileged classes. The other architectural tradition found in Ireland is what's called vernacular housing. Every area of the country had its own variation on the basic pattern of a rectangular whitewashed single-storey building built using cheap materials – mud, straw and stone. They generally had a central hearth, small windows and a half-door that prevented hens and other animals coming into the house. The earlier houses had animals and people living together under the same roof. This tradition probably reflects a much more ancient tradition of byre houses dating back to pre-Christian times. Houses tended to have gable ends in Connacht, Munster and west Ulster whereas the rest of the country used hipped roofs (roofs that run all the way around), possibly reflecting an evolution from earlier oval or circular patterns. Most of these thatched houses have disappeared; others have had thatch replaced with corrugated iron.

Other Housing

Later, towards the end of the 19th century, as farmers became more affluent, two-storey slate-roofed farmhouses were built using the same basic one-room-wide pattern. In the second half of the 19th century many larger farmhouses were built that reflected larger Georgian houses. The features adopted were large windows, fanlights above the door and walled gardens. Some of these are among Ireland's most attractive houses; they are not too large to manage but have some of the feel of the grand Georgian mansions. The architectural historian Maurice Craig has pointed out that it is possible to map a logical stylistic progression from the humblest cottage right up to the grandest Palladian mansion.

There's no clear cut-off point when Georgian becomes Victorian. Some country houses were built in the Victorian style; in cities terraced houses were built for the new middle class and large houses started to fill the new suburbs in Dublin, Cork and Belfast. Ireland also has a long tradition of public housing in rural areas. From the 1880s the Congested Districts Board built labourers' cottages; county council cottages were built in the 1940s; and small two-storey terraced houses were built in towns and villages. Many of these are very much in demand today.

Nowadays the majority of houses in rural and urban landscapes are relatively newly built. Traditional houses tended to be tucked into the landscape for shelter, but many modern bungalows with central heating and good insulation no longer need this protection and have been built on the tops of hills, facing the ocean and in other exposed locations. Some people believe that the new bungalows represent a rejection of the Irish vernacular tradition that is associated with poverty, dispossession and the famine. Others point out that these

Urban Sprawl

One-off houses in the countryside have become a battleground in rural Ireland. On one side conservationists and environmentalists say that they wish to preserve the rural landscape and prevent ribbon development outside towns. On the other, farmers and local representatives argue fiercely that they should have the right to build on their own land and sell sites to augment falling farm incomes.

Whatever your view is on the controversy, you will certainly notice the spread-out settlement patterns in the countryside, where in some cases bungalows and ribbon development have ruined beautiful vistas. Houses with no farms attached and no apparent connection to the land often face the road, even when the view is the other way. A clear distinction between town and country is becoming more and more blurred.

The reasons for this are equally disputed. Some believe that the Irish are returning to ancient Celtic patterns of dispersed settlement. Others point out that Ireland was never influenced by Roman urban culture. Others argue that in Ireland, the only post-colonial society in Western Europe, there is no general consensus on the need for rules and regulations. Another view holds that towns and villages represented centres of anglicisation and military power and that people preferred to live away from them.

You might also simply say that the countryside is a more attractive place to live – few Irish towns are pretty in the way that English villages can be. A positive aspect of this for house-hunters is that houses in villages or towns are often considerably cheaper than houses in the countryside. Another thing to keep in mind is that it is getting harder to obtain planning permission in some areas of the country (see 'Planning in Ireland', pp.110–13).

bungalows are quite similar to the traditional vernacular house with long, low outlines. Many of the designs come from Bungalow Bliss, a manual of architectural plans and contracts for affordable bungalows that has been hugely popular in Ireland since its first printing in 1971.

Property Types Today

Castles

Anglo-Norman castles are found all across Ireland; many are completely ruined so restoration is extremely expensive. You will able to find some restored castles and some, rarely, that have been continually inhabited since medieval times, for a substantial price.

Estates and Georgian Houses

The homes of the Anglo-Irish ascendancy are dotted throughout the country. These range from fairly modest rectories to grand Palladian mansions. Such houses have often lost the estates that they once had but generally have a few acres of land and many outbuildings.

Farmhouses and Cottages

Many old-style farmhouses come on the market without land as the farmer has built a more modern house. Usually these are simple rectangular buildings with smallish windows and a range of outhouses behind.

The picture-postcard-perfect Irish cottage is on the verge of extinction and its price tag reflects this. However, many attractive cottages were built throughout the 20th century, often in pairs, and you'll find these quite frequently although many have been renovated and extended so few retain their original footprint.

Modern Holiday Homes and Bungalows

You'll find many modern holiday homes along the coast. Usually they are grouped together, sometimes around a central green. The quality varies widely – some are very attractive and others are can be obtrusive. More recently traditional designs have been winning out, often with non-traditional additions like dormer windows.

Single-storey houses are probably the most common house type in the country. Some of these houses can be very attractive, others can be overblown with a mish-mash of architectural features: Greek style porticoes, picture windows and eagle-headed gateposts.

More recently two-storey houses have been built across the country. Again, some are beautifully designed while others can be ugly.

Farmland

If you want to farm you can probably find a parcel of land without too much difficulty, but if you are looking for land to build a house on you should read the section on planning permission (*see* 'Planning in Ireland', pp.110–13). It will be much harder than you may imagine (*see also* **First Steps**, 'Farming and Land Prices', pp.12–13)

City Houses

City dwellings can be anything from a huge Georgian mansion to a comfortable brick Victorian house. In many towns the typical house stands two or three storeys high with a shop or pub on the ground floor. Small two-room cottages, most of which have now been extended, are common in cities.

Houses in Modern Suburban Estates

These are houses that are very similar to their semi-detached counterparts outside any British city with three to four bedrooms and front and back gardens. Those in more developed estates can be very nice places to live; those in very newly built estates can lack services.

Pubs and Other Commercial Properties

Residential pubs come on the market quite often but tend to be expensive. The Irish pub licensing system dates from the Intoxicating Liquor Act 1902 when the number of pub licences was frozen. Subsequent population decline meant that this wasn't a problem, until the boom of the 1990s when the price of pub licences rose to exorbitant levels. Despite some moves towards deregulation, pub licences remain extremely valuable.

Restaurants, shops and other commercial properties come on the market quite often but it is not difficult to get a licence to open a new one.

Guide Prices

Prices in Ireland, unlike the rest of Europe, are always per property rather than per square foot or metre. This means that it is difficult to assemble indicative prices for different-size properties. In this book the average prices for new and second-hand houses in the Republic are given, with more details for Northern Ireland. The next section (compiled in early 2004) gives an indication of what you can expect to find in different price brackets. The key thing to remember is that Dublin and its environs are much more expensive than the rest of the country, and that property prices in Galway and Cork are rising. A one-bedroom apartment in Dublin will cost the same as a four-bedroom house elsewhere.

Prices in the Republic (from the Permanent TSB House Price Index in 2003)

County	Average house price (€)	County	Average house price (€)
Carlow	201,000	Limerick	199,000
Cavan	182,000	Longford	183,000
Clare	200,000	Louth	207,000
Cork City	244,000	Mayo	181,000
Cork County	218,000	Meath	241,000
Donegal	172,000	Monaghan	203,000
Dublin City	326,000	Offaly	182,000
Dublin County	320,000	Roscommon	186,000
Galway	241,000	Sligo	211,000
Kerry	192,000	Tipperary	179,000
Kildare	264,000	Waterford	202,000
Kilkenny	210,000	Westmeath	196,000
Laois	185,000	Wexford	190,000
Leitrim	181,000	Wicklow	288,000

Permanent Trustee Savings Bank (Permanent TSB) and the Economic and Social Research Institute (ESRI) publish a national house price index quarterly. This will give you a good indication of trends and percentage increases in house prices for the preceding three months. It is available on the Permanent TSB website (**www.permanenttsb.ie**). The website also has a handy house-price calculator that works out current house values based previous sale prices. In Northern Ireland the University of Ulster and the Bank of Ireland publish a similar but more detailed house price index. It is also a good idea to contact estate agents in the town near to where you are thinking of moving. They are generally very helpful and will give you an indication of prices in the area.

Examples of Listings for Different Prices

Some examples of what you might find in different price brackets are given below. Without wanting to pour cold water on your enthusiasm, please note that the sites and cottages at the lower end – anything under €100,000 – are liable to have a lot wrong with them: be on boggy land, have very out-of-the-way locations, be completely dilapidated or simply rather unattractive.

€30,000

- Three-room country cottage requiring extensive renovation on half an acre, Carrick-on-Shannon, County Leitrim.
- Three-acre plot of mostly rushy land, in a somewhat out-of-the-way location, Peterswell, County Galway.
- Five-room farmhouse in need of major repairs at Garvagh, Dromahair, County Leitrim.

Prices in Northern Ireland (from the Northern Ireland Quarterly House Price Index, Quarter 4, 2003)

Region	All	Terrace	Semi-detached house	Detached house	Semi-detached bungalow	Detached bungalow	Apartment
Northern Ireland	£105,863	£78,043	£96,704	£158,942	£88,294	£132,208	£94,995
Belfast	£105,242	£82,976	£114,410	£184,660	n/a	£171,762	£96,844
North Down	£113,589	£81,053	£98,839	£177,686	£93,967	£148,600	£75,915
Lisburn	£121,532	£88,900	£109,539	£175,020	n/a	£156,103	n/a
East Antrim	£90,665	£67,428	£82,923	£137,898	£85,517	£119,022	£98,406
Londonderry and Strabane	£87,408	£60,806	£83,359	£127,274	£77,350	£106,292	n/a
Antrim and Ballymena	£102,601	£66,225	£81,837	£150,486	£85,171	£132,731	n/a
Coleraine, Limavady and North Coast	£109,911	£76,568	£95,328	£168,558	£86,929	£113,589	£106,981
Enniskillen, Fermanagh and South Tyrone	£119,193	£79,917	£88,390	£146,747	n/a	n/a	n/a
Mid Ulster	£104,722	£85,597	£87,925	£139,456	n/a	£107,850	n/a
Mid and South Down	£117,456	£71,239	£91,538	£155,539	£95,963	£146,141	£97,100
Craigavon/ Armagh	£99,577	£66,892	£78,578	£150,776	£87,407	£112,325	£78,073

€40,000

- Traditional two-storey cottage needing extensive work in Arigna, County Sligo
- Detached one-bedroom cottage near Toomevara, County Tipperary.

€50,000

- Cottage in need of substantial repair on one acre on elevated site with scenic views in Glenbrohane, County Limerick.

€70,000

- Two-bedroom thatched cottage in Ballymacward, North Galway.
- Period former-workman's stone cottage on an estate with some of its original features, Boyle, County Roscommon.

€80,000

- Two-bedroom holiday cottage, recently renovated in Carrick-On-Suir in South Tipperary.
- Two-bedroom house on half an acre in Rearcross, County Tipperary.

€90,000

- Newly redecorated two-bedroom cottage with out-buildings, situated close to fishing, lakes and country walks in Elphin, County Leitrim.
- Small two-bedroom cottage in Bawnboy, County Cavan.

€100,000

- Three-bedroom two-storey town house on the main street of Collooney, County Sligo.
- One-bedroom holiday apartments in Liscannor, 4 miles from the town of Lahinch, County Clare.
- Cottage in need of renovation on half an acre, Hollymount, County Mayo.
- Three-bedroom house just outside Belfast.

€120,000

- Three-bedroom traditional cottage, with outbuildings on one acre, in Cootehall, County Roscommon.
- Derelict traditional farmhouse on 2 acres near Gearhies, Bantry, County Cork
- 600-year-old ruined tower on half an acre without planning permission near Midleton, County Cork.

€140,000

- Three-bedroom semi-detached house between Balla and Castlebar, County Mayo.
- One-bedroom apartment in Belfast.

€160,000

- 19th-century two-storey farmhouse in Gowran, County Kilkenny.
- Three-bedroom semi-detached house in Kiltimagh, County Mayo.
- 14-acre farm in County Limerick.

€180,000

- Three-bedroom semi-detached house in new development in Ballinrobe, County Mayo.
- Three-bedroom semi-detached house in Bridgend, County Donegal (close to Derry City).
- Two-bedroom holiday cottages in Liscannor, County Clare.
- Traditional station house with four bedrooms and original features in Castlebar, County Mayo

- 0.19 acre site with full planning permission in Dungarvan town, County Waterford.

€200,000

- Three-bedroom cottage needing work on 23 acres with access to a lake near Mohill in County Leitrim.
- Three-bedroom semi-detached house in 18-house tax-designated development close to Carrick-on-Shannon, County Leitrim.
- Three-bedroom holiday home with 3-star rating in Ballyferriter, Dingle, County Kerry.

€220,000

- Three-bedroom semi-detached cottage in need of modernisation and repair on half an acre with a number of outhouses in County Meath.
- Three-bedroom holiday home in upmarket development, Kenmare, County Kerry.

€250,000

- Three-bedroom house, 950 square feet, with back garden, Ashbourne Village, County Meath.
- Four-bedroom detached house near the beach at Enniscrone, County Sligo.
- Cut-stone derelict former Roman Catholic church on half an acre in Ballybunion, County Kerry.
- Ground-floor apartment in Dun Laoghaire, Dublin.

€270,000

- Four-bedroom house in a new development with lake views in Castlebar, County Mayo.
- Five-bedroom family home with detached garage near Donegal Town, County Donegal.
- Organic farm with a whitewashed three-bedroom farmhouse on 11 acres near Castlecomer in County Kilkenny.
- Modern four-bedroom cottage on one acre in Gowran, County Kilkenny.

€300,000

- Stone three-bedroom house on half an acre in Carrick-on-Shannon, County Leitrim.
- Two-bedroom end of terrace house in Drumcondra, Dublin.

- 6-acre site with sea views and full planning permission for one single storey dwelling house 4.3 miles from Castlegregory, County Kerry.

€350,000
- Three-bedroom converted and extended schoolhouse in Letterkenny, County Donegal.
- Restored two-bedroom artisan cottage in Broadstone, Dublin,
- Three-bedroom cottage, with adjoining self-contained guest apartment in Kinsale, County Cork.
- Traditional two-storey farmhouse, completely renovated, in Thomastown, County Kilkenny,
- 22 acres of land with two ruined cottages (no planning permission) near Cong in Galway overlooking Lough Corrib.

€400,000
- Five-bedroom modern house in Athlone, County Westmeath.
- Three-bedroom bungalow outside Wicklow town.
- Small three-bedroom town house in Dundrum, Dublin.
- Two-bedroom mid-terrace house in Portobello, Dublin.

€450,000
- Four-bedroom modern bungalow in West Cork.
- Five-bedroom house outside Newry in County Down.

€500,000
- Four-bedroom detached bungalow in Kinsale, County Cork.
- B&B with five bedrooms in Ashbourne, County Meath.

€550,000
- B&B with 18 bedrooms (11 en suite) on a 3-acre site near Athlone, County Westmeath.
- Four-bedroom semi-detached house in Dalkey, Dublin.
- Four-bedroom bunglow with spectacular sea views in Wicklow town, County Wicklow.

€600,000
- Derelict County Monaghan village with 23 houses, dance hall and old mill, once home to over 150 people.
- Georgian rectory on 10.7 acres at Enniskeane, County Cork.

- 45-acre dairy farm in Mallow, County Cork, with farmbuildings and traditional farmhouse with five bedrooms.

- 53-acre farm in Kilkenny with original house (in need of major repair).

€650,000

- Late-Victorian lodge on 2.4 acres in Enniscorthy, County Wexford.

- 18th-century house on 2 acres with views of Mulroy Bay, Kerrykeel, County Donegal.

- Five-bedroom newly restored house with 14 acres, a walled garden and a stableyard near Moneygall in County Tipperary.

- Two-bedroom Victorian terraced house on Cherryfield Avenue, Ranelagh, Dublin.

€700,000

- Three-bedroom mews house on Garville Lane, Rathgar, Dublin.

- Four-bedroom architect-designed house with self-contained apartment and 2 acres of garden in Ballylickey, West Cork.

€800,000

- Six-bedroom split-level house on half an acre with views of Kinsale Bay in County Cork.

- 72-acre residential farm in Wicklow with three-bedroom cottage in good repair and outbuildings including an old dairy.

- Georgian guest house with 10 bedrooms, restaurant and tea rooms near Cappoquin in County Waterford.

- Victorian rectory with outhouses and stables on 0.81 acres just outside Cork city with views over Owenabue river valley.

- Large modern house (12 bedrooms, formerly used as B&B) on Inish Mór (the largest of the Aran Islands).

€900,000

- 17th-century fortified manor house on 20 acres near Lismore in County Waterford.

- Georgian town house needing refurbishment with four bedrooms and grounds to rear of 5.7 acres on the Square, Mountmellick, County Laois.

€975,000

- Two-bedroom Lutyens-style house on 1.3 acres of garden in Ratoath, County Meath.

€1,300,000–2,000,000

- Large Georgian house needing some modernisation on 19 acres, with 20 loose boxes and other outbuildings in Carrigadrohid, County Cork.
- Inishturkbeg Island, small island 1 mile off the mainland, with two separate residences and its own pier in Clew Bay, County Sligo.
- Five-bedroom French château-style house on 4 acres with swimming pool and frescoes in County Tyrone.

€2,000,000

- Five-bedroom property (4,500 square feet) on 12.7 acres in Kilbride, County Meath.
- Large three-storey redbrick Victorian house in need of some renovation on Dartmouth Square, Dublin.

€2,500,000+

- Palladian mansion designed by Richard Castle on 14 acres in County Meath.
- 23-bedroom country house hotel on the sea in Ardfert, County Kerry.
- 12.64-acre development site with outline planning permission for 29 detached dwellings, 22 semi-detached dwellings and one retail shop in Claremorris, County Mayo.
- Detached five-bedroom house on Brighton Road in Foxrock, Dublin.

Research and Information Sources

Websites

One of the good things about Ireland is that you won't be completely over-whelmed by the number of websites and information sources. However, you'll find a range of Irish websites dealing with property. The biggest, and the place to start, is **www.myhome.ie**, a joint venture between Sherry Fitzgerald, Gunne Residential and Douglas Newman Good. MyHome.ie carries property listings for over 350 agents nationwide. Ascot First (**www.ascotfirst.com**) is another basic site that has lots of suburban property with an associated newspaper (**www.irishproperty.ie**). There is a good property site (**www.daft.ie**) that has won awards and has advice as well as property listings.

There are lots and lots of estate agents who will send you brochures on request. Many, in addition to their own websites, have clubbed together in groups like the Real Estate Alliance (**www.realestatealliance.ie**) or the Property Team (**www.propertyteam.ie**), which is mainly Dublin-based but is growing rapidly. The site of the Institute of Auctioneers and Valuers in Ireland (**www. iavi.ie**) provides pages for many of its members. ReMax (**www.remax-ireland. com**) is an international organisation aiming to undercut the main players, which has been expanding in the past couple of years. Green Valley properties (**www.gvp.ie**) covers the mid-west region and takes particular pride in telling it how it is. Look here for a genuine description of a tumbledown corrugated iron-roofed cottage in the middle of a forest rather than a bijou residence with tons of potential that's perfect for the DIY enthusiast. The website **www.eproperty gold.com** is a good site for Cork and around. Country Homes Ireland (**www. countryhomesireland.com**) and Michael Daniels (**www.michaelhdaniels.com**) deal in the upper end of the market.

In Northern Ireland, look at Property News (**www.propertynews.com**) and Northern Ireland Property (**www.niproperty. net**).

Property Sections in the Papers

The *Sunday Times* (Irish edition) has a 'Home' section that includes a comprehensive weekly guide to property, and also publishes a yearly overview of the market in January that gives a snapshot of prices in each county. The *Irish Times* publishes a property supplement on Thursdays, the *Irish Independent* on Fridays. The *Irish Examiner* has more property in the Cork region. The *Belfast Telegraph* also has a property supplement and the *Farmers' Journal* has farms and country houses. *See* **Settling In**, 'Media', pp.220–21, for information about these papers and *see* **References**, 'Newspapers in the Republic', p.279, and 'Newspapers in Northern Ireland', p.280, for the addresses of local papers. You may see country homes advertised in magazines like *Country Life* in the UK.

Estate Agents

Estate agents in Ireland are usually called auctioneers, not because they always sell at auction but because they must hold an auctioneer's licence or a house agent's licence. To become an auctioneer all you have to do in practice is to lodge a €12,700 bond in the District Court – there is no need to pass any exams or have any experience. Most reputable auctioneers are members of either the **Irish Auctioneers and Valuers Institute (IAVI)** or the **Institute of Professional Auctioneers and Valuers (IPAV)** and both organisations have rigorous entry requirements to ensure that their members are properly trained and professional. They have insurance and have drawn up rules of practice that their members must follow. So try to make sure that your agent is a member. However, many country auctioneers don't hold membership of these organisations and it is possible that you'll fall in love with a house being sold by one of these agencies. In this case it is best to be careful – use a solicitor to check the title and other legal matters (*see* **Making the Purchase** for more on the solicitor's role) and make sure you ask the agent to clarify anything you are not sure of.

The most important thing for you to keep in mind as a buyer is that the agent has a duty of care, in legal terms, to the vendor and not to you. The agent's job is to get the highest possible price for the vendor. In fact, the more you pay for the house the higher their commission will be – so essentially this means that they are not on your side! But you are protected by a rule stipulating that an auctioneer cannot misrepresent facts about a house. If they do so they are in breach of the code and risk their reputation and practice. But this does not mean that they have to tell you everything that might be wrong with the house. It is therefore a very good idea to have a list of questions to ask the auctioneer, to which they must give truthful answers. Remember too that you are concerned with the product – the house – whereas they are concerned with the price. So the agent will tend to ask you 'How much do you want to pay?' while you are trying to tell him that you are looking for a two-bedroom house with a sea view. In Ireland you will also have to do much of the leg work yourself. Don't expect the agent to turn up with a sheaf of properties that might suit you, unless you are searching in the very top price bracket. That said, agents will

Case Study: Never Give Up

Caroline and Roger Macken moved to Ireland from Coventry six years ago, when Robert was offered a management role in his company, which was expanding into the Irish market. 'We had copies of local newspaper property sections sent over every Thursday,' says Caroline. 'I preferred the newspaper to the Internet. We looked through them with the kids, and Phoebe who was eight at the time, went through them ringing round all the ones with paddocks and stables. We had to explain to her that not everyone in Ireland had ponies of their own, but we did promise her a dog...' In the end, the family fell in love with a house. A conversion of a 200-year-old cottage, near Lucan village, appealed to all of them, and so they arranged a visit to look at the property. 'There was a mix-up at the bank, and we couldn't get the finance to bid at the auction,' says Roger. 'It was all a bit new to us, anyway, as most homes in England are sold by private treaty so the whole auction thing was a bit beyond us at the time.' Upset at missing out on her dream home, but still intrigued about the house, Caroline rang the auctioneers to find out how much it had gone for. 'We'd heard so much about spiralling house prices, I was prepared for a real shock,' she remembers. 'But the house hadn't actually sold – so I immediately said – we're buying it! And that was that.' 'I think the lesson is that you need to keep in touch with the auctioneers and estate agents,' says Roger. 'It is the house you're going to live in for years and years, and it is worth being a bit persistent to get what you want. And obviously make sure that your finances are in order in advance,' he adds.

Types of Sale in Ireland: Summary

• **Private treaty**: This is the most common method. The estate agent quotes a price and the purchasers make offers based on this price. The vendor and purchaser then negotiate until they reach an agreement.

• **Auction**: The property is advertised with a guide price. The sale itself takes place through a bidding process involving at least two parties. The vendor sets an undisclosed reserve price below which she or he will not sell. The property is sold to the highest bidder in excess of the guide price on the auction day. The purchaser must pay a deposit of 10 per cent immediately after the auction and sign an unconditional contract.

• **By tender**: The vendor invites offers in writing from potential purchasers by a specified time and date. The offers are not disclosed and the vendor can accept any of them or refuse them all.

• **Best and final offer**: This is a particularly nerve-racking method that gained popularity during the height of the boom when there were often several would-be purchasers competing for a property. All the parties are invited to make a best and final offer in writing by a certain date and time. The offers are not disclosed and the vendor may accept any offer or refuse all.

See **Making the Purchase**, pp.155–7, for much more detailed information about types of sale.

be helpful and will certainly try to suggest properties – they just won't do it in a highly organised fashion.

The vendor pays the estate agent's fees. As a rule fees are around 2 per cent of the sale price, not including VAT (at 20 per cent) or additional costs such as advertising. You, as buyer, have to pay solicitor's fees – about 1 per cent of the purchase price although some solicitors charge a fixed fee. These fees don't include additional costs such as land registry or legal search fees. You will have to pay stamp duty (a government tax) on the purchase price unless you are an owner-occupier of a new house or apartment not exceeding 125 square metres (*see* **Making the Purchase** for much more detailed information on fees and stamp duty).

One thing that you should be aware of is that Ireland, and particularly Dublin, has a nasty little distinction between what the auctioneer plans to get for a property and the guide price he or she gives out to the hapless house-hunter. A guide price is simply the price recommended by the auctioneer. (A reserve price is the price below which the vendor will not go.) Don't be too hopeful when you see a guide price of €250,000 for a two-bedroom cottage in Ballsbridge; it is very likely that it will go for up to 25 per cent more, even though in theory the guide price shouldn't be more than 10 per cent below what the vendor expects to get for the property.

The Big Estate Agents

- **Douglas Newman Good (www.douglasnewmangood.com; t** (01) 673 1400): a large, mainly Dublin-based agency.

- **Gunne Residential (www.gunne.ie; t** (01) 618 5501): a large agency, mainly Dublin-based, but with offices in Carrickmacross, Drogheda, Monaghan, Mullingar and Navan.

- **Hamilton Osbourne King** (HOK; **www.hok.ie; t** (01) 663 4300): a long-established agency with offices in Cork, Dublin and Belfast. HOK Residential deals with second-hand homes, country property, fine art and antiques.

- **Hooke and MacDonald (www.hookemacdonald.ie; t** (01) 631 8402): specialises in apartments and new homes. It has a Belfast office that deals with many of the new developments in Belfast and a good letting service.

- **Jackson Stops (www.jacksonstops.ie; t** (01) 633 3777): specialist in country property.

- **Lisney's (www.lisney.com):** a well-established commercial and residential agency with offices in Belfast and Cork.

- **Sherry Fitzgerald (www.sherryfitz.ie; t** (01) 639 9200): has a countrywide network of franchised agents (over 90 offices) and runs a yearly property exhibition in London with a large range of Irish properties on offer.

Surveyors

There are generally two types of survey. The first is a valuation survey, generally insisted on by lending institutions, which guarantees that the property is worth what you intend to pay for it and that therefore the lender will be able to get their money back if anything goes wrong. This type of survey is cheaper than the other sort, a structural survey, but won't identify all possible problems with the property. The structural survey gives you an accurate assessment of the property and should give you a 'schedule of dilapidations on the property', which you can then cost out before committing to buy. If buying a second-hand home it is essential to get a proper survey done. Surveys usually cost between €200 and €400 plus VAT at 20 per cent. Surveyors, structural engineers or architects can carry out a survey. Ensure that these professionals are properly qualified – membership of a professional organisation generally guarantees this – and are covered by professional indemnity insurance. This means that if anything goes wrong you have some comeback. If you are there when surveyors are carrying out a survey note that it should take at least 2 hours on a standard house and they should come equipped with things like ladders so they can gain access to attics and other hard-to-reach areas. (*See* also **Making the Purchase**, pp.129–33.)

Surveyors, Structural Engineers and Architects

- **Society of Chartered Surveyors in the Republic of Ireland (www.scs.ie;** t (01) 676 5500; 5 Wilton Place, Dublin 2).

- **Architects and Surveyors Institute (t** (01) 269 4462; 7 Woodbine Park, Blackrock, Co. Dublin).

- **The Royal Institute of Architects of Ireland (www.riai.ie; t** (01) 676 1703; 8 Merrion Square, Dublin 2).

The Institution of Engineers of Ireland (www.iei.ie; t (01) 668 4341; 22 Clyde Road, Ballsbridge, Dublin 4).

Viewing Trips

Before you start viewing sit down, preferably without any distractions, and write down a wish list divided into 'must have' and 'nice to have'; then stick to it – although this is considerably easier said than done. Invest in a digital camera, if you don't already have one. Taking good pictures of any property that you are interested in, internally and externally, will help fix it in your mind, particularly if you have several properties to view in one day. Pictures will also help you demonstrate what you are talking about to someone who hasn't seen the property. Bring a notebook and a copy of Appendix 1 of this book. Ensure that you identify all your notes, with the address, agent and asking price for the property. Make sure you take thorough notes of anything that strikes you about the property and any questions you'd like to have answered. Again, remember that it is the buyer who must be wary so make sure that you ask plenty of questions; your estate agent must answer them truthfully although he or she doesn't have to volunteer information. Take it easy, there is no point in viewing several properties in a row and having them all blur into one by the end of the day. If you know instantly when you see something that it isn't for you, tell the agent or vendor so and leave; don't waste time trekking around a property that you have no intention of buying.

Radon

Some areas in Ireland, particularly regions where granite is the underlying rock, have problems with radon gas in homes. Radon is a naturally occurring radioactive gas. If you're concerned about this you can get your home tested and it is quite easy to install measures that remove the gas. The Radiological Protection Institute of Ireland has a map that shows which areas are liable to have dangerous levels of radon gas and can also advise on radon protection.

- **Radiological Protection Institute of Ireland (www.rpii.ie; t** (01) 269 7766; 3 Clonskeagh Square, Clonskeagh Road, Dublin 14).

Case Study: Be Informed

Like so many people the Smiths never really intended to settle in Ireland. 'We did everything totally wrong,' explains Betty 'We had no intention of buying here. When we started to think about retiring, we looked in the home counties, then we gradually moved across England but what we wanted was always a bit too expensive.' Eventually the couple took an Irish holiday three years before Peter's retirement. Plans to stay with friends fell through and willy-nilly they found themselves in a hotel in Dromineer on the shores of Lough Derg in Tipperary. 'So we thought we'd have a look at houses, just for fun, just to pass the time really,' says Betty. But these fun house-hunting trips do have a way of sneaking up on you when you least expect it and so it was for Betty and Peter.

After looking at a couple of houses they didn't like much, they were getting ready to return to England when the last house they went to see, an early Georgian house overlooking Lough Derg with a walled garden and old stone outbuildings, turned out to be the one. 'We just thought "that's it",' Betty explains. But, as can be expected, there was a glitch. Peter continues the story: 'The owner, who turned out to be English as well, was absolutely charming but he was asking too much, for our budget, but also for what we thought it was worth. He kept on saying "make me an offer" but we really wanted to halve what he was looking for and we thought that it would be insulting.' The couple left and returned to England, half-resolved to forget about the house. 'But we knew he'd only been there for a year, so we kept on thinking, if only we could find out what he paid for the house, then we'd know what he might accept.'

They found out in the most unexpected way. Betty was leafing through an old *Country Life* and there it was – an ad for the house a year before for less than half of the asking price. 'I screamed, we got on the phone straight away and made an offer just a bit above half of what he was asking. He accepted it, and here we are today almost 15 years later.' It turned out that the man was in fact an investor who specialised in buying houses, living in them for a year or so and then selling them on at considerably more than he'd paid for them. So the moral of the story is that it pays to be informed – find out as much as you can about the house and the seller.

Tips and Questions to Ask

Here is a list of some of the things to ask about properties and to keep in mind when viewing. There is a much more detailed list in Appendix 1.

General

- See if you can view during the day and in the evening. This will help you get a better feel for the house and for the neighbourhood.
- Check how the property compares to your wish list.

• If possible don't view alone, even if you are buying the property on your own. Second opinions are always useful and it tends to be more relaxing to have a partner. Ideally have someone with you who is an old hand at house-buying, especially if you are not that experienced.

• Ask if you can look around alone; it is often hard to look thoroughly when on a guided tour.

• How long has the property been on the market? If it is been around for a long time there may well be a reason.

• What is the water supply to the house. Is it mains, group scheme or well? (*See* box 'Water and Waste', p.115.)

• How is waste treated? (*See* box 'Water and Waste', p.115.)

• Get a proper survey done – it will be worth it.

External

• Check the house externally: walk around it if possible and look at the walls, window frames, roof and gutters. This inspection can highlight potential problems to look for, for instance dampness, when viewing internally.

• Have a look at the other houses on the street or in the neighbourhood. How does this one compare?

• Is there room to extend if you need more space in the future?

• Have any extensions or alterations been carried out and if so did they have proper planning permission? You'll be liable if they were carried out illegally. The vendor should be able to give you a certificate of compliance with building regulations.

Internal

• Has the house been well maintained? What's the overall condition? If it has been painted recently, look out carefully for signs of dampness.

• What way does the house face? Which rooms get morning and evening sun?

• Check the woodwork for woodworm (little circular holes in the wood) or any rotting. Are the floorboards steady or do they bounce (this can be a sign of deteriorating joists underneath).

• Are any fixtures or fitting included in the sale? If so, do you want them?

• Is there enough storage space? Newly built Irish homes tend to be very short of storage.

• When was the central heating installed? Is it oil-fired? Check the running costs. (*See* **Settling In**, 'Home Utilities and Services', pp.212–14, for more on heating.)

Damp

You won't be surprised to hear that damp is a big problem in second-hand Irish houses and one of the most common causes of rising damp is guttering. Rainwater can flow off the roof on to the ground to be absorbed straight up into your walls. Make sure that down pipes don't fall short of the ground and that a gully takes the water some distance away from the house to a soak pit. Check gutters regularly: leaves, birds' nests and sticks can all cause blockages; grass growing out of a gutter is a very bad sign.

Another major cause of damp is earth banked up against the walls. Many older houses have a cellar to avoid this. At the very least make sure that the ground level outside is below the level of the floor inside. French drains (a trench around the house filled with stones) can also improve drainage and reduce damp. Internal drylining isn't such a good idea as it can encourage damp and fungus growth behind the lining. You are strongly advised not to put waterproof paints and sealants on external walls – this has the effect of trapping moisture internally. However, it is also not advised to strip all the plaster off leaving the stone exposed – this was very popular in the 1980s but can lead to water ingress and cause even more damp. The best solution is generally a traditional render that will allow the house to breathe.

- Is the home properly insulated, and are the windows double-glazed? Poor insulation will increase your heating bills.

Legal and Title

- Is the title freehold or leasehold? If leasehold, when does the lease expire?
- Are there any rights of way through the property? Be particularly careful if your access to the property is through a right of way; this can cause major difficulties with neighbours.

The Area

- Ask the sellers about the neighbours and take a walk or drive around the neighbourhood (if in the city). Go into the local shops and pubs. Ask about the neighbourhood.
- How close is the nearest shop, pub, public transport, school? What other facilities are important to you?
- Telephone or visit the local Garda station to ask about crime in the area. They are usually very forthcoming and friendly and will give you an honest answer.
- If it is in the country, have any tree plantations been planted nearby? In the 1990s many farmers received large grants to plant mixed plantations of broadleaf trees. Over the next 20–30 years as these come to maturity they will change the views and landscape considerably.

Temporary Accommodation

Ireland originally had two tourist boards: Bord Fáilte in the Republic and the Northern Ireland Tourist Board in the North. Under the terms of the Good Friday Agreement these two have been amalgamated into an island-wide organisation called **Tourism Ireland (www.ireland.travel.ie)**. Tourism Ireland publishes a range of booklets on different types of accommodation – bed and breakfasts (B&Bs), guest houses, farmhouses, country houses and hotels.

The booklets and website also explain the differences between the various types of accommodation. B&Bs are probably the most economical but can vary hugely in quality. The best offer warm comfortable rooms, generally with en-suite bathrooms, and a huge Irish breakfast from €35 up. The worst, sadly, feature scratchy nylon sheets, copious holy statues, and minuscule bathrooms shoehorned into the corner of the bedroom. A green shamrock is Tourism Ireland's sign of approval showing that the place has reached a minimum standard. But if you like the look of a place, don't be put off by the lack of a green shamrock – some B&Bs don't want to pay the fees required and prefer to advertise separately. Single travellers should be aware that most B&Bs have the unpleasant habit of charging a single person a double rate. This is the case even during the off-season. The rationale is that they could rent the room to two people; but if you ring around you should find someone who'll put you up for a single rate.

If you are travelling around, have a little extra to spend and want to stop for just a night or two try Ireland's *Blue Book* or the *Hidden Ireland*. These are lists of wonderful country houses, usually run by families. They are generally reasonably priced although more expensive than B&Bs. *Hidden Ireland* (**www.hidden-ireland.com**) is a list of private country homes chosen for country house atmosphere and architectural merit. Ireland's *Blue Book* (**www.irelands-blue-book.ie**) has many similar houses, although some are very grand, and includes a wider selection from the north of Ireland.

You can book by contacting the individual accommodation, through Tourism Ireland and through booking services like **Gulliver (www.gulliver.ie)** or the **Hotel Association (www.irelandhotels.com)**.

Short-term and Holiday Rentals

If you just wish to rent for a week or two while house-hunting, a short-term let is probably your best option. Tourism Ireland produces several self-catering accommodation guides that are available from any tourist office or by contacting them directly. You can also browse and book accommodation online. The *Discover Ireland* brochure (**www.discoverireland.ie**) and its network of regional tourism offices is a useful point of reference. Remember that summer,

Easter and bank holiday weekends are the most popular times and prices can reach €750 or considerably more per week. Off-peak you can find houses for as little as €250 per week.

Some of the grander houses also have cottages or converted stables for weekly rent. These are often quirkier and more characterful than the average holiday cottage. You'll find many of them on **www.hiddenhr.com**, which is run by the Hidden Ireland people. Other websites are **www.holiday-rentals.co.uk** and **www.elegant.ie**.

If you are looking for something unusual try the **Landmark Trust (www.irish-landmark.com**; **t** (01) 670 4733; 25 Eustace Street, Dublin 2). The Trust rescues small buildings of historical and architectural interest, restores them and then maintains them through short-term letting to the public. You can choose from a range of exquisite and unique houses including lighthouses, gate lodges and a romantic medieval miniature castle in County Cork.

Short-term lets in Dublin can be very expensive, although the corporate letting market collapsed in late 2000 with the result that many very upmarket houses and apartments came on to the market at considerably reduced rents compared to beforehand.

Renting before Buying

Unless you already know the country very well and know exactly what you want to buy and where, it can be a very good idea to rent for 6 to 12 months before buying. Ireland might be a little slower to seduce than Provence or the Mediterranean coast. The climate is unpredictable; it is also very damp (very good for the complexion, however!) and you may find that the short winter days get you down. In country areas you could ask about a longer lease for properties advertised as short lets. Owners may be happy to let to you for a few months or longer. In Dublin rental properties are advertised in the *Evening Herald*. The website **www.daft.ie** is the first port of call for students but you can find very good houses and apartments there – if you can disentangle private renters from all the agents on the site. Otherwise there are lots of letting agents who will show you apartments; the landlord pays their fee so this is often the most convenient way to go (*see* **Letting your Property**, 'Long-term Lets', pp.272–4 for a list of agents).

Rents are generally based on the number of bedrooms. As a result some houses or apartments advertised as two-bedroom may, on viewing, appear to have pushed the broom cupboard into service as a bedroom (*see* **Letting your property**, 'Long-term Lets', p.273, for a list of average rents in the cities and around the country). Remember too that there is a lot of very low-quality housing in the cities and what seems to be a bargain often won't be. However, you can find wonderful apartments in the cities and often a city apartment can be a good base for house-hunting forays.

Most apartments are furnished. Unfurnished apartments are almost unheard of, and landlords are generally reluctant or unable to take away furniture you don't want. In the country you may occasionally find an unfurnished house for rent but this is quite rare. Generally landlords ask you to pay a deposit of one month's rent in advance. Most landlords will also require you to pay monthly by direct debit from your bank account so you may have to set up an Irish bank account to do so. This can be a bit of a Catch-22 situation as you can't open a bank account without evidence of residency – generally a utility bill will suffice but you may not be able to transfer the utility bill into your name without setting up a direct debit to guarantee payment. As a rule you pay all gas and electricity expenses; you usually transfer these bills into your name for the duration of your tenancy (see **Settling In** for information on utilities, banks and much more).

Buying to Let

It may seem like the perfect solution – buy a house in Ireland, spend some time in it yourself and let it out the rest of the time. You enjoy the property when you can, and it pays for itself. If this is your plan, stop and consider all the issues very carefully before proceeding.

First of all, there are two ways to approach buying to let. The first is to buy purely and simply for income-generation. This means buying a property that you can let out for most if not all of the year and that will pay for itself. The second is a home that you plan to use yourself and let out when you are not using it. The first is a business, the second is not. The first means that you will probably choose a property in a city or town or a region where you will find an adequate supply of tenants. The second might mean that you choose a property in a 'holiday' location, by the sea, on a lake or simply somewhere you like. It is unlikely that you will be able to cover all the costs of a holiday home from rental income. Oversupply is one reason why holiday properties are difficult to let all year round. Thousands of new holiday homes have been built in seaside resorts under the **Seaside Resort Renewal Scheme** and many of these lie empty for much of the year. Weather is another reason: people do not head to Connemara for winter sun.

Prices are high. Some would say they are astronomical at peak season, but they can be as much as a quarter less off-peak. Rentals covering summer (June, July, August, part of September), perhaps Christmas and Easter and bank holiday weekends are unlikely to fund the entire cost of the house. These times may well be when you will wish to use the property. That said if you have a high-quality property with character and unusual features you may be able to let it more frequently. Some parts of the country, particularly more exclusive towns like Kinsale in West Cork, have a shortage of rental properties. If your property is close to a golf course or other amenity you should find tenants for other times of the year, but finding tenants, arranging for someone to meet them, organising cleaning and so on can all be a headache, particularly when you are on the other side of the Irish Sea. Management companies can be an answer but add quite a bit to running costs and don't operate in many rural areas.

What all this means for you is that you need to research very carefully before buying a holiday home that you cannot afford without extra rental income. This means checking the rents on similar properties in the area. Don't take the selling agent's word for this, do your own research. Find out what the occupancy rates in similar properties are and analyse what your costs are likely to be in detail. A lot of holiday homes were built in large groups during the 1990s to take advantage of tax breaks; now owners find these very hard to let outside peak season. Tenants seem to prefer more intimate developments or houses that stand alone.

If you plan to buy a property simply to fund the mortgage and perhaps make a capital appreciation at the same time, you will need to do just as much homework. Check what the yield will be – the amount of rent as a proportion of the value of the property. Buying a Dublin city centre property might not be the best investment; rents across Dublin are relatively flat – meaning that your rental income for a more expensive property may not match what you paid for it. Rents in the country are considerably lower than rents in the cities (see **Letting Your Property**, 'Long-term Lets', p.273, for a list of average rents). Dublin rents are much higher than rents in the provincial cities, but have dropped considerably over the last three years: the average rental income for a two-bedroom apartment was 1,200 Irish pounds and it is now the equivalent in euro.

Make sure you establish your investment goals. How long do you wish to keep the property? Are you looking mainly for capital appreciation or for rental income (or both)? Will the rent service the loan fully? Would you be able to pay the mortgage if interest rates were to rise?

There is a student accommodation tax relief scheme and you could perhaps take advantage of this to buy a property near a recognised third-level college and use it for yourself in the summer or perhaps rent it out to tourists. Towns like Sligo with large transient student populations that are also near the sea and have other amenities might be suitable for such a plan. The good news, for you as landlord, is that tenants don't have as many rights in Ireland as they do in other European countries. Detailed guidance and information on letting property, albeit from the landlord's point of view, is given in **Letting your Property**, pp.261–74.

Building from Scratch

Buying a site and building your own house seems to be the ideal way to cut costs and create exactly what you want, where you want it. Ireland has very rigorous planning laws and before you make any plans to build you *must* understand these planning regulations. If you buy a site without planning permission and are subsequently refused permission to build you'll be left with an almost worthless piece of land. It is well worth your while checking out the county development plan (*see* below, and available in any public library) and getting professional advice before buying land to build on. The planning authority will also give you advice on whether your plan will comply with the development plan and design standards.

The County Development Plan

The county development plan is the agreed blueprint for planning and development in a county. Each local authority, in consultation with the public, lays out the planning policies for the area for the next 6 years. Generally it is a written statement together with a series of maps showing the council's objectives for different areas in the county. Each county development plan should also take into account the National Spatial Strategy – this is a plan for balanced regional development that runs right up to 2020. Some areas may be zoned residential, others industrial, others may be part of a green belt where no building is permitted. All planning applications in the area are measured against this plan. You can see the county development plan for each county in the local library, on the county council's website or you can contact them directly (*see* **References**, 'Irish County Councils', pp.282–6).

Unfortunately, since rezoning land can result in huge windfalls for the owners of that land, development plans are often subjected to political pressure, causing much hand-wringing in the media. This does not seem to stop county councillors from disregarding the plans when the interests of a constituent or, in some cases, personal interests, override the plan.

Note also that some county development plans have triggered other types of controversy. Wicklow, for example, included a provision that only permanent native residents – meaning that the person had been living in the area for at least 10 years – could build in certain parts of the county. This was supposed to prevent villages being overwhelmed by Dublin commuters but led to all kinds of claims and counter-claims of racism and élitism. Make sure that you consult the development plans and the local council before making a commitment to build, and remember that where *you* want to build – beside a lake, somewhere with a wonderful view or high in the mountains – is often the least likely place you will get planning permission, since the aim of the development plan is to protect areas of high amenity.

Planning in Ireland

You need planning permission for any development of land or property unless the development is specifically exempted. Development includes everything from building and making alterations to the demolition of a habitable building. If you own a listed property you need permission to carry out any changes whatsoever. However, minor additions to existing houses – adding small conservatories, porches, walls and garages – don't need permission. Don't be too daunted, as this section takes you through all the planning regulations, and the Department of the Environment, Heritage and Local Government produces useful leaflets on every aspect of the planning process (*see* box 'Planning Leaflets', p.113, for a list of titles).

You apply to your local planning authority for planning permission; this may be a county council, a borough council, a city or a town council (*see* **References**, 'Irish County Councils', pp.282–6, for a full list of county councils and contact details). There are two main types of planning permission: permission and outline permission. Permission is usually called 'full permission' or 'full planning permission' (the magic words attached to so many sites for sale). To obtain full planning permission you'll need to submit an official application that shows the location of the proposed building site, the layout and what the development will look like when it is finished. This means, incidentally, that if you purchase a site with full planning permission you can't build just anything, you have to build precisely what the original permission was for, and that includes things like number of bathrooms, windows and doors as well as finishes and square footage. If you'd like to change the plans you need to apply for a new

Planning Permission

To apply for planning permission you will need to submit:

- the page of the newspaper showing the notice of intention to seek planning permission.
- a copy of the site notice erected on the land.
- a plan showing where the site notice has been placed on the land.
- six copies of the location map showing exactly where the development will be sited.
- six copies of a site or layout plan (scale of not less than 1:500).
- six copies of plans, elevations and sections of the building to a scale of 1:200.
- the appropriate fee (the current fee for an application to build a house is €65 but this can be more depending on size; the fee for a house extension is €34).
- a schedule listing the plans, drawings and maps.

Timescale for Planning Permission

At start	Notice published in newspaper and site notice erected
Two weeks later	Latest date for lodging application
2–5 weeks later (statutory period is 8 weeks)	Application is validated by the planning authority; submissions or objections are considered and notice of decision is issued
4 weeks after issue of notice of decision	If no appeal is made, the planning authority will issue grant of permission, or outline permission (if they have not already indicated a decision to refuse)

permission. Most rural areas in Ireland don't have public sewers so you may need to include information about the type of sewage treatment you plan to install (see box 'Water and Waste', p.115). You must announce your intention to build in a local newspaper and put up a similar notice on the land itself. (If you are buying a house, it is a good idea to take a walk around the area to see if there are any applications nearby – they have to be displayed prominently.)

Outline permission means that the planning authority has agreed in principle to the development. To get this you only need to supply documentation relating to siting and the layout. After getting outline permission for your site you'll need to supply detailed drawings and specifications before getting full permission to build. Generally, outline permissions last for three years. Developers sometimes apply for outline permission before going to all the expense and trouble of full permission, though as a private person you'll be unlikely to do this – if you plan to build, get full permission.

Once you've assembled all your plans, forms and fees for the planning application and sent them off to the planning office with the appropriate fee, you sit back and wait for up to eight weeks while the council mulls over your application. During this time anyone can view your application and, upon payment of a fee (€20), make a written observation or submission on it (based on planning considerations not personal opinions), which the planners must consider. The planning authority can ask you for further information and extend the decision time at their discretion. Once they've made a decision they issue notice of their intention to grant or refuse and anyone who wishes to object to the development can do so (this was free but objectors now have to come up with €50 to lodge their complaint). If an objection is made the application is then sent off to a nationwide body called An Bord Pleanála (**www.pleanala.ie**; not hard to guess this one – it is the Planning Board), which makes a final decision on the application. If on the other hand your application is refused or you don't like the conditions attached (permission is often granted with conditions – that you move the septic tank or lower the roof-line or something like that) you also have the right to appeal to An Bord Pleanála (on payment of a further fee of €200). Once granted, full permission lasts for five years. If you don't build anything in this time, the permission lapses and you'll have to reapply in full all over again.

As you can see, the process is pretty long and involved, and although the actual fee is low you will need to pay architects, planning consultants (if the building may be controversial) and other professionals. You should be pretty sure that your application will meet all the requirements of the county development plan; you'll also need to consider things like overlooking a neighbour, interference with a right of way, building in a special area of conservation (EU habitat directives are the same all over Europe) or breaking the skyline – all grounds for refusal or additional conditions. You may find this rather hard to believe, having seen some of the buildings that have been granted permission in the past, but that's the way it is in Ireland. That said, don't be timid when putting in your application and feel that it must be a traditional design. One very innovative design was submitted with much trepidation to Cork County

Case Study: Planning and Linguistics

Jane Andrews' love of Connemara ponies first brought her to Ireland, to the Clifden Pony Show, where enthusiasts from all over the world come to buy and admire Ireland's only native breed of horse – a tough, intelligent and agile animal that has been bred to survive in the harsh, rocky terrain of the west. Legend has it that when the Spanish Armada sank off the Connemara coast in the 16th century, the horses managed to swim ashore and bred with the native ponies running wild in the mountains. After 20 years of travelling back and forth, breeding ponies, becoming a member of the Irish Connemara Pony Society and making many many friends, Jane realised that Ireland was where she wanted to live.

In June 2002 she finally sold her farm in Wiltshire and started her search. 'I knew exactly what I wanted,' she explains, 'a cottage near Clifden with some land where I could breed ponies, but it was very hard to find anything; land is at a premium in this area.' Eventually, realising that property prices were rising and that she needed to put her money into something, she bought a small B&B and started to run the business. 'It was totally new and totally different but I've enjoyed it.' She kept looking for a small farm for her 12 remaining ponies. A short time later she thought she had found the perfect solution, some land near Clifden that she could build on with plenty of space for the ponies. However, the county development plan for this Gaeltacht region states that all applicants for planning permission must be able to speak Irish. Jane is 58 and doesn't think that she'd be able to learn the language. Regretfully she had to abandon her plan to build. She's waiting to hear whether the proviso will become law or will be repealed, and is still searching for her farm. The only consolation for Jane is that the B&B, bought and refurbished for about €300,000, is now valued at €560,000.

Planning Leaflets

The following leaflets on planning can be obtained from the Department of the Environment:

- PL1 – A Guide to Planning Permission
- PL2 – Making a Planning Application
- PL3 – Commenting on a Planning Application
- PL4 – Building a House – The Planning Issues
- PL5 – Doing Work around the House – The Planning Issues
- PL6 – Agricultural & Farm Development – The Planning Issues
- PL7 – Planning for the Business Person
- PL8 – The Development Plan
- PL9 – Enviromental Impact Assesment
- PL10 – Making a Planning Appeal
- PL11 – A Guide to the Building Regulations
- PL12 – A Guide to Architectural Heritage

Council and was granted with no conditions, with the comment that it was a breath of fresh air to see a good modern design.

Finally, you should also know that most planning authorities are planning to introduce levies on new homes across the country. The levies are not for services like water and electricity (which you pay for separately), but for community facilities. Eleven councils will apply a single flat levy on all houses regardless of size and the others will charge a varying amount depending on the size of the house. They vary widely: Kildare plans to charge €14,000 per house whereas Limerick will charge €3,700; Wicklow plans to levy €140 per square metre and Kilkenny will levy only €45. These levies apply to all developments that secure planning permission after 10 March 2004 and could add quite a considerable amount onto your building costs. If you buy a listed property you will need to delve even deeper into the intricacies of planning. This is explained in more detail in 'Renovation and Conservation', pp.116–18.

The Department of the Environment, Heritage and Local Government produces a series of leaflets on every aspect of the planning process. These are available on-line, directly from the Department's Planning and Land Section, Custom House, Dublin 1 (**www.irlgov.ie**; **t** (01) 679 3377), or you can pick one up from Enfo at 17 St Andrew Street, Dublin (**www.enfo.ie**; IRL only **t** 1890 200191).

Building a New Home

Once you have your planning permission, you can start to build. You should consult a guide such as the National House Building Guarantee Scheme's House Building Manual or the RIAI's Build your Own House and Home to familiarise yourself with all the issues as this book cannot hope to deal with all of them, but we'll touch briefly on some of the things you need to consider.

When building, your options are to hire an architect to design the house for you or to buy ready-made plans and get a builder to do the work. Many Irish houses are built using such plans, which explains why so many of them look so similar. The advantage of using an architect is that you get something tailor-made for you and your needs. Architect-designed homes also tend to be worth more when reselling.

Most new houses in Ireland are block-built (two layers of cement blocks with an insulated cavity wall between them) but timber-frame houses (with a wooden frame and external weatherproof finish in stone, brick or cement) are gaining popularity despite strenuous efforts from the Irish Home Builders' Association to persuade people that they are likely to rot, collapse and do all kinds of other undesirable things. In fact they are cheaper and quicker to construct than traditional building methods and are just as well insulated as other house types, but Irish builders are likely to be more experienced with the traditional methods. Research both before making up your mind. Another, far less usual, method is to import prefabricated log houses from Scandinavian countries – there are a few of these lurking, slightly incongruously, in the Irish landscape. And you'll find a few eco-homes built with straw bales, earth and other environmentally friendly materials.

There are two ways to go about any building project. The first is the self-build option where you hire and manage all the professionals yourself. This means that you can knock as much as 20–30 per cent of the cost of building off your total but also means that you need to know what you are doing and have plenty of time to focus on the project. The other way is to ask a professional – an architect, engineer, builder or professional project manager – to manage the project for you. This costs more but ensures, in theory, that everything goes smoothly and to schedule, without you needing to give up the day job. In practice, you do need to know what's going on at different stages of the building project so it is a very good idea to read up on terminology and the issues that might arise. Pricing varies widely – a rule of thumb is probably per between €100 and €200 per square foot depending on the specifications and finishes. Your architect or builder should be able to advise you.

Builders and Other Craftspeople

Builders in Ireland have a fairly good reputation for quality but it is wise to make sure that you are covered for all eventualities. In an ideal world your builder and all the other professionals you need – plumbers, electricians, plasterers, tillers, glaziers and roofers – would be registered with the Construction Industry Federation (the Irish Home Builders Association is part of this organisation), but many otherwise excellent builders are not. This leaves you in

Water and Waste

Despite Ireland's watery reputation, in rural areas a good water supply is not a given. Although 90 per cent of the population has access to a public mains supply, many less built-up areas rely on individual wells or a group scheme – a supply shared by a small group of houses. You should always enquire about the water situation before you buy a site or an older house. If you're building a new home in the countryside you may have to drill a well; grants are available for up to 75 per cent of the cost from the local authority. Positioning of wells is limited by where the septic tank is located and they must be a certain distance from the front and back doors of a property. You'll often employ a water diviner to find the best spot if drilling a well – they use forked sticks to find the water and, believe it or not, are almost never wrong. Average well depths are 150–200ft deep but many are far deeper than that – it all depends on the rock strata underlying your house. The well for Ballygowan mineral water is 1,000ft deep.

Before you can drink your well water you must get the water tested by the local health board for bacteria and for chemicals. Most Irish groundwater is not chemically polluted but high levels of bacteria, from animal and human waste, have been found in some areas. If the water isn't up to standard you can treat it with UV light and filters. The local health officer can give advice on this.

Waste disposal is another thorny issue. If you are building in the country you'll get to know a lot more about sewage and its idiosyncrasies than you ever imagined. And if you buy a house in the country, find out what the waste disposal system is. You might find yourself having to get a tank pumped out once or twice a year. Septic tanks are the most common method used – concrete tanks sited underground with a percolation field – but there are all kinds of other systems: Puraflo peat filter systems, reedbed biological systems and other bio-cycle methods. You'll need to supply detailed information on the sewage treatment system you plan to use with your planning application if building in the country; lack of attention to this could mean that your application is summarily refused.

something of a quandary: how do you establish the credentials of your builder and other workers? One thing you can do is ask in the local hardware shop. They know who's got a good reputation, who's busy and who buys good-quality materials. Make sure you get a proper contract with stages clearly laid out. You can also ask them for a list of jobs they've done recently.

If you are buying or building a new house it should be registered and covered by the National House Building Guarantee Scheme or HomeBond. This is a scheme established by the Construction Industry Federation and the Irish Home Builders Association to ensure that proper building standards are maintained – the guarantee should ensure that you are covered against any structural faults for six years. A supervising or bonded engineer visits the site during construction and ensures that the work is to standard. If she or he is not satisfied that the work meets building regulations they will not sign off the house. Don't be surprised to find Romanian plasterers and Polish stonemasons working on your property. Many Eastern European craftspeople have come to work in Ireland over the past five or six years. They are usually sponsored by a builder and are here perfectly legally.

Builders

- **Construction Industry Federation (www.cif.ie; t** IRL (01) 497 7487; Federation House, Canal Road, Dublin 6).
- **HomeBond (t** 1850 306300; The National House Building Guarantee Scheme, Federation House, Canal Road, Dublin 6).
- **Irish Home Builders Association** (IHBA) **(www.cif.ie; t** (01) 406 6000; Construction House, Canal Road, Dublin 6).
- **National Guild of Master Craftsmen (www.nationalguild.ie; t** (01) 473 2543).

Architects

Architects are not allowed to advertise so you'll have to do some investigation to find one. If you know anyone who has used an Irish architect ask them for information and suggestions. The **Royal Institute of Architects (www.riai.ie; t** (01) 676 1703; 8 Merrion Square, Dublin 2) can give you a list of architects who specialise in different areas – renovation and conservation, extensions, one-off buildings and so on. Their website also offers a good architect search (Arch-Search) facility, which allows you to stipulate a range of criteria. While you're on the site, have a look also at the picture gallery of buildings that have won Irish Architecture awards.

Architect fees vary but are generally calculated as a percentage of the total – perhaps 10 per cent of the build budget, sometimes more, sometimes less, depending on the complexity of the project.

Renovation and Conservation

Renovation is often a good bet. Since so many Irish people have abandoned old and damp houses for modern bungalows, you will find quite a number of very dilapidated houses in need of total renovation. That said, in parts of the country, particularly West Cork, they have all been snapped up. You can also find quite a number of unusual buildings that can be turned into homes – old schoolhouses that are now too small for modern class sizes, abandoned and deconsecrated Church of Ireland churches, stationhouses on abandoned railway tracks, light-houses, Martello towers, even ruined Norman tower houses have been rescued and renovated by enterprising and imaginative individuals.

Renovating and reselling will almost always be a profitable exercise – providing – and this is a huge proviso – that you know what you are getting into. This means you have to plan carefully, be very clear about the expenses you are liable to incur before starting, and be ready to deal with glitches, recalcitrant builders and the various problems that can and will occur. There's renovation and there's renovation. Are you planning to upgrade a heap of stones to a habitable property or are you starting with a habitable property and making larger or smaller changes? The professionals you'll require and the labour involved may be very different. Things you don't expect will inevitably throw out the best-laid plans. A renovator in Dublin found that she couldn't put a fitted kitchen into her house because the walls didn't meet at 90 degrees and the floors were uneven – an extra expense to factor in after she'd done her budget calculations. When you ask for advice you get differing opinions from every expert, so you have to decipher what's most appropriate for your operation.

Pink Castles and Statuettes

Jeremy Irons, the Oscar-winning actor, stirred up more controversy than he expected with his purchase and renovation of an Irish property. An Irish castle to be precise, seven-storeys and 100ft high, looking over Roaringwater Bay in west Cork. Kilcoe Castle, built around 1450, is the former seat of the McCarthy clan and was the last castle in the district to hold out against the English, although the locals were eventually unsuccessful and the castle fell in 1603. It was an austere, grey, uninhabited ruin when Irons bought it. After extensive research Irons and his architect Bena Stutchbury (*see* box 'Case Study: A Vernacular Architect', p.39, for her story) discovered that the castle would have originally been covered with a thick coat of render painted with white lime wash to protect it against the salty winds. Deciding that white would be too stark and make the building look like a lighthouse, they eventually settled on adding ferrous sulphate, or 'copperass', to the lime. When painted on to the castle walls this turned them a colour variously described as peach, terracotta or plain old pink, depending on the time of the day, on how close you are to the castle or on whom you ask.

Although Dúchas, the Irish Government's heritage department (now disbanded and absorbed into the Department of the Environment), didn't object to the colour, saying that it would fade eventually, local opinion wasn't so forgiving. The Cork-based *Southern Star* ran a piece on it and the story was picked up all over the world with headlines ranging from 'Irons's Peachy Irish Castle' to 'Life in the Pink'. Irons ruefully points out that when old masters are restored there will always be someone who 'preferred it as it was', but so far is sticking to his guns. Over time the colour has faded and all the controversy has ended up being a storm in a paintpot – to paraphrase yet another of the tabloid headlines.

If your house is of special interest, be particularly careful. A nationwide 'Record of Protected Structures' has replaced the previous system of listed buildings (which was similar to that in the UK). This new system has been criticised because there is just one classification rather than several categories of listing, so a cottage with an unusual porch and a 17th-century castle are considered equal under the legislation. Usually minor works to houses don't need planning permission (changing windows, adding on a conservatory, moving a bathroom) but if your house is a protected structure such works do require permission. The Department of the Environment and Local Government's leaflet states: 'Such works can be carried out without planning permission only if the works would not affect the character of the structure or any element of the structure that contributes to its special interest.' And, as you can imagine, this covers quite a few things.

There are grants to help the owners of protected structures carry out work to the necessary conservation standards (usually 50 per cent of the cost of works up to €13,000). You can find out about these by contacting your local county or borough councils (see **References**, 'Irish County Councils', pp.282–6). The Irish Heritage Council (**www.heritagecouncil.ie**) also provides grants and information; it is worth getting in touch with them as they may be able to help out with things that seem minor like restoration of walls or replacing uPVC windows with the original wooden sash windows. The Department of the Environment publishes a series of Conservation Guidelines that ranges from shopfronts to ironwork (available from **www.environ.ie** or Government Publications, Molesworth Street, Dublin). The one on mortars, pointing and renders gives the quantities and types of hair to add to lime mortars (ox or goat of 50–75mm in length). Apparently yak hair is sometimes imported for the purpose!

Making the Purchase

By Joseph McArdle
Barrister at Law (King's Inns, Middle Temple)

Buying a property in the Republic of Ireland is not very different from buying a property in England. It is certainly as safe as buying a property in the UK. On reading a book such as this – which must explain the potential pitfalls if it is to serve any useful purpose – it can seem a frightening or dangerous experience. But remember that the same or similar dangers arise when buying a house in the UK, particularly given the similarities between the two legal systems. Irish law and English law were identical until 1922. Take a quick look at a textbook on English conveyancing and all the horrible fixes that people have got themselves into. There is much the same system in Ireland, north and south. In practice, you (and other people like you) do not worry about these dangers because you are familiar with them and, more importantly, because you are shielded against contact with most of them by your solicitor.

This is not a textbook and does not represent itself as giving legal advice any more than a guidebook can guarantee that the quality of food in a restaurant or the amount of traffic on a particular by-road will be what it was when the author ate in a particular hotel or drove through a particular region. Regard this book as a snapshot, something to answer some of your questions and to help you decide whether or not you really want to go ahead with a plan which had been maturing in your head or which you and your partner had been discussing casually as a possibility. When you decide to act, however, you must ask an Irish lawyer to advise you about any issues that worry you and leave it to him to avoid the landmines. He speaks English, so there is no language barrier as there might be in Spain or Italy and if you have already bought or sold a property in the UK, much of what he says will be comfortingly familiar.

If it will make you happier, you can always consult your own lawyer in England for general advice, but this may add to your costs and, in any event, he or she will most probably tell you that he/she is not qualified to give definitive advice on detailed questions of Irish law.

Preliminary Points

Money

Ireland is part of the euro zone and the currency is, therefore the euro.

At the time of writing (June 2004) €1 = £0.66544 sterling approximately or, to put it another way – £1 sterling = €1.513 approximately. Prices in euro can therefore be divided by 1.5 for a rough estimate. Obviously, the more money you change the more important the figures after the decimal point become.

Generally speaking, at present this rate is pretty stable, only changing at the third decimal point.

Prices

Prices quoted are usually only rough estimates. At the moment, prices are high because there is a lot of disposable income and demand is great. The Irish economy is booming. At the time of writing, the clouds on the horizon are Iraq and the price of oil. Every week the experts prophesy that the housing bubble will burst but it has not happened yet. The decision is yours – do you buy now knowing that, in the short term at least, the odds are in favour of an increase in your net worth, or do you wait in expectation of a fall in prices from which there will be no recovery? Although the chances of no recovery are slight, it is always a question of how long you are prepared to wait.

The Law

This book is intended primarily for people from England and Wales and refers mainly to the twenty six counties of the island of Ireland which make up the Republic of Ireland (from here onwards, I shall refer to the country as 'Ireland'). For this reason I have drawn comparisons with English law. Scots law is somewhat different.

Although Northern Ireland is part of the United Kingdom and the sterling area, land law in England and Wales differs in various aspects from Northern Ireland. This section is not qualified to comment on these differences.

If you are interested in property in Northern Ireland and are looking for legal advice, it is best to get in contact with the **Law Society of Northern Ireland** which is based at Law Society House, 98 Victoria Street, Belfast BTI 3J2, Northern Ireland, United Kingdom. As of 14 April 2004, there were also at least 17 local solicitors' associations. The names and addresses of their Secretaries and Chairpersons may be found on the website of the Law Society of Northern Ireland at **www.lawsoc-ni.org**.

Until 1922, Irish and English law were identical. Since then new legislation has been introduced in both countries but often the changes have been on much the same lines. Judgements in English courts are still cited in the Irish courts. They are not binding but are certainly regarded as persuasive.

Disclaimer

Although we have done our best to cover most topics of interest to the buyer of a property in Ireland, a guide of this kind cannot take into account every individual's personal circumstances and the size of the book means that the advice cannot be comprehensive. The book is intended as a starting point that will enable people who are thinking of buying property to understand some of the issues involved and to ask the necessary questions of their professional advisers. **It is no substitute for professional advice.** Neither the author nor the publishers can accept any liability for any action taken or not taken as a result of this book.

Preparing to Buy a Property in Ireland

Make a Preliminary Selection of a Type of Property

This is not always as obvious as you might first think. Once again the application of common sense can help inform your decision but, mercifully, the human spirit often ignores such considerations. If you, or your spouse, falls in love with an abandoned school-house in the middle of the countryside whereas reason tells you that you ought to be looking for an apartment near an airport, you will probably buy the school-house. And you will probably enjoy every minute of owning it. This does not mean, however, that it isn't worth spending a little time thinking about the type of property that would suit you best *before* you travel to Ireland to look at buildings. Buying an inappropriate type of property can prove very expensive and, worse still, can put you off the whole idea of a property abroad.

As well as helping you to focus your ideas, thinking about these issues will help you to give auctioneers a clear brief as to what you are looking for. This will help them to help you and avoid your time being wasted looking at totally inappropriate properties. Always discuss your requirements with the local agents who are helping you find a property rather than dictating those requirements to them. They may well say that what you are looking for is not obtainable in their area – but that something very similar is, and at reasonable cost. Do not be afraid to change your mind. It is quite common for people to start off looking at rural properties for restoration and to end up deciding that, for them, a new property is a better bet. Or the other way round. If you do change your mind you *must* tell the auctioneers with whom you are working. Better still, you should be discussing your developing views with them and getting their confirmation that what you want is 'do-able'.

A checklist of key points to think about is at the end of this chapter.

Understand the System

As I say above, there are more similarities than differences in the purchase or sale of property in Ireland and England. Do not, however, allow this to lull you into a sense of false security or to say to yourself 'I know all about it'. There *are* differences and, with one exception, only an Irish auctioneer or lawyer will be able to give a definitive answer to individual queries. The exception is the English or Welsh auctioneer who specialises in purchasing property in Ireland. They do exist, although the majority would deal more often in commercial than residential properties except for period country houses/stately homes which are usually outside the budget of anyone except pop stars or Queen's counsel.

Choose a Solicitor

Talk to your English Lawyer?

Although it may seem premature, many think that it is prudent to consult your English lawyer *before* you have started to look for a property in Ireland. In spite of what I have said above, it is not impossible that he or she has already been involved in such a purchase. The main point of a consultation at this preliminary stage is that you are not under pressure and, therefore, can weigh up all the pros and cons at your leisure without feeling that you are already committed.

It will give you a clearer picture and even give you a certain reassurance to have examined and come to at least a tentative conclusion on matters such as:

- **the ownership of the property, which may have serious tax implications, particularly in relation to inheritance.**

- **to have mortgage finance or not to take out a mortgage – and from an Irish or an English lender?**

- **acquiring the euro to pay for the property (NOTE: the plural of 'euro' is 'euro' and of 'cent' is 'cent' and the symbol for the euro is €).**

- **considering whether the purchase might not be in sterling.**

- **deciding how to structure your purchase to minimise taxes and costs in the UK if you continue to be so liable.**

- **if you plan to live in Ireland and not just to use the property as a holiday home, consideration of the implications as regards tax and other issues in the UK.**

You will find that much of the advice that your UK lawyer gives you (with the usual lawyerly caveats) will be relevant to Ireland but only as a general guide, to permit you to get the feel of what you are letting yourself in for. For all other matters, you will need to engage an Irish solicitor. It is quite possible that your UK solicitor will be in a position to recommend auctioneers, architects, surveyors, banks, mortgage lenders, etc. in England or Wales who have contacts in Ireland or even have branches across the Irish Sea. The firm may have its own contacts in particular areas, such as Waterford, west Cork, Galway, Mayo or Donegal, all areas which have attracted many second home owners from the UK, France, Germany, the Netherlands and even further afield.

As you will see later, many of the Irish versions of such bodies or institutions have links with the UK, particularly the banks and building societies.

Once you have set foot in Ireland and certainly once you have reached at least a tentative decision about a particular property, you should be dealing with (a) an Irish auctioneer, (b) solicitor, (c) surveyor/engineer and (d) architect or engineer.

Irish Solicitors

Unlike the UK, it can be said that solicitors have, by virtue of s.58 of the Irish Solicitors Act, 1954, been given a 'conveyancing monopoly' in Ireland, in other words, a solicitor is the only professional person who may check the legal title to land. Accordingly, you cannot have a land transaction without the use of a solicitor. In any case, if you are getting a mortgage, the lending institution will insist on your using a solicitor.

Therefore, unless there are overwhelming reasons for using your own UK lawyer whom you know and who knows you, there is a lot to be said for consulting an Irish solicitor as soon as possible. He or she will be operating on home ground. As in the UK, the Irish legal profession is divided into two branches, solicitors and barristers but, remember that the devil is in the detail, and there are differences in the law of the two jurisdictions. It is not merely a question of points of law. An Irish solicitor will most probably know the auctioneer and the property and may also know the vendor. He or she will almost certainly be familiar with your bank or building society.

Unless something goes badly wrong with your purchase, you will, as you would in the UK, deal with a solicitor and not a barrister. Every solicitor is a member of the Incorporated Law Society of Ireland. Many solicitors, particularly in the major centres, operate in partnerships. In small country towns, you may find that the local solicitor is a 'sole practitioner', that is, a one-person firm. This does not mean that you will get less satisfactory service, although it could mean that he or she is under greater pressure. In theory, in a large partnership, where work can be divided out among the partners, service should be more speedy. This does not necessarily follow. The large city firms have sections which specialise in different branches of the law but often they are more concerned with large sales concerning commercial property and unless you know a particular employee or partner of the firm they may not be so interested in residential property. In addition, the local solicitor tends to be more of a jack-of-all-trades but has his ear to the ground and will be familiar with the current planning issues and the local Planning Office.

How to pick an Irish solicitor? The best way is always word of mouth from a friend who has already done what you are planning to do or from some other reliable source in Ireland. Failing that you can consult the *Yellow Pages* of the telephone directory (in Ireland called the '*Golden Pages*'). The normal telephone directory is divided into 'Residential Listings' and 'Business Listings'. Solicitors' names and addresses are to be found in the latter. Finally, you can get advice from the Law Society. Your UK solicitor may have contacts there.

If you worry that a country solicitor may not be up to the job, remember that, if a particularly difficult point of law arises in relation to your purchase, he can always refer your case to a barrister.

English Solicitors

You have had a preliminary discussion with your own English solicitor. You have contacted an Irish solicitor. At this stage, you may feel that the services of the Irish lawyer may not give you all the information or help you need to cover the **UK consequences of your proposed purchase**. You may require advice about inheritance issues, the UK tax implications of your purchase, how to save taxes, surveys, mortgages, currency exchange, etc. It may well be that an Irish lawyer is already familiar with all such matters to a certain extent. However, any Irish lawyer will tell you that, although he may help you in relation to UK law, he cannot stand by what he says and for a definitive answer you must consult a UK lawyer. Even in England it is wiser to retain the services of a specialist UK lawyer familiar with these issues. Your usual solicitor is unlikely to be able to help as there is only a handful of English lawyers with the necessary expertise.

In Ireland, expertise concerning purchases by English tax residents of property in Ireland is most likely to be found in the big city firms in Dublin, and in areas where foreigners have been buying second homes for some time now.

Decide on Ownership

The question of ownership has long-term taxation implications depending on whether you are single, married or divorced and re-married and whether or not you have made a will and the terms of the will.

Inheritance rules in Ireland are much closer to rules in the UK than to France, for example, and so should not give rise to unpleasant surprises. There is a close relationships between the Inland Revenue in Great Britain and the Revenue Commissioners in Ireland (which from now on we shall call 'the Revenue') and there are mutual arrangements in this regard but, if money is not to be lost, it is important to be aware of the pitfalls from the very beginning and make your choices accordingly. Getting the ownership wrong can lead to unnecessary tax during your lifetime and on your death. *See* pp.146–51 later in this chapter.

Arrange Finance

Before you decide to purchase a property, whether at home or abroad, it is vital to decide how you are going to finance the purchase. This will depend on many things, for example whether or not you have disposable income. If you do have some spare cash, you must ask yourself whether it will be more profitable and/or safer to invest in property in Ireland than to invest in attractive shares or safe government bonds.

If, on the other hand, you will need finance, it is wise to have some assurance beforehand that a mortgage is possible and to have a clear idea as to whether it will be coming from an Irish or an English institution.

Get an Offer of a Mortgage

If you do decide that you want to borrow money to part-finance your purchase, it makes sense to get clearance before you start looking at property.

Always remember, that no matter how similar house purchase in Ireland may be to house purchase in the UK, the transaction will take place in another country and another island and time and distance must be taken into account in a way that they need not be if you are buying in your home town. It does not take any longer to send a fax or an e-mail to or from Galway than Gloucester, but some things need to be done face to face and they must be factored into your overall plan of campaign.

Whether you want to borrow on your UK property or on the Irish property, your lawyers should be able to put you in touch with suitable lenders. The latter will process your application and give you a preliminary clearance to borrow up to a certain amount. This, of course, is subject to the property and its title later proving satisfactory. Doing this removes the need for an embarrassing call to the auctioneer a week after you have bought the property to tell him that you can't raise the finance. Getting a preliminary clearance in this way does not restrict your freedom to take up a better offer if one turns up while you are still looking at properties. See pp.133–45.

The Exchange Rate Risk

If the funds to repay the mortgage are coming from your sterling earnings, the amount you will have to pay will be affected by fluctuations in exchange rates between sterling and the euro. Check with your local bank or some other knowledgeable financial advisor as to how these fluctuations have varied and what the forecast is for the immediate future. If the variations are great it can make a tremendous difference to your monthly mortgage repayments. Fortunately, they have not varied greatly in the recent past.

If sterling were to fall in value, then your debt as a percentage of the value of the property would increase in sterling terms. Your property would be worth more in sterling terms but your mortgage would also have increased in value. You might feel that it was worth it.

If, on the other hand, sterling were to rise then the situation would be reversed: a lower mortgage but less money to take home if you decide to sell up.

Think about How You Will Pay a Deposit

Similar considerations apply to the question of a deposit. Do you have enough money immediately available? How much is it likely to be? Here again, forewarned is forearmed.

You will often need to put down a booking deposit of 1–5 per cent of the price of the property. The booking deposit is fully refundable if the sale does not proceed. How should you make this payment?

Normally, in Ireland the booking deposit is paid to the auctioneer and the balance is deposited with the purchaser's solicitor.

There is, however, a further option that people are increasingly using in the UK. This is to leave the amount likely to be needed as a deposit with their lawyer in the UK. Then, when they have found the right property and the auctioneer is asking them to sign some form of contract, they can tell him that it is their lawyer who has the money.

The most prudent thing you can do is to contact a lawyer before you talk seriously to auctioneers because he will need to understand something about your circumstances before being able to give sensible advice about, for example, the special clauses needed in any contract even before the serious possibility of a contract is raised .

Capital Growth

People buy houses for various reasons. The most obvious is that they need a place to live. In the case of the purchase of a house abroad, it means either that they have decided to live in the new country, they intend to holiday there or they contemplate having an income from the rental of the property. In relation to the first two options in particular, it would be pleasant to know that your property is not only a home or a holiday retreat but is also an investment which will increase in value. Mark Twain said something to the effect that land is the only thing to invest in because they have stopped making it.

It is certainly true that in Ireland the price of property is continuing to increase. As we said earlier, this is not a bubble but because of pressure of population. The stock exchange, as in the case of the dot.com bubble a few years ago, can be notoriously fickle. A property in attractive surroundings can give you, your family and friends great enjoyment *and* be a sound investment.

It is advisable, therefore, to get advice from experts concerning the trends in the market and the state of the economy in Ireland, although it is not unusual for experts to differ. But even fallible experts should be able to give an indication of which areas have potential for capital growth, such as seaside places which have not been spoiled, where there are amenities and where prices have not already gone through the roof. At the time of writing (2004), interest rates in the UK have risen and, if, in response, they rise in Ireland this could mean a slowing up of the market and make it more attractive for purchasers.

A word of warning – if you are looking for a place to retire or to spend frequent holidays, the prospect of a quick (or even postponed) killing should not be your dominant consideration. It might be nice to know that your asset is increasing in value, but if you end up heartily disliking your surroundings, no amount of gain for your children or grandchildren will compensate for making your golden years miserable. The worst-case scenario is that you are so cheesed off that you get rid of the place at a significant loss.

Stop and Consider the Alternatives to Buying

Rental

The possibility of being trapped in a place inhabited by people whom you loathe, where you cannot see your favourite TV programmes, where you do not have access to broadband or where it rains all the time, is a good reason for temporarily renting a place in the area in which you are thinking of living. It is best to do this for a full year before deciding whether or not to live there. Allowing for time thereafter to find and buy a property probably means a 12–18-month rental. Try to rent something similar to what you are thinking of buying and do not rent unseen – take a short holiday to find your rental property.

If you rent you are less likely to commit yourself to a purchase in an area which does not come up to your expectations. It also avoids the expensive process of having to sell the property and buy another, either in Ireland or the UK. Moving house is expensive, whether within Ireland or between Ireland and England. There is also the question of the fees incurred – let us say 10 per cent being the fees and taxes on the purchase of the new property and 2–3 per cent being the auctioneers' fee for selling the old one. A move back to England (depending on the value of the property bought) could possibly cost about 5–8 per cent sales expenses in Ireland and 3 per cent purchase expenses in the UK.

Needless to say, there are drawbacks to renting:

- **Property prices may continue to rise. A delay of say 18 months might even cost you about 15–20 per cent in increased property cost. This is a lot more than your money would have made if invested, so the delay would have cost you money.**

- **The rent you paid out is dead money. This would probably be about 5 per cent of the value of a property per annum.**

- **You want to get on with your life, especially if you have just retired.**

- **Moving is classified as one of life's major stressful events. You will have to do it twice rather than once (and, if you have rented an unfurnished house, pay removal expenses twice).**

- **Moving into temporary accommodation can produce a lack of attachment to the area, which can mean that you don't commit to it or give it a fair try. You don't make an effort to get to know people. You are always looking back over your shoulder to England rather than enjoying what Ireland has to offer.**

- **It can be hard to find good accommodation available on an 18-month let.**

If you are thinking of a holiday home it can also certainly make sense to rent rather than buy. The biggest drawback to owning a property overseas is that you feel compelled to take all your holidays there and deprive yourself of the possibility of visiting other parts of the globe. You are paying for it so you should use it! If you invested the money spent on the home it would generate a good income, which would pay for a holiday anywhere in the world. Of course, renting is never as good as owning your own home. You do not know the quality of what you will find on arrival. You won't be able to leave your clothes there and so travel light. You won't have friends there and so feel part of the community. You won't be able to offer the use of the property to family and friends.

Another bonus – a holiday home in Ireland can be exchanged for a holiday home in Spain, Greece or Australia (*see* below).

Exchanges

If you do not want to move permanently or to deprive yourself of the possibility of variety in your annual (or more frequent) holidays, exchanging houses may be for you. It is increasingly popular and many people find that it is a cheap and pleasant way of having a new experience. Your home (permanent or temporary) is not lying idle and you are not paying rent in that luxury villa in the exotic location.

Of course, every exchange is a gamble and you can win the jackpot or be a sorry loser. You may return to find your home vandalised. The exchange property and its surroundings may bear no relation to the glowing description that accompanied the original offer.

But if you are lucky, you can be very lucky. A few years ago, a man in County Kerry, in the southwest of Ireland, who lived in a medium-sized cottage near the sea, answered an ad for an exchange inserted by a family in the southwest of France. The deal went through and he headed off to what he expected to be the French equivalent of his own modest home. When he arrived, he felt that there must have been a mistake. He had come to an 18th-century château with ornamental garden and swimming pool. But, no, this was the correct address. His wonderment and embarrassment grew when he discovered that the staff of the château lived in and had remained to take care him, his family and the château. Luckily, the owner of the château fell in love with Ireland and the two families became great friends. Their exchanges continued for many years.

Property Inspection

Whatever property you are thinking of buying, you should think about having it inspected *before* you commit yourself to the purchase. It can cost nearly as much and can cause just as much disruption to repair property in Ireland as it does in England, so you don't want any surprises.

Of course, you cannot inspect a house which has not yet been built, but at least most new properties will be covered by a short guarantee running from the date of handover and covering minor but not trivial defects in a new property. The property will also benefit from a guarantee in respect of major structural defects that will last for 10 years. As a subsequent purchaser you assume the benefit of these guarantees. After 10 years you are on your own! For property more than 10 years old (and, arguably, for younger property too) you should consider a survey.

If you decide on a survey there are a number of options available to you.

Do-it-yourself

There are several things that you can do yourself. These will help you to decide when to instruct a surveyor to do a proper survey and help direct him to any specific points of interest. *See* **Appendix 1**, p.294.

Auctioneer's Valuation and 'Survey'

It is not the custom in Ireland for auctioneers to carry out surveys. Nonetheless, it may be possible to arrange for a local auctioneer, *other than the one who is selling to you*, to give the property a quick 'once over' to comment on the price asked and any obvious problem areas. This will be far short of a survey but it is better than doing nothing. It is likely to cost in the region of €200 plus VAT.

Mortgage Lenders' Survey

Have a quick survey if you want to but remember that there is no substitute for a proper survey. Don't skip it just because the bank does not ask for one. Most lenders do not ask for a survey and, when they do, it is normally fairly peremptory, limited to a check on whether the walls are imminently about to fall down. They will ask for a valuation but do not confuse this with a survey. This is just to check whether the property is worth the money that the bank is lending you. You cannot legally rely on such a valuation.

Irish Builder's Report

If you are going to do a virtual demolition and rebuild job, then it might make sense to get a local builder to do a report on the property. A reputable and experienced builder will also be able to comment on whether the price is reasonable for the property in its existing state. Make sure you ask for a written quotation for any building work proposed. As in any country, it is as well to get several quotes, though this might be easier said than done: there is a lot of work for builders at the moment.

How to Get a Reputable and Experienced Builder

Usually, the best way is by word of mouth from a reliable source (which may not include the auctioneer). If you are Irish or have Irish ancestors, you may have contacts already. If you have friends or acquaintances who have bought property in the area and have lived or holidayed there for several years, they should be able to help you. The architect or surveyor may have contacts in the area. An architect, in particular, may be hesitant about recommending anyone but, if he or she does, the chances are that the person will be reliable. An architect would have too much to lose in recommending an unskilled or unreliable builder.

Irish Surveyor/Engineer's Survey

Your lawyer can put you in touch with the right people. Across the country, there are many engineers or quasi-engineers who are the most common type of 'surveying' professionals and would be quite up to the job. Otherwise, you can obtain a list of approved surveyors from the Society of Chartered Surveyors in Ireland (5 Wilton Place, Dublin 2, **t** (01) 676 5500; **info@scs.ie**). Normally, the people that they would recommend would be surveyors who would only deal with commercial properties or large country houses. The Law Society, the Institute of Engineers of Ireland (IEI) (22 Clyde Road, Ballsbridge, Dublin 4; **www.iei.ie**) and the Royal Institute of Architects of Ireland (RIAI) (8 Merrion Square, Dublin 2; **www.riai.ie**) have agreed certain surveyor qualifications that are acceptable to them.

The cost of a survey of a three-bedroom house in Dublin by such a chartered surveyor is typically €400 plus VAT at 21% i.e. €484. A survey of a larger house will cost more. As most chartered surveyors are based in Dublin, a survey elsewhere will cost more to take account of travel expenses – you can be thinking of €500 plus VAT.

A report from an Irish surveyor will be much the same as the report that you would get from an English surveyor.

Architect's Survey

It is one thing to engage the services of an architect to design your house and oversee the building, it is another to use an architect merely to carry out a survey. Most architects are reluctant to do a survey unless they know the would-be purchaser personally and do it as a favour. Your own lawyer can put you in touch with an English architect for survey purposes but, unless the property is very highly priced and has a potential for high risk and the possibilities of expensive restoration (an 18th- or early 19th-century country house, for example) it is probably cheaper to engage an Irish architect because he can make site visits and the cost of travel will be accordingly less. Obviously, these costs are proportionally greater for a survey than for drawing up new plans.

An architect's survey will, as you might expect, tend to focus on issues of design and construction although it should cover all of the basic matters relevant to a survey. Architects can be ruthless or realists (depending on your point of view) and it is not unknown for an architect, called in to comment on a picturesque old building, to recommend that the whole structure be razed to the ground and that the purchaser should start again from scratch. On the whole, it is probably better not to use an architect for a survey.

Very often, outside the cities, the house that you look at may have been designed by an engineer, a practice of which architects do not approve. If all you want is a house for a few weeks a year which keeps out the rain and is not likely to fall down, then you might consider it more convenient to use a local engineer. At the same time, the phrase 'architect-designed' is often used and may carry weight when you are selling. In addition, engineers, like builders, are much in demand and you may face delays if you use one.

UK-based Surveyor

There should be little difficulty in getting a UK-based surveyor to provide a report. However, as with an architect, if the site or building is in a scenically beautiful but remote area, the cost of travel will add to the cost. Make the same checks as for a UK surveyor based in Ireland. Unless the property is particularly expensive, it may not be worth the extra expense.

Timescale

How long will it take to have a survey done? How long is a piece of string? This will depend on the urgency of the need for a survey, your impatience and persistence and your indication of willingness to pay promptly for prompt service. Between the availability of the surveyors, the phone calls, the visit and the writing of the report, it could be done in seven days.

Contracts 'Subject to Survey'

This is negotiable. Everything will depend on how anxious either the vendor or yourself are to have the sale completed. Ask your lawyer for his opinion. Obviously, it is to your benefit if the clause is included in the contract. A survey could take time and, if there is no such clause, the vendor could become impatient and sell to someone else. This again will depend on how much demand there is for the property.

The Survey

Your surveyor should know what he is doing. In addition, to the checks on the condition of the house, he will also check the access roads, the boundaries of the property, the planning status, business regulations affecting the house and any alterations and any adjacent planning proposals.

Checklist – Things You May Ask Your Surveyor to Do

- **Electrical condition and continuity check.**
- **Drains check, including assessment of drains to point where they join mains sewers or septic tank.**

- Water quality check.
- Septic tank check.
- Adequacy of foundations.
- Rot check.
- Check on cement quality in property constructed out of cement.
- Check of underfloor areas, where access cannot easily be obtained.
- Check on heating and air-conditioning.
- Wood-boring insect check.
- Evidence of asbestos.
- Evidence of radon gas – if it is in an affected area.

Raising Finance to Buy a Property in Ireland

In these days of low interest rates, many more people in the UK are taking out a mortgage in order to buy property abroad, although it is probable that the property is in countries with a sunnier climate than Ireland. For many people, their own money will be better employed in their business, or even in other investments, than in a home in Ireland. If, however, a property is viewed simply as an investment, a mortgage allows you to increase your benefit from the capital growth of the property by 'leveraging' the investment. If you buy a house for £200,000 and it increases in value by £50,000 that is a 25 per cent return on your investment. If you had only put in £50,000 of your own money and borrowed the other £150,000 then the increase in value represents a return of 100 per cent on your investment. If the rate of increase in the value of the property is more than the mortgage rate, you have won. In recent years property in Ireland has gone up in value by much more than the mortgage rate. The key questions are whether that will continue and, if so, for how long.

If you decide to take out a mortgage you can, in most cases, either mortgage (or extend the mortgage on) your existing UK property or you can take out a mortgage on your new Irish property.

You may wish to consider fixed-rate mortgages so that you may know your commitment over, say, the next few years. Currently, fixed-rate mortgages are for a term of five years. Again, there are advantages and disadvantages.

Mortgaging Your UK Property

By a UK mortgage I mean a mortgage of your UK property. At the moment there is fierce competition to lend money and there are some excellent deals to be done, whether you choose to borrow at a variable rate, at a fixed rate or in one of the hybrid schemes now on offer. Read the Sunday papers or the specialist mortgage press to see what is on offer, or consult a mortgage broker. Perhaps most useful are mortgage brokers who can discuss the possibilities in both the UK and Ireland.

It is outside the scope of this book to go into detail about the procedures for obtaining a UK mortgage.

A number of people have found that, whenever interest rates are falling, re-mortgaging their property in the UK has reduced the cost of their existing borrowing so significantly that their new mortgage – including a loan to buy a modest Irish property – has cost no more, in monthly terms, than their old loan. Remember, however, that this is only the case *when interest rates are falling and are likely to stay low*. Some commentators (probably British) hold the view that a UK mortgage is generally the better option for people who need to borrow relatively small sums and who will be repaying it out of UK income.

Advantages

- **The loan will probably be very cheap to set up.**

You will probably already have a mortgage. If you stay with the same lender there will be no legal fees or land registry fees for the additional loan. There may not even be an arrangement fee. If you go to a new lender, many special deals mean that the lender will pay all fees involved.

- **The loan repayments will be in sterling.**

If the funds to repay the mortgage are coming from your sterling earnings then the amount you have to pay will not be affected by fluctuations in exchange rates between the pound and the euro.

Equally, if sterling falls in value then your debt as a percentage of the value of the property decreases. Your property will be worth more in sterling terms but your mortgage will remain the same.

Disadvantages

- **You will pay UK interest rates, which may be higher than euro rates.**

Check this out. Make sure you compare the overall cost of the two mortgages. Crude rates (which, in any case, may not be comparable as they are calculated differently in the two countries) do not tell the whole tale. What is the total monthly cost of each mortgage, including life insurance and all extras? What is the total amount required to repay the loan, including all fees and charges?

- **If sterling increases in value against the euro, a mortgage in euro would become cheaper to pay off.**

- **Some academics argue that, in economic terms, debts incurred to buy assets should be secured against the asset bought and assets in one country should be funded by borrowings in that country.**

- **Many people do not like the idea of mortgaging their main home – which they may only just have cleared after 25 years of paying a mortgage!**

Irish Mortgages

By an Irish mortgage, I mean a mortgage taken out over your Irish property. This will either be from an Irish bank or from a British bank that is registered and does business in Ireland. You may find that you cannot take a mortgage on your new Irish property from your local branch of a UK building society or high street bank. Check in advance that this is, indeed, the case before you start making plans or pursuing serious enquiries. Remember to get advice from your accountant about the effect that taking out a mortgage from a UK bank may have on your tax liabilities in Ireland and/or the UK.

You may also get mortgages from foreign banks in Ireland (including UK banks) or from offshore banks. Given the buoyancy of the market, these institutions are currently showing interest in Ireland.

If you decide to mortgage your Irish property, you may find it more difficult to obtain a mortgage from an English lender, which may require more guarantees

The Irish Mortgage Council

The Irish Mortgage Council (IMC) is made up of banks, building societies and mortgage-lenders. All the significant domestic lenders are members of the IMC and it is estimated that its members account for the largest amount of mortgage lending in the Republic of Ireland. The IMC is a member of the European Mortgage Federation (EMF).

The current members of IMC are Permanent TSB, IIB Homeloans, Bank of Ireland, Ulster Bank, AIB, EBS Building Society, Irish Nationwide, First Active, ACC Bank, the Bank of Scotland-Ireland, ICS Building Society and the National Irish Bank. All these institutions have websites.

All these bodies are subject to control in varying degrees by the Irish Financial Services Regulatory Authority (IFSRA), the Central Bank of Ireland and the Department of the Environment and Local Government.

Many of the IMC members have links with the UK. Set out below are some of the more obvious cases.

Allied Irish Bank plc operates in the UK through Allied Irish Bank (AIB) (GB), a wholly owned subsidiary of the Irish bank. The bank has many offices throughout the UK and new branches are planned.

The **Bank of Ireland Group** has its head office in Dublin but its operations extend geographically throughout Ireland and the UK. In the UK, it operates mainly through Bristol & West plc which was acquired in July 1997 as well as through the bank's branch network. UK Financial Services operates in selected markets and provides mortgages, savings and investment products to personal and business customers.

The **Ulster Bank**, which has its headquarters in Belfast, Northern Ireland, is a member of the Royal Bank of Scotland Group. It operates in the Republic of Ireland, Northern Ireland and the Isle of Man.

as to the value of the property. On the other hand, if you are borrowing from an Irish lender and paying from English income, the Irish lender may require more proof that your income will be forthcoming for the life of the mortgage.

Mortgage Options

Repayment or Annuity Mortgage

This is the traditional mortgage and the majority of people who borrow money to purchase a new home opt for a repayment or 'annuity' mortgage, a type of mortgage with which UK borrowers will be familiar. The loan is normally taken out for 20 or 25 years. The early payments are eaten up by the interest element while very little comes off the loan. Obviously, therefore, the amount borrowed reduces very slowly initially. It is only at a much later stage that you find you are paying off the capital. This is more attractive than it might seem at first sight, because in Ireland there is significant tax relief on mortgage interest.

The borrower will be presented with a choice. Do you opt for fixed-rate repayments over a variable term or variable rate repayments over a fixed term? Fixed-rate repayments, as the name implies, means that, no matter whether interest rates are rising or falling, you pay the same amount every month, but if interest rates go up you will be paying over a longer period and, if they fall, you will clear your mortgage more rapidly. Variable rate repayments are a mirror image of the fixed-rate repayments. The term – 10, 15 or 20 years – stays the same but every month, you may find yourself paying a different amount.

Which is best for you? When interest rates are going up, fixed rates are popular, when they are falling, borrowers often change to variable rates.

There is another way to deal with changes in interest rates. Some institutions will allow you to pay off part of your mortgage at a fixed rate and the rest at a variable rate.

Fixed-rate Mortgage

Fixed rate loans can be fixed for 1–10 years, but be warned that there can be expensive penalties if you pay them off early.

Capped-rate Mortgage

It is also possible to get a capped-rate mortgage. In this case, a premium is paid which guarantees that the mortgage rate will not go beyond the original agreed rate. It is possible to increase the monthly or annual payment. This can be done as a certain percentage of the payments or else the borrower can pay lump sums. One disadvantage of a capped rate mortgage is that, if the property is sold or the mortgage is redeemed before the term set by the mortgage agreement, there may be a redemption fee to pay.

A change from a capped or fixed rate to a variable rate can give rise to a 'funding fee'.

Low-start Mortgage

A low-start mortgage postpones payment of some of the interest that is normally paid at the beginning of the loan by adding it to the amount of the loan, so that the loan increases over time. Again beware. You are only postponing the inevitable and will probably pay more than you would have paid with another type of mortgage.

Deferred-start Mortgage

A repayment mortgage may provide that no repayments are made for the first one to three months.

Endowment Mortgage

An endowment mortgage combines the mortgage repayment with savings through a life assurance policy. You make an interest payment to the bank or building society and another payment to an assurance company which invests your money on your behalf. If the assurance company has chosen wisely (and the market does well), by the end of the mortgage term the value of the endowment policy should have grown sufficiently to repay the mortgage and leave you with a surplus. On the other hand, there is no guarantee that the proceeds of the policy will be sufficient to repay the mortgage loan, and you may be required to increase your monthly contributions.

In Ireland, the following benefits have been claimed for endowment mortgages:

- **Interest is paid on the full capital sum throughout the life of the loan.**

- **Monthly contributions are paid into an endowment policy. This includes sufficient life assurance to pay off the loan in the event of death. By the end of the mortgage term, the value of the policy should have grown to repay the mortgage in full.**

Be aware: at present endowment mortgages are not popular. They have not performed well lately.

Pension Mortgages

Pension mortgages are offered to the self-employed or to employees whose employer does not operate an occupational pension scheme. This type of mortgage is not unlike an endowment mortgage. Monthly repayments are made but they only pay the interest on the loan. Simultaneously, payments are made to a personal pension plan. At the end of the fixed term, the capital is paid from the money in the pension plan and anything over will help to pay the bills when you retire.

The benefits of pension mortgages include:

- **The mortgage is linked to a pension scheme.**

- **It is similar to an endowment policy: interest only is paid on the full capital sum over the life of the loan, while the pension pund is also being built up.**

- Pension mortgages are suitable if you are not part of a company pension scheme, are self-employed or are a propriety (owner) director with a 21 per cent share in the company.

Flexible Mortgage

It is possible with repayment and endowment mortgages to arrange to make no repayment for one or two months each year and to pay whatever was due as part of other monthly payments.

In the case of endowment mortgages this is dependent on your paying the endowment part (towards the pension every month).

Mortgage Break

It is also possible to arrange to suspend payments for up to three months in a year but you must respect the original agreed term.

Mortgage Indemnity Bond

If the sum borrowed comes to 70 to 80 per cent of the price of the property, it is usual for the borrower to pay a mortgage indemnity fee or bond or guarantee. This can be 3 per cent of the difference between an 'agreed' percentage of the purchase price and the amount borrowed.

How Much Can I Borrow?

Different banks have slightly different rules and slightly different ways of interpreting their rules. Generally speaking, banks will lend you an amount that will give rise to monthly payments of up to about 30–33 per cent of your net available monthly income.

In the UK, the starting point is your net monthly salary after deduction of tax and National Insurance but before deduction of voluntary payments such as to savings schemes. If there are two applicants, the two salaries are taken into account. If you have investment income or a pension this will also be taken into account. If you are buying a property with a track record of letting income, this *may* be taken into account. If you are over 65, your earnings will not usually be taken into account, but your pension and investment income will be. If your circumstances are at all unusual, seek advice, as approaching a different bank may produce a different result.

e.g.	Mr Smith – net salary per month	£3,000
	Mrs Smith – net salary per month	£2,000
	Investment income per month	£1,000
	Total income taken into account	£6,000 per month

The maximum loan repayments permitted will be 30 per cent of this sum (i.e. £1,800 per month), less any existing fixed commitments. Regular monthly commitments would include mortgage payments on your main and other properties, any rent paid, HP commitments and maintenance (family financial

Irish Interest Rates

Currently (July 2004) the top five Irish interest rates on mortgages are:

- Top 5 Fixed rates: 3.3–3.5 % APR
- Top 5 Variable rates: 3.35–3.6 % APR
- Top 5 Discount rates: 3.4–3.5 % APR

These rates are charged by the following lending institutions – the AIB Group, ICS Building Society, Permanent TSB, First Active and IIB Homeloans.

If only it were that simple.

Recently published figures in relation to above mentioned institutions and the other members of the IMC show that lending rates and APRs can vary tremendously according to the product offered and the timescale. This depends on whether it is a matter of new business or an existing customer; on the period of the loan (one, two, three, four, five years or more); on whether it is a variable rate or a tracker rate. The basic rate as at 1 June 2004 went from 2.54 per cent for one year to 6.5 per cent for 20 years. The lowest APR rate, which reflects the real cost of borrowing, was 2.9 per cent and the highest, 6.7 per cent. This last was the 20-year mortgage. The cost per €1,000 on a 20-year mortgage can vary from €5,320 to €6,870. It pays to shop around.

provision) payments. Repayments on credit cards do not count. If there are two applicants, the commitments of both are taken into account.

e.g.	Mr and Mrs Smith – mortgage on main home	£750
	Mr and Mrs Smith – mortgage on house in Ireland	£400
	Mrs Smith – HP on car	£200
	Total pre-existing outgoings	£1,350 per month

Maximum loan repayment permitted = £1,800 – £1,350 = £450 per month. This would equate to a mortgage of about £60,000 over 15 years.

If you are buying a property for investment (rental), the bank may treat this as commercial lending and apply different criteria.

Payments for New Property

If you are buying a property which is still being built, you may only need to make a deposit or you may be required to make periodic payments as the building progresses but will not have full title until the whole process has been completed. The banks may not be happy with this arrangement, as you do not own anything that you can mortgage and they have no cover. In such a case, it is likely that the mortgage will only be granted to cover the final payment. As the final payment will probably be a substantial amount, say, 60 to 70 per cent of the overall price, you should not be unduly inconvenienced. If, however, the initial payments are high, the bank may offer you a credit facility to enable you to meet those payments. Once the property has been delivered to you, the normal monthly payments will begin.

Property Needing Restoration

Not all banks will finance a property which needs serious restoration. If, however, you have the money to buy the property but not to renovate it, it is important that you apply for the mortgage before buying the property. You may find it very difficult to do so afterwards.

Applications for an Irish Mortgage

Once again the information needed will vary from bank to bank. It will also depend on whether you are employed or self-employed.

Applications can receive preliminary approval (subject to survey of the property, confirmation of title and confirmation of the information supplied by you) within a few days. Allow at least four days from the date of your application to receive a written mortgage offer, because your application needs to be processed. Do not worry if you have to wait for a longer period.

Let us take AIB Bank in Ireland as an example. It offers the following terms:

- The bank pays your Mortgage Indemnity Bond (see p.138).
- It offers 2 months' free life assurance through an associate.
- It gives an optional budget account facility.
- It lends up to 90 per cent of property price/valuation.
- There are variable or fixed interest rate options.
- You can get loans up to 35 years.
- You can increase your repayments when you want – you may pay your loan quicker with increased payments either by making a lump sum payment or by increasing your normal repayment amount.
- Flexible payments are available – e.g. you may pay over 10 or 11 months rather than 12 to allow a little extra cash for Christmas or summer holidays.
- Interest is calculated daily, which saves you money compared to lenders who calculate interest on a monthly or annual basis.
- It offers mortgage mobility – you can change property without breaking a fixed-term contract.
- There is a mortgage top-up facility – you may top up your existing mortgage if additional funds are required for extending, renovating, refurbishing, educational or medical expenses.
- A bank protection plan is available – it offers you a payment protection plan (PPP) which protects your mortgage repayments in case of accident, illness or involuntary employment.

This bank also grants a **foreign currency home mortgage**, i.e. a loan in any currency other than euro for the purpose of buying a residential property in Ireland (see p.145). It does so with the caveat that, while there are advantages in borrowing a foreign currency to purchase your new home, equally, borrowing in a foreign currency brings attendant financial risks. It is important to recognise that your liability is at all times in the foreign currency (which may be sterling).

The bank also offers a **tracker mortgage** which is designed to meet the needs of those who wish to avail themselves of a variable rate of interest but want a guarantee on the margin that will be charged for the life of the mortgage. ('Margin' in this context means the difference between the interest rate paid to depositors or for funds on the money market and the rate charged to borrowers.) The margin payable depends on the amount you wish to borrow and the value of your home (loan to value). The tracker mortgage guarantees the full European Central Bank (ECB) rate changes will be passed on to the customer within five working days.

Home insurance is also available through an insurance company operating with the bank which claims to offer you maximum protection and total security at a competitive price.

Finally, the bank offers a **buy-to-let** mortgage:

- **Up to 85% of the purchase price/valuation will be considered.**

- **Fixed, variable or tracker mortgages are on offer.**

- **A flexible term allows normal repayment terms up to 20 years, with up to 25 years considered where appropriate.**

- **A tailored buy-to-let insurance package is available with up to 50 per cent discount on home insurance.**

The European Standardised Information Sheet

If it has not already been supplied, you should ask the lender institute with whom you are in contact to provide you with a copy of the 'Voluntary Code of Conduct on Pre-Contractual Information for Home Loans'.

This document contains a European Standardised Information Sheet, a completed form of which should be supplied, in any case, by the lender institution and which should be an accurate representation of the offer that the lender would make to you under prevailing market conditions based on the information which you had given to the lender. It will, most probably, contain a proviso that the figures supplied could fluctuate with market conditions.

- **The information sheet will warn you that your home is at risk if you do not keep up payments on a mortgage or any other loan secured on it.**

- **It will set out the name of the lender, your name and a description of the particular product, i.e. the type of loan interest, the address, etc. and may require a third-party guarantee as a special condition set out in the letter.**

- It will state the nominal rate of interest and the annual percentage rate (APR), for example – 3.30 per cent varying. For variable rate loans, the payment rates may be adjusted by the lender from time to time.

- It will state the amount of credit advanced, the duration of the loan agreement, the number of payments due, the intervals at which they must be made and the amount of each instalment.

- If you are taking out an interest-only loan, it will state the amount of the interest.

- The information sheet will also remind you of the need to provide for additional non-recurrent and recurrent costs and will state whether or not a loan may be repaid in full or in part without penalty. Normally, there will be a redemption fee for repayment of a fixed-rate loan.

- It should also give you an address to which complaints may be addressed.

If you decide to repay the capital sum by way of an endowment policy, pension or other repayment vehicle, the monthly repayment will be advised by the provider of this repayment vehicle but keep in mind that there is *no guarantee* that the proceeds of an insurance will be sufficient to repay the loan in full when it becomes due for repayment and make it your business to have some alternative strategy up your sleeve.

See **Appendix 2**, p.299, for a typical example of this sheet.

Contracts 'Subject to Mortgage'

If you chance your luck and sign a contract before your mortgage has been confirmed, it is advisable that you ensure there is a clause in it which states that the purchase is dependent upon a mortgage and that, if no mortgage is provided, then the agreement is cancelled. This means that you will not be bound if the proposed lender lets you down.

It is very important that the clause covers your situation precisely so as to give you maximum assurance. It would be very foolhardy to sign such a contract without it being checked by your solicitor.

The Cost of Taking Out a Mortgage

Taking out a mortgage will normally involve charges amounting to about 3 per cent of the sum borrowed. These charges are in addition to the normal expenses incurred when buying a property, which normally amount to 2–3 per cent of the price of the property before stamp duty.

Although you will most certainly be required to take out life insurance for the amount of the loan, the bank may accept a suitable existing policy. Dependent on your ages or other relevant factors, you may be required to have a medical report. You will definitely be required to insure the property (*see* below) and submit details of your policy.

The offer may be subject to early redemption penalties. Early payment penalties are of particular concern in the case of a fixed-rate mortgage.

The Exchange Rate Risk

As we said above, if the funds to repay the mortgage are coming from your sterling earnings, the amount you have to pay will be affected by fluctuations in exchange rates between sterling and the euro. Lately these fluctuations have not been excessive but this is no guarantee that things cannot change. If, on the other hand, your income is in euro, because, for example, it comes from renting in the euro-zone, you do not have a problem.

Mortgage Interest Relief

If you are liable for tax in Ireland, tax relief is available on the interest paid on a mortgage, and for owner-occupiers this is subject to upper limits depending on the purchaser's situation. This is deducted at mortgage source, which means that the mortgage repayment is reduced by the amount of tax relief. Mortgage interest relief is also available on loans taken out to buy residential investment property. This relief is not subject to the limits imposed on owner-occupiers, but it is offset against rental income received.

Repayment in Euro

If the funds to repay the mortgage are coming from rental income paid to you in euro, this will give you something to spend them on!

Stamp Duty on Irish Mortgages

This is exempt on mortgages up to and including €254,000 (2004 figure). All mortgages exceeding €254,000 and representing 80 per cent or more of the value of the property are subject to a stamp duty rate of 0.1 per cent, rounded down to the nearest zero, to a maximum of €630.

Direct Debit Mandate

A direct debit mandate must be set up for mortgage repayments before a lending institution will issue the loan cheque.

Life Assurance

Before you will be loaned money, you must have in place, at least one week before the completion of the purchase, a life assurance policy providing, in the event of the death of the borrower, for payment of a sum equal to the amount of the principal estimated by the mortgage lender to be outstanding in the year in which the death occurs.

Property Insurance

You will also be required, not later than one week before completion of the purchase, to take out comprehensive property insurance against fire and other usual risks for the full *reinstatement* and *not the market price* of the property which may be much higher or even lower.

Payment Protection Plan (PPP)

You may be asked (and it will certainly be recommended) by the lender institution to take out a payment protection plan (PPP), which would cover your mortgage repayment for up to 12 months if you were unable to work as a result of accident, illness or involuntary unemployment.

Land Registry

If the title must be registered in the Land Registry, registration of a mortgage (called in Land Registry terminology a 'charge') will cost approximately €131. It is always possible that the fee has been increased, so check with your lawyer.

Not all property or transactions must be registered in the Land Registry. I shall discuss later the types of property where registration is mandatory and where it is voluntary; *see* pp.152–4.

Saving Money on Your Euro Repayments

Your mortgage will usually be paid directly from your Irish bank account. Unless you have lots of rental or other euro income going into that account, you will need to send money from the UK in order to meet the payments.

Every time you send a payment to Ireland you will face two costs. The first is the price of the euro. This, of course, depends on the exchange rate used to convert your sterling. The second cost is the charge that will be made by your UK and Irish banks to transfer the funds – which can be substantial. Some Irish banks make no charge for transferring funds to pay off mortgages. These deals are worth looking out for if the other terms are competitive.

There are steps you can take to control both of these charges.

As far as the exchange rate is concerned, you should be receiving the so-called 'commercial rate', not the tourist rate published in the papers. The good news is that it is a much better rate. The bad news is that rates vary from second to second and so it is difficult to get alternative quotes. By the time you phone the second company, the first has changed. In any case, the fact that you have signed a direct debit mandate may also slow things up.

There are various organisations that can convert your sterling into euro. Your bank is unlikely to give you the best exchange rate. Specialist currency dealers will normally better the bank's rate, often significantly. If you decide to deal with a currency dealer, *you must deal with one that is reputable*. They will be handling your money and, if they go bust with it in their possession, you could lose it. It is not likely that a local solicitor in the UK or Ireland will be familiar with any such organisations.

Another possibility for saving money arises if you 'forward-buy' the euro that you are going to need for the year. It is possible to agree with a currency dealer that you will buy all your euro for the next 12 months at a price that is, essentially, today's price. You normally pay 10 per cent down and the balance on delivery. If the euro rises in value you will gain, perhaps substantially. *If the euro falls in value* – you have gambled and lost! The main attraction of forward-buying is not so much the possibility for gaining on the exchange rate as the certainty that the deal gives you. Only enter into these agreements with a reputable and, if possible, bonded broker.

Bearing in mind the cost of conversion and transmission of currency, it is better to make fewer rather than more payments. You will have to work out whether, taking into account the loss of interest on the funds transferred against the bank charges saved, you should choose to send money monthly, quarterly or half-yearly.

Foreign Currency Mortgages

It is possible to mortgage your new home in Ireland but to borrow in another currency – US dollars, Swiss francs, Japanese yen. It may be that you work full time or intermittently in one of these countries and have a source of income there. This option is mainly of interest to people who either do not have sufficient equity in their UK home or who, for whatever reason, do not wish to mortgage the property in which they live.

Other Loans

Many people may not need to incur the expense of mortgaging their property in Ireland. You may intend to move to Ireland permanently. You have already paid off your UK mortgage and your UK home is on sale. You have found the perfect place in Ireland and have, say, £180,000 of the £200, 000 (€302,600) available from savings and pension lump sums. The balance will be paid from the sale of your UK home, but you are not sure whether that will take place before you are committed to the purchase of the house in Ireland in a few weeks' time.

It is probably unnecessarily complicated to mortgage your UK home for such a short period and, indeed, it could be difficult to do so if the bank knows that you are selling and if you are, for example, 65 years old and not working.

In this case, it is often simplest to approach your bank for a short-term loan or overdraft. This might be for the £20,000 shortfall or it could be that you don't really want to cash in some of your investments at this stage, in which case you might ask for a facility of, perhaps, £50,000.

Some people choose to take out two- or three-year UK loans for, say, £15,000 each while still resident in the UK and prior to leaving for Ireland in order to cover a gap such as waiting to receive a pension lump sum. Despite the high interest rates on such loans, the overall cost can be a lot less than taking a short-term mortgage on the Irish property and paying all the fees relating to that mortgage.

Who Should Own the Property?

There are many ways of structuring the purchase of a house in Ireland. Each has significant advantages and disadvantages. The choice of the right structure can save you a lot in tax and expenses during your lifetime and on your death. The consequences of making the wrong decision will not be as great as it would be in a country with a different system of inheritance like France, Greece or other civil law countries, but caution is always required, particularly if you are in a second marriage or are cohabiting without being married.

The Options

When reading this section and, indeed, the remainder of 'Making a Purchase' it is important to remember that *lex situ* (the law of the place) applies in the case of immovable property in Ireland. This means that Irish law will apply to any land or house that you buy in Ireland. *See* also **Financial Implications**, 'Inheritance', pp.195–201.

Sole Ownership

In some cases, it could be sensible to put the property in the name of one person only, if, for example, the husband is very old and the wife in her twenties, or if one party is a life risk. On the other hand, it is seldom a good idea from the point of view of tax or inheritance planning.

In order to give security to a surviving partner, it is wise for the owner of the property to make a will in which the property is left to the other partner.

Joint Ownership

Joint ownership is more complicated than sole ownership in the sense that, if it is not made clear from the beginning what the intentions of the owners are, difficulties can arise in the case of the divorce of a married couple or the death of one of the joint owners whatever their relationship. If a husband or a wife buys a property in Ireland, he or she probably does not think about the details of ownership. It will be 'their' house. Their intention, without knowing it, most probably is that they will be 'joint tenants'.

If two people who are not married or in a similar relationship are buying together, they will normally buy in both their names. Your half is yours and your fellow owner's half is his or hers. Your intention will most probably be that you should be 'tenants-in-common'.

I should, therefore, say something briefly about joint tenancies and tenancies-in-common. (By the way, 'tenant' in these cases does not mean someone who rents the property. It means 'owner'.) As I said above, you and your co-owner can hold your property either under a joint tenancy or a tenancy-in-common. These two types of ownership give you different rights.

The first, **joint tenancy**, means that each of you has an equal right to possession of the entire property.

The second, **tenancy-in-common**, is a different kettle of fish. Both tenants-in-common have a right to possession of the entire property, even though they may not have equal shares in it. You could have rights over three-quarters of the property, while the second tenant-in-common could only lay claim to a quarter. You may have different interests in the property. You may have acquired those interests at different times, for example, you bought the property in Ireland but a year later you transferred a portion of it to your brother or your child.

If you purchase your new property with someone else, but you do not pay the same amount –you pay two-thirds and the other person pays one-third – there is what is called a 'rebuttable presumption' that you share the equitable estate as tenants-in-common, in proportion to the amounts of your contributions. The term 'rebuttable presumption' means that a court will presume that you are not joint tenants unless you can show that, in fact, your common intention was that you would be joint tenants.

Alternatively, the Court may decide that the legal owner of property is holding it in trust for someone else. A resulting trust may be presumed where one person provides the money to buy property, but it is conveyed in another person's name.

Survivorship

The most important distinction between the two types of tenancy relates to survivorship. In the case of a joint tenancy, the surviving joint owner automatically succeeds to the share of a joint tenant who dies, i.e. takes the whole property. If a tenant-in-common makes a will and then dies, the property is inherited by the person or persons to whom it has been bequeathed in his or her will. In such a case, if your spouse has children from another marriage, your stepchildren would inherit from him or her and they could insist on the sale of your home. If he/she dies intestate (i.e. has not made a will), there are precise rules in Irish law laying down what will happen to the property (see p.199).

You must keep this in mind when you are buying your new home.

It is possible to end joint tenancy. It may be ended by partitioning the property, i.e. dividing it in two (which is not a very practical solution) or by sale in lieu of partition, under s.4 of the 1868 Partition Act. On the request of one of the co-owners, the court will order the sale, 'unless it sees good reason to the contrary'.

If you do decide to end a joint ownership, get the advice of your solicitor before you start the process.

There is something else that must be taken into account in relation to joint ownership. On application by or on behalf of an interested party, a court may decide that the legal owner of property is holding it in trust for someone else under a 'resulting trust'. A resulting trust may be presumed where one person provides the money to buy property, but it is conveyed in another person's name (see 'The Presumption of Advancement', below). The court may also decide that a person holds a property under a 'constructive trust', a device which can be imposed by the court in any situation, no matter how novel, to achieve justice.

Something else to be aware of is, that if you buy a property in the name of yourself and your spouse, you will both have to take into account the Irish Family Home Protection Act 1976 whenever you decide to mortgage the property or to sell it. The act requires that, before such a property is sold or used as security for a loan, the written consent of both of you will be required. This applies even if you have registered your home in one of your names only.

The Presumption of Advancement

When a person voluntarily transfers property, owned by him or her, into joint names or provides the majority of the funds for an asset held in joint names, the presumption of resulting trust arises, which in effect means that the courts will presume that the property will be deemed to fall into the estate of the donor on his/her death and not to the surviving owner. The survivor, however, can rebut or set aside this presumption, by providing proof of a clear intention to the contrary. The considerations to take into account in this situation are the intentions of the donor at the time the account was opened, the control or power the donor has over the asset and the contributions of the parties.

One exception to the presumption of resulting trust, is the 'presumption of advancement'. As discussed above, where a person puts property into joint names, but provides all the funds for the asset, controls it during his lifetime and receives the entirety of the income from the asset, the presumption of resulting trust would apply and it would be likely that the asset would revert to the donor's estate on his death, unless a contrary intention can be established. If, however, the person who survives is a spouse or child of the deceased, the courts will presume that the property was intended to be a gift to the surviving joint owner, and the property will not revert to the estate of the deceased, but will go to the surviving owner, unless the estate can establish and prove that the deceased did not intend to gift the property.

Each individual situation must be examined to determine who is entitled to the proceeds of a joint account on the death of one of the owners. A way of avoiding any confusion would be for the joint owners to sign a form of mandate or statement, detailing their clear intentions when setting up the account.

The English Approach

Although your Irish property-holding will be governed by Irish law, it may be of interest to have some idea of the English approach to these matters. Where property is conveyed into the name of one party only, a non-legal-title-holding partner may claim a beneficial interest in that property in several ways: first, by producing an express contract in writing; secondly, by producing a trust in her/his favour evidenced in writing; or, thirdly, by establishing the existence of an oral declaration of a trust relied and acted upon to his or her detriment.

In the absence of one or more of these declarations, evidence of direct contributions may give rise to the creation of a 'constructive trust'. The notion of common intention between the parties must be established for indirect contributions – unpaid housework, contributions to renovations, unpaid work in the family business – to give rise to a beneficial interest in favour of the non-legal title-holder.

An agreement in writing will dispose of any doubts. An oral agreement is less satisfactory. If one of the parties is trying to show that he/she has an interest in the property, it will be necessary to convince a court that, before the property was bought, he/she and the other party talked about the situation and agreed to share. This conversation need not have spelt everything out in legal language. A court may be less happy with an alleged agreement or discussion which took place after the property had been acquired.

Given the risk of a house being sold, why should a couple decide on tenancy-in-common? It could be that you have three children and your wife has two, and you are anxious to be as fair as possible to them all, then to secure each of those children an equal share on your death you might think about buying 60 per cent in your name and 40 per cent in your wife's name. This is less drastic if you are talking about a holiday cottage than if it is a question of your permanent home.

It is very important to seek clear advice from your lawyer about the form of ownership that will suit you best, with regard to the consequences both in the UK and in Ireland. It is certainly advisable to consult an Irish lawyer.

Limited Company

Some people consider owning a property through the medium of a limited company to be a very attractive option. You own the shares in the company; the company owns the house.

There are various types of company. Your most likely choice would be a limited liability company with two shareholders. Nowadays, it is possible to incorporate a 'one-man' company and, in this case, some of the legal obligations are less onerous, for example, the requirement to hold board meetings. Nevertheless, there are disadvantages in setting up a company. In the UK and Ireland, companies are regulated, board meetings (with the exception of one-man companies) must be held, minutes must be kept and accounts must be audited. In Ireland, the company must be registered in the Company Registration Office and Annual reports must be filed. You will need to employ an auditor. The company itself must pay tax on any profits and, if you draw money out of the company, this will be regarded as your income and will be subject to tax. Corporation tax is low in Ireland (12.5 per cent) much lower than income tax, but if you are not making a handsome income from it, the other expenses could outweigh the benefits of low corporation tax. (*See* also **Financial Implications**, pp.183–4, and consider the consequences of receiving 'benefits in kind' from the usage of a house owned by a company.)

UK Company

It is rare for a purchase through a UK company to make sense for a holiday home or single investment property abroad. This is despite the fact that the ability to pay for the property with the company's money without drawing it out of the company and paying UK tax on the dividend is attractive. It will, however, be liable to corporation tax. Once again you need expert advice from someone familiar with company law and taxation laws in both the UK and Ireland. Unless you have been offered foolproof advice (an endangered species), it is always good advice to keep it simple.

Irish Company

There is little difference between setting up a company in Ireland or in England. The procedures are much the same and Irish and English company laws resemble each other.

Although you reduce your personal tax bill, you will have obligations similar to your UK duties and will have to meet the resultant outgoings.

Offshore (Tax Haven) Company

In Ireland, as in the UK, there is a difference between tax *avoidance* and tax *evasion*. The former – using legitimate means and legal loop-holes to reduce your exposure to taxation – is lawful. The latter – filing false returns, not disclosing assets, transferring assets improperly to someone else and similar dodges to hide your liability – is very much unlawful. Transferring property to or buying property through a company incorporated in a no-questions-asked, low tax jurisdiction can, depending on the circumstances, spill over from avoidance to evasion. Unless there are very good reasons, think hard before you buy an investment property in Ireland through an offshore company.

In any case, there is the added disincentive that the Irish government has now passed laws to combat such ownership. Land is treated as a 'qualified asset' and, therefore, even if it is owned by an offshore company, rental income obtained from it will give rise to a tax liability in Ireland.

These new measures have more or less killed off ownership via such companies.

If the person who controls the offshore company is tax resident in the UK or Ireland, he may be treated as a director or shadow director of the company. He may thus be liable to UK (or Irish) income tax on the 'benefit in kind' he gets if the company allows him to use the property in Ireland. If the property rents out for £1,000 a week, this could amount to a lot of benefit and a lot of tax.

This does not mean that this type of ownership is never a good idea. If you are a 93 year old buying a £10,000,000 property, or someone who wishes to be discreet about your ownership of the property, or a famous film star, you might think the cost is a small price to pay, either for the avoidance of inheritance tax or for the protection of your privacy.

Which is Right for You?

The choice is of fundamental importance. If you get it wrong, you will pay massively more tax than you need to, both during your lifetime and on your death. The tax consequences arise not only in Ireland but also in the UK.

For each buyer of a home in Ireland, one of the options set out above may suit perfectly. Another might just about make sense. The rest would be an expensive waste of money.

The trouble is that it is not obvious which is the right choice! You should take advice in *every case*, in the UK from a UK lawyer and/or accountant, in Ireland from an Irish lawyer and/or accountant. If your case is simple, so will be the advice. If it is complex, the time and money will be repaid many times over. It is better to spend some money at the beginning than to pay out large sums at a later stage when you may be in vulnerable position due to a bereavement or other reasons. Avoid being 'penny wise and pound foolish'.

The Process of Buying a Property in Ireland

The Law

As I have already pointed out, until 1922 the law of England and Wales and the law of Ireland were the same law, and even today laws adopted by the British parliament prior to 1922 are valid in Ireland unless specifically amended or replaced. The doctrine of precedence, i.e. the binding nature of judicial decisions still holds true in Ireland today and 19th-century judgments of English judges may still be quoted in court. Even post 1922 English judgements have a persuasive value. If you show Irish legal documents to your UK solicitor, he or she will feel comfortable with them because they will be drafted in terms that are very familiar, particularly in land law where Norman French terms may still be used.

As with other areas of law, land law in Ireland and England were identical until 1925 when the English system was reformed and sweeping legislation was brought in, to modernise the English law.

There was, however, one big difference. In the latter half of the 19th century, a series of legal reforms called the **Land Purchase Acts** was adopted in Ireland, which made it possible for tenants to buy out their landlords with the aid of long-term loans from the London government.

In 1891 a **Registration of Title Act** made registration of title compulsory in the case of all land bought out under the Land Purchase Acts. This meant that all subsequent transactions affecting such land would have to be registered.

In 1964, another Registration of Title Act was passed which further provided for the extension of the system by making compulsory the registration of ownership of:

- **land acquired after 1 January 1967, by any Statutory Authority.**
- **land sold in an area in which the Minister for Justice has made an order making registration compulsory. At present, registration is compulsory in Counties Carlow, Meath and Laois.**

Land Registry

In 1892, a Land Registry was established to provide a system of compulsory registration of title which would be simple, inexpensive and easily accessible.

When title is registered in the Land Registry, the deeds are filed in the Registry and all relevant particulars concerning the property and its ownership are entered on registers called 'folios' which are then maintained in the Land Registry. In conjunction with the folios, the Land Registry maintains maps.

A folio is a document which describes:

- **the property registered and refers to a plan on the Registry maps.**
- **the registered owner.**
- **any burdens (e.g. rights of way, charges) affecting the property (there are also certain burdens to be found in s. 72 of the 1964 Land Act which affect land even though they have not been registered).**

What is so important about this system is that the register is *conclusive* evidence of title to property and any right, privilege, appurtenance or burden appearing on the property. The Land Registry operates a non-conclusive boundary system which means that the map does not indicate whether a boundary includes a hedge or wall or ditch, etc. However, the physical features along which the boundaries run must be accurately identified. The title shown on the folio is guaranteed by the State, which is bound to indemnify any person who suffers loss through a mistake made by the Land Registry.

If you want to find out about the property which you are anxious to buy – whether the proposed vendor is really the owner, whether the land is mortgaged or has rights of way across it or whether anyone else has the right to cut turf (peat) on the land, you may go to the Land Registry and inspect the folio on payment of the prescribed fee. If you wish to go further and examine the instruments 'behind' a folio (the actual document which transferred land from father to son or created a burden, etc.), you will need the permission of the owner or his personal representative, i.e. his solicitor, or an order of the court or any other requirement set out in the Land Registration Rules 1972. Normally, you would look first at the names index, then the folio and finally the map. Often the folio will have an individual filed map attached to it. Folios are updated on foot of applications (called 'instruments' lodged in the Registry. These include transfers of registered property, mortgages and leases, or releases of existing burdens. Only leases of 21 years or more are registrable.

New folios are created on foot of applications for first registration of title or subdivisions of existing folios.

Duplicates of folios are kept in various local offices in the Circuit Court offices of each county except Dublin and Waterford. Duplicates of the maps are not available in the local offices.

An index of names of registered owners linking the name with the relevant folio number is maintained. An index corresponding with the folio number is also kept. The folios, maps and indexes and the duplicate folios and names index are available for public inspection and copying.

Over 80 per cent of land in Ireland is registered land for the purposes of the Land Registry.

Nowadays, the Land Registry, because of the sheer volume of documentation that it stores, and as part of a decentralisation programme, is based in different parts of the country.

- The sections that deal with the counties of Cavan, Donegal, Leitrim, Longford, Louth, Meath, Monaghan and Westmeath are located in Dublin in Chancery Lane, Dublin 7 behind the principal courts, the Four Courts.

- The sections that deal with the counties of Clare, Dublin, Galway, Mayo, Roscommon and Sligo are also located in Dublin, in the Setanta Centre, Nassau Street, Dublin 2 near Trinity College.

- The sections that deal with the counties of Kildare and Wicklow are also located in Dublin, in the Irish Life Centre, Block 1, Lower Abbey Street, Dublin 1, not far from Connolly Station.

- The sections that deal with the counties of Carlow, Cork, Kerry, Kilkenny, Laois, Limerick, Offaly, Tipperary, Waterford and Wexford are located on Cork Road, Waterford City beside the Holy Ghost Hospital.

Registry of Deeds

The Registry of Deeds was founded in 1708 to provide a system of *voluntary* registration for deeds and conveyances affecting land and to give priority to registered deeds over unregistered registrable deeds.

When a document is registered in the Registry of Deeds it is not filed there; it is returned to the party who delivered it for registration.

The document filed in the Registry of Deeds is a **memorial**, which is essentially a synopsis of the deed and also contains other statutory requirements.

If you are purchasing unregistered land, you can carry out a search in the Registry of Deeds to discover the existence of deeds affecting the property. However, you need to read the actual deeds in order to examine the title to the property. A memorial of a deed may serve as evidence of the contents of a lost deed. There are two types of search – a **hand search** made by any member of the public and an **official search** after which a certificate of its result is issued.

Official searches are themselves of two kinds:

- A **common search**, which is carried out by one official and is initiated but not warranted.

- A **negative search**, which is made by two officials. A certificate is issued signed by the Assistant Registrar or authorised HEO. This certifies that no memorial is registered which comes within the terms of the Search Requisition and is not abstracted in the certificate.

The Registry of Deeds is located at Henrietta Street in Dublin beside Kings Inns. It is divided into two main units: the Registration Unit, which registers deeds relating to unregistered property and the Search Unit, where hand, official searches and genealogical searches can be conducted.

The Price

This can be freely agreed between the parties. Depending on the economic climate there may be ample or very little room for negotiating a reduction in the asking price. At the moment (2004) the scope is limited for popularly priced properties in the main cities and tourist areas, where it is a seller's market.

Brown Paper Envelopes

Because of the liability for capital gains tax, it is not unknown for a vendor or his auctioneer to propose that a portion of the purchase price be handed over in a 'brown paper envelope' i.e. in cash and that the price inserted in the deed of sale does not include this amount. This may also seem attractive to you as it might seem to save you stamp duty.

If you accept such a proposal you are breaking the law. What seems like a harmless scheme in which you oblige someone who may become your neighbour, can, in fact, get you into very hot water.

In addition, although an under-the-counter payment like this will reduce your tax and fees, when you come to sell, your profit on the sale of the property will be increased by the amount that was handed over unofficially and your own CGT liabilities will be accordingly greater. The vendor's gain has now become your loss.

Nevertheless, there is scope for quite legitimately reducing the price declared and so reducing tax. For example, if your purchase of a holiday home includes some furniture, a boat or a caravan, there is no need to declare the value of these items and to pay stamp duty on the price paid. You can enter into a separate contract for the 'extras' and save some money for the vendor. Don't forget, however, that their value will affect the rate at which stamp duty is charged.

Different Methods of Buying Property

A house may be bought in Ireland by private treaty, at auction, by tender or by a procedure called 'Best and Final Offer'.

By Private Treaty

This is the most common method of purchasing a house. In this situation the auctioneer quotes a price and the potential purchasers make offers based on this quoted price. Negotiations then take place between the vendor and potential purchaser until an agreement is reached.

By Tender

In this situation, the vendor invites offers in writing from potential purchasers by a specified time. These offers are not disclosed and the vendor may reserve the right to accept any offer or refuse all.

Best and Final Offer

This situation arises when there are a number of potential purchasers making offers for the property. All interested parties are invited to submit their best and final offer in writing by a certain time. These offers are not disclosed and the vendor may accept any offer or refuse all.

At Auction

This involves the sale of a property through a bidding process involving two or more parties. A reserve price, which is not disclosed, is set for the property and this represents the minimum price at which the vendor will sell, although the vendor may withdraw the property at any time during the auction before the reserve has been reached. Once the reserve has been reached, the auctioneer has to inform the auction that this has happened. The property will be sold to the highest bidder in excess of the reserve price. The party to whom it is sold must sign an unconditional contract and pay a non-refundable deposit of 10 per cent of the purchase price immediately after the auction.

Why Sell at Auction?

Auction is a traditional method of selling goods and chattels including land and property. In the past, properties put on the market for sale by public auction were more likely to have been of a unique style or perhaps be period homes for which there is high demand and a shortage in supply. However, recently, due in the main to the rising market (particularly in Dublin) and an increase in competition for properties, a much wider range of properties is now sold by this method. Selling by auction tends to maximise the price available through increased exposure to the market over an intensive three- or four-week sales campaign, attractive brochures and pictures in the property pages of the leading newspapers. An auction campaign also gives interested purchasers a definite timescale to work within, and at the auction itself they are in a position to opt out of the process at any time should the bidding go beyond their initial expectations.

The Guide Price

Your auctioneer will propose a guide price to you. This is a figure which is invariably lower than the price expected to be achieved at the auction, and is offered as a guide only. It is a price which is approximately 10 per cent less than the anticipated reserve and is set by the auctioneer and the vendor. In other words, if the reserve price on a house is likely to be €600,000 the guide price will be €540,000. In addition, the Irish Auctioneers and Valuers Institute's (IAVI) policy is that guidelines should be within 10 per cent of the anticipated reserve. Therefore, purchasers should generally expect that the reserve price on a property will be not more than 10 per cent higher than the guideline. Currently, some disappointed would-be purchasers have complained that this is a rule which is more honoured in the breach than in the observance because the guide price is not sacrosanct. If there is a high level of interest in the property or other similar properties which have sold for exceptional prices during the campaign, the guide price can be revised upwards. Prospective purchasers with a strong interest in the property should be advised to keep in touch with the auctioneer during the campaign.

The reserve is the minimum figure for which a vendor will sell. This figure is normally agreed between the vendor and the auctioneer on the day of the auction. Ultimately, it is up to the vendor to decide on the reserve as it is his property which is being sold. The sale is not over when the reserve has been reached. Bidding can continue and the auctioneer declares the property to be 'on the market', indicating to bidders that the highest bid from that point on will secure the property.

If on the other hand the property fails to reach the reserve, it is withdrawn at the auction. At this point, most auctioneers will negotiate exclusively with the highest bidder in an effort to achieve a price level acceptable to both the vendor and purchaser. In this case, the prospective purchaser has a tactical advantage because he knows that he has no competition in the market for the property. However, if the negotiations are conducted professionally the outcome can be a 'win-win' situation for both vendor and purchaser.

You may not have been the highest bidder but do not despair. You still have the opportunity to negotiate for a property withdrawn at auction. You should indicate to the auctioneer your desire to negotiate. In the event of negotiations breaking down with the highest bidder, you may then get the opportunity to negotiate for the property.

Buying at Auction

Once you make the decision to pursue a property that is for auction, you should arrange through the auctioneer to have the property surveyed; put your financial arrangements in place; consult your solicitor in good time so that all legal issues are clarified and, finally, decide what the property is worth to you and at what level you are prepared to lose it!

At the auction itself, try to get in a good position in the auction room so that you can see what is happening around you. Ideally you should be accompanied by your solicitor or advisor who is authorised to bid on your behalf.

What to do if you are successful in bidding for a property is generally covered by the **Conditions of Sale**, a legal document which is available prior to the auction for examination by purchasers' solicitors so that they can be satisfied with title, the procedures to be followed after the auction and so on. In general, the purchaser and the vendor sign a binding contract setting out a closing date immediately after an auction and a 10 per cent deposit is paid there and then.

Purchasing the Property

When you finally decide to buy a property (by whatever method) and instruct your solicitor to carry out the necessary legal work – the conveyance – this is a summary of the steps that follow.

General Enquiries and Special Enquiries

Certain enquiries are made routinely in the course of the purchase of a property. These include, in appropriate cases, a check on the planning situation of the property. This enquiry will reveal the position of the property itself but it will not, at least directly, tell you about its neighbours and it will not reveal general plans for the area.

If you want to know whether the authorities are going to build a prison in the village or run a new road through your back garden (both, presumably, bad things) or build a motorway access point or railway station 3km away (both, presumably, good things), you will need to ask. The best place to go is the local Planning Authority, which will have maps showing all planning applications *actually lodged*. If you are concerned about what might happen in the area then you will need to discuss the position with your solicitor at an early stage. Your solicitor can organise this, but if you have the time and inclination you can do it yourself. It will help you to become familiar with the area and with the local officials with whom you may have dealings in the future. You will find the staff to be helpful and supportive. On the other hand, it is quite normal for your solicitor to carry out these searches.

Normal enquiries also include a check that the seller is the registered owner of the property and that it is sold (if this has been agreed) free of mortgages or other charges.

In order to advise you what special enquiries might be appropriate, your lawyer will need to be told your proposals for the property. Do you intend to let it out? If so will it be on a commercial basis? Do you intend to use it for business purposes? Do you want to extend or modify the exterior of the property? Do you intend to make interior structural alterations?

Agree in advance the additional enquiries that you would like to make and get an estimate of the cost of those enquiries.

Draft Purchase Contract

When a preliminary oral understanding has been reached and both vendor and yourself are satisfied (in so far as this is possible) with the price, and with the results of the general and special enquiries, the first step will be taken by the vendor's solicitor.

He or she will draw up a contract containing the information that you have supplied and the information supplied by the vendor – the names of the parties, a description of the property, the price and various conditions.

He or she sends this draft contract to your solicitor who will check it and inform you whether or not he or she is satisfied with its contents. If he or she is not satisfied, he or she may enter into correspondence with the vendor's solicitor. If he or she is satisfied, he will recommend that you sign.

It is important to realise that there is a *significant difference between Irish and UK practice concerning the time of signature of the contract*. In the UK, contracts are exchanged at the end of the transaction. In Ireland, this used to happen soon after the start of the transaction.

The advantage of the Irish practice is that there is much less chance of a would-be purchaser being gazumped or, if there is a chain of purchases to be got through, that the chain could break down. The down side is that there is greater pressure to make sure that everything is 100 per cent correct. Partly because of this pressure, it is the practice nowadays, if any aspect of the sale is tricky or not straightforward, to allow for a longer pre-contract period than was accepted in the past. Normally a contract will now be signed about four weeks before closing.

At the time of signing the purchase contract, there may be unresolved matters which, if they are not sorted out satisfactorily, could make the purchase pointless. These are usually matters which are not in the hands of either yourself or the vendor. Your solicitor will have these written into the contract as 'conditions'; see E) and L) below. Most purchase contracts in Ireland are based on the 'Standard Incorporated Law Society' contract. This model contract lists:

- the address of the property
- the selling price
- the date of purchase
- general conditions
- conditions special to your case (see E) and L) below)

A contract with a builder is usually in a different standard form. It may be that you will need to sign one contract for the purchase of the site and another for the building work on your new home.

The normal procedure may therefore be summarised like this:

A) You find a house that you want to buy.

B) Your auctioneer sends instructions to the vendor's solicitor.

C) The vendor's solicitor draws up a contract which is sent to the purchaser's solicitor. Neither party is bound to sell or buy the house until this contract has been signed by all the parties and a full deposit paid.

D) It is usual nowadays for there to be a period of two to three weeks before the contract is signed. This period is used to identify gross defects in the title.

E) The contract may be subject to any of the following conditions if they are relevant: (1) survey approval, (2) obtaining loan approval, (3) special conditions in relation to closing dates or other special requirements, say, inclusion of furniture or similar objects in the sale, (4) obtaining planning permission. All such conditions will be included in the contract eventually. (See L) below for further remarks about these conditions.)

F) There may also be negotiations between the parties over how these matters are to be dealt with and what are to be the real time limits allowed for this.

G) Once these negotiations have been concluded, the contract is signed and a deposit is paid. This means that the vendor is now obliged to sell and the purchaser is now obliged to buy. It is unheard of that you should not be required to pay this deposit, usually about 10 per cent, when you sign the contract. This money is held by the vendor's solicitor or by the auctioneer.

H) The signature normally takes place four to five weeks before closing.

I) Once the contract has been signed, neither party can walk away from it except grounds that have been included in the contract and drafted in a water-tight manner.

J) If the vendor tries to walk away, he or she will be compelled by the court to complete and to pay costs.

K) If the purchaser refuses to complete, he or she will pay interest set out in the contract, normally 15 per cent per annum, which is a high rate of interest, and, once the closing day has passed, the vendor can send the purchaser a **28-day notice**. If the purchaser misses this date, he or she will forfeit his deposit and the vendor can sell to someone else or get a court order to compel him or her to complete the transaction.

L) In a recent Irish case, the court decided that most of the conditions referred to above, about loans, planning, etc., are not what are called **conditions precedent**, i.e. conditions which must be satisfied before any contract at all becomes binding on either party but are instead **conditions subsequent**, which means that, if they are not met, the binding contract can cease to be binding, usually as regards one of the parties only and then at his option. This makes the notice provisions and determining provisions very important.

Valuation Report

It may be that you are obtaining a loan or taking out a mortgage in order to buy. In this case, a condition of the contract will be that you are given the loan, otherwise the contract will not come into force.

The lending institution will want assurance that its *from* loan is secured and will, therefore, require that the property be valued and a valuation report submitted to them.

A sensible solicitor for the vendor will not accept a contract if your solicitor cannot show that the lending institution has already approved the loan.

Title

Your solicitor will check the title, i.e. assure him or herself that the vendor is really the owner of the property and that there are no other claims to it or encumbrances which affect the vendor's ability to sell. In order to do so, he will need to see the documents which evidence such title: a folio in the Land Registry, or title deeds registered there or in the Registry of Deeds.

Investigations of Title: Requisitions and Queries

Your solicitor will almost certainly by this point be of the opinion that there are questions relating to the property and its title and will send a list of these questions to the vendor's solicitor. These are called **requisitions** and are usually in a standard form plus particular matters which have aroused his suspicions. Very often they are based on the Law Society's standard form of *Objections and Requisitions of Title*, from which your solicitor, although it is basically designed for use by him or her *after* the contract has been signed, can select and make enquiries or requisitions before the contract has been signed. That it might not be necessary to enquire into all the matters listed is evident when you consider

INDEX to Requisitions on Title

that there are 44 headings, under each of which a number of questions may arise. There is no need to go into these in this book but it is useful to know what are the areas that may be queried (*see* above for the contents of the 1996 edition of the *Law Society Objections and Requisitions*). It is obvious even from a glance that many of the topics will not affect you unless you are willing to keep a dairy herd or to open a nightclub.

Queries

Your solicitor will also seek assurance from the vendor's solicitor about matters which would prevent you from obtaining full title to the property or would interfere with your full enjoyment of the property.

• As stated above, these queries will ask for assurances that the vendor has the power to sell the property. The easiest way to demonstrate this is to show that it is registered in the vendor's name in the Land Registry.

- If the property is registered in the Registry of Deeds, good title is regarded as established if the property has been registered in the vendor's name for 30 years.
- If it is a comparatively new property or one which has been renovated or has had additions built on in the recent past, the vendor must show that it was built, renovated or added to in accordance with planning permission, local government requirements and building regulations.
- The vendor must show that there are no unpaid loans (mortgages, etc.) in existence.
- The vendor must show that there are no utility bills outstanding, for which you will be liable once you have signed the deed of sale.
- There may be fixtures and fittings in the house, mirrors, cupboards, book-cases, lights, chandeliers, etc. even washing machines, which you are buying. It must be made clear that they are governed by the agreed price and that the vendor cannot come back looking for separate payment for such items.
- Your solicitor will also insist that the vendor should certify that the property is not liable for any estate duty, succession duty, rent or land improvement charges. There will be a similar enquiry as to any rights that the public may have over the property, any rights of way or any short-term tenancies.

Sequence of Exchanges of Draft Deeds of Title

Following consultation with you and possibly further correspondence with the vendor's solicitor, your solicitor will draw up a deed transferring the title in the property to you.

Once the vendor's solicitor (and, naturally, the vendor) accepts this deed, it goes back again to your solicitor for **engrossment**, i.e. the preparation of the final deed in its traditional format.

The engrossed deed is sent to the vendor's solicitor for signature.

Searches

There may be mortgages outstanding or somebody, for example an aged rela-tive, may have a right of residence in the property. To make sure that neither is the case, your solicitor will conduct a search in the Land Registry or the Registry of Deeds.

If you are buying from a company and not an individual, your solicitor will make a search in the Companies Registration Office to make sure that the company is as it should be and that it has the power to sell the property free from any debt, lien or other encumbrance.

It is also important to ascertain whether or not there is *current* or *past* litigation concerning the property, either in relation to ownership or to any charges on it, or even a debt which could, if judgment is given against the vendor, result in a judgment mortgage being registered against your new home. To make sure that this is not the case, your solicitor will most likely make a search, called a **judgment search**, in the Central Office of the High Court. Your solicitor will also make what is called a **bankruptcy search** to make sure that the vendor is not bankrupt or that no bankruptcy proceedings are pending which might prevent him for transferring the title to you. Finally, a prudent solicitor will conduct a **sheriff and revenue sheriff search** in relation to property which is held by a lease to check that the vendor does not have outstanding debts.

To sum up, searches should or will take place in the Land Registry and/or the Registry of Deeds in relation to title and possible bankruptcy, the Judgments Office, the Sheriff's Office, the Bankruptcy Office and the Companies Office.

Final Checks: Some Practical Safeguards

If you want to be a prudent purchaser, you will take nothing for granted and it is important to remember that there can be last-minute difficulties. During the period that negotiations and/or the legal formalities have been taking place, something may have happened to the property which damaged the very features with which you fell in love.

Accordingly, before the sale is closed you should inspect the property (preferably in the company of your solicitor or your auctioneer) to make sure that it has not been damaged or altered in any way since you last saw it. It's not impossible that such alterations could have happened by accident or by the future vendor's moving fences or even parts of the building, windows, doors, etc. If the building has been vacant, it might even have been vandalised.

You will already have a list of the fittings and fixtures that are included in the price of the building and property generally, trees, plants, fences, etc., and you should make sure that they are all as you saw them last, have not been damaged in any way and have not be replaced by cheap substitutes. The future vendor is obliged to make good the damage or to return such fittings and fixtures and restore them to good working order. Otherwise, you should arrange that an amount equal to your loss be deducted from the purchase price.

Do not agree to a closure of the sale until such matters have been sorted out! If this is denied, you may have the right to demand the return of your deposit and any fees paid by you.

Fixing the Completion Date

This is one of the most important things that the solicitors on both sides must settle: the date when the vendor hands over to you the title deeds and keys of your new house in exchange for the balance of the purchase money. It is their responsibility to meet that date because, if they do not, either you or the vendor could be out of pocket. You, for example, may be liable for extra interest costs.

For all the above reasons, the date must be one which will have a reasonable chance of being respected.

Of course, either you or the vendor may have your own ideas of what is a suitable date. You may be selling your home in the UK and be waiting for the funds from the sale. In such a case, you may not want completion before you have the money in the bank. You may be waiting for loan approval. It is most likely that the vendor would want an early date but, if he or she is planning to move into a new house which is under construction, it may be he/she who wants a delay.

Whichever scenario is the case, your solicitor or the vendor's solicitor may raise the possibility of time being made of the essence of the contract. This would be so that interest can be charged if there is a delay in completion.

You may find that, if there is going to be a long delay, it will be suggested that the balance of the purchase money be put on joint deposit in the names of your and the vendor's solicitors until the problem has been solved.

There is another possibility. You may ask to be allowed to take possession of the property before completion, for example, to carry out repairs or make improvements, but, if this is granted, you will most certainly, unless the vendor and his solicitor are idiots, either be subject to special conditions in the contract dealing with the situation or to other restrictions imposed by the vendor. It is case law in Ireland since 1851 that you implicitly have agreed to pay interest on the outstanding balance of the purchase money. In addition, you will be liable for repairs and payment of outgoings while you are in possession and, if you make improvements to the property, you cannot recover the cost even though the sale eventually collapses through the vendor's default.

Closing the Sale

Normally, closing will take place about five to eight weeks after the purchase contract has been signed. This gives your solicitor time to complete his or her work. It must be said, however, that, in Dublin, where the atmosphere is more competitive, contracts can insist on completion within three weeks.

Officially a sale is closed in the office of the vendor's solicitor (completion). However, across the country where solicitors and their fathers and their fathers' fathers have known each other and built up trust, it is more and more the practice for completion to take place by post except where the contract contains special conditions. Apart from commercial transactions, it is rare for the clients to be present. The vendor's solicitor has the deed of purchase signed by the vendor and all the documents relating to the property. Your solicitor has a bank draft for the outstanding purchase price.

Final searches made prior to completion are carried out to make sure that no dealing with the property has been registered in the relatively short period

Power of Attorney

It may be that you are not available when signatures are required, because you are working at home, are in another country or are completely tied up in the sale of your English home. In this case, you can always give a power of attorney to someone to act on your behalf. Sometimes, this can be your spouse who will go over to Ireland and sign documents while you continue to sort things out at home.

Remember that anything signed by a person with your power of attorney is legally binding on you.

Do not give a power of attorney to anyone, unless you have absolute trust in them. It might be more time-consuming but it might be wiser to use the Royal Mail, An Post or a courier service to receive and send contracts. Money can be sent by other means and a solicitor can always obtain a bank draft as soon as you have paid the requisite sum into his or her account.

between the contract and completion in order to gain priority over you, the purchaser. If such a dealing is discovered, your solicitor will insist that anyone having rights under the dealing must join in the conveyance to release those rights and, if this is not done, you will be entitled to call off the sale.

Final searches are examined and explained, the bank draft is exchanged for the vendor's documents and the property is yours.

The Final Payment

The normal method of payment nowadays is by banker's draft. The most eminent textbook on conveyancing in Ireland – *Irish Conveyancing Law*, by J.C.W. Wylie, is emphatic on this point, saying, 'The vendor's solicitor should never accept a personal cheque from the purchaser or his solicitor no matter how eminent he may be. Such a cheque may not be honoured and this is a risk which the vendor's solicitor must avoid at all costs. If he has accepted such a cheque and it is not honoured, he will be liable in negligence for the amount of the cheque.'

Do not, therefore, feel insulted if your own solicitor does not agree to pay your cheque to the vendor but insists that you provide him with funds which he lodges to cover the amount of the banker's draft.

All this can take time, so it is advisable to set everything in motion as soon as possible. If the money is coming from a bank or a building society, it is important to make sure that this is available on time. It has been common practice in the UK for the bank or building society to appoint the purchaser's, i.e. your, solicitor to act as its agent for the completion of the mortgage. This was not usually the case in Ireland although this is now changing.

When you hand over the money to your solicitor, he must give you a receipt.

Getting the Money to Ireland

Payment can be sent from the UK to Ireland by electronic transfer, banker's draft, cheque, even cash (which is not very sensible).

There are no exchange controls between Ireland and the UK.

Capital Gains Clearance Certificate

If you are paying more than €500,000 for your new property, you are obliged to deduct 15 per cent of the purchase price and send it to the Revenue Commissioners if the vendor has not produced to your solicitor a copy of a **CG 50A clearance certificate** which puts the Revenue Commissioner on notice that the property is to be sold and that Capital Gains Tax (CGT) will be due.

After the Deed of Sale Has Been Signed

If **stamp duty** is payable, it must be paid within 28 days. Otherwise, penalties will apply. Once this has been done, the title deed will be lodged for registration in the Land Registry or in the Registry of Deeds.

If the property has been mortgaged, the title deed is sent to the lender institution, which holds it until the mortgage has been repaid.

Registering the Property

When the house is on registered land, you are required, through your solicitor, to register your ownership in the **Land Registry** and thereafter your name and details are entered on the appropriate Register.

It is not legally binding but is common practice and will, in fact, be required by any lending institution, to also have your ownership of the property registered in the **Registry of Deeds**.

The Cost of Buying a Property in Ireland

It is emphasised that these are only ballpark figures giving an indication of the type of expense that you might reasonably expect. Obviously, every purchase is unique and varying factors can cause differences in the amounts that you will be required to pay. In addition, as in the UK, taxes, levies and stamp duties can change with every budget in Ireland. VAT is charged on all fees.

Mortgage arrangement costs are not covered here; see pp.133–45.

Auctioneer's Fees

Auctioneer's fees are in the region of 2 per cent in Dublin and generally exceed this in regions outside Dublin. However, this figure is negotiable and if you are selling a desirable property the auctioneer may accept a lower rate, 1.5 per cent, 1.2 per cent or even, if you are lucky, 1 per cent. Look around.

Solicitor's Fees

Solicitor's fees are typically 1 per cent of the purchase price plus VAT. Alternatively, some solicitors charge a fixed fee. These fees exclude additional costs such as land registry and legal search fees.

Stamp Duty on Mortgage

This is exempt on mortgages up to and including €254,000. All mortgages exceeding €254,000 are subject to a stamp duty rate of 0.1 per cent, rounded down to the nearest zero, to a maximum of €630.

Registration in the Land Registry and Registry of Deeds

Registration of mortgage in the Land Registry: €131.
Registration of ownership in the Land Registry is dependent on property value:

Value of the property being registered	Fee
Up to €13,000	€125
€13,000–€26,000	€190
€26,001–€51,000	€250
€51,001–b255,000	€375
€255,001–€385,000	€500
Over €385,000	€625

There is also a fee of €60 if you only buy part of an existing folio and consequently a new folio has to be opened.

Total fees for registration in the Registry of Deeds should be around €120.

Stamp Duty on Property Purchase

The rates charged vary according to purchaser and property; see table, overleaf for current rates. All owner-occupiers are exempt from stamp duty on **new houses and apartments** provided that the area does not exceed 125 square

Residential Property: Rates of Stamp Duty for Conveyances on Sale or Lease Premiums

Aggregate Consideration	First-time Buyer as Owner-occupier	All others
Up to €127,000	Exempt	Exempt
€127,001–€190,500	Exempt	3%
€ 190,501–€254,000	3%	4%
€ 254,001–€317,000	3.75%	5%
€317,501–€381,000	4.5%	6%
€381,00–€635,000	7.5%	7.5%
Over €635,000	9%	9%

Non-Residential Property: Rates of Stamp Duty for Conveyances on Sale or Lease Premiums executed on or after 4th December 2002

Aggregate Consideration	Rate
Up to €127,000	Exempt
€127,001 – €190,500	3%
€190,501 – €254,000	4%
€254,001 – €317,500	5%
€317,501 – €381,000	6%
€381,001 – €635,000	7.5%
Over €635,000	9%

metres. Properties exceeding 125 square metres are subject to stamp duty at the appropriate rate on either the site cost, or a quarter of the site cost plus the house cost less VAT, whichever is greater. Stamp duty is applicable for all purchasers of **second-hand properties** at the appropriate rates.

Investors

If you are buying a property as an investment only, you are obliged to pay stamp duty on both new and second-hand houses and apartments, *see* above.

Miscellaneous Other Costs

Property Insurance

If you own a property in the UK, you will be familiar with home insurance. You will find little difference when you go to Ireland.

A number of major British insurance companies are expected to begin quoting for business in the Irish market soon. It may be that your current UK insurer will be glad to retain your business when you move to Ireland.

Local Taxes

There are no rates on non-commercial property in Ireland. Depending on where you live, there may be charges for refuse collection and possibly water charges.

Other Expenses

There will, inevitably, be other expenses involved with owning property as there would at home. This will include routine repairs, maintenance, insurance, standing charges for electricity. In rural areas, you may need to join a local water scheme. Sometimes, this could involve a one-off payment; in other areas it may mean a one-off payment and an annual contribution.

Key Points to Consider when Purchasing Different Properties

Property under Construction

• Make sure you understand exactly what you are buying. How big is the property? What will it look like? How will it be finished? What appliances are included? What facilities will it enjoy?

• Think about who should own the property so as to minimise tax and inheritance problems.

• Make sure the contract has all of the necessary clauses required to protect your position.

• Make sure there is a bank guarantee if you are buying 'off plan'.

• Be clear about the timetable for making payments.

• Think about whether you should forward-buy currency.

• Before you take delivery of the property, consider carefully whether it is worth incurring the expense of an independent survey to confirm that all is in order with the construction and to help draft any 'snagging list'.

Key Points – Second-hand Properties

• Make sure you understand exactly what you are buying. Are the boundaries clear? What furniture or fittings are included?

• Think about whether to have the property surveyed, especially if it is nearly 10 years old and any existing guarantee will soon be expiring.

• Think about who should own the property (see pp.146–51).

• Make sure the contract has all the necessary clauses required to protect your position.

• Think about whether you should forward-buy currency.

• Before you take delivery of the property, make sure that everything agreed is present.

Special Points – Older Properties

When buying an old property – a property built more than, say, 50 years ago – there are one or two additional special points to look out for:

• Are you having a survey? Not to do so can be an expensive mistake.

• Are you clear about any restoration costs to be incurred? Do you have estimates for those charges?

• Are there any planning problems associated with any alterations or improvements you want to make to the property?

• When you take delivery of the property, make sure that everything agreed is present.

Special Points – Rural Properties

• Are there access routes to your property, i.e. does the property adjoin the road or do you have to cross another property? If the latter, do you have an undisputed legal right of way by foot and by any means of transport?

• Such properties have often acquired a number of rights and obligations over the years. Are you clear about any obligations you might be taking on?

• You are probably buying for peace and quiet and the rural idyll. Are you sure that nothing is happening in the vicinity of your property that will be detrimental to this?

• If you have any plans to change the property or to use it for other purposes, will this be permitted?

Special Points – City Properties

• City properties will usually be apartments, concerning which *see* below.

• Unless you are used to living in a city, do not underestimate the noise that will be generated nearby. If you are in a busy area (and you are likely to be) this will go on until late at night. How good is the sound insulation?

• If you intend to use a car, where will you park?

Special Points – Apartments and Houses Sharing Facilities

• Have you thought about a survey of the property? Will it include the common parts? This can be expensive.

• Is there a tenants' association? Make sure you understand the association's rules. Make sure you understand any charges that may be levied by it.

• Make contact with the spokesperson of the association. Ask about any issues affecting the area. Are there any major works approved but not yet carried out? Make sure that the contract is clear about who is responsible for paying for these.

• Make contact with other owners. Are they happy with the tenants' association and the way it is run? Expect a range of answers!

• Understand how the association is run. Once you are an owner, try to attend the general meetings of the association regularly.

Other Things to Do when You Buy a Property

• Make arrangements for your bank to pay your refuse charges, if any, and telephone and electricity bills, etc.

- Insure the property and its contents.

- Make a full photographic record of the property. This is useful in the event of an insurance claim and for your scrapbook.

- Make a will to include your assets in Ireland (*see* pp.195–201). Get yourself a local accountant. This is your point of contact with the Irish tax office. He will also usually complete and file your annual tax return on the basis of the information supplied by you. Your lawyer may provide this service or should be able to suggest a suitable person.

Renovation or Building

If you are buying a new property or one that does not need major repair, this section is not for you. On the other hand, you may have taken a fancy to a particular area and bought a vacant plot because you want to start from scratch and build the home that you have always dreamed of. You may have bought a house that needs substantial improvement to meet your particular needs or even a derelict house. In such cases, this section suggests some general guidelines.

Fix a Budget

Whichever choice you make, the most sensible thing to do is to begin by fixing a budget for the operation. What is the maximum that you are prepared to spend in order to end up with a house ready to live in? Include the cost of purchase, any essential repairs or improvements and the taxes and fees payable. If you are buying a house in need of repair, fixing a budget is clearly more difficult. You will always underestimate the cost of the repairs. *Very few jobs finish exactly on budget!* That is as true in Ireland as it is in England.

You can save yourself a lot of heartbreak, and many sleepless nights, if you respect the following simple guidelines:

- If you are buying a property that needs major work, do not commit yourself until you have had a survey and builders' estimates for the work shown to be necessary.

- If possible, have an independent third party with knowledge of current building expenses verify the builder's estimates.

- Have every stage of the operation itemised and costed.

- Agree time limits for each stage of the work with the builder.

- Have clear and binding arrangements from the beginning on how payment is to be made, preferably on completion of the different stages.

- If possible, have a written contract with the builder leaving no loose ends. On smaller jobs across the country, you may find that the builder does not ask for a written contract. This is a matter of judgement. If you, or your surveyor, architect or other advisor, feel that delay or a botched job will cause undue upset or even give rise to extra expense, it is advisable to have a contract drawn up which provides for eventual pitfalls.

• If you are told by the seller (vendor in legal language) that there is no time for all this preparation and that you will lose the property if you do not sign today/this week/before Easter, walk away.

• If you have agreed to pay for the different stages of the job, have regular meetings with the builder to discuss what he has done, examine the work and compare what he has done with your checklist or contract. This may be difficult and expensive if you are still in the UK. In such a case, it may save time and money to pay a professional person to do it for you. It is not advisable to accept the builder's assurance that 'the job will be done by 1st July' and go home and have no contact until the 30th of June. Builders in Ireland are, as in England or Wales, very human and will have other clients closer at hand who will be pestering them to finish work or to carry out repairs, and they often respond to the person who is most persistent and present. Their too=human response will be, 'Sure, Mr Smith is in no hurry. He'd be on to me if he was. I'll just finish this little job for Tommy and no harm will be done.' Builders are deliberately not mind-readers and if you do not make clear that you have a deadline, do not expect them to second-guess you.

• You are not out to make friends but to move into your house or holiday home. You must balance prudence and common sense against unnecessary interference. Show polite interest in the progress that is being made but do not be pushy. Turning up regularly and asking 'How's it going, lads?' will pay dividends. Diplomacy will get you much further in Ireland than apparent lack of interest followed by exasperation and bad blood. A smile and a kind word can go a long way. Harsh language in an English accent can be counter-productive.

• If you must stay in the UK while the work is being carried out, find a reliable person to visit the site and keep an eye on things.

There are model contracts available, for example, the Standard Building Agreement and a standard contract proposed by the Construction Industry Federation of Ireland (CIF).

I repeat, unless you are in the happy position that money is no object, do not exceed your budget. It is too easy, after a good lunch and in the company of a silver-tongued auctioneer, to throw your financial plans to the wind. 'Another £30,000 won't break me' is a statement you may later come to regret.

It is sound practice to keep some money in reserve. The unexpected is to be expected where building or restoration is concerned.

Financial Implications

by Joseph McArdle
Barrister at Law (Kings Inn, Middle Temple)

06

Taxation

If you are liable to pay tax in Ireland, you will not be in for major surprises, because the tax systems of the UK and Ireland are not so very different from each other. Individual rates will differ and different emphasis will be placed on different ways of raising money for the government, but on the whole Ireland has inherited its tax system from Great Britain.

Planning of Tax Affairs – Decisions You Must Make

The most basic decisions that you will have to make when planning your tax affairs is whether to cease to be resident in the UK, whether to cease to be ordinarily resident in the UK or whether to change your domicile to Ireland. Each of these has many consequences, many of which are not obvious.

The next decision is when in the tax year to make these changes. Once again, that decision has many consequences.

It is vital that you seek proper professional advice before making these decisions. You will need advice from specialist lawyers, accountants or financial advisers all of whom should be able to help you.

Are You Resident or Non-resident for Tax Purposes?

The biggest single factor in determining how you will be treated by the tax authorities in any country is whether you are resident in that country for tax purposes. This concept of tax residence causes a great deal of confusion.

Tax residence is nothing to do with whether you have registered as resident in a country or whether you have a home (residence) in that country – although a person who is tax resident will normally have a home there. Tax residence is a question of fact. The law lays down certain tests that will be used to decide whether or not you are tax resident. If you fall into the categories stipulated in the tests then you will be considered tax resident whether you want to be or not and whether it was your intention to be tax resident or not.

You will have to consider two different questions concerning tax residence. The first is whether you will be treated as tax resident in the UK and the second is whether you will be treated as tax resident in Ireland.

The Rules that Determine Residence in the UK

In the UK there are two tests that will help determine where you pay tax. These assess your domicile and your residence.

Domicile

Domicile is a legal concept that means residence in a particular country with the intention of residing permanently in that country. Everybody acquires a domicile of origin at birth. If you were born in the UK that is your domicile unless you formally elect to change it. You can change your domicile but it is often not easy to do so. Changes in domicile can have far-reaching tax consequences and can also be a useful tax reduction tool.

Residence and Ordinary Residence

Residence falls into two categories. Under English law there is a test of simple residence – actually living here other than on a purely temporary basis – and of ordinary residence.

A person will generally be treated as **resident** in the UK if he or she spends 183 or more days per year in the UK. A visitor will also be treated as resident if he or she comes to the UK regularly and spends significant time here. If he or she spends, on average over a period of four or more years, more than three months here, he or she will be treated as tax resident.

A person can continue to be **ordinarily resident** in the UK even after he or she has actually ceased being resident here. A person is ordinarily resident in the UK if his or her presence is a little more settled. The residence is an important part of his or her life. It will normally have gone on for some time.

The most important thing to understand is that, once you have been ordinarily resident in this country, the simple fact of going to Ireland will not automatically bring that residence to an end. If you leave this country in order to take up permanent residence elsewhere then, by concession, the Inland Revenue will treat you as ceasing to be resident on the day following your departure. But they will not treat you as ceasing to be ordinarily resident if, after leaving, you spend an average of 91 or fewer days per year in the UK over any four-year period. In other words, they don't want you to escape too easily!

The Rules that Determine Residence in Ireland

Tax residence in Ireland is also tested by similar rules, the main ones of which are explained in **First Steps**, pp.17–19. Your residence status for the purpose of calculating Irish tax is established by the number of days you spend in Ireland during the tax year (in Ireland this coincides with the calendar year and runs from January to December). Purchasing a property in Ireland does not automatically make you a resident but could be relevant in determining a single country of residence under the double taxation agreement between Ireland and the UK (*see* p.178).

Residence

You are considered **resident** in Ireland if you spend **183 days or more** in Ireland during that tax year. If you spend **280 days or more** in Ireland over a period of two consecutive tax years you are regarded as resident in Ireland for the second tax year. For example, if you spend 140 days in Ireland in Year One and 150 days in Year Two, you will be deemed to be resident in Ireland for all of Year Two. If, however, you satisfy the residence required in the first year and spend no more than 30 days in the second year, this does not make you resident in Ireland in the second year e.g. 300 days in Ireland in Year One, 20 days in Ireland in Year Two, you have only been resident in Ireland in Year One. A 'day' of residence in Ireland is a day in which you were in Ireland at midnight. *Residence does not need to be consecutive*: it does not matter how often you leave Ireland during a particular year. What counts are the actual number of days that you spent in the country. If they add up in total to 183 i.e. one day more than half the year, you have been resident in Ireland.

Ordinary Residence

If you are resident in Ireland for three tax years (for example, you spend more than 183 days in Ireland per year) you are considered **ordinarily resident** from the beginning of the fourth tax year. You stop being ordinarily resident if you are non-resident for three years in a row. IWith the exception of certain types of income, if you have become ordinarily resident but happen to be non-resident for a particular tax year, you will still be regarded as being resident for that year of absence.

Electing for Residence

If you come to Ireland in a particular tax year and do not spend a sufficient number of days to become resident as set out above, you may **elect to be resident** for that tax year in order, for example, to avail of full personal income tax credits. A condition of making an election is that you must establish to the satisfaction of your local tax office that you will be resident in Ireland in the following tax year under any one of the tests mentioned above. But remember that once an election has been made, it cannot subsequently be cancelled. As a resident you will be liable to tax on your worldwide income earned or arising during the entire tax year during which you came to Ireland. However, income from employment will be taxable only from the date of your arrival in Ireland. If you wish to make an election, you can do so by writing to your local tax office.

Domicile

Domicile is a concept of general law in Ireland as in the UK. It may be broadly interpreted as meaning residence in a particular country *with the intention of residing there permanently*. Everyone acquires a domicile of origin at birth. A domicile of origin will remain with a person until such time as a new domicile of choice is acquired. However, before the domicile of origin can be shed, there has to be clear evidence that the person has a positive intention of permanent residence in the new country and has given up all idea of ever returning to live permanently in his or her home country. So basically, if you were born in the UK, that remains your **domicile** unless you formally elect to change it.

Liability to Irish Tax (from the Irish Revenue Commissioners)

Resident, ordinarily resident and Irish domiciled	Taxable on all Irish- and foreign-sourced income in full.
Not resident, ordinarily resident and Irish domiciled	Taxable on all Irish- and foreign-sourced income in full, but income from the following sources is exempt from tax: • a trade, profession, office or employment, all the duties of which are exercised outside Ireland (*see* note 1) • other foreign income, e.g. investment income, provided that it does not exceed €3,810 in the tax year in which it is earned.
Not resident, ordinarily resident and not Irish domiciled	Taxable on Irish-sourced income in full and taxable on remittances (*see* note 2) of foreign-sourced income, but income from the following sources is exempt: • a trade, profession, office or employment, all the duties of which are exercised outside Ireland (*see* note 1) • other foreign income, e.g. investment income, provided that it does not exceed €3,810 in the tax year in which it is earned.
Resident and ordinarily resident but not Irish domiciled	Taxable on Irish-sourced income in full and on remittances (*see* note 2) of foreign-sourced income.
Resident and domiciled but not ordinarily resident	Taxable on Irish-sourced income in full and on remittances (*see* note 2) of foreign-sourced income.
Not resident, not ordinarily resident and not Irish domiciled	Taxable on Irish-sourced income in full and on foreign-sourced income for a trade, profession or employment exercised in Ireland.

Note 1: In the case of an employment, if an inconsequential number of days are spent working in Ireland and are incidental to the foreign duties of an employment, those duties exercised in Ireland will not affect your exemption from Irish tax. Normally any number of days up to a maximum of 30 in a tax year will be regarded as incidental days.

Note 2: The **remittance basis** of assessment applies to foreign-sourced income (excluding UK-sourced income). It provides that for any tax year during which you are not Irish domiciled, or if you are an Irish citizen who is not ordinarily resident in Ireland, you will only be taxable to the extent that you bring that income into Ireland.

Double Taxation Agreements

It is possible to be tax resident in more than one country at the same time. In this case you could end up, under the rules of each country, liable to pay the same tax in both countries. Also, a particular item of income could under each country's different rules be taxable in both the country in which it is sourced and also in the country in which the recipient of that income is resident.

For these reasons, many countries have concluded agreements called double taxation agreements with other countries to protect individuals from being required to pay tax twice. Ireland and the UK have such an agreement.

If, for example, your income is chargeable to tax in Ireland and in the UK, a double charge is prevented by one of the following:

- **exempting the income from tax in one of the countries.**

- **allowing a credit in Ireland or the UK for the tax paid in the other country on the same income.**

The main points of relevance to you will be that:

- **Any income from letting property in the UK will normally be outside the scope of Irish taxation and, instead, will be taxed in the UK.**

- **Pensions received from the UK – except for government pensions – will be taxed in Ireland but not in the UK.**

- **Government pensions will continue to be taxed in UK but are neither taxed in Ireland nor do they count when assessing the level of your income to calculate the rate of tax payable on your income.**

- **You will normally not be required to pay UK capital gains tax on gains made after you have settled in Ireland except in relation to real estate located in the UK.**

- **If you are taxed on a gift made outside Ireland, then the tax paid will usually be offset against the gift tax due in Ireland.**

- **If you pay tax on an inheritance outside Ireland, the same will apply.**

If you feel that you might be at risk of double taxation, it is important to familiarise yourself with the double taxation agreement between Ireland and the UK and to get advice from a professional who is familiar with this field and who is acquainted with your personal circumstances.

If you do become resident in Ireland but, at an earlier stage in your life, have been working outside Ireland or the UK and have an income arising in a country which has not signed a double taxation agreement with Ireland (for a list of further countries that have agreements with Ireland, *see* p.291), your income in Ireland for the purposes of taxation will be whatever is left to you after you have paid tax in that third country. There is no credit available for foreign tax paid against your Irish tax liability on the same income.

Taxes Payable in the UK

Both Ireland and the UK assess your domicile and your residence. Expressed in a simplified way – once you have left UK to live in Ireland:

- **You will continue to have to pay tax in England on any capital gains you make anywhere in the world for as long as you are ordinarily resident and domiciled in United Kingdom.**

- **You will continue to be liable to British inheritance tax on all of your assets located anywhere in the world for as long as you remain domiciled in the UK. This will be subject to double taxation relief (*see* below). Other, more complex rules also apply in certain circumstances.**

- **You will always pay UK income tax (Schedule A) on income arising from land and buildings in the UK – wherever your domicile, residence or ordinary residence.**

- **You will pay UK income tax (Schedule D) on the following basis:**

  - **Income from 'self-employed' trade or profession carried out in the UK (Cases I & II) – normally taxed in the UK if income arises in the UK.**

  - **Income from interest, annuities or other annual payments from the UK (Case III) – normally taxed in the UK if income arises in the UK and you are ordinarily resident in the UK.**

  - **Income from investments and businesses outside UK (Cases IV & V) – normally only taxed in the UK if you are UK domiciled and resident or ordinarily resident in the UK.**

  - **Income from government pensions (fire, police, army, civil servant, etc.) in all cases taxed in the UK.**

  - **Sundry profits not otherwise taxable (Case VI) arising out of land or building in the UK – always taxed in the UK.**

- **You will pay income tax on any income earned from salaried employment in the UK only in respect of any earnings from duties performed in the UK unless you are resident and ordinarily resident in the UK – in which case you will usually pay tax in the UK on your worldwide earnings.**

If you are only buying a holiday home and will remain primarily resident in the UK, your tax position in the UK will not change very much. You will have to declare any income you make from your Irish property as part of your UK tax declaration. The calculation of tax due on that income will be made in accordance with UK rules. The UK tax man will give you full credit for any taxes already paid in Ireland. On the disposal of the property, you should disclose the profit made to the UK tax man. He will again give full credit for Irish tax paid. Similarly, on your death, the assets in Ireland must be disclosed on the UK probate tax declaration but, once again, you will be given full credit for sums paid in Ireland.

Taxes Payable in Ireland: Non-residents

Your liability for tax in Ireland depends on your personal circumstances and your residence status. There may be situations when you will be liable to pay tax in Ireland whether or not you are domiciled or ordinarily resident there.

However, in general, a person who is non-resident for tax purposes has few contacts with the Irish tax system and any such contacts are fairly painless.

Local Taxes

Both residents and non-residents pay these taxes where they exist. Rates on private dwellings have been abolished in Ireland. Some local councils have charges for refuse collections or for water.

Income Tax

As a non-resident you will generally only pay tax on:

- **income generated from land and buildings located in Ireland.**
- **income from Irish securities and capital invested in Ireland. There are certain exemptions and the rules change frequently.**
- **income from business activities in Ireland.**
- **earned income if you are employed or self-employed in Ireland.**

Income tax is calculated on these amounts at various band rates going currently from 20 per cent to 45 per cent.

Taxes on Capital Gains

You will pay tax on the capital gain you make on the sale of real estate in Ireland. However, if the gain is a result of the sale of a principal residential property which was purchased more than five years previously, the gain will not be taxed. If the property was purchased within the previous five years then the gain will be taxed, not under capital gains tax but as income tax.

Taxes on Death

Inheritance tax is paid in Ireland on the value of any assets in Ireland as at the date of your death.

Selling your home in the UK

If you sell your home in the UK (or any property elsewhere) in a tax year in which you are neither resident nor ordinarily resident in Ireland, there will be no liability to Irish tax when the proceeds from the sale are brought into Ireland.

Taxes Payable in Ireland: Residents

As in the UK, there are many types of Irish taxes and duties. In alphabetical order the **taxes** are – capital acquisition tax, capital gains tax, corporation tax, dividend witholding tax, income tax, relevant contracts tax, residential property tax, retention tax, tax clearance, value added tax (VAT) and withholding tax. In alphabetical order, the **duties** are – customs and excise, tonnage tax, stamp duties, vehicle registration tax and environmental levy.

Don't worry! Many of the above will not apply to you and in respect of those which might affect you, there are many personal credits and personal reliefs and exemptions to be deducted.

Generally speaking you will be chargeable to Irish tax on your worldwide income earned or arising in a tax year during which you are resident, ordinarily resident and domiciled in Ireland for tax purposes. For any tax year during which you are non-resident and non ordinarily resident in Ireland, you will be chargeable to tax on your income from Irish sources only. The extent of your liability to Irish tax may also be influenced by your domicile status.

Unless you have formed a company, your main taxation concern will be with **income tax**, which, as in the UK, is levied on your earnings or on other money that you receive from investments, such as rent from your property or from shares. If you form a company, any income that it earns will fall under the **corporation tax** system. If you make a profit from the sale of your property or if someone gives you a gift, these windfalls are taxable under **capital gains tax** (CGT) or **capital acquisitions tax** (CAT). The details of these rules, particularly in relation to rates, can change in the annual budget just as they do in the UK.

Filing a Tax Return

In Ireland since 2002, the **tax year** has run as the calendar year, from 1 January to the following 31 December. Ireland operates a system of **self-assessment** of income tax. It is up to you to see that your tax affairs are in order. You must pay your tax and make your tax returns at the following times:

- **An initial tax based on your calculations of the amount for which you will be liable (Preliminary Tax) – payable on/before 31 October in the year of assessment. This is a forecast of the tax that you will be liable to pay in the coming year.**

- **Income Tax Returns, CGT Returns and Forms 46G must be submitted on/before 31 October following year of assessment.**

- **The balance of your tax liability must be paid on/before 31 October following year of assessment ('Pay and File').**

For tax purposes, you are described as a 'chargeable person' and, as such, you must submit a tax return within the given time limit and not wait for a request from the Revenue Commissioners. It is up to you to inform the Revenue Commissioners what you consider your liabilities to be.

These rules do not apply if you are employed in Ireland under the PAYE (Pay As You Earn) system where your tax is deducted at source by your employer. As long as you do not have any income other than your salary, you are not usually required to file a return. If, however, you are a company director, you will normally be obliged to submit a Return even if all your income tax is deducted at source.

Bringing Funds into Ireland

If you are settling in Ireland for the first time and have earned income before you arrived, any savings that you have from the income which you earned prior to the 1st of January of the year in which you became resident will not be liable to Irish tax. However, income, other than employment income, earned or arising outside Ireland between the 1st of January and the date of your arrival will be taxable if brought ('remitted') into Ireland, unless a double taxation agreement provides for a different treatment.

Selling your Home in the UK

If you sell your home in the UK (or any property elsewhere) in a tax year during which you were resident or ordinarily resident in Ireland, you may be liable for capital gains tax. Get advice from an experienced professional who is familiar with rates for capital gains tax in Ireland and the UK. He or she will be able to advise you as to when to sell in order to get the better tax rate.

If, however, the property was your principal private residence for the full period of ownership, the proceeds will be exempt from capital gains tax. Remember that this will only apply if the property is sold within 12 months of being vacated. So if you leave it, come to Ireland and sell it 18 months later, you will be liable for capital gains tax.

Foreign Pensions

If you are in receipt of a pension from a source outside Ireland, the UK or elsewhere, the general rule is that it will be liable to Irish tax unless it is relieved under the provisions of a double taxation agreement. Such an agreement may provide that pensions paid in respect of past services of a governmental nature are to be taxed only in the source country. Certain other pensions which would have been exempt from tax in the UK (if such exist), had you continued to reside there, may also continue to be exempt from Irish tax when you go to live there. Your Irish tax office will advise; see also **Settling In**, 'Pensions', pp.245–7.

Income Tax

If you are not looking for a holiday home or to retire to Ireland but have found a job there or intend to become self-employed, your salary/income will be taxable in Ireland from the date of your arrival unless it is relieved under the Irish/UK double taxation agreement. Your residence status will be irrelevant.

Health Insurance – Personal Credits and Authorised Insurers

A claimant who has paid a premium to an authorised fund or society on behalf of himself/herself, children and dependents and, if assessed under aggregation, his/her spouse may claim these payments aganst tax.

The following are the institutions which are recognised for this purpose by the Revenue: BUPA Ireland Ltd., CIE Clerical Staff Hospital Fund, ESB Marina Staff Medical Provident Fund, ESB Staff Medical Provident Fund, Goulding Voluntary Medical Scheme, HSBC Group Medical Scheme, Irish Life Assurance (plc), Medical Aid Society, Irish Life Assurance (plc), Outdoor Staff Benevolent Fund, Lotus Development, Ireland Medical Benefits Society, Motorola Medical Aid Society, New Ireland/Irish National Staff Benevolent Fund, Prison Officers' Medical Aid Society, Saville Medical Benefits Society, St Pauls Garda Medical Aid Society, Sun Alliance Insurance Co., Transport Hospital Fund, VHI, Viking Ireland Medical Benefits Society, XiLinx Ireland Medical Benefits Society.

If it happens that you are an Irish citizen, not ordinarily resident in Ireland and not Irish domiciled, your foreign employment income, *from any country except the UK*, will only be taxable to the extent that it is remitted into Ireland.

If you are resident for Irish tax purposes in the year that the income is earned, you will be entitled to full personal tax credits and reliefs.

Employees will pay tax under the PAYE system (usually weekly or monthly). If you are **self-employed** or have **income from outside Ireland** you use the self-assessment system (tax is payable in one lump sum or by direct debit at intervals) and must complete returns by the correct dates (*see* p.181)

Irish income tax is calculated at the appropriate rates on your gross pay earned in a tax year (less superannuation and contributions to a Revenue-approved health scheme; *see* box, above). In order to estimate the tax payable, gross tax is then reduced by whatever tax credits are due to you.

See **Settling In**, 'Working and Employment', pp.226–9, for fuller details on income tax for the employed and self-employed, including tables of recent tax bands and examples of the effect of income tax and tax credits on net pay.

Benefits-in-Kind and Perquisites

This section relates to employed people only: you may be taxed not only on your income but also on benefits-in-kind. These are benefits received from an employer which *cannot be converted into money*, but which nonetheless would save you money. Most benefits are taxable if total remuneration (including benefits-in-kind) is €1,905 or more in any tax year but, if you are a director of a company and receive benefits, they will be taxable regardless of the level of remuneration. Perquisites are remuneration in non-monetary form which *is convertible into money or money's worth*, for example, vouchers in various forms, the payment of club subscriptions or medical insurance by an employer.

Examples of benefits are the **private use of a company car or van, free or subsidised accommodation, preferential loans** (a loan on which no interest is payable or is payable at a lower rate than a rate fixed by the Minister for Finance), etc.

As a general rule, the amount assessable by the Revenue is the cost to your employer of providing the benefit-in-kind, less any amount contributed to your employer by you.

The responsibility for notifying the revenue about benefits *will not fall on you* but on your employer who is obliged to make an annual return on a form called P11D and to make the appropriate deductions from your pay packet.

Withholding Tax on Professional Fees

If you are a professional and plan to work as such in Ireland, you may find that a certain percentage of your fees for 'professional services' are deducted at source. However, this only arises when you have supplied these services to 'accountable persons', which means government departments, local authorities, health boards, state bodies and similar organisations.

The withholding tax is 20 per cent of your gross income from the work. This tax does not apply to payments already covered by PAYE or under a scheme called the 'construction industry tax deduction scheme'. The withholding tax will also be levied on your earnings even if you are non-resident but, in such a case, you are entitled to a full refund of the deduction.

Even though a deduction takes place at the standard rate, it does not affect the overall calculation of your profits or gains for tax purposes although it will, of course, be set off against the tax chargeable on your profits.

Tax on Social Welfare Pensions

Pensions paid by the Irish Department of Social and Family Affairs (DSFA) are taxable and should be declared in your tax returns. Tax is not deducted at source by the Department. If a Social Welfare pension is your only source of income it is unlikely that there will be any tax due, as your tax credits or exemption limit will generally cover this income. If you have income in addition to your pension, your tax credits will be reduced by the amount of your Social Welfare pension for PAYE purposes. If you pay tax under self-assessment, your Social Welfare pension will be included in your notice of assessment.

Tax on Rental Income

Perhaps you will decide to rent out all or a portion of your property, full time or for part of the year. If so, given the normal conditions concerning residence and being ordinarily resident, you will be liable for income tax on the **rental income**.

You may also allow people to build signs on your land or you may lease out grazing rights to a neighbouring farmer. These are **easements** and, if you earn money from granting them, you will be liable for tax. You might have a barn or a warehouse on your property and rent it for business purposes. If the lease is less than 50 years some of the premium charged will be treated as rent.

If you buy and rent out a property in Ireland but continue to be resident in the UK (or go to Croatia!), your tenant must deduct the tax from his or her payments at the standard rate and remit it to Revenue.

If you let a room or rooms in your principal private residence as residential accommodation, a gross annual rental of up to €7,620 is exempt from tax under the **rent-a-room scheme**.

There are, of course, deductions that may be made from taxable rental income. Generally speaking they are:

- **Ground rent, an insignificant amount if it still exists.**
- **Maintenance.**
- **General repairs.**
- **Management fees paid to an agent which may indeed by the case if you are renting out to holiday makers.**
- **Service charges, water/ refuse etc.**
- **Accountant's fees for preparing rental accounts.**
- **Wear and tear – depreciation of furniture and fittings i.e. 15 per cent of cost of items allowed in years 1–6 and 10 per cent in year 7.**
- **Building expenditure if you live in a renewal incentive area.**
- **Interest – relief is due for interest paid on loans to purchase, improve or repair a residential premises (with some exceptions).**

Pay-related Social Insurance

In addition to income tax you have to pay national insurance. This is called pay-related social insurance (PRSI). As a PAYE employee you pay 4 per cent PRSI (up to a threshold, currently €42,160) and a further 2 per cent health contribution on your entire salary. You are exempt from PRSI on the first €127 you earn per week. If you earn less than €287 you are exempt from PRSI and if you earn less than €356 you are exempt from the health contribution. Your employer pays a further amount (usually 10.25 per cent). If you are self-employed your PRSI contribution is 5 per cent on your entire income.

If you are aged 66 or over you are not liable to pay PRSI. A separate Health Contribution is payable to age 70, on income other than Social Welfare payments. Recipients of a Social Welfare Family Payment or Deserted Wife's Benefit or Allowance do not have to pay the Health Contribution, even if their total income is more than €356 per week.

Further information is available from the Department of Social and Family Affairs, t (01) 704 3000.

Corporation Tax

This is a tax on the earnings of companies which are treated differently from private individuals. It will not affect you if you are not a company and, if you are, you should already have UK or Irish solicitors or accountants to advise you. If not, you are sailing out into deep waters without a compass.

Valued Added Tax (VAT)

Apart from paying the VAT which is added to your bill when you purchase goods in a shop, you are hardly likely to be troubled with VAT and VAT returns if you do not intend to carry on a business in Ireland and become a VAT-registered trader. If you have no such intention, you can skip this section.

VAT is a consumer tax. It is collected by VAT-registered traders on their supplies of goods and services. Persons supplying taxable goods or services in the course or furtherance of business must register and account for VAT if their turnover is in excess of certain limits. The main annual limits (2004 figures) are:

- **€51,000 for persons supplying goods.**
- **€25,500 for persons supplying services.**

Persons established in Ireland whose turnover does not exceed the appropriate limit may opt to register but are not obliged to do so.

Exemptions

If you do intend to become a VAT-registered trader, the Revenue will give you full information about your responsibilities and will let you know which goods and services are exempt from VAT. In general, persons supplying such goods and services, e.g. schools, universities and hospitals, are treated as being exempt for VAT purposes. This means that these persons must pay VAT on their purchases but they have no obligation, or entitlement, to register and account for VAT.

Capital Acquisitions Tax

Capital acquisitions tax includes gift tax, inheritance tax, discretionary trust tax and probate tax

Gift Tax and Inheritance Tax

Gift tax is charged on taxable gifts and inheritance tax is charged on taxable inheritances. The tax is charged on the taxable value of the gift or inheritance. The taxable value is arrived at by deducting permissible debts and encumbrances and any payment by the person receiving the gift or inheritance (the 'beneficiary') from the market value of the gift or inheritance.

Group Threshold

Beneficiaries of gifts or inheritances are entitled to receive a tax-free amount before tax is calculated under capital acquisitions tax. The tax-free amounts vary depending on the relationship between the person providing the gift or inheritance (called the 'disponer') and the person receiving the gift or inheritance. For gift and inheritance tax purposes, these tax-free amounts are known as 'group thresholds'.

Three group thresholds were introduced on the 1st December 1999 in respect of gifts and inheritances taken between 1st December 1999 and 31st December 2001. The group thresholds are indexed by reference to the consumer price index (CPI) and the indexation factor for 2004 (1st January 2003 to 31st December 2003 inclusive) is 1.198.

The indexed groups thresholds for 2004 (after indexation) were as follows:

Group	Relationship to Disponer	Group Threshold
A	Son/Daughter	€456,438
B	Parent*/Brother/Sister/ Niece/Nephew/Grandchild	€45,644
C	Relationship other than Group A or B	€22,822

*In certain circumstances, a parent taking an inheritance from a child may qualify for the Group A threshold.

Further information may be obtained from the Capital Taxes Division, Taxpayer Information Service, Dublin Castle, **t** 1890 20 11 04.

Gifts or inheritances of Irish property are liable to tax *whether or not the disponer is resident or domiciled in Ireland*. Foreign property is liable to tax where either the disponer or the beneficiary *is* resident or ordinarily resident in Ireland at the relevant date.

Various exemptions from gift and inheritance tax have been provided for. For example, the first €3,000 taken as a gift by a beneficiary from a disponer in any one year is exempt from tax, as are gifts and inheritances taken by one spouse from the other. There are exemptions in favour of certain charities, heritage property, superannuation benefits, and foreign donees of certain Irish government securities. Qualifying insurance policies to the extent that they are utilised in the payment of gift tax or inheritance tax are also exempt.

In addition to the exemptions, various reliefs, which are subject to certain conditions being satisfied, apply, e.g.:

- **Agricultural relief: operates by reducing the market value of agricultural property (this will only apply if you are farmer in Ireland).**

- **Business relief: granted by reducing the taxable value of business property.**

Leaflets explaining all this may be obtained from the Revenue Commissioners.

Exemptions

Ask for information leaflets CAT1, 'Gift Tax', and 'CAT2, 'Inheritance Tax'.

Gifts from a spouse are entirely exempt from gift tax regardless of the amount involved. Similarly, **inheritances from a spouse** are exempt from inheritance tax. Each **child** can receive gifts or inheritances of up to a certain amount tax-free from their parents provided that no previous gifts or inheritances were taken by the child since 5th December 1991.

For gifts and inheritances of **certain dwellings** received since 1st December 1999, capital acquisitions tax does not apply provided that:

- **the recipient has been living in the house as his or her only or main residence for the 3 years prior to the transfer.**
- **the recipient continues to live in the house for at least 6 years after the transfer.**
- **the recipient must not be beneficially entitled to any other dwelling house or to an interest in any other dwelling house.**

If you are **permanently incapacitated** because of physical or mental infirmity, a gift or inheritance taken by you to meet your medical expenses (including, for example, the cost of nursing home care) is exempt from gift or inheritance tax.

Probate Tax

Probate tax is much more likely to affect you, or rather your heirs, but, it is hoped, not for a long time in the future. It is charged at the rate of 2 per cent on the estates of persons dying after 17th June 1993. Foreign property, for example, your house in the UK, is not liable to probate tax unless the owner dies domiciled in Ireland. Assets passing otherwise than under the will or intestacy are excluded.

Funeral expenses and debt owing by the deceased at the time of death are allowable in arriving at the taxable value. Exemptions include estates below €50,790 in 2000, property passing absolutely to a surviving spouse, the principal private residence (where there is a surviving spouse or where certain dependent children or relatives succeed), property passing to a charity, heritage property, superannuation benefits, certain government securities, unit trusts and policies taken by foreigners, qualifying insurance policies (to the extent that they are utilised in the payment of probate tax or inheritance tax) and property which has already within one year prior to the death borne probate tax on the death of a predeceased spouse (or within 5 years where there is a dependent child).

Capital Gains Tax

If you decide to sell some of your assets while resident in Ireland you may be liable to capital gains tax (CGT), a tax arising in the words of the Revenue 'on gains arising on the disposals of assets'. Does this mean that you will be required to pay out a large sum of money if you decide that you are not happy in Ireland or if other compelling reasons force you to sell up? Not necessarily.

If your house in Ireland is your principal private residence you are exempt provided that you have been occupying it as your only or main residence during the period in which you owned it. 'House' in this context includes one acre of land but not more. The exemption is restricted where the house has been partly let or partly used for business or if you did not reside in it for long periods or where the house or gardens are being sold for development purposes.

The standard rate (2004) is 20 per cent of the price of the property less deductible expenditure.

The deductible expenditure which will be taken from the money you have been paid by the purchaser will be:

- **The amount that you paid for the property including the incidental costs of the purchase.**

- **Any 'enhancement expenditure', i.e. all renovations and additions that you have made to the property. There are multipliers to be taken into account.**

- **The incidental costs of selling the property such as legal and advertising costs.**

Returns of capital gains must be made by the 31st of October in the year following the year of assessment without being required to do so by the Inspector of Taxes.

Ask for information booklet CGT1: *Guide to Capital Gains Tax.*

Exemptions

At age 55 years or over you may be entitled to relief from capital gains tax on the sale or transfer of assets used for the purpose of farming, or a trade, carried on by you, or of shares in your family company which you have owned *for at least 10 years.* Relief may also be available where an interest in the land is transferred under the scheme for early retirement from farming or, in certain instances, if you sell land to a local authority for road construction, widening or extension purposes where that land has been let prior to sale.

A transfer of land from a parent to his/her child to enable that child to construct a main residence on the land is exempt from capital gains tax in certain circumstances.

Deposit Interest Retention Tax (DIRT)

A tax which might affect you is this retention tax. This means that, if as a resident in Ireland you have money on deposit with an Irish bank, building society, Post Office Savings Bank or similar institution, the institution is required to deduct 20 per cent of the interest paid or credited to you on your deposits.

This deduction is not made if you are non-resident in Ireland and your deposit is in a foreign currency (which includes £ sterling).

You are not required to make returns to the Revenue of payments of interest that have been subject to deduction of tax.

If you are aged 65 years or over or permanently incapacitated and would not, because of personal reliefs, age exemption, etc., be liable to income tax ,you are entitled to a refund of the money deducted.

Questions and Answers: Tax and Your New Home

• *Do you need to tell Revenue if you buy a house?*

Yes – you should inform your district office as soon as possible so that correspondence can be sent to your new address.

• *Can you claim tax relief on your mortgage?*

Yes – if the house is situated in Ireland, Northern Ireland or Great Britain and is used as your sole or main residence.

• *What is a 'sole or main residence'?*

A sole or main residence is the residence which is your home for the greater part of the time. It does not have to be owned by you, e.g. your parents' residence may also be your sole or main residence, if you normally live there.

• *If you intend to let part of your house to help with the mortgage repayments, what tax relief can you claim against your personal income tax and against the rental income?*

In this situation, part of the mortgage interest may be claimed as a normal interest credit against your personal income tax. However, the balance of the interest may not be claimed as a rental deduction. The mortgage interest applicable to the let part of the house will be determined on a just and reasonable basis. For example, the apportionment of the interest may be by reference to the number of rooms let.

• *Does residence only mean a house?*

No. It also includes a flat; any garden or grounds of an ornamental nature which are used along with the house or flat; and a mobile home/caravan – provided it is on a permanent site, is of a reasonable size to fulfil the requirements of use as a permanent residence, has electricity and other services supplied to it, and is immobilised (i.e. wheels removed and mounted on blocks).

• *Can you claim tax relief on a loan for home improvements?*

Yes. You can claim tax relief on a loan used by you to purchase, repair, develop or improve your sole or main residence or to pay off another loan (or loans) used for that purpose.

• *What can the loan be used for?*

The loan can be used for most work done on your sole or main residence except for money spent on furniture or removable fittings (e.g. light fittings, curtains, carpets, etc.). Examples of what the loan may be used for are:

• Extensions, purchase/construction of garage, garden shed, greenhouse, etc.
• Construction of driveway, path, etc.
• Conversions, painting and decorating.
• Installing central heating.
• Rewiring or replumbing (including bathroom suites).
• Replacing or installing windows.
• Purchase and/or installation of burglar/fire alarms.

• Purchase and installation of bedroom and kitchen units which are affixed to and become part of the building.
• Treatment for damp, dry rot, woodworm, etc.
• Landscaping gardens (including garden walls).
• Contributions to group water and sewerage schemes.

• *How much tax relief will you get?*
Tax relief is granted on the amount of the interest paid, at the standard rate subject to the overall limits. You can find these overall limits in Revenue Leaflet IT60, 'Home Loan Interest Relief' – 2000/2001 onwards. Special provisions apply for first time buyers. The period for which relief is available is 7 years.

• *How can you claim the relief?*
Before 1 January 2002, tax relief for home mortgage interest was given through the tax system. Now, it is granted at source. This means that your mortgage lender gives you the benefit of the tax relief element on the mortgage interest on behalf of the Revenue Commissioners.

Your mortgage repayment is reduced by the amount of the tax relief. Your lender in turn claims this amount from the Revenue. Any future adjustments in the tax relief (for example, arising from changes in interest rates) will be made automatically by the lender on behalf of the Revenue. It is not necessary to claim mortgage interest relief in the annual tax return, and it no longer appears on your Notice of Tax Credits. Borrowers who are taking out new mortgages must complete a TRS1 form. Your lender will supply you with this form. Forms can also be obtained from the TRS Section, Collector-Generals, Sarsfield House, Francis Street, Limerick.

If you wish to pursue the matter yourself, you can also get details from the Revenue Leaflet TRS 'Mortgage Interest Tax Relief at Source'.

• *If you sell your house, will you have to pay capital gains tax?*
No. If the house (including grounds of up to one acre) has been occupied as your sole or main residence throughout your period of ownership you will be exempt from capital gains tax on the sale.

• *What happens if you had let part of the house or used part of the house for business purposes?*
Full exemption may not be due if only part of the house has been used as your residence. In this case an apportionment will be made to arrive at the exempt portion of the total gain and you will have to pay capital gains tax on the balance.

• *What happens if your property has 'development value'?*
Where your property has development value, i.e. if it is sold for a price higher than its normal current use value, then the relief from capital gains tax as outlined above is confined to what it would be if the property did not have development value.

Personal Reliefs and Exemptions

Do not despair. Ireland offers a series of personal reliefs and exemptions to deal with specific situations and encourage certain activities.

For example, if you are a writer, sculptor, painter, or practise one of the arts you may be eligible for the artist's exemption; see p.229.

Other areas covered for exemptions include business expansion schemes, car expenses, deposit interest retentions tax (DIRT) repayments, donations/deeds of covenant (usually to charities), exemption and marginal relief, foreign earnings deduction, leasing farm land, lump sum payments, retirement annuities, seaside resort relief, seed capital, tuition fees, trade union subscriptions, trans border workers, urban renewal relief, and tax credits and reliefs for over 65s.

If you feel that any of the above might apply to you, you will have little difficulty in getting information; ask for information leaflet IT1, 'Tax Credits, Reliefs and Rates'. Here are more details on a few of the most common reliefs, exemptions and credits.

Note: Capital acquisitions tax, capital gains tax and VAT exemptions are covered in the previous section under each tax.

Age Credit

The age credit is available when either you or your spouse reach 65 years of age at any time during the tax year. You should contact Revenue when you reach that age, by telephoning your regional Revenue LoCall number (see p.193).

Blind Person's Tax Credit

The blind person's tax credit is available if you are registered as blind. This credit is also due for your spouse if he/she is registered as blind. Ask for information leaflet IT35, 'Blind Person's Tax Credits and Reliefs' – large print.

Deeds of Covenant

Tax relief of up to 5 per cent of the covenantor's total income is available on a deed of covenant in favour of a person aged 65 or over. Unrestricted tax relief can be claimed on covenants in favour of permanently incapacitated adults.

Ask for information leaflet IT7, 'Covenants to Individuals'.

Dependent Relative Tax Credit

Available if you maintain at your own expense:

- **A son or daughter who lives with you and on whom you depend because of old age or infirmity.**
- **A widowed father or mother of yourself or your spouse regardless of the state of his/her health.**
- **A relative, including a relative of your spouse, who is unable, due to old age or infirmity, to maintain himself/herself.**

Ask for information leaflet IT46, 'Dependent Relative Tax Credit'.

Allowance for Employing a Carer

If you, your spouse or a relative are incapacitated and you employ someone to care for the incapacitated person, you can claim for the cost of the employment. Ask for leaflet IT47, 'Incapacitated Person – Allowance for Employing a Carer'.

Low Income Exemption

Neither you nor your spouse need to pay tax if your total income is less than a certain limit. The income limits vary depending on your age and marital status. Marginal relief is available when your income is slightly over the limit.

Rent Relief

Rent relief is available, up to a maximum amount, in respect of rent paid for private rented accommodation. The upper limits are given in leaflet IT1, 'Tax Credits, Reliefs'. Ask for form Rent 1.

Health Expenses

Ireland's health system is not as broad as the NHS; you will have to pay for many medical and dental services unless you are eligible for a means-tested medical card (*see* pp.238–42). Tax relief may however be claimed in respect of qualifying unreimbursed (i.e. after VHI, BUPA, Health Board or compensation refunds) medical and non-routine dental or ophthalmic expenses incurred by a taxpayer and/or his/her dependants.

The first €125 per person does not qualify for relief. Where several dependants are the subject of a claim, the overall restriction is €250 for a group.

You, as an individual, may claim tax relief in respect of health expenses incurred by yourself, your spouse, your child or any other child, who for the year of the claim, is in your custody and maintained at your expense and under 18

Revenue Commissioners: LoCall Regional Contact Numbers

If you need further information or clarification on any point, telephone your regional office whose LoCall number is listed below. All calls are charged at local rates. A list of specific county tax offices and their contact details is given on pp.282–6.

- **Border Midlands Region, t** 1890 777 425
  Cavan, Monaghan, Donegal, Mayo, Galway, Leitrim, Longford, Louth, Offaly, Roscommon, Sligo, Westmeath.

- **Dublin Region, t** 1890 333 425
  Dublin (City and County).

- **East and Southeast Region, t** 1890 444 425
  Carlow, Kildare, Kilkenny, Laois, Meath, Tipperary, Waterford, Wexford, Wicklow.

- **Southwest Region, t** 1890 222 425
  Clare, Cork, Kerry, Limerick.

years of age, or if over 18 years of age, is receiving full-time education.You may claim for a relative who is aged 65 years (or over) or who is permanently incapacitated. Ask for information leaflet IT6, 'Medical Expenses Relief'.

Qualifying health expenses include:

- **Certain costs of doctor/consultant fees, dentist fees.**
- **Diagnostic procedures carried out on the advice of a practitioner.**
- **Drugs or medicines prescribed by a doctor.**
- **The supply, maintenance or repair of any medical, surgical, dental or nursing appliance used on the advice of a practitioner.**
- **Maintenance/treatment in an approved hospital or approved nursing home.**
- **Transport by ambulance.**
- **Reasonable travelling and accommodation expenses if qualifying health care is only available outside Ireland.**
- **Home/special nursing – in certain circumstances.**
- **Educational psychological assessments and speech and language therapy services for children, applicable for 2001 and subsequent years.**

Qualifying **dental treatment** includes: crowns, veneers, tip-replacing, gold inlays, endodontics (root canal treatment), periodontal treatment, orthodontic treatment, surgical extraction of impacted wisdom teeth, bridge work, dental implant treatment. From 2004 tax relief at the standard rate of tax applies to premiums paid for dental insurance to an authorised insurer for non-routine dental treatment where the policy is for dental insurance only.

The following do not qualify for tax relief:

- **Routine ophthalmic care – i.e. sight testing, spectacles, contact lenses.**
- **Routine dental care – i.e. extraction, scaling, filling of teeth, dentures.**

Note: Receipts, although not submitted, must be retained for at least 6 years. LoCall Number for ordering Forms Med1: **t** 1890 30 67 06.

Tax Planning Generally

Do it and do it as soon as possible. Every day you delay will make it more difficult to get the results you are looking for.

There are many possibilities for tax planning for someone moving to Ireland. Some points worth considering are:

- **Time your departure from UK to get the best out of the UK tax system.**
- **Arrange your affairs so that there is a gap between leaving UK (for tax purposes) and becoming resident in Ireland. That gap can be used to make all sorts of beneficial changes to the structure of your finances.**

> ### Tax Clearance Certificate
>
> It is possible that, in your new home, you will be looking for a government grant or subsidy from a public authority, even possibly a contract or a licence. If this is of a value of €6,500 or more within any twelve-month period, you may be required to produce a tax clearance certificate. This is a written confirmation from the Revenue that your tax affairs are in order as the date of issue of the certificate. In some instances, a certificate may be issued to a customer who has tax arrears provided such arrears are covered by an instalment arrangement that has been agreed with the Revenue.

- Think, in particular, about when to make any capital gain if you are selling your business or other assets in the UK.

- Consider disposing of some of your assets as free gifts. You will not have to pay wealth tax on the value given away and the recipients will generally not have to pay either gift or inheritance tax on the gift.

Inheritance

Irish Inheritance Rules

Irish inheritance rules are based on the Irish Succession Act of 1965. The fact that this Act was needed to repeal English and British statutes beginning with the Curtesy Act of 1226 in the reign of Henry III and ending with the Wills (Soldiers and Sailors) 1918 only goes to show how closely Irish and English law are linked. The language, the general terms and procedures of succession law are almost identical to UK law and will be familiar, if not to you, certainly to your UK solicitor.

Who Gets What under Irish Law?

Before we embark on this section, we must bear one principle in mind. Under common law, it is usual that movable property – cash, shares, jewels, furniture, etc. – passes in accordance with the law of the country in which you are domiciled and that immovable property – land, houses, etc. – passes according to the law of the country in which it is situated. Until further notice, we shall, generally speaking, be dealing with property which is subject to the law of the country in which you are domiciled.

In order to answer this question, we must remember that what lawyers call the 'process of succession' is either testamentary or intestate. In other words, if you make a will, your estate will be divided out in accordance with the requirements of the will. If you die 'intestate', i.e. you have not made a will, your estate will be passed on in accordance with the provisions of the Succession Act, 1965.

You and Your Will

If this book can give you one sound piece of advice, it is that you should make a will, not just because you are considering moving to Ireland but because everyone with any means or assets should make a will. You will save a lot of people a lot of trouble after you have gone and there is no point in protesting that you don't have any means. Most people own more bits and pieces and have more assets than they realise (see 'Investments', p.202).

A will does not have to be detailed. It can be short and sweet and, however disappointed some of your loved ones may be, with two exceptions there is little they can do about it.

Making a will does not bind you forever. As long as you are alive you can alter or revoke it and make a new one. By making a will, you are making things easier for your spouse, your children or your friends. You can make sure that your affairs will be handled properly by appointing trustworthy executors. You avoid having your heirs' inheritance being eaten up by legal disputes. If there are personal belongings that for sentimental reasons you would like different people to have, you can ensure that they get them. You can have the peace of mind of knowing that what will happen to your property after your death is what you want. Failure to make a will subjects your estate to the often hard rules of intestacy and to certain assumptions in favour of a spouse or children or even distant relations which were not at all what you would have in mind.

After all, making a will is not such a big deal. Anyone who is 18 years of age, or, if under 18, is or has been married and is of sound disposing mind, can legally make a will. 'Sound disposing mind' merely means that you understand that a document is being made that disposes of assets on death, that you are capable of knowing the nature and extent of your estate (see below), and that you are able to consider those persons who might be expected to benefit from your estate and decide whether or not to benefit them.

A lawyer, when asked when a person should make a will, replied that it would be prudent to so on reaching any of the following stages in life:

- **Getting married.**
- **Going abroad.**
- **Getting divorced or separated.**
- **Buying a house.**
- **Having children.**
- **Inheriting property (or winning the Lottery!).**
- **Retiring, getting older or suffering illness.**
- **Now!**

The same language is used in Ireland as in the UK when talking about succession matters. 'Estate' is a case in point. Your *estate* simply means whatever assets (e.g. bank accounts, stocks and shares, house, land, livestock, jewellery, car, etc.) can be passed on to beneficiaries following your death.

Making a Will

For your will to be valid, you must satisfy the criteria mentioned above.

Your will must be in writing and signed at the foot or at the end of it (a) by you or (b) by some person in your presence and (c) by your direction. The signature must be made or acknowledged by you in the presence of each of two or more witnesses, present at the same time, and each witness must attest your signature by his or her signature in your presence. No form of attestation is necessary, nor is it necessary for the witnesses to sign in the presence of each other. The rule about the position of your signature is satisfied as long as it is clear that you intended to show by your signature that what is written down is your will.

Warning – any gift to either of the witnesses or their spouses is void.

Revocation of a Will

If you marry after making your will, this makes it void except when you have made the will in contemplation of marriage (whether or not this is expressly stated in the will). Apart from this, no will, or any part of a will, is revoked except:

- **by another will or codicil (an appendix added to a will) executed as described above.**

- **by some writing declaring an intention to revoke it and executed in the manner in which a will must be executed.**

- **if you burn, tear up or destroy your old will.**

- **if someone does this in your presence on your orders with the intention of revoking it.**

Simultaneous Deaths and Interpretation of Wills

The Irish Act keeps the common law presumption that if two or more people die in circumstances rendering it uncertain which of them survived the other or others, for the purpose of the distribution of the estate of any of them, they are deemed to have died simultaneously.

As regards the 'construction' of a will (the interpretation of it by a court), as a general principle, subject to limited exceptions, only the words of the will should be considered in determining your intention. In other words, nobody can come forward and claim that, where you wrote 'black', you really meant 'white'. Any evidence like this will only be allowed if it not only shows your intention but also *explains any contradiction* in your will. If there is any difficulty in interpreting your intentions, the reading which permits a bequest to be operative is the one which will be preferred.

This is what is good about making a will. With only two exceptions, outlined below, your property goes to the person or persons to whom you have decided to leave it.

Rights of Surviving Spouse

If you have no children and leave a spouse, your spouse has a right to half your estate even though you have made other provisions in your will.

If you leave a spouse and children, the surviving spouse has a right to one-third of your estate (the 'legal right'). To avoid this possibility, your future spouse can renounce his or her legal right in a pre-nuptial agreement made in writing or he or she can renounce the right in writing after the wedding and while you are still alive.

The surviving husband or wife must choose which to take: the legal right or whatever rights have been given by the will itself. If he or she makes no choice, then he or she takes the rights under the will, even if they amount to less. Why should any spouse take this course? It may be that the will gives property to him or her, for example, a pleasant holiday home in Ireland, which he or she would not automatically get if the estate had to be sold in order to meet the legal rights of the spouse and the children.

If, before 1 January 1967, you have made permanent provision for your spouse, whether by way of a contract or otherwise, all property which is included under this provision (other than periodical payments for his or her maintenance) are regarded as given in or towards satisfaction of the legal right and their value is deducted from the legal right. Accordingly, if they are equal to or greater than one-third of your estate, the spouse is not entitled to take any share as a legal right. If their value is less than the legal right, your spouse is only entitled to receive so much of your estate as, when added to the value of the property, is sufficient to make up the full amount of his or her share.

Rights of Children

No matter what you write in your will, any of your children will have the right to apply to the court for an order granting such provision as the court thinks just, out of your estate, where the court is of opinion that you failed in your 'moral duty' to make provision for him or her in accordance with your means.

The court must consider the application from the point of view of a 'prudent and just' parent, taking into account the position of each of your children and any other circumstance which the court may consider of assistance in arriving at a decision that will be as fair as possible to the child to whom the application relates and to the other children. This rule has given rise to a lot of litigation, often by widows on behalf of minor children. On the other hand, if your son is aged 55 and is a dot.com millionaire, it is to be imagined that the court will not look too favourably on such an application. The Supreme Court in Ireland has held that it is not enough to establish that the provision made for a child was not as great as it might have been or not as generous as the bequests to other children or beneficiaries. What counts is a positive failure in moral duty.

If it can be shown that, during your lifetime, the financial support which you gave to your children was indicative of concerned assistance to all the members of your family and that you had a good relationship with them, the court will be very reluctant to vary the dispositions of your will. If, however, there was marked hostility between yourself and one particular child, the court might well take a different view.

It is felt that this judgement was pronounced to prevent a spate of applications by 'avaricious and frivolous' children.

Since 1987, children whose parents were not married to each other have a right to apply to the court under this provision of the Succession Act, 1965.

What If I Don't Make a Will? (Intestacy)

If you die intestate, i.e. you have not made a will, your estate, after the payment of all expenses, debts and liabilities and any legal right properly payable, will pass to your heirs in the following manner:

- **If you leave a spouse and no children, your spouse takes the whole estate.**
- **If you leave a spouse and children, your spouse takes two-thirds and the children one-third.**
- **If there are children but your spouse is dead, the children inherit all.**
- **If you leave no spouse or children, your parents take equal shares.**
- **If only one parent outlives you, he or she inherits everything.**
- **If both parents are dead, your brothers and sisters and their children inherit.**
- **If there is none of the above in existence, your estate will be distributed in equal shares among your next-of-kin.**
- **If no next-of-kin can be found, the State takes the estate as the ultimate intestate successor.**

The Irish rules for identifying next-of-kin are the same as those in the UK.

The court has the power to make further orders in relation to the administration of your estate as may appear to it just and equitable.

Other Issues and Rules Relating to Inheritance

The Dwelling

Subject to certain limitations, your surviving spouse can require the personal representatives (*see* p.201) to appropriate the dwelling in which he or she was ordinarily resident in satisfaction of his or her share.

Unworthiness to Succeed and Disinheritance

A sane person who has been found guilty of murdering or attempting to murder you or of your manslaughter cannot take any share in your estate except when the will has been made in the interval *between* the commission of the crime and your death and, possibly, when it is understood that you were aware of his or her guilt.

Desertion

If your spouse has deserted you more than at least two years before your death, he or she is precluded from taking any share in your estate as a legal right or on intestacy.

If your spouse has been found guilty of an offence punishable by a maximum period of at least two years' imprisonment or by a more severe penalty, against you, or against your new or former spouse or your child (including an adopted child or anyone to whom you were *in loco parentis* at the time of the offence), he or she may not take any share in your estate.

Immovables and Movables

It is a long-established rule that succession to movable property in the case of intestacy is determined by the law of the country in which the testator is domiciled at the time of death and that succession to immovable property is determined by the law of country in which the immovable property is situated. This is also the legal position in the UK.

If you have retained your English domicile, the fact that your assets must be administered according to Irish law will not detract from this principle, since the duty of an Irish executor will still be to distribute your movable property to the persons entitled under English law.

Over the years in both Ireland and the UK, there have been problems about the formal validity of wills of movables made in a country in which the testator is not domiciled. This has been taken care of in the Succession Act of 1965 which makes a will valid if its form complies with the internal law of a number of possible countries.

The Assets

The assets which will pass under your will or intestacy will be:

- **Assets owned in your sole name.**
- **Assets owned by you but placed in the name of another person for convenience or some similar reason.**
- **Assets placed by you in the joint names of yourself and another person without the intention of benefiting that other person.**

The assets which will pass outside your will or intestacy will be:

- **Assets passing by nomination, e.g. you may have instructed An Post (the Irish equivalent of the Royal Mail) to pay saving certificates on your death to a particular person called the nominee.**

- **Death benefits passing under a life insurance policy or pension scheme where the beneficiaries are particular family members named in the policy or scheme.**

- **Assets in which you had an interest for your life only.**

- **Assets placed by you in the joint names of yourself and another person with the intention of benefiting that other person on your death.**

The Personal Representative

The personal representative is the person who is responsible for finalising your affairs. If you have made a will, it is likely that you have appointed the personal representative by naming him or her the will as your **executor**. If you die intestate, the personal representative will probably have taken on the responsibility simply because he or she is your spouse or one of your next-of-kin.

A personal representative who has not been appointed by will is known as an **administrator**.

Trustee

If your children are very young, you may provide in your will that, for a specified period, your estate is to be held on trust on their behalf by trustees named in the will. You may also create such a trust if you wish the property to be held for the benefit of one person for life and, on the death of that person, to be transferred to another beneficiary. The trustees will take over the management of the trust property only after the estate has been administered by the personal representative. The trust will then continue until the time specified in the will for the ultimate handing over of the property.

Investments

The Need to Do Something

Most of us don't like making investment decisions. They make our head hurt. They make us face up to unpleasant things – like taxes and death. We don't really understand what we are doing, what the options are or what is best. We don't know whom we should trust to give us advice. We know we ought to do something, but it will wait until next week – or maybe the week after. Until then our present arrangements will have to do.

If you are moving to live overseas you *must* review your investments. Your current arrangements are likely to be financially disastrous – and may even be illegal.

What Are You Worth?

Most of us are, in financial terms, worth more than we think. When we come to move abroad and have to think about these things it can come as a shock.

Take a pencil and list your actual and potential assets in the box below.

This will give you an idea as to the amount you are worth now and, just as importantly, what you are likely to be worth in the future. Your investment plans should take into account both figures.

Asset	Value – Local Currency	Value – £s
Current Assets		
Main home		
Holiday home		
Contents of main home		
Contents of holiday home		
Car		
Boat		
Bank accounts		
Other cash-type investments		
Bonds, etc.		
Stocks and shares		
PEPs, Tessas, ISAs		
Value of your business		
Other		
Future Assets		
Value of share options		
Personal/company pension – likely lump sum		
Potential inheritances or other accretions		
Value of endowment mortgages on maturity		
Other		

Who Should Look After your Investments?

You may already have an investment adviser. You may be very happy with his or her quality and the service you have received. The odds are that he or she will have a pretty good idea of the investment picture in Ireland.

Similarly, an Irish investment adviser will most probably be well acquainted with the money market in the UK but may not be so sure about UK tax and inheritance rules that could still have some importance for you.

Choosing an investment adviser competent to deal with your affairs once you are in Ireland should not be difficult. By all means seek guidance from your existing adviser. The financial world, particularly in these islands, can be quite a small one. It is quite possible that he may have contacts in Ireland. Ask for guidance from others who have already made the move. Do some research. Meet the potential candidates. Are you comfortable with them? Do they share your approach to life? Do they have the necessary experience? Is their performance record good? How are they regulated? What security/bonding/guarantees can they offer you? How will they be paid for their work? Fees or commission? If commission, what will that formula mean they are making from you in 'real money' rather than percentages?

Fortunately, there are some excellent and highly professional advisers with good track records. Make sure you choose one.

Where Should You Invest?

For British people the big issue is whether they should keep their sterling investments. Most British people will have investments that are largely sterling-based. Even if they are, for example, a Far Eastern fund they will probably be denominated in sterling and they will pay out dividends, etc. in pounds sterling. You will be spending euro.

As the value of the euro fluctuates against the pound, the value of your investments will go up and down. This, of itself, isn't too important because the value won't crystallise unless you sell. What does matter is that the revenue you generate from those investments (rent, interest, dividends etc.) can fluctuate in value. Take, for example, an investment that generated you £10,000 per annum. Rock steady. Then think of that income in spending power. Your income will vary as the difference between sterling and the euro varies. If the euro increases in value compared to sterling your income will increase, but if it falls then you will have a drop in income. The same result follows when you look on it as sterling changing in value.

Keeping Track of Your Investments

Whatever you decide to do about investments – put them in a trust, appoint investment managers to manage them in your own name or manage them yourself, you should always keep an up-to-date list of your investments and assets *and tell your family where to find it.* Make a file. By all means have a computer file but print off a good old-fashioned paper copy also. Keep it in an obvious place known to your family. Keep it with your will and the deeds to your house, preferably in a safe box with your bank or your solicitor. Also keep in the same place the originals of bank account books, share certificates, etc. or a note of where they are to be found. For a lawyer it is very frustrating – and expensive for the client – when, after a parent's death, the children come in with a suitcase full of correspondence and old cheque books. The lawyer has to go through it all and write to what may well be a series of banks lest there should be £1,000,000 lurking in a forgotten account. There never is, and it wastes a lot of money.

Conclusion

Buying a home in Ireland, whether to use as a holiday home, as an investment or to live in permanently is as safe and as simple (or complicated) as buying one in the UK. Many British people have bought homes in Ireland without major problems. In the last few years; many have seen their properties rise substantially in value. For a trouble-free time you simply need to keep your head and to seek advice from experts who can help you make the four basic decisions:

- **Who should own the property?**
- **What am I going to do about inheritance?**
- **What am I going to do about controlling my potential tax liabilities?**
- **If I am going to live in Ireland, what do I do about my investments?**

If you don't like lawyers, remember that they make far more money out of sorting out messes you get into by not following advice than by giving advice to you in the first place.

Coming Back to England

You are, of course, free to return to England at any stage.

Many people wonder whether they should preserve an escape route by, for example, keeping their old house and letting it out until they are sure of their intentions. People in the know consider this to be a bad idea. The house will be a worry and a distraction. How do you manage it? Are the tenants ruining your lovely home? The house will probably not be ideal for investment purposes and may generate less income than you could get by putting the value elsewhere. It may not be in an area with good capital growth. The income (and capital value in euro terms) will be at the mercy of exchange rate fluctuations. The house might not even suit your requirements if you do return to England. It also encourages you to look backwards instead of forwards. It is usually better to sell up and invest the proceeds elsewhere.

Settling In

07

Once you've signed on the dotted line there are a million new things to start thinking about. You can forget all about estate agents and surveyors, but questions about schools, supermarkets and how to get the phone connected will start to rear their ugly heads. This chapter aims to help you with all these questions and is therefore something of a mixed bag. You'll find practical information about phones, electricity, rubbish collection and all the other things you'll need to know when setting up house. You will also find an overview of the health system, the language, the food, education, politics, employment and a host of other areas. The chapter doesn't pretend to be fully comprehensive but gives plenty of advice about where to look for further information. The **References** chapter at the end of this book also gives suggestions for further reading for anyone interested in investigating politics, literature and other aspects of life in Ireland.

Making the Move

Decide what you are going to bring with you. Furniture and electronic goods are probably going to be comparatively expensive in Ireland so work out what you need and whether the shipping costs are worth it. Some people rent large vans and do it all themselves (remember that ferry travel costs considerably less in the spring, autumn and winter). Rental companies can give you a good idea of the size of the vehicle you'll need. Check what their insurance covers and if your own insurance will cover the move. Professional removal companies may make life much easier if you have lots to move. Ideally your movers should be licensed members of a trade body such as the British Association of Removers or the Irish Road Haulage Association. Call around for a range of quotes before choosing one (a list of companies is given in **References**, 'Removal Companies, pp.281–2) and discuss the estimates for what's involved. Do remember that the cheapest is not necessarily the best.

You should always get a written estimate. Usually estimates are based on the number of items being moved, the shipment size, the services rendered and the

---

Moving Costs

Sample average moving costs from London to Dublin including packing (January 2004):

- **Allens (www.allenremovals.ie; t** (01) 451 3585):
  €1,350 (plus 15% insurance + 21% VAT).

- **Cronin (www.theartofmoving.com; t** (01) 809 7000):
  €1,685 (plus 1% declared goods value insurance at 2.5% plus 21% VAT).

- **Oman (www.oman.ie; t** 1850 668464 (Republic only) or **t** (045) 886300):
  €1,950 to €2,450 (plus 1.5/2% declared goods value insurance plus 21% VAT).

length of travel. They may include conditions to account for possible unknowns at the other end (difficult staircases, for example). Once you know what the costs are likely to be, you can decide what you want to bring and what you will leave behind. Ensure that the mover knows what items are not to be moved on the day.

Moving Checklist A

Here is a checklist of jobs to remember to do before you move:

- **Make an early booking with furniture movers – you may not be able to book your preferred date unless you book well in advance.**

- **Decide whether you will use professional packers. Leaving everything to the movers, including the packing of clothing, linen, crockery and books, might be more convenient for you although doing it yourself will reduce their price for the job. Movers should provide you with crates and special containers should you decide to do your own packing. Some movers offer full unpacking services.**

- **Arrange insurance or check whether your existing policy covers all risks. Note that some companies do not insure goods that haven't been professionally packed. Check that the insurance covers unpacking and transit.**

- **Prepare a time schedule to avoid overlooking things, such as final gas and electricity meter readings.**

- **Give the contractor a list of the items you will be leaving behind and keep a copy so that you can check with the foreman on the day.**

- **Try to let the movers know what's going where on arrival – this will save you having to move large pieces of furniture again.**

Moving Checklist B

As you leave, make sure you bring these things with you:

- **Proof of your last UK address – preferably utility bills; you are generally advised to bring several.**
- **The name and address of your last employer.**
- **Your NHS card.**
- **Your National Insurance number.**
- **Your driver's licence and insurance details.**
- **All documents associated with ownership if you are bringing a car.**
- **Correspondence associated with transferring pensions and entitlements.**
- **Personal documentation, birth certificates, marriage certificate ,etc.**
- **Passports and extra photocopies of them.**

- Children's school records.
- Sheets of British postage stamps – these are very useful if you need to send stamped addressed envelopes to the UK.

The Irish Language

Most of Ireland speaks English. No monolingual Irish-speakers remain. Although Article 8 of the Irish Constitution states firmly that 'The Irish language as the national language is the first official language' and 'The English language is recognised as a second official language', English is spoken universally. The only time you might need a little Irish is in the west of Ireland where many traffic signs tend to be monolingual.

Irish is used as a community language only in the **Gaeltacht** areas along the west coast (*see* p.47), and even there the numbers of Irish-speakers is decreasing partly because more English-speaking families have been moving in and partly because Irish-speaking families continue to move to English. Despite this, Irish is unlikely to die out completely. All Irish schoolchildren must study it until their school-leaving exam and it is required for many civil service jobs (although exemptions are possible). Many Irish-speaking families are scattered across the country especially, oddly enough, in Dublin. Of late there have been optimistic signs for the language including TG4, the Irish-language television

Hiberno-English and Other Dialects

Hiberno-English is the name given to the variety of English used in Ireland. Modern Hiberno-English has many forms and pronunciations that come from Early Modern English (used in the late 16th to early 17th centuries when English settlements in Ireland became more established) and also has many words and expressions directly derived from the Irish language. The word 'oxter' for armpit and 'cog' for cheating in exams are still used in Ireland although they have not been used in standard English since the 1800s. Grammatical particularities include the non-standard use of 'have' and 'do' – 'I'm after doing something' instead of 'I've just done something' and 'I do be here everyday' to express the habitual, both direct translations from the Irish.

Some of the usages and expressions can be traced to different parts of the country but many of these regional differences are disappearing as people become more mobile. It is likely that many of the unique characteristics of Hiberno-English will die out over time as Ireland becomes more globalised and children in schools continue to learn grammar based on Standard English. In recent years, Ulster-Scots, a West Germanic language very similar to English and very closely related to Scots or Lallans (but with no connection to Scottish Gaelic), has seen a revival, perhaps as a reaction to the popularity of Irish among the Nationalist population in Northern Ireland.

station established in 1996, and the popularity of Gaelscoileanna, schools where all subjects are taught in Irish.

If you are interested in learning Irish you should have no difficulty in finding a language class for adults in your area. Údarás na Gaeltachta (the Gaeltacht Authority; **www.udaras.ie**) is the development authority for Gaeltacht areas and Bord na Gaeilge (the Irish Language Board; **www.bnag.ie**) promotes the use of Irish as the vernacular across Ireland.

Shopping

The biggest difference between shopping in Ireland and in Britain is probably the variety on offer. If you are spending sterling you will find most things good value; if you are earning in euro things will be quite expensive, particularly everyday products. Many familiar names are here: M&S, Boots, Tesco, B&Q and almost all the high street fashion names. In fact shopping in the cities, particularly in Dublin, is almost the same as shopping in any British city of the same size. Grafton Street, for example, Dublin's main shopping street, features in rapid succession: McDonald's, Burger King, the Body Shop, Boots, Next, Monsoon and Laura Ashley. Away from the main streets, however, you will find your shopping trips enlivened by many shops you won't have come across before.

In rural areas you'll certainly notice less variety and higher prices for any goods seen as exotic in some way – things like melons and chillies come under this heading. If you like to cook Indian or anything ethnic at home you'll have to stock up on ingredients in the cities. Ireland has very good-value shoes and clothes, especially in lower-end retailers like Penney's and Dunnes. Even shopping in a cutting-edge boutique will cost you less than it would in the UK.

Local Shops

Most villages have a local grocery and newsagents shop that sells most of the basic necessities. The majority of these are now franchised chains (SuperValu,

The Cost of Booze

Wine and other alcohol costs considerably more than in Britain. This is because every bottle is subject to standard government duties and VAT at 20 per cent. These taxes remain the same for cheap and expensive bottles. The excise duty works out at €2.05 per bottle for wine and €4.10 for sparkling wine. When you add VAT prices stack up very quickly and you will find very little for under €10. In fact you are probably better off buying a more expensive bottle of wine, since the taxes will amount to a smaller proportion of the overall price. Many British people (and an increasing number of Irish) bring wine in from Britain or France to avoid these taxes.

The Cost of Living in Ireland

Irish people are forever complaining about how life is getting more and more expensive, and they do have a point. Although inflation is dropping, to an estimated 1.7 per cent in 2004, Ireland's cost of living is still about twice the EU average.

In 2003 Mercer HR Consulting found that Dublin was the 21st most expensive city in the world in a study that measured the cost of 200 everyday items in over 144 cities – up from 73rd the year before! In 2003 Forfás, the national policies advisory board, found that Ireland was the second most expensive country in the euro zone and might overtake Finland as the most expensive in the next couple of years.

Ireland is the most expensive country in the euro zone for basic foodstuffs: things like eggs, mineral water, corn oil, potatoes, onions, tomatoes, oranges, chips, salt and instant soup. Other non-food items – washing powder, razor blades, toothpaste, shampoo, toilet paper, tampons and batteries – are more expensive than in many other EU member states. But it is not all bad news – clothing and footwear, communications and household utilities such as water, electricity and gas are cheaper in Ireland than in most other EU countries. Some goods such as butter, teabags, cornflakes, cola and deodorant are among the least expensive in Europe. Remember also that the statistics are skewed by the high cost of alcohol, cigarettes and eating out here. So if you don't smoke or drink (or drink abstemiously) life should be relatively cheap. Even if you do, the overall cost of living is roughly equal to that in Britain. In Northern Ireland it is considerably cheaper mainly because property costs so much less.

Centra, Spar and Londis are the names you'll see often). Most larger towns also have small family-owned butchers (since the Irish are confirmed carnivores) and often a bakery. Some will also have a vegetable shop. Locally grown vegetables like potatoes, cabbage, onions and carrots shouldn't be expensive but often are. Imported fruit and vegetables can be very expensive; it is well worth shopping around, as they can be cheaper in another shop just around the corner. If you are lucky you might have some of the wonderful farmhouse cheese producers or organic farmers for which Ireland is famed selling produce locally.

Supermarkets

The biggest supermarkets in Ireland are Tesco, Dunnes Stores and Superquinn. Dunnes Stores is an Irish family-owned, mass-market retailer in food, clothing and housewares. Superquinn is another Irish-owned chain based mainly in Dublin but with some supermarkets dotted around the country. Tesco is the largest supermarket chain with about 80 stores nationwide. Marks & Spencer has several stores in Dublin and Belfast and you will find branches of Sainsbury

The Plastic Bag Tax

It may sound bizarre but it is been a resounding success. In March 2002 the Irish Government introduced a 15-cent environmental tax on plastic bags in supermarkets and other shops. Within a couple of months the use of plastic bags had dropped by 95 per cent and the remnants of bags littering the countryside and floating in seas and rivers had dropped to almost nothing. So expect to pay 15 cents per bag when you are shopping or else bring your own. The tax is spent on environmental projects.

in Northern Ireland. The German discount supermarkets Aldi and Lidl are also making inroads into Ireland and can be found in many towns.

The Irish government protects smaller shops and retailers with a law that doesn't permit supermarkets or other retail units with a floor area above 3,500 square metres in Dublin (and 3,000 square metres elsewhere in Ireland). This means that you won't find huge hypermarkets and superstores in Ireland. Incidentally it also means that IKEA doesn't have an Irish presence – much to the chagrin of those trying to furnish houses cheaply. IKEA has said that they'll open a store somewhere off the M50 in Dublin if this cap is lifted at any stage.

Speciality Shops and Markets

Small delicatessens and specialty shops are gaining a foothold all over the country. Morton's, a very upmarket supermarket in Ranelagh, Dublin, has just opened its first branch in Salthill in Galway citing demand from prosperous residents. Wholefood and healthfood shops are also springing up across rural Ireland. These vary widely; some sell mainly supplements, others stock a wide variety of goods – from organic vegetables to biodegradable cleaning products. Along with the traditional street markets (one of the most famous is Moore Street in Dublin) you will find newer farmers' markets in many towns (and read about the famous English Market in Cork in **Profiles of the Regions**, 'Cork', p.40). The website **www.irelandmarkets.com** gives a list of markets countrywide.

Metric or Imperial?

Although Ireland officially went metric almost 30 years ago, in practice the old measurements have not completely died out. You can ask for a pound of sausages and the butcher will give you a half-kilo or so of them; many food-stuffs have measurement in pounds *and* kilos on the packet; beer is always sold by the pint or half-pint – although milk is always in litres. Metric is the only form of measurement taught in schools, so the younger generation tends to use it more. You will notice that, unlike in Britain, nobody feels terribly strongly about the issue either way so it is likely that, as EU regulations bite, metric will become more and more usual.

Home Utilities and Services

Irish houses are often not very well insulated, perhaps because the climate is quite mild year-round, and damp can be a problem. Formerly many homes were heated with wood or turf-burning ranges and open fires. Today most homes are centrally heated and use electricity, gas or oil to run the system. Running costs vary depending on the modernity of your systems and how well your house is insulated; gas is usually the cheapest. Unfortunately it is not available country-wide. Sustainable Energy Ireland publishes fuel cost comparisons for various fuels and you can access this on their website (**www.irish-energy.ie**). Many houses have open fires or solid fuel stoves in addition to central heating. Bord na Mona (the Irish Turf Board) supplies coal and peat briquettes to homes, and most areas also have a local fuel supplier who will deliver.

Electricity

The **Electricity Supply Board (ESB)** network (**www.esb.ie**, **t** 1850 372 372 in Ireland only) owns and operates the electricity network in the Republic of Ireland. It is responsible to all customers for connection to the network. The ESB was formerly a monopoly supplier – since deregulation of the market the ESB is in theory just one among many other suppliers and has been split into Networks and Customer Supply. Many industrial and commercial companies use alternative suppliers but as a domestic customer your only option is still the ESB. The ESB is responsible for supply, meter readings, emergency reconnections and so on. They also run the Shop Electric chain of shops nationwide where you can buy appliances and pay for them in instalments via your electricity bill. The ESB offers cheaper rates for appliances and heating that run overnight.

You might need an enhanced supply if you plan to run everything on electricity (showers, under floor heating, and so on). It is a good idea to check with the company when applying for a connection. Many Irish houses use electric night storage heating. Its advantages are that it is very easy to install and is often much less intrusive than other forms of central heating in older houses. However, electricity is a relatively expensive heating method and you might be better off considering other options if you wish to cut costs.

Electricity Basics

Mains electricity is supplied at 220 volts. Plugs are flat with three pins. All appliances, no matter how small, must have a three-pin fused plug for connection to the mains. The fuse in the plug should be rated to suit the appliance; a 3-amp fuse is used for low power appliances such as razors and computers; a 5-amp fuse is used for appliances up to 1 kilowatt; and a 13-amp fuse is used for all other appliances including hair dryers, kettles and travel irons.

Once you are hooked up to the grid you generally get **bills** every two months. These include a small standing charge and VAT (currently 13.5 per cent). You can pay bills in a variety of ways – by direct debit, cheque, in banks, post offices or ESB shops and through many ATM machines. Note that many banks only accept payments from their own customers.

Getting Connected to Electricity

In most cases you'll simply arrange to transfer the account from the previous owner's name into yours, but if the house is new or if the electricity has been off for some time you'll have some extra work to do.

New Houses

If you are building a new house on a site you must apply to the ESB for a connection. Application forms are available from the ESB Networks office or by calling **t** 1850 372 757. You need to supply a site location map and site plan with your application. After you have sent your form to the ESB you will receive a quotation with costs and the timescale for connection. ESB Networks will include the actual costs of erecting poles and installing cables to bring a supply to your home, so bear this in mind if you are building somewhere very remote. You'll also need a Certificate of Completion recognised by the Electro-Technical Council of Ireland (ETCI).

House with no Electricity (6 months to 2 years)

You must get the house checked by an approved electrical contractor, and you also have to get an ETCI Certificate of Completion before getting reconnected.

House with no Electricity (over 2 years)

You will have to apply for a new connection using the standard application form (contact the ESB networks office for one).

Gas

Bord Gáis (the Gas Bord; **www.bge.ie**) manages the gas supply in Ireland. **Natural gas** (a colourless non-polluting fossil fuel) is piped from Irish and North Sea gas fields to homes and industries in various parts of the country. At present all the main cities have piped gas supply and a new pipeline from Dublin to Galway linking Enfield, Mullingar, Tullamore, Athlone and Ballinasloe to the network is being completed. If you don't have a direct connection to the pipeline you can cook with a **butane gas** cylinder (obtainable from local suppliers, shops and hardware stores). Many houses run central heating from an outdoor liquefied petroleum gas (LPG) tank that is refilled. **Flogas** (**www.flogas.ie**) is the main LPG supplier in the Republic (others use oil-fired central heating). Bord Gáis estimates that the typical cost of running heating, hot water and cooking using natural gas is €14 per week (based on a typical annual usage of 22,000 kilowatt hours).

Getting Connected to Mains Gas

If your house was previously connected to a gas pipeline it is a simple matter to change over the account. If you need a new connection and live within 15 metres of a gas main the connection service is free, but if you live further than 15 metres you will have to contribute to the costs of bringing the pipe to your home. The standard contribution for domestic houses is €250 for a 15-metre service and €73.78 per metre for every metre over and above 15 metres (both include VAT at 13.5 per cent).

Water

We reviewed many watery issues in **Selecting a Property**, 'Water and Waste', p.115. Key things to remember are that although there are no water charges in Ireland, you may be liable for some charges if you are connected to a group water scheme (where a community creates its own piped water supply).

Telephone

Although in theory the telephone system has been completely deregulated, in practice most people still use **Eircom** (**www.eircom.ie**), the main Irish fixed line provider and formerly the monopoly operator. This is probably because Eircom is responsible for the general land network and the installation of new phone lines. If you use another provider you still have to pay a monthly line rental fee to Eircom and pay for your calls separately. Irish people are accustomed to one phone bill and have been reluctant to switch to two – so far only 200,000 people use services provided by rivals to Eircom.

Before choosing a provider, think about your usage patterns and investigate offers from Eircom and competitors to see which suits you best. You might like to know that the Consumer's Association of Ireland found that Eircom was the second most expensive of 13 fixed-line operators it surveyed and that line rentals in Ireland are the highest in the EU (at around €290 a year) following

Changing Telephone Company?

ComReg suggests that before changing to an alternative telephone company you should ask:

- for a printed price list.
- if the company has a minimum chargefor each call or a set-up charge.
- how the company charges for calls – per second or per minute.
- if there are any additional charges such as connection fees.
- what the peak and off-peak times are.
- how long it will take to change over.
- if you need to sign up for a set time period.
- if you have to spend a set minimum amount per month.
- if there are any special discounts available.

a hike by Eircom at the start of 2004. If you make a lot of international calls, an alternative provider will probably save you money. The competition includes **Esat BT** (**www.esatbt.ie**), **Smart** (**www.smarttelecom.ie**), **Cinergi** (**www. cinergi.ie**), **Swiftcall** (**www.swiftcall.ie**) and a horde of others. A list of the providers is given in the consumer's section of the Commission for Communications Regulation (**www.comreg.ie**). If you plan to use one of the alternatives, make sure that their prices suit your call usage pattern and check any other charges that may apply – things like service connection fees, call set-up fees and extra charges for itemised bills or call barring (*see* the list of questions to ask in the box 'Changing Telephone Company?', below). You could also use a telephone card (available in most newsagents) to save money on long-distance calls.

Getting Connected

If the house you move into already has a telephone in place, you may just need to transfer it into your name. If there is no telephone or the previous occupant has taken the account (and number) with them, you'll have to pay a fee of €127 for installation. These days Eircom are good at installing phones and can generally do it within a week. Unless you request otherwise, your name and number will be published in the local telephone directory (this is supplied free to you along with a *Golden Pages* (the Irish equivalent of *Yellow Pages*), but if you want telephone directories for other areas you'll have to pay extra).

The Internet

Eircom.net (**www.eircom.net**) is the main Internet supplier, and Esat BT and NTL also provide access.

Your options are:

- A free service where you pay per call for dial-up connections and pay a substantial amount for a technical helpline.
- A similar subscription service where calls and technical help cost less but you pay a monthly fee.
- A dial-up flat-rate Internet package (of for instance 10 or 15 hours).
- An always-on broadband package.

There is a distinct digital divide between the Dublin area, which is typically well served by broadband suppliers, and regional areas where often little or no broadband is available – although Eircom have ambitious plans to make broadband available countrywide. You will need to contact Eircom.net or one of the other suppliers to see whether your line will support broadband services. At present about 30,000 people subscribe to flat-rate Internet packages. Broadband take-up is quite poor, probably because rental costs are amongst the highest in the EU.

Mobile Telephones

Mobile telephones have taken off in Ireland in a very big way – nearly everyone (83 per cent of the population) has one. The Irish system runs on the digital GSM network and coverage is pretty good countrywide, although rural areas tend to have the occasional gap. Try and find out what network works best in your area before deciding on a provider. Older houses with thick walls also deflect signals.

Three mobile networks operate in Ireland. Two of these will be familiar to you: **O2** (**www.o2.ie**), owned by BT, and **Vodafone** (**www.vodafone.ie**); there is also **Meteor** (**www.meteor.ie**). O2 and Vodafone are by far the biggest with 96 per cent of the market between them, and Meteor is a relative newcomer. The prefixes for each company are 086, 087 and 085, respectively, although you can now keep your old number and prefix if you change from one network provider to another. It won't surprise you to learn that tariffs are more expensive than in the rest of Europe – although the providers vociferously argue that prices only seem higher because Irish people use their phones more than other Europeans. The Irish do talk a lot but it is hard to argue that they talk much more than the Italians or the Spanish and the enormous profits made by Vodafone and O2 in Ireland would also seem to contradict this (combined pre-tax profits of over €300 million in 2003 alone).

You have the option of a pay-monthly contract (usually for a 12-month period) with different plans depending on level of use, or a prepaid system (usually called pay-as-you-go) where you pay in advance for calls and can't make more after the money has run out. As in Britain you generally get a free or very cheap phone with a monthly contract – if you want an upmarket lightweight phone with lots of extras it will naturally cost more. If you intend to use the phone to make frequent calls the pay monthly contracts make far more sense – prepaid options are prohibitively expensive, especially if you use your telephone during the day. However, if you plan to use the phone mainly to receive calls, the prepaid option may work for you.

You can pick up a phone in many outlets across the country and they can generally be activated the same day. You will need identification and a utility bill if you wish to purchase a pay-monthly calling plan. Some companies also require you to set up a direct debit to pay the bill if you have not owned a mobile telephone in Ireland before. Staff selling the telephones often don't give very good advice about the best calling plan for you, and comparing the different plans can be fiendishly complicated. It is generally best to choose a plan that seems to be a bit more than you think you'll need.

Television

Once upon a time, not so long ago, most households in Ireland only had access to two channels – RTÉ1 and 2 – via a simple aerial. Later many Dublin homes got access to a range of British channels via cable. Now almost everybody can access multi-channel television via cable, **Multipoint Microwave Distribution System (MMDS)** – a system that uses a rooftop mini-dish to decode low-power microwave signals – or digital satellite. **NTL Ireland (www.ntl.com/locales/ie/)**, **Chorus (www.chorus.ie**; the name may change since the company was in financial difficulties in early 2004) and a couple of regional operators supply cable and MMDS. **Sky Digital** supplies digital satellite television. Perhaps because people are used to paying extra for TV channels, Ireland outstrips the UK for *per capita* satellite TV uptake.

Your options depend on how much television you want to watch and how much you want to pay – starting with a simple rooftop aerial, which gives you free access to the four Irish channels RTÉ1, Network 2, TV3 and TG4 (your licence

Television Licences

Every home or business with a television set (even if it is for watching videos) must also have a current TV licence. An Post collects fees and also maintains a database with records of who's paid and who hasn't (99 per cent of Irish households have a television). TV licence inspectors visit regularly and you will be found out if you don't have a licence. The cost is €152 in 2004. You can pay for your licence:

- directly in post offices with cash, cheque, TV savings stamps or Laser card (though not all post offices take Laser).
- by credit or Laser card on LoCall, **t** 1890 228528.
- by annual direct debit from your bank current or credit card account/
- on the web at **www.billpay.ie** (for renewals only) and by post.

fee pays for these). If you live in the city you will probably have cable – basic or digital. The price depends on what package you choose but you'll generally have to pay a hefty installation fee in addition to a monthly bill. In rural areas with no cable access you can choose between digital satellite or MMDS. You can access a range of free-to-air channels via digital satellite but you will need to pay for the set-up box and dish to be installed. If you are using MMDS you will have to pay for any channels you receive. Generally speaking, if you want a wide range of channels including all the British ones you will need to subscribe and pay a monthly fee for your chosen package. For example NTL's basic cable package gives you all the Irish and British channels along with CNBC, the Discovery Channel, MTV and so on. You can add movies, sports and other options on for an extra fee. In rural areas it is a good idea to check with your neighbours what the reception is like and what supplier they would recommend.

Rubbish Collection

Ireland's waste management record is distinctly patchy. The Environmental Protection Agency (EPA) estimates that in 2001 the average individual was producing 35 per cent more waste than in 1995. At 13.5 per cent, the recycling rate is well below that in other EU countries, and 90 per cent of household and commercial waste is consigned to landfill, compared with 60 per cent else-where. Protests against the siting of incinerators and landfill sites are often in the news. Local authorities tend to take different approaches to waste; collec-tion charges vary widely depending on where you live, from €270 up to €460 per year; and some authorities actively encourage recycling while others don't.

In cities collection takes place once a week on a designated day, although in some parts of the country it is only once a fortnight. You are generally supplied with a wheelie bin, which can't be overfilled, or your rubbish won't be collected. Some authorities sell bin tags and you must tag your bag of rubbish to ensure collection. Most local authorities will also supply you with a composting bin for a small fee. Some authorities supply different coloured bins for kerbside paper and other types of rubbish collection but in most cases you will have to bring bottles, cans, paper and other recyclable waste to a bring centre or civic amenity centre. Contact **Repak** (**www.repak.ie**) or your local authority to find out where your nearest bring centre is. If you have lots of rubbish to dispose of or are clearing out a house, you will probably need to hire a skip.

Bin Tax Battles

Rubbish collection used to be free (or at least was funded from general income taxes and other government revenue), but over the last 20 years direct payment for rubbish collection has been introduced all around Ireland by local authorities. This 'bin tax' has met with strenuous opposition in many areas with anti-bin tax protestors jailed in late 2003 for non-payment of bin charges.

Media

Television

The state-run broadcaster, **RTÉ** (Raidió Telefís Éireann) – runs three television stations (RTÉ 1, Network 2 and TG4) and four national radio stations. Every owner of a television set must pay a licence fee that supports RTÉ (*see* p.217).

RTÉ 1 broadcasts around 70 per cent of home-produced programmes: crowd pleasers like the televised National Lottery programme, the soap *Fair City*, the world's (reputedly) longest-running talk show *The Late Late Show* and lots of current affairs, news and documentaries. More recently RTÉ has tried to depict the new Ireland with shows like *The Big Bow Wow* and *Bachelor's Walk*.

Network 2 is more lowbrow and broadcasts children's programmes, lots of bought-in shows from the USA (often before they are screened in the UK) and sports. Late in the evenings it often broadcasts interesting, quirky programmes.

TV3, the first privately owned Irish station, went on air in 1998. Unlike RTÉ, TV3 doesn't need to consider public service broadcasting so most of the programmes are imported and there is a focus on entertainment. *Coronation Street*, poached from RTÉ early on, is a particularly big draw.

TG4 broadcasts mainly in Irish (with English subtitles) but also has films in English (with Irish subtitles!). Some of these are art house and foreign language films. Some of TG4's programmes have been surprisingly popular and it has won plaudits for innovative programming.

You'll be able to access all the **British channels** if you have a cable or satellite connection (*see* p.217).

You'll find information about all the channels in the *RTÉ Guide* – Ireland's biggest selling magazine.

Radio

RTÉ operates four national radio stations: **Radio 1** broadcasts news, talk-shows and sports during the day and some excellent documentaries and music in the evenings; **2FM** broadcasts wall-to-wall pop all day and night; **Lyric FM** has arts programmes and classical music – particularly good in the evenings; and **Raidió na Gaeltachta** broadcasts in the Irish language. A privately owned pop-based national station, **Today FM**, was launched in 1997. RTÉ's dominance has been challenged in Dublin by **98FM** and **FM104** – all fairly bland music stations. Newly established **Newstalk 106**, doing exactly what it says on the box, is sassier but hasn't yet bitten into RTÉ's ratings for news and commentary. Local radio is very widely listened to in rural areas – some are mainly pop and others have a mix of music and call-in programmes.

Newspapers

Newspapers have been published in Ireland for over 300 years and the *Belfast Newsletter*, first published in 1737, is one of the oldest continuously published newspapers in the world. Today there are six daily papers in Ireland: the *Irish Independent*, the *Irish Times*, the *Irish Examiner*, the *Star*, the *Belfast Newsletter* and the *Irish News*.

Of the broadsheets the *Irish Independent* sells the most, reflecting a wide country readership and perhaps its less intellectual and more populist approach. The *Irish Times* is generally regarded as the most serious newspaper but with something of a Dublin bias. The *Irish Examiner* was formerly the *Cork Examiner* and most of its readership is from Munster and the south of the Republic. The *Star* is Ireland's only indigenous tabloid although the British *Sun* and *Mirror* publish Irish editions. In Dublin the *Evening Herald* is required reading for flat-hunters and covers local news. It falls somewhere between a broadsheet and a tabloid although it is in tabloid format. On Sundays, indigenous papers are the *Sunday Tribune, Sunday Independent, Sunday World, Ireland on Sunday* and Belfast's *Sunday Life*. Newshound (**www.nuzhound.com**) is an excellent website for keeping up to date on events in Northern Ireland and has an extensive archive of articles dealing with the Troubles and their aftermath.

You'll find **British newspapers** in most large towns and everywhere in Northern Ireland. The *Sunday Times* publishes an Irish edition, which is the biggest-selling Irish Sunday paper. There are lots of locally produced magazines: *U, Irish Tatler, Social and Personal* and *Image* are the Irish competitors to *Tatler, Vogue, Harpers and Queen* and so on. Reading these and other local glossy magazines will bring home to you just how small the population of Ireland is, since the same faces and events feature throughout. The *Phoenix* is a satirical magazine with news, current affairs and politics although you'll probably be bemused by the names and references on first reading.

Reading the *Irish Times* may not prepare you for life outside the Pale, however. Local newspapers (generally published weekly) will give you a better insight into life and the issues of the day in rural areas. Their quality varies: some can be very conservative and Catholic in tone, while others can compete with the national broadsheets. Many also carry advertisements for property in the region. Most counties have one or two local papers, making up over 60 nationwide. The *Irish Independent* website (**www.unison.ie**) hosts the online editions of over 27 newspapers.

Banks, Building Societies and Post Offices

Banks and Building Societies

Banks in the Republic, like many other institutions, make massive profits but claim that these are not excessive. You can make your own mind up on this but do make sure that you compare the charges levied by the different banks before selecting one. All banks now offer online and telephone banking facilities and most actively discourage you from going to the bank to carry out transactions like bill payments (by loading a surcharge on to such payments). Most banks have abolished yearly service charges and introduced transaction charges – which, you won't be surprised to hear, often add up to considerably more than the old service charges. **Building societies** are owned by their members and compete with the banks for many services. **Credit unions** are a network of non-profit making community-based organisations owned by their members. They originated with a Co-operative Development Society formed in Dublin in the

Opening Hours of Banks and Building Societies

Most banks are open from 9.30 to 4 on weekdays, with late opening (to 5) on Thursdays. In some towns late opening may be on another day. Building societies are generally open until 5.30 and some are open on Saturdays as well.

Banks and Building Societies

The main banks are:

- ACCBank (**www.accbank.ie**).
- Allied Irish Bank (AIB; **www.aib.ie**).
- Bank of Ireland (BOI; **www.bankofireland.ie**).
- National Irish Bank (**www.nib.ie**).
- Permanent TSB (**www.permanenttsb.ie**).
- Ulster Bank (**www.ulsterbank.com**).

The main building societies are:

- Educational Building Society (EBS; **www.ebs.ie**).
- First Active (**www.firstactive.ie**).
- ICS Building Society (**www.mortgagestore.ie**).

mid 1950s and offer saving and loans facilities. At one stage they offered better interest rates than the banks but as interest rates are so low they are no longer as competitive. There are over 530 in Ireland and you'll find one in most towns. Most are affiliated with the Irish League of Credit Unions (**www.creditunion.ie**).

Types of **accounts and services** offered don't differ very much from those in the UK but you won't find any familiar names here. The main types of account available are **current**, **deposit** and **loan accounts**, and a couple of hybrids – the cashsave account offered by AIB is a cross between a current and deposit account. Banks and building societies deduct tax – called deposit interest retention tax (DIRT) – at source on interest on savings. **Cheques** have been virtually superseded by **Laser cards**, a type of debit card. All banks and building societies offer **credit cards** – check out interest rates before choosing one.

Credit-rating doesn't work the way it does in the UK. Your bank manager has discretion about whether to give you a loan or an overdraft based on the bank's analysis of your record, so it is a good idea to get to know the manager and to pay any money due regularly and on time.

Opening an Account

Opening a bank account is relatively straightforward; you must supply:

- a current valid passport or driving licence.
- a recent household bill such as gas, electricity or telephone in your name.

If you can't supply these forms of ID the bank may request other confirmations of identity and address such as:

- an identification form containing a photograph signed by a Garda.
- documentation or cards issued by a government department.

- a letter or statement from a person in a position of responsibility, such as a solicitor, doctor, community employment scheme supervisor or social worker.

- a letter or statement from an employer.

The bank also has the right to know the nature of your business, so you may be asked about the type of business you plan to transact through an account and the origin of funds you wish to deposit. However, there are no exchange controls in Ireland. Any sums of money in any currency can be freely brought into or taken out of the country without disclosure or other formalities.

Bank Machines

All the banks, building societies and some credit unions issue ATM cards enabling you to withdraw cash from bank machines around the country. You'll find ATM machines in most cities – though you won't believe how long queues can be in city centre locations on weekend nights. In cities ATMs are also starting to appear in convenience stores. Country areas can be a different story, with the nearest machine sometimes being up to 20 miles or more away. Come equipped with cash on your first visit to remote locations and find out the situation from locals as regards the nearest 'hole in the wall'.

Post Offices

An Post (**www.anpost.ie**) runs the postal system. Every village and town has at least one **post office** (Oifig an Phoist). You'll identify it by the white on green 'An Post' sign outside. Post boxes, always bright green, are common in Dublin and in most towns. If you look carefully you may see older ones dating from before independence with VR or ER still visible (for Queen Victoria and King Edward). Collection times vary but they are always posted on the post box or in the post office. In 2004 standard **stamps** (used for post anywhere in Ireland or Europe) cost 48 cents (open or closed); letter postage for non-European countries was 57 cents. You can also open tax-free **post office accounts** that offer a considerable saving on the banks – you can't withdraw very much at one time, though. Some social welfare benefits are paid at some post offices. Utility bills can be paid in most post offices and online (**www.billpay.ie**). Some post offices offer a pass-port express service that saves a trip to the passport office when you need a new passport. An Post also offers a range of **banking services** – withdrawals, cash lodgements and so on – for AIB.

Opening Hours of Post Offices
Post offices are open from 8.30 to 5.30, Monday to Friday, and from 9 to 12 noon on Saturdays. The General Post Office on O'Connell Street is open from 8 to 8, Monday to Saturday, and 10 to 6.30 on Sundays.

Addresses

Ireland doesn't use postal or zip codes – frustrating if you are trying to fill out online forms. Addresses can therefore seem rather vague. In country areas the 'townland' and the name of the house are generally used to pinpoint the exact location of a house. So when house-hunting in the country, make sure you get detailed directions and be prepared to stop to ask for directions several times. Remember also that the Irish sense of distance can be vague so 'a mile down the road' may be considerably further than you expect. Dublin on the other hand has a system of postal districts numbering 1 to 24 (even numbers are south of the Liffey and odd numbers are to the north) and the postal address can make a major difference to the price of a house. One of many recent scandals involved bribery of an elected representative to change the postcode of a new development since the neighbouring one was more desirable.

Working and Employment

Overview

The employment outlook in Ireland is bright at present. Unemployment is low, at around 4.8 per cent, and a far cry from the levels of the 1980s. Despite this it is important to research the market for your skills carefully before committing to buying a property. If you have your heart set on a particular area of the country and have a specialised area of expertise opportunities may be far and few between. Demand in some sectors (IT particularly) has fallen off considerably in the last couple of years, but if you are a medical or pharmaceutical professional or work in construction you should have little problem as these industries are crying out for personnel. You will find specific information on skill shortages and vacancies in Ireland from **Fás**, the State Training and Employment Authority (**www.fas.ie**; **t** 1800 611 116 in the Republic only) and from **Forfás**, a state body promoting industrial and technological development (**www.askireland.com**).

The average working week in Ireland is 37.2 hours (in Northern Ireland it is 35 hours). Increased numbers of part-time workers, many of them immigrants, are driving this figure down. Nine out of 10 Irish people say they are generally satisfied in their jobs and a whopping two-thirds of workers say that they would continue to work even if they were wealthy enough not to bother!

Looking for a Job

Everything that you would do in the UK applies here. If you are sending CVs to companies it is a good idea to follow up with a phone call making sure that it has arrived. Personal contacts can be helpful, so ask people you meet if they know of anything in your line of work. Persevere – it can take a bit of time to find something.

The website **www.irishjobs.ie** is one of the main sources for recruitment and **www.monster.ie** is the Irish branch of the international group. There are hundreds of recruitment agencies; check to see if one you are familiar with in the UK has a branch in Ireland. All the Irish newspapers have recruitment sections. The biggest recruitment section is probably in the *Irish Times* on Friday; the *Evening Herald* is good for more casual jobs.

Getting a PPS Number

You already know that you must be an EU citizen or have a work permit to be allowed to work in Ireland. You need to apply for a PPS number (formerly known as an RSI number) before you can work legally. This number registers you with the Revenue Commissioners (**www.revenue.ie**). If you are returning to Ireland after a long period abroad you probably already have a PPS number and the Revenue Commissioners should be able to track this down for you.

As a UK national (or resident of Northern Ireland) you will need the following proofs of identification to get your PPS number:

- a current valid passport or birth certificate (long form preferred).

- valid photographic ID, such as full driving licence, employment ID (with photo).

- evidence of either work/claim/residency/tax liability/education history in the UK or Northern Ireland and evidence of address.

Business Etiquette in Ireland

Nothing differs radically from the UK, but you may find that people use first names almost immediately and often behave rather informally from the first meeting. Irish people are often late for meetings and appointments (don't copy this behaviour). If you are going out to dinner with business acquaintances they will generally insist on paying the bill. Connections and mutual acquaintances are very important in business and you will probably find that Irish people will spend some time trying to find someone you both know when they first meet you.

You may notice that the Irish are reluctant to mention their qualifications and achievements and are uncomfortable if you do so. They hate a 'show-off' and wouldn't like to be seen as one themselves. Allied to this, the Irish are not easy to impress and even if you do impress them they are very unlikely to tell you so. Another thing that you may notice is more bad language than you are used to in the workplace. It isn't because Irish people find their work particularly infuriating but because they swear lots outside work, and it tends to carry over.

Important Forms

• **Form P60** At the end of each tax year your employer has to give you a certificate showing pay and the tax and PRSI deducted during the year. This certificate is called form P60 and comes in two parts. It records:

- the pay you received from your employer.
- the tax deducted under PAYE.
- the PRSI contributions deducted.

If your tax liability needs to be reviewed, you send one part of the form P60 to the tax office. If you need to claim benefit you bring the second part to the social welfare office as evidence that you have paid PRSI contributions.

• **Form P45** This is a certificate given by your employer, when you leave employment, showing that tax and PRSI have been correctly deducted from your pay. You must give this form to your new employer when starting employment. Form P45 shows:

- gross pay to date of leaving.
- tax deducted to date of leaving.
- PRSI deducted to date of leaving and number of insurable weeks.
- the tax credits, standard rate cut-off point and tax table in operation.

• **Form 12A** You'll need this form when starting work for the first time. You fill it out to apply for a certificate of tax credits and standard rate cut-off point. This certificate sets out the amount of tax credits due to you and will be required by your new employer. Otherwise you might find yourself paying emergency tax until your tax-free allowances have been calculated.

How the Tax System Works

The income tax system in Ireland now operates on a tax credit system. This means that your tax is initially calculated on your gross income without any allowances. Then tax credits (*see* box 'Some Tax Tables', below) are deducted to arrive at the total tax payable. Individuals have different credits based on marital status, whether they are paying a mortgage, number of dependants and so on. Married couples can choose to be assessed together or separately. You pay tax under the **Pay As You Earn (PAYE)** system (usually weekly or monthly) if you are an employee. If you are self-employed or have income from outside Ireland you use a **self-assessment** system (tax is payable in one lump sum or by direct debit at intervals). Currently the lower rate of tax is 20 per cent (up to the standard cut-off point, currently €28,000 for a single person) and 42 per cent on anything above €28,000 (*see* 'Tax Tables', opposite, for examples of take-home pay for various incomes).

If you are paid through an Irish payroll you have to pay PAYE. Your employer is obliged to deduct this from your salary based on the information in your tax-free allowance certificate. Tax is also payable on earnings that result from your employment (including bonuses, overtime, non-cash pay or 'benefits-in-kind' such as the use of company car, tips, and so on). You do not pay tax on payments to approved pension schemes and some savings accounts. *See* **Financial Implications**, 'Taxation' pp.174–95.

Pay-related Social Insurance (PRSI)

In addition to income tax you have to pay national insurance. This is called **pay-related social insurance (PRSI)**. The main benefits based on PRSI payments include unemployment benefit, disability benefit, maternity benefit, health and safety benefit, widow/widowers and/or old age pension, dental and optical treatment benefit and carer's benefit.

As a **PAYE employee** you pay 4 per cent PRSI (up to a threshold, currently €42,160) and a further 2 per cent health contribution on your entire salary. You are exempt from PRSI on the first €127 you earn per week. If you earn less than €287 you are exempt from PRSI and if you earn less than €356 you are exempt from the health contribution. Your employer pays a further amount (usually 10.25 per cent). If you are **self-employed**, your PRSI contribution is 5 per cent on your entire income.

Tax Tables

The tables below give information for the tax year January–December 2004.

Personal Tax Credits (income on which no tax is payable)

Single Person's Tax Credit	€1,520
Married Person's Tax Credit	€3,040
Widowed Person's Tax Credit	
– qualifying for One-parent Family Tax Credit	€1,520
– without dependent children	€1,820
– in year of bereavement	€3,040
One-parent Family Tax Credit (with qualifying dependent children), widowed, deserted, separated or unmarried	€1,520

Tax Rates and Bands

Single or widowed without dependent children	€28,000 @ 20% Balance @ 42%
Single or widowed qualifying for One-parent Family Tax Credit	€32,000 @ 20% Balance @ 42%
Married couple (one spouse with income)	€37,000 @ 20% Balance @ 42%
Married couple (both spouses with income)	€37,000 @ 20% (with an increase of €19,000 max.) Balance @ 42%

Sample Take-home Pay for a Single Person after Tax

Gross Income (€)	Net Pay Monthly (€)	Gross Income (€)	Net Pay Monthly (€)
25,000	1,757	70,000	3,851
32,000	2,115	76,000	4,130
38,000	2,375	82,500	4,433
44,500	2,669	90,000	4,782
50,500	2,923	100,000	5,248
57,000	3,248	115,000	5,947
63,500	3,550	125,000	6,412

Sample Take-home Pay for Married Couple with Two Incomes after Tax (assessed jointly)

Gross Income (€)	Net Pay Monthly (€)	Gross Income (€)	Net Pay Monthly (€)
25,000	2,053	70,000	4,491
32,000	2,457	76,000	4,751
38,000	2,774	82,500	5,037
44,500	3,175	90,000	5,384
50,500	3,545	100,000	5,846
57,000	3,927	115,000	6,542
63,500	4,209	125,000	7,006

Sample Take-home Pay for Married Couple with Two Incomes after Tax (assessed separately)

Gross Income (€)	Net Pay Monthly (€)	Gross Income (€)	Net Pay Monthly (€)
25,000	1,884	70,000	4,143
32,000	2,315	76,000	4,422
38,000	2,667	82,500	4,725
44,500	2,961	90,000	5,074
50,500	3,238	100,000	5,539
57,000	3,539	115,000	6,238
63,500	3,481	125,000	6,704

Self-employment

The number of self-employed people outside agriculture (where numbers fell) increased rapidly during the 1990s in Ireland. If you work for yourself you pay income tax under the **self-assessment** system. Most self-employed people use an accountant to help them work out their liabilities.

Whether you need to register for VAT or not depends on the turnover of your business – if you exceed €51,000 for the supply of goods and €25,500 for the supply of services you must register. You will also need a PPS number (*see* 'Getting a PPS Number', p.225).

The Artist's Exemption

There are mixed opinions on the legacy of former Taoiseach (Prime Minister) Charles Haughey. Although these days he's probably best known for massive corruption and tax evasion, many artists retain a soft spot for him since he was responsible for introducing what's called the artist's exemption. Creative artists who are resident or domiciled in the Republic are exempt from income tax. The only catch is that your work must be original, creative and have cultural and artistic merit. The work should fall into one of the following categories:

- book or other writing
- play
- musical composition (musicians' performances are not tax-exempt)
- painting or other similar picture
- sculpture

You must apply to the Revenue Commissioners for approval, giving examples of your work, testimonials as to its artistic and cultural merit and evidence that your work has been published, produced or sold. You can apply for an exemption for one piece of work or for a general exemption that is valid for all your work. If you are thinking of moving to Ireland to avail yourself of the exemption you can apply for an advance opinion on your work.

You can get a useful explanatory leaflet and all the necessary forms from the Revenue Commissioners (**www.revenue.ie**).

In Ireland since 2002, the **tax year** has run as the calendar year, i.e. from 1 January to the following 31 December. It is up to you to see that your tax affairs are in order.

You must pay your tax and make your tax returns at the following times:

- An initial tax based on your calculations of the amount for which you will be liable (Preliminary Tax) – payable on/before 31 October in the year of assessment. This is a forecast of the tax that you will be liable to pay in the coming year.

- Income Tax Returns, CGT Returns and Forms 46G must be submitted on/before 31 October following year of assessment.

- The balance of your tax liability must be paid on/before 31 October following year of assessment ('Pay and File').

Starting Your Own Business

If you've decided to give up working for someone else and be your own boss you will need to think about the kind of business entity that you will use to trade. In Ireland there are three main entities: sole trader, partnership or limited liability company.

Sole Trader

This is probably the simplest way to set up on your own. A sole trader is in business on his or her own account. You need to register for taxes and pay income tax under the self-assessment system. The risk associated with running a business as a sole trader is that there is no separate legal entity, so that your personal assets are liable if the business does not go according to plan.

Partnership

If you want to go into business with one or more other people where neither is an employee of the other you generally form a partnership. A partnership is rather like a sole trader but with two or more people involved. It is not a separate legal entity so, rather like a sole trader, both partners are liable for the debts of the partnership. Generally it is wise to draw up a legal agreement at the start of the partnership. This document should summarise the agreed position in the case of various eventualities: how the bank account is set up, how profits (or losses) are to be divided up, what happens on the death of a partner and how decisions are to be made.

Limited Liability Company

As the name implies, a company is a separate legal entity, meaning that the shareholders are not personally liable for any losses or debts. This means that you, as a shareholder, are liable only for the amount of capital you contributed to the company. You must register your company name with the Companies Registration Office and file an annual statutory return with them. The accounts of the company are available to the public for inspection. Limited liability companies are quite complicated to set up and register and many people start off as a sole trader before setting up their companies. Companies in Ireland pay a standard corporate tax rate of 12.5 per cent on their profits.

Another option is to use a co-operative model for a partnership or a limited liability company. Co-operatives are jointly owned by a group and conform to certain ethical principles.

Things You Need to Do when Setting Up a Business

• Decide the legal structure for your business – sole trader, limited company, and so on.

• You must register your new business with the tax office when you start in business. There are different forms for businesses with a yearly turnover of more or less than €127,000. The Revenue Commissioners can organise a New Business Visit from an official to make sure you are clear about your tax obligations and liabilities. When you register for tax you must state the purpose of the company and what it will do in the way of business.

- If you plan to employ someone in your business you must register as an employer for PAYE and PRSI. Note also that Ireland has a minimum wage – currently €7 per hour.

- You must register for VAT if you are a taxable person and if your annual turnover exceeds the following limits: €51,000 for the supply of goods and €25,500 for the supply of services. You must also register for corporation tax if you are a company.

- You must have a PPS number before you can complete any business forms.

- You must keep full and accurate records of your business from the start. This involves setting up proper accounting systems and opening a business bank account.

- You must ensure that your business meets all the relevant legislation and regulations (for instance, pubs need a special licence).

Contacts

Ireland has a host of government agencies that give advice, information and, in some cases, grants to those setting up businesses in Ireland. **Business Access to State Information and Services (www.basis.ie)** is a site that provides businesses with a single access point to all government information and services. **Enterprise Ireland (www.enterprise-ireland.com)** is the organisation that helps

Business Permission for Non-EEA Nationals

Business permission is the written permission of the Minister for Justice, Equality and Law Reform to allow a person to engage in business in Ireland. A non-EEA national who wants to run a business must obtain this permission. Once you obtain the permission you are allowed to live in Ireland. Anyone can apply, as long as they can show that the grant of business permission would:

- result in the transfer to Ireland of assets and capital worth at least €300,000.

- create employment for at least two EEA nationals for a new project (or maintain existing employment).

- add to the commercial activity and competitiveness of the state.

- result in the substitution of Irish goods for goods that would otherwise be imported.

- provide a viable trading concern, which would provide the applicant with enough money to provide for themselves and any dependants without resorting to social welfare or employment for which a work permit would be required.

Applicants must have a valid passport or national identity document and be of good character.

the development of Irish enterprise. It generally deals with companies employing 10 or more people and can help start-ups with training and financing. The local county or city enterprise boards are often the best place to begin for people starting smaller businesses. They provide training, financial assistance, mentoring and advice to start-ups.

The website **www.startingabusinessinireland.com** provides a useful directory of contacts for new businesses.

Education

Overview

The Irish education system is very well regarded and is generally seen as being a major factor in Ireland's dramatic economic success – estimated to contribute an additional 1 per cent to growth each year. In the 2003 annual OECD review *Education at a Glance*, Irish 15-year-olds were ranked fifth of 27 OECD states in reading literacy. They scored well above average in scientific literacy and average for mathematical literacy. The introduction to the report noted that the Irish education system was particularly successful at preparing Irish students for lifelong learning – mainly because the scope of the curriculum is very broad. Many high-tech companies established Irish bases in the 1990s precisely because this broad education is particularly appropriate for the fast-changing knowledge economy.

Education is compulsory for children aged from 6 to 15. In practice most children begin school at age 4 or 5 and finish at 18. Special-needs children are generally educated within the mainstream in Ireland – especially those with mild- to moderate-level delays. 35 per cent of Irish school-leavers go on to study at third level (in Britain the figure is only 26 per cent) and universities have an excellent reputation. A recent survey of attitudes to employment also showed that people who work in education are the most likely to be happy in their jobs.

If you are among the numerous British parents moving to Ireland specifically for high-quality education and small class sizes, you probably know most of this

Home Schooling in Ireland

Parents have a constitutional right to educate their children at home if they so wish. The National Educational Welfare Board (NEWB) maintains a register of children being educated outside the main school system and you must add your child to this list before starting home schooling. Education welfare officers will visit your home periodically to ensure that the child's education meets minimum standards. Unfortunately these standards have not yet been established by law so there's something of a grey area about what exactly the child should be learning.

> ### Exemption from Studying Irish at Post-primary Level
> The Department of Education and Science excuses some students from studying Irish in post-primary school, although the circumstances in which a student will be given this exemption are very limited. Usually residence abroad is a valid reason for exemption and students with certain disabilities may also be exempted. If your child has never learnt Irish and is at post-primary level they will probably be exempted, but enquire at the school before enrolling.

already. Note, though, that there is no easy way for you to judge the quality of a school since there is no ratings system in Ireland (schools in Northern Ireland have also scrapped school performance tables and publish their results independently). Visiting the school and enquiring about its reputation in the locality is the best way to glean information. Discipline is not a serious problem in most schools but some inner city schools have difficulties with drugs and absenteeism.

Education in Northern Ireland

Students in Northern Ireland score higher in standardised exams than they do elsewhere in the UK – almost 38 per cent of those sitting A-levels achieved the top pass mark ratings compared with the national average of 29 per cent. The system is similar to that in the rest of Britain – pupils follow the same national curriculum and take the same standardised exams. The main difference you will notice is religious segregation. There are very few integrated schools. Another difference is that the 11-plus examination is to be abolished in Northern Ireland by 2008.

Visit the **Department of Education in Northern Ireland (www.deni.gov.uk)** and **BBC Northern Ireland (www.bbc.co.uk/northernireland/learning/)** for more information.

Schooling Levels

Primary Level

A child's first school is called a primary or national school. The vast majority of these are state-aided and don't charge fees. Parents do pay for books and uniforms (if the school requires uniforms – many don't). They are almost always co-educational. Alternatively, children can attend a private fee-paying primary school. In practice almost all primary school children attend state-aided schools. School is compulsory for children from age 6 but nearly all 5-year-olds and over half of 4-year-olds attend school. Children can't be enrolled in school before their fourth birthday and there are virtually no state-funded pre-schools (the few that exist are usually for disadvantaged children or children with special needs). This means that crèches, Montessori schools and other types of

The Ethos of Primary Schools

Even though almost all primary schools are state-funded they are generally privately owned – usually by church authorities. This means that the owners set the ethos of the school, although the state is responsible for how the school is run and managed. The vast majority of schools are Catholic although many larger towns will also have a Church of Ireland primary school. There is also a Muslim National School in Clonskeagh in Dublin. Multi-denominational schools are becoming more popular particularly in Dublin. Gaelscoileanna (Irish Schools) are national schools that teach through Irish. These schools are very popular – because the teaching is reputed to be of a very high standard. In many schools pupils are expected to attend a religion class (an hour or so a week) and partake in morning prayers – regardless of their own denomination. Ask the school about this at the onset if you prefer your child not to attend.

playschool have to be funded by parents and, to add insult to injury, childcare and pre-school expenses are not tax-refundable. (Until recently crèche facilities provided by an employer were taxed as benefit in kind!)

The primary school cycle is eight years long and the school year for primary school children runs from 1 September to 30 June. Generally infant classes are taught from 9.30 to 2 and the rest of the pupils finish at 3 (creating headaches for parents with children at both levels). Children start off in junior infants, followed by senior infants (parents bringing their little ones to school for the first time will be touched to hear that infant classes are often called 'Low Babies' and 'High Babies') before moving into first class and so on up to sixth class. Most children leave primary school at age 12.

A new curriculum for all primary schools was introduced in 1999 and is now fully operational. The curriculum is child-centred and stresses activity- and discovery-based learning. Irish is compulsory for all children in primary school – no exceptions. Children who don't speak English as a first language are entitled to remedial English lessons. (At present one in 20 primary school children are non-nationals and schools are struggling to adjust to the new situation.) Generally other languages aren't taught at primary level, although there are a few pilot schemes throughout the country.

Even though the quality of education is excellent, there are a couple of things that you should be prepared for. For example, school buildings can leave a lot to be desired – under-maintained classrooms, leaks and problems with damp are more common than they should be, especially in rural areas. Many schools do not have any physical education facilities so children will be taken outside to do a few exercises once a week (although most of them get lots of exercise playing football or hurling during breaks). Although all primary schools are now connected to the Internet, there may be only one or two computers for a whole class. Schools will be happy to have you visit and you'll find teachers very willing to talk to you about what your child can expect, but don't expect a speedy (or indeed any) response to written or e-mail enquiries – most schools don't have administrative systems in place to deal with these.

If you plan to enrol your child in a primary school, contact the school directly to enquire about places. In Dublin some schools, particularly multi-denominational ones, are oversubscribed and you may be asked to put your child's name on a waiting list. In rural areas schools may be falling over themselves to have your children – if the number of children in the school falls below a certain level they may lose a teacher. Most schools give priority to children from the local parish, and schools run by minority religions will usually give priority to children of that religion.

Second Level

Again, the post-primary or secondary system is of a high standard but is sometimes criticised for being very exam-orientated. This isn't surprising when you consider that students' chances of a university place are completely dependent on the number of points gained in their final school exam, the Leaving Certificate. Most schools are free (although students pay for books, uniforms and exam fees) but there is a wide range of private schools – some of them boarding schools – and many of Ireland's great and good are alumni of the most prestigious.

Post-primary education starts with a 3-year junior cycle followed by a 2-year senior cycle. At the end of the **junior cycle** students sit the **Junior Certificate**. A

Case Study: Choosing a School

David and Fiona Stewart inherited an old farmhouse near Carlow from David's grandmother in the late 1980s. For years they used it for holidays and spent whatever extra money they had on renovations. After the birth of their two children (now aged 10 and 8) they decided to move permanently to Ireland and run a small guest house in 1999. One of the main reasons for their decision was the quality of education in Ireland. But choosing a school was difficult – the family's new home was equidistant between two schools. They didn't initially realise that competition between the two for new pupils was fierce but they soon found out: 'One of the local schoolteachers was the friendliest of all the people we met. We met him in the local pub at first and then he dropped into the house one day for a chat and a cup of tea.' On his departure he gave each child 20 pounds. 'I nearly died,' says Fiona. 'Our youngest, Sam, was only three and wasn't going to school for another couple of years anyway! Later on I realised that giving money to children was quite common and lots of people would give them a pound or two (nowadays euros) when they came to visit, but this was really blatant bribery!' In the end they sent the children to the rival school. 'They'd made friends with more children from that one so the money didn't really figure in the decision, but I still laugh when I think of it!'

Types of Secondary School

You'll find secondary schools, vocational schools, community schools, comprehensive schools and community colleges. The differences are mainly in who owns the schools (often religious orders in the case of secondary schools) and how they are managed and, in some cases, funded; but since all students study the same curriculum these differences are often quite minor.

Secondary schools, community schools and comprehensive schools are generally denominational schools whereas vocational schools and community colleges are non-denominational. About 35 per cent of secondary schools are single sex. Most vocational and community schools are co-educational.

transition year before starting the senior cycle is optional (over 75 per cent of schools offer a **transition year programme**). During transition year students focus on personal development and cultural studies, improving skills and getting some work experience. Schools devise their own programmes based on Department of Education guidelines. After transition year the 2-year **senior cycle** begins. The final exam is called the **Leaving Certificate**. Most students take seven subjects for this exam – English, Irish, maths and four other subjects of their choice. There are also vocational and applied Leaving Certificates for those less academically inclined. Each subject can be taken at pass or honours level. Students are awarded points for their grades and their combined total decides which course and university they'll be accepted into. If you have second-level pupils in the family you'll soon learn all about the points system and the difference between an A1 at pass level and a D2 at honours.

The **Central Admissions Office** (www.cao.ie) administers the centralised university admissions process. Earlier subject specialisation in the UK means that the Leaving Certificate is probably about a year behind A-levels. Irish universities accept A-levels and one or two tutorial centres in Dublin offer them to pupils (for example, the **Dublin Tutorial Centre**; www.dtc.ie).

The curriculum for the International Baccalaureate exam is taught at one Dublin school; there is also a German school in Dublin and a Japanese boarding school in County Kildare.

In rural areas you generally won't have much choice over where to send your children. One large secondary school will serve the surrounding area and take in pupils from a range of primary schools. In cities, particularly Dublin, you'll have a wider choice. The **Oasis** site (**oasis.gov.ie**) supplies a useful list of questions to ask when selecting a secondary school.

Third Level

There are seven universities and 14 institutes of technology (ITs) in Ireland. Third-level education has an excellent reputation and is widely seen as a key element of the Republic's economic success. As a result, since 1997 investment in the third-level sector has increased by 74 per cent; it now stands at close to €1.5 billion per year. If you live in the EU, tuition is free for all accredited third-level courses. Keep an eye on the news, though, as the government is muttering about reintroducing fees at some stage despite widespread opposition.

Ireland has a centralised system for applications to third level and competition is fierce. Points are not assigned based on the difficulty of the course but on the number of applicants divided by the number of places on the course. Clearly things like medicine and pharmacy have always required high points but there are many anomalies. Trinity College in Dublin, for example, has fewer places than University College Dublin for many of its courses and these courses require higher points as a result. But the numbers of students coming out of the secondary system and applying to university is just beginning to drop off (Ireland's baby boom took place in the 1970s and 80s, with peak births in 1980), so the points required for courses will probably start to drop somewhat over the next 10 years.

To qualify for free fees:

- **You must be an Irish national or a national of another EU member state who has been living in the EU for at least 3 of the 5 years before starting your course.**

- **The course you wish to take must be an undergraduate course of at least 2 years' duration.**

- **You must not have a previous qualification at the same level.**

- **You must not be repeating the year.**

An 'Expert Group on Future Skills Needs' investigated future needs in Ireland and identified career sectors that are likely to experience shortages in the

Further Research

The Irish government website **Oasis (www.oasis.gov.ie)** gives lots of information about schools and universities in Ireland. The Irish educational system is run by the **Department of Education and Science (www.education.ie)**, which publishes a list of all primary schools in the country. Many of them also have their own websites. You can find out all about the primary and secondary curricula at the website of the **National Council for Curriculum and Assessment (www.ncca.ie)**. Skool.ie **(www.skoool.ie)** is an award-winning site (also rated one of the top five e-learning projects in the world). Here you'll find a huge amount of educational content, including all the key syllabus topics for junior and senior cycles. The site should give you a good idea of what students will be learning at second level. It also has a useful schools guide with information about secondary schools in each county. **Scoilnet (www.scoilnet.ie)**, another portal site for Irish education, includes the primary sector and gives a good overview of what pupils are likely to be doing at different ages and stages.

future. So you might want to give your child a discreet push towards one of the following:

- software engineering
- agricultural and food engineering
- food science
- microbiology
- biology
- chemistry
- biochemistry

- civil engineering
- electrical engineering
- mechanical engineering
- electronic engineering
- town planning
- systems analysis
- pharmacy

Health and Emergencies

Irish people's health compares favourably with international standards – life expectancy at birth is 78.5 for women and 73 for men (74 in Northern Ireland). Interestingly, Irish people tend to report lower levels of ill health than the rest of the EU, suggesting that they are more optimistic than their fellow EU citizens. Cardiovascular diseases and cancer are the major causes of death among Irish people, perhaps because over 30 per cent of the population smoke – a statistic that hasn't changed much over the last 20 years despite rising costs and ever more terrifying health warnings. Alcohol consumption is also the highest in the EU. Alcohol consumption *per capita* has risen with increasing affluence – before the 1990s it was one of the lowest in the EU. The birth rate has been dropping but is still one of the highest in the EU (14.5 per 1,000 of population).

Ireland's health system is run by eight regional health boards under the control of the Department of Health and Children. In general you will find good health care standards, but Ireland is a small country and its health service has been under-funded for some time. This means that specialised services are generally only offered in Dublin; rural hospitals can be run-down and there can be long waiting lists for public patients across the country. In winter elderly or convalescent patients who would be better cared for in a nursing home occupy

Travelling to Ireland

EU citizens are entitled to free health care when travelling in the EEA. In most countries you need to produce an E111 form when claiming treatment, but you don't need an E111 form when travelling to Ireland. All you need is evidence of residence in the UK (an NHS medical card or a driving licence (and if neither is available, a DHS exemption notice, a current passport or similar - documentation may be accepted). The UK Department of Health (**www.doh.gov.uk/traveladvice/**; UK **t** 0800 555 7777) publishes a leaflet called 'Health Advice for Travellers'. This gives detailed information on everything you're likely to need when travelling abroad and includes an E111 form.

many hospital beds leading to shortages and queues. The health service has also been criticised for a lack of co-ordination between its various sectors. At the moment the health service is being reviewed and reform is planned. A recent report recommended that each region should have one major hospital providing the full range of acute services. This would mean that all the remaining hospitals would become local hospitals without accident and emergency services or maternity services.

Ireland's health system is not as broad as the NHS; you will have to pay for many medical and dental services unless you are eligible for a means-tested medical card (*see* 'Medical Cards', below). Nationals of other countries resident in Ireland normally have exactly the same rights as Irish citizens. If you are an EU national or ordinarily resident in Ireland you are eligible for the following medical services:

- **All in-patient public hospital services in public wards, including consultant services; there is a daily charge of €45.**
- **All other outpatient hospital services, including consultants (again subject to some charges).**
- **Accident and emergency (A&E) departments; if your doctor refers you, there is no charge, otherwise it costs €45 per visit.**
- **Maternity and infant care services including the services of a general practitioner during pregnancy and for up to six weeks after the birth.**
- **Drugs and medicines for the treatment of some long-term illnesses.**
- **A refund of expenditure on prescribed drugs and medicines in excess of a specified amount.**

If you are eligible for a medical card (*see* below) you are also entitled to the following free medical services:

- **GP services (if you are registered with a GP).**
- **Any prescribed medicines.**
- **In-patient hospital treatment in a public ward.**
- **Outpatient hospital treatment.**
- **Dental, ophthalmic and aural services.**
- **Community care services.**

Clearly if you don't have a medical card you are liable to pay for GP visits, prescription drugs and some hospital charges.

Medical Cards

You qualify for a medical card if your total family income (for a married couple under age 66) is less than €206.50 a week. A single person (under age 66) living alone qualifies when their income minus pension taxes is €142.50 or less. A

Medical Card Income Guidelines with Effect from 1 January 2004

Category	Weekly income limit* Aged under 66	Aged 66–69
Single person living alone	€142.50	€156
Single person living with family	€127	€134
Married couple	€206.50	€231
Allowance for child under 16	€26	€26
Allowance for dependants over 16 (with no income)	€26	€26

*Gross without PRSI and health contributions

medical card normally covers the cardholder, his or her spouse, all children under age 16 and any dependants over 16. Various other adjustments are made based on the number of dependants and age (*see* the table above). Once you've satisfied the means test you will receive a medical card from your regional health board.

If you don't qualify for a medical card you are liable for visits to your GP and for any prescribed medicines and for dental, optical and aural services.

Anybody aged **70 and over** is entitled to a medical card irrespective of income. This card, which is not means-tested, covers the applicant only, not dependants.

The E128 Form

If you come to work in Ireland temporarily for up to a year and continue to pay UK NI contributions (this must be confirmed by the DSS) you are entitled to form E128. This gives you all the rights of an Irish medical cardholder.

Hospitals

Rather like schools, many hospitals provide a good service but the buildings can be dilapidated and equipment fairly basic. There is a lack of qualified staff, so many nurses and doctors are recruited from abroad. The most common public hospitals are health board hospitals, owned and funded by the health boards. There are also voluntary public hospitals, which are sometimes owned by religious bodies; others are incorporated by charter or statute and are run by boards appointed by the Minister for Health. Public hospitals often provide private care but must distinguish between public and private beds. There are also some private hospitals, which receive no state funding. If you wish to have private care in hospital you or your health insurance company must pay for the costs involved.

Doctors

Doctors in Ireland are generally known as general practitioners (GPs), as in Britain. There are no set fees for GP services so it is a good idea to check the cost of the consultation before making an appointment. Local GPs charge around €30 for a consultation although this can rise to €45 in Dublin. Traditionally most doctors would make house calls, although this practice is being phased out in many parts of the country. Most towns have a local surgery where one or more doctors practise. Many doctors have clinics, which operate on a first come first served basis and others (particularly in the cities) require you to make an appointment. Public health nurses visit new mothers.

Dentists

Dental treatment is provided by local health boards and private practitioners. You'll find a dentist in most towns. Local health boards provide dental services for the following groups:

- **all children under the age of 6.**
- **children who attend national school.**
- **children, up to their 16th birthday, who have left national school.**
- **adult medical card-holders and their adult dependants.**
- **patients in health board hospitals and institutions.**

Everyone else has to attend a private dentist. You generally have to make an appointment to see a dentist a couple of weeks in advance unless it is an extreme emergency. If you have worked in Ireland for a certain number of years and amassed the requisite number of PRSI payments (this varies depending on your age) you can get check-ups and certain treatments free and pay only part of the costs for other types of treatments. Standard dental treatments are free for medical card-holders. Orthodontic treatment for children is extremely over-subscribed and the waiting lists are extraordinarily long. Most parents, if they can afford it, opt for private orthodontic care.

Health Insurance

Private health insurance in Ireland is calculated using a 'community rating system'. This means all consumers pay the same premium for a particular health plan, regardless of their age, gender and current or likely future state of their health (except children under 18 years of age, who are charged a lower 'child rate'). Currently about 50 per cent of the population holds private health insurance with either **VHI** (**www.vhihealthe.com**) or **BUPA Ireland** (**www. bupaireland.ie**). This insurance pays for private or semi-private care in hospital or from consultants. Both can offer some cover for doctor and dentist bills as an add-on policy. BUPA set up business here seven years ago and is still regarded as the 'new kid on the block'. The Irish seem to prefer to stick with what they know – only 6 per cent of people with private health insurance have ever changed provider (80 per cent of people with private insurance are with the VHI – about 1.55 million people) even though BUPA works out slightly cheaper than the VHI.

Apart from this the two don't differ radically. VHI's most popular plan – Plan B – costs €38.86 per month for an adult, and a similar plan with BUPA (Essentials Plus) costs €37.56. VHI provides cover at 101 hospitals, BUPA at 92. In general, VHI also offers longer-lasting cover for in-patient psychiatric treatment and higher maximum benefits for emergency overseas medical expenses. BUPA has a more extensive range of outpatient benefits and covers more alternative therapies.

The **Health Insurance Authority (HIA)** has produced a useful leaflet comparing private health insurance costs. This gives details of the main benefits provided by each insurer together with costs and is available on their website (**www.hia.ie**). You can claim tax relief on your subscription to private healthcare.

Social Services and Welfare Benefits

The Irish social welfare system doesn't distinguish between nationals and non-nationals. This means that anyone from outside the state complying with the laws covering entering the country, living here and working here is entitled to social welfare assistance and benefits. However, in early 2004 the government announced plans to bring in a law requiring EU citizens to have been 'habitually resident' for two years before being eligible for certain welfare benefits. This is to prevent citizens of the 10 EU accession states claiming welfare benefits and it is not clear yet how it may affect UK citizens who wish to claim social welfare in Ireland.

The **Department of Social and Family Affairs** (**www.welfare.ie**) runs Ireland's social welfare system. This department manages a range of social insurance and social assistance schemes that provide for unemployment, illness, maternity, caring, widowhood, retirement and old age. The department produces a good range of leaflets explaining every aspect of the welfare system and you should consult their website or visit any social welfare office to find out more about the areas that directly affect you.

UK Benefits

At present EU rules stipulate that you can transfer unemployment benefit from your country of origin (provided you registered in the UK as a jobseeker at least four weeks before you left) and it will be paid to you in Ireland for up to 13 weeks. After that period you may qualify for means-tested unemployment assistance. Usually you must show that you are actively looking for work to qualify. Your national insurance record in Britain can help you to qualify for contributory welfare benefits in Ireland. Make sure that you bring any P60s (employee annual pay, tax and National Insurance record) you have to Ireland with you as they may help you to qualify for contributory benefits. You can also transfer your UK state pension to Ireland (*see* 'Pensions', pp.245–6, for details).

Irish Benefits

Payments are divided into three groups:

- **Social insurance (or contributory) payments, made on the basis of pay-related social insurance (PRSI) contributions.**

- **Social assistance (or non-contributory) payments, made on the basis of a means test.**

- **Universal payments (such as child benefit or free travel for people aged over 65), which are not dependent on PRSI contributions or a means test.**

Social insurance schemes are paid for by the individual, in some cases over a lifetime's employment. They include an old age contributory pension, retirement pension, widow's/widower's contributory pension, orphan's contributory allowance, deserted wife's benefit, invalidity pension, disability benefit, unemployment benefit, pay-related benefit, maternity allowance, treatment benefit and death grants.

Social assistance schemes are financed entirely by the Exchequer and you must satisfy a means test before qualifying for payment under any of these schemes. They include old age non-contributory pension, widow's/widower's non-contributory pension, orphan's non-contributory pension, deserted wife's allowance, prisoner's wife's allowance, lone parent's allowance, unemployment assistance, pre-retirement allowance, supplementary welfare allowance, family income supplement, carer's allowance and rent allowance.

Child Benefit

Child benefit is payable to all parents with children under 16 and is extended up to age 18 for children in full-time education. This is paid monthly and is not subject to a means test. You can get application forms from social welfare offices or post offices nationwide. Currently the children's allowance is for the first and second child is €131.60 (from April 2004) and for third and subsequent children €165.30 (from April 2004).

Retirement and Pensions

Many retirees move to Ireland for the lifestyle, cheaper housing and a country generally regarded as being respectful towards its older citizens. Most retirees in Ireland are fit, active and healthy and play an important role in the life of the community.

Benefits for Retirees in Ireland

There are several benefits you can expect as a retiree in Ireland and your income from UK pensions or other assets does not affect them. Generally, if you are eligible for one, you are eligible for all.

- **Free electricity**: all persons over 70 are entitled to this, regardless of means or of whom they live with. Those over 66 in receipt of most social welfare pensions or who meet a means test are also eligible. It covers monthly standing charges and a set usage amount per month.

- **Free natural gas**: this is offered as an alternative to free electricity, for those who have a gas supply in their homes. Qualifying conditions are similar to those for free electricity. You are also eligible for free bottled gas if you are connected to neither gas nor electricity!

- **Free television licence**: if you qualify for free electricity or gas you are also eligible for a free annual television licence.

- **Free telephone rental**: you are also entitled to free telephone rental and b2.42 plus VAT towards calls in each two-month call period. If you are

---

Facts and Figures about Older People in Ireland

- In 2002 those aged 65+ numbered 436,001 (246,846 women and 189,155 men).

- The average retirement age is 63.1 (there is no set retirement age although it is generally 65).

- 25.8 per cent of these lived alone (30.3 per cent of women and 19.8 per cent of men).

- There are now more older people in urban areas (238,301) than in rural locations (197,700).

- Over 85 per cent of older people living in the community owned their own homes.

- Over 93 per cent of Irish older people were satisfied with their housing.

- 80 per cent of older people in Ireland rated their quality of life as good or very good.

- 67 per cent rated their health as good or very good.

hearing- or visually impaired you are also eligible for a second socket and a special phone.

• **Medical card**: everyone over age 70 is entitled to a medical card. This entitles you to most medical services free of charge (*see* pp.239–240).

• **Free travel**: everyone aged over 66 automatically qualifies for a pass entitling them and a person living with them to free travel (with some restrictions at peak times) on bus and rail services, including cross-border services.

• **Carer's allowance and carer's benefit**: if you need full-time care your carer may be entitled to either a carer's allowance (a means-tested payment) or carer's benefit (based on PRSI contributions).

The **Department of Social and Family Affairs** administers all these allowances (collectively known as the Household Benefits Package or the free schemes) and you can learn more by contacting the department. The leaflet SW 107, available from your local social welfare office or any post office, explains the benefits available to retirees and those over age 70 in detail. There are also several organisations that aim to raise older people's profiles in society and give information and advice on retirement, pensions and other entitlements. These include the **National Council on Ageing and Older People** (**www.ncaop.ie**), **Older in Ireland** (**www.olderinireland.ie**), **Positive Age** (**www.positiveage.net**) and **Age Action** (**www.ageaction.ie**).

Pensions

UK Pensions

You can have your **UK state pension** paid directly to you (with an extra amount if you are aged 80 or more) in any other EEA or agreement country – which includes Ireland. This pension will also be increased in line with inflation each April. Payments can be made into a UK or an Irish bank account and are paid every 4 or 13 weeks. If you have paid contributions in other EEA countries your pension from there can be paid to you in the same way.

Private and company pensions vary. Some will pay your pension into any bank account, in or outside the UK, whereas many will only pay the pension into a UK bank account. Bear in mind that your UK pension may go up and down as sterling moves against the euro.

If you plan to transfer **other UK benefits** to Ireland, be aware that not everything is transferable. Bereavement allowance (formerly known as widow's pension), widowed parent's allowance (formerly known as widowed mother's allowance) and industrial injuries disablement benefit will all transfer, but certain other allowances won't.

If you have not yet retired and move to Ireland, your entitlement to a UK pension is frozen and the pension will be paid to you when you reach UK retirement age. If you are quite near retirement age it might be worth making additional voluntary payments while you are resident overseas.

For further information on transferring pensions and benefits to Ireland contact the **Pensions and Overseas Benefits Directorate**, Department of Social Security, Tyneview Park, Benton, Newcastle Upon Tyne NE98 1BA; UK **t** (0191) 218 7777. The **International Pension Centre** will also be able to advise you (UK **t** (0191) 218 7777; **typ-customer-care@dwp.gsi.gov.uk**).

Double Taxation Agreements and Pensions

Ireland has a double taxation agreement with Britain (*see* p.178) that should ensure that you don't pay tax twice on the same income. Double taxation agreements generally make a distinction between pensions payable by governments to former employees and pensions payable by private employers.

As a rule, pensions for non-governmental employees are taxed in the country of residence. So, if you are living in Ireland and getting an occupational pension from the UK (or another country), you should generally receive it gross and then pay Irish tax on it. You need to contact the Inland Revenue in the UK and claim relief on the basis of residence in Ireland. The Inland Revenue should then authorise the payment of your pension without deduction of tax. Most double-taxation agreements work like this – you pay tax only where you are resident.

However, most governmental pensions are generally taxed in the country where they are paid and you will need to inform the Irish Revenue Commisioners of this when making your tax return in Ireland. They should then give you a tax credit for the tax already paid in the UK.

See Appendices for countries Ireland has double taxation agreements with.

Irish Pensions

The Department of Social and Family Affairs pay Irish state pensions. There are three pensions specifically for those aged 65 and over: the **retirement pension** (payable from age 65), the **contributory old age pension** (payable from age 66) and the **non-contributory old age pension** (payable from age 66). The retirement pension is paid to those who are no longer in insurable employment and meet the required number of PRSI payments. Old age contributory pensions are paid to those over 66 who also have the required number of contributions. You

Yearly Exemption Limits in 2004

Status	Aged under 65	Aged 65+
Single or widowed person	€5,210	€15,500
Married couple	€10,420	€31,000
First two dependent children	€575 each	€575 each
Subsequent dependent children	€830 each	€830 each

can continue to work without affecting your contributory pension. If you haven't paid enough contributions you may qualify for pro-rata payments. Old age non-contributory pensions are paid to people over 66 who don't have enough contributions to satisfy the requirements. This pension is means-tested. As a UK citizen you are eligible for this if you satisfy the means test.

All income from pensions in Ireland is subject to taxation and you pay taxes on your pension entitlements in the normal way (for instance under the PAYE system without the PRSI element), but when you are over 65 the tax exemption limits are much higher and there are some extra tax credits. If you are in receipt of social welfare pensions you are likely to be under the limits, but if you have an occupational pension *and* a contributory pension you will probably have to pay some tax.

Cars and Other Private Transport

Owning a Car

Ireland is the fourth most expensive place to buy a new car in the EU – and don't think that you'll be able to escape by importing a car from abroad; there are very specific rules governing what you can bring into the country and you'll have to pay duty if you have owned the car for less than six months. VAT on cars is 20 per cent. However, you can import a car (and other goods) that you've previously owned (for at least six months) if you decide to take up permanent residence in Ireland.

Second-hand cars are a little more reasonable but will probably cost more than their equivalent in Britain. You will find second-hand car dealers all over the country. *Buy and Sell* magazine (**www.buyandsell.ie**) is a good starting point for seeing how much you can expect to pay for second-hand cars (and can also be very good for second-hand furniture and lots of other things).

Petrol currently costs an average of 90.8 cents per litre nationwide. The AA (**www.aaireland.ie**) gives up-to-date estimates of the cost of fuel and the overall cost of running a car in Ireland. Currently the AA estimates that a smallish car (1251–1500cc) would cost about 1 euro a mile to run (this figure includes operating costs, depreciation, tax and insurance).

Bringing a Car into Ireland

You must have a certificate of permanent export or a vehicle registration document to bring a car into Ireland from abroad. If you plan to bring the car into Ireland permanently you must register the car with the Revenue Commissioners and pay vehicle registration tax (VRT) by the end of the working day following your arrival into Ireland. You will be given a new registration number for the car, which you must display within three days, and a form that allows you to apply for motor tax.

VRT is calculated as a percentage of the expected selling price. This is called the open market selling price (OMSP) and is calculated by the VRT official. Unfortunately what you actually paid for the car has no bearing on its designated value. Revenue will give you a VRT quotation but emphasises that nothing is certain until you've formally brought the car to them for inspection. VRT rates vary depending on the size of the engine from 22.5 per cent up to 30 per cent of the OMSP. You can avoid payment of VRT if you can prove that you owned and used the vehicle for at least six months before transfer and that the appropriate local taxes have been paid and not refunded. To prove this you will usually need to supply:

- **the vehicle registration document.**
- **the certificate of insurance.**
- **the sales invoice, receipt of purchase or other similar document.**
- **evidence of the date on which the vehicle was brought into the state (for example a sailing ticket).**
- **documents proving your residency abroad – utility bills, evidence of having paid tax, rental or council tax receipts – the more the better!**

Before you can drive the car legally in the state you must also pay motor tax and pay insurance (*see* 'Vehicle Insurance', p.250). The whole process and the names of the forms you will require is described in detail on the **Revenue Commissioner**'s website (**www.revenue.ie**). You can also contact the Vehicle Registration Unit directly at the **Department of the Environment, Heritage and**

The National Car Test

All cars over 4 years old must pass a national car test (NCT). This test was introduced in 2002 as part of an EU directive making car testing compulsory in all member states. It covers things like brakes, exhaust emission, wheels and tyres, lights, steering and suspension, chassis and underbody, electrical systems, glass and mirrors, transmission, interior and fuel system. The test is strict and minor things such as broken windscreen wipers, wing mirrors or indicators will fail the car just as surely as more serious problems – high emission levels, faulty steering or bad brakes. Once the car has passed it is issued with an NCT certificate – which will be required for tax and insurance.

If you import a car from the UK it will have to pass the NCT on the appropriate date even if it has already received an MOT in Britain or Northern Ireland. If you are buying a second-hand car always find out if it is passed the test and when the next one is due. Cars must be tested every 2 years. Visit the National Car Test Service website (**www.ncts.ie**) to learn more about the test and test centres countrywide.

Local Government (www.environ.ie), Shannon, Co. Clare (**t** (061) 365000; LoCall **t** 1890 411 412 for calls charged at local rate from anywhere within the Republic). This unit also deals with changes of vehicle of ownership, so if you buy a car in the Republic you must contact the unit to register the vehicle in your name.

Avoidance Measures

If you don't want to deal with all the hassle of getting your car to the VRT centre the day after your arrival you can request a 'Green Card' from your UK insurer. Don't tell them that you are moving to Ireland permanently but that you will be living there for a few months and need an extension of your UK insurance. They should be able to issue you with the card for a small fee – this allows you to drive your car in Ireland and be fully insured. They are generally issued for three months at a time.

Licences

If you hold a licence from any of the EU/EEA states, you can exchange it for an Irish licence with no difficulty. If your licence was issued in Australia, Gibraltar, Isle of Man, Japan, Jersey, South Africa, South Korea or Switzerland you can also exchange it for an Irish one. If your licence was issued anywhere else, you can only use it to drive in Ireland for 12 months. You then have to apply for and sit the Irish driving test. Currently there is over a year's waiting list for tests and this waiting period doesn't look as if it is going to be reduced any time soon. Before sitting the test you must apply for a provisional driving licence. This is a licence issued specifically for the purpose of learning to drive. In practice, as we saw in **Selecting a Property**, lots of Irish people drive for years on a provisional licence despite the extra insurance costs involved for provisional drivers. You then apply for a driving test and if you pass this you will be issued with a full driving licence. You must be resident in Ireland to sit the test here (i.e. have spent 183 days in the state and have an Irish address, see pp.174–7). The Department of Transport has a special driving test website with all the information you need (**www.drivingtest.ie**). You must always carry your licence with you when driving in Ireland.

Car Taxes

Motor tax is compulsory. It is calculated on engine size so the bigger your engine, the more tax you pay. You pay the tax at your local motor tax office – every local authority has one. Contact details for every local authority are listed at the front of public phone directories and addresses are also given at the back of this book (see **References**, 'Irish County Councils', pp.282–6); you can also pay online at **www.motortax.ie**. The table overleaf gives an indication of some of the rates that applied in January 2004 – a much more comprehensive list is published on the Motor Tax website or is available from your local motor tax office.

You must display evidence that you've paid the tax, in the form of a motor tax disc on the windscreen of your car. Tax and insurance spot checks are common on Irish roads. Motor taxes can be paid yearly, half-yearly or quarterly; paying the full amount up front every year will save you about 11 per cent on paying half-yearly and 13 per cent on paying quarterly. You must show evidence of insurance to get your motor tax disc.

Car and Motorbike Taxes

Cars		Motorbikes	
1000–1100cc	€227	Under 75cc	€37
1301–1400cc	€292	76–200cc	€51
1601–1700cc	€414	More than 201cc	€67
2000–2100cc	€689		

Vehicle Insurance

You must have insurance to drive in a public place and to obtain a motor tax disc. Car insurance is a thorny subject in Ireland. Irish people feel extremely aggrieved about the cost of insurance and feel, justifiably, that they pay far more than other EU countries. However, Ireland is currently rated third in the EU for road accident frequency and it also has the highest fatality rate in Europe. In 2003, 341 people were killed on Irish roads. The Irish Insurance Federation also claims that there is a particularly litigious environment in Ireland with large awards handed out by the courts to victims of car accidents.

Whatever the reasons for the high premiums, you can certainly save by shopping around – checking prices online, contacting insurance companies directly and using a broker. Brokers tend to be able to get the cheapest deals – approaching the insurer directly rarely pays dividends in the form of lower premiums. You'll find an insurance broker in most towns and the Professional Insurance Brokers Association (PIBA; **www.piba.ie**) can also give you the names of local brokers. A recent survey published by the Irish Financial Services Regulatory Authority (IFSRA) found that drivers can save as much as 50 per cent by shopping around for insurance. Another piece of good news is that a new directive by the European Union, due to come into force before Christmas 2004, will allow Irish motorists to insure cars in other EU member states and legally drive the car with full coverage in Ireland. But these directives can often be held up so it is best to base your insurance cost estimates on what's available now.

If you are involved in an accident you must remain at the scene of the accident for a reasonable amount of time and give your name, address, registration number and insurance details to the driver of the other vehicle. If anyone is injured you must inform the Gardaí but it is not compulsory to inform them of the accident if there are no injuries.

Sample Driver Profiles and Insurance Costs

- Dublin-based cleaner aged 30, driving a Fiat Punto: €1,565 from Axa and €804 from FBD for fully comprehensive cover

- Cavan-based teacher aged 36, driving a Renault Laguna: €898 from Axa and €526 from FBD fully comprehensive cover

- Longford-based civil servant aged 52, driving an Opel Astra: €1,006 from Axa and €501 from Quinn Direct for third party, fire and theft

- Cork-based student aged 19, driving a Nissan Micra on a provisional licence: €2,113 from Axa and €1,676 from Eagle Star for third party, fire and theft.

Based on survey published by IFSRA in March 2004; visit **www.ifsra.ie** for more detailed profiles.

Parking

Most towns of any size have disc parking – discs are usually available from local shops. Cities generally have metered parking. Dublin is particularly notorious for a shortage of parking spaces. If you are planning to buy an apartment and want to keep a car, make sure a parking space is included or purchase one separately as you generally won't be able to park your car on the street. Residents of a house can apply for a resident's parking permit for a nominal fee. Contact the local county council for information on parking permits.

Taking Your Pet to Ireland

The good news is that there are no restrictions on bringing pets to Ireland from the UK. The bad news is that if your pet is coming from outside the UK, the Channel Islands or the Isle of Man you must have an import licence for it. To obtain an import licence you have to put your pet into approved quarantine in Ireland for at least six months. If the animal has come from certain countries and has a current rabies vaccination certificate you can place it into approved quarantine for just one month and then keep it under approved private arrangements for another five months. However, attentive readers will already have realised that, since pets can travel freely between Britain and Ireland, once your pet has been through the UK pet importation process (where an approved pet passport may avoid the need for quarantine) it can travel freely on to Ireland. You can get all the information you need about the UK Passports for Pets scheme from the UK Department of Environment, Food and Rural Affairs.

There is just one approved quarantine facility in Ireland and this is Lissenhall Quarantine Kennels and Catteries (**t** (01) 840 1776/840 9776; Lissenhall, Swords, Co. Dublin). If you want to bring animals other than cats and dogs into the

> ## How the Irish Regard Dog Licences
> An elderly Irish farmer is driving down the road in an ancient rust bucket when he's stopped by the Gardaí. The Garda walks around the car making detailed notes on missing headlights, broken mirrors, bald tyres and so on. Eventually he notices a dog sitting up on the passenger seat. 'Do you have a licence for him?' he asks. 'Oh, no,' replies the old man. 'Sure I do most of the driving myself.'

Republic you should contact the Department of Agriculture and Food to see what the relevant regulations are (forms for import licences are available from them as well.)

You are supposed to have a licence for your dog (although many people don't seem to bother and the rule is not strictly enforced) and all dogs should wear collars with a tag with the name of their owners. Certain breeds (pitbull terriers among them) have to wear muzzles outside and be kept under strict control. Licences are available from post offices and cost €12.70 per year; a general dog licence (one for an unspecified number of dogs – probably only relevant to those of you who want to breed dogs) costs €253.95. One doggy thing to be aware of is that sheep-chasing is taken very very seriously in country areas. A farmer has the right to shoot a sheep-chasing dog on sight. If you are not sure how your dog will react to sheep, keep it under strict control until you are sure that it won't cause any problems. Farmers also tend to take a dim view of people who walk dogs on their land. Even if you don't feel this is justified, always ask before setting off on a tramp with your dog. This might avoid considerable bad feeling with your neighbours.

Crime and the Police

Crime rates in Ireland are very low by international standards (although Ireland's prison population is the highest in Europe *per capita*, most prisoners have committed minor crimes, often drug-related). Crime in rural areas is generally far less than in the cities – particularly the Dublin area. A survey shows that 50 per cent of all recorded indictable offences from 1948 to 1998 were committed in the Dublin region. Crime against property (burglary) is on the decrease whereas crimes against people (robberies) seem to be rising some-what. Despite this, the overall crime rate has fluctuated around the same level for the last 20 years. In spite of this, crime features largely in the newspapers and politicians often use minor increases in crime rates as a stick to beat one another with. Pay no attention to alarmist headlines: Ireland is generally very safe and Northern Ireland has particularly low crime rates.

The police force there (formerly the RUC) is now called the **Police Service of Northern Ireland (PSNI)**.

> **Emergencies**
> Dial **t** 999 or 112 and ask for the service you require.

The police force in the Republic is called **An Garda Síochána**, which means the Guardians of the Peace. The **Gardaí** (pronounced Guardee, singular is **Garda**) are generally trusted and well regarded. They do not carry guns. Particularly in rural areas the local Garda is very much part of the community and will probably know most of the people in his or her area. Many areas have a local Neighbourhood Watch or Community Alert scheme where volunteers from the community report any suspicious behaviour to the Gardaí. If you plan to live in the country and have many valuable antiques or paintings you will need an alarm and other safety features to obtain insurance. This is because professional burglars have been known to target country properties, often stealing to order. Similarly, if you plan to leave a house empty for part of the year, it would be wise not to keep many valuables there and to have a neighbour or friend check it occasionally. There is even an organisation that will make spot checks on a vacant property for you (*see* **Letting Your Property**, 'Management Agencies', p.271, for more details).

Irish Politics

The System

The Republic of Ireland is a parliamentary democracy governed by the Oireachtas or parliament. This consists of two houses – Dáil Éireann (House of Representatives) and the Seanad (Senate). The Dáil has 166 members, or TDs, who are elected by a proportional representation system. The Seanad has 60 members: university graduates elect six; a number of vocational panels elect another 43; and the Taoiseach (or Prime Minister) appoints 11. The Taoiseach is the head of the government and looks after the day-to-day running of the country. The Tánaiste (deputy prime minister) stands in for the Taoiseach if he or she is absent or incapacitated. The administrative structure of the government is set out in the Constitution of Ireland (Bunreacht na hÉireann), enacted by referendum in July 1937 and periodically modified by referendum since. The Constitution also describes the fundamental rights of every Irish citizen.

The President (An tUachtarán) is elected by a direct vote every 7 years. The President is the official head of the state and of the defence forces but has little power. The position took on great symbolic resonance when Ireland's first woman president, Mary Robinson, was elected in 1990. The current president is Mary McAleese, a barrister and Fianna Fáil nominee. In 2004 she is coming to the end of her 7-year term and will run again in October 2004.

Political Parties

Ireland gained independence from Britain in 1921 under a treaty negotiated by Sinn Féin (the political party that came to power after the 1916 Rising seeking Irish independence) and the British Government. The treaty partitioned the island, creating what was known as the Irish Free State, the 26 counties that now make up the Republic, and allowing the remaining six counties in Ulster to stay part of Britain. The divisions created by the Treaty led to a civil war between pro- and anti-treaty sides and split Sinn Féin down the middle. Irish politics remain dominated by the two political parties that grew from these divisions, Fianna Fáil and Fine Gael, pro- and anti-treaty respectively, and changes in the party system have been gradual, despite efforts by the Labour party to create an alternative left–right alignment. In the most recent general election (2002) Fianna Fáil gained 41.5 per cent of first preference votes; Fine Gael, 22.5 per cent; Labour, 10.8 per cent; Sinn Féin, 6.5 per cent; Progressive Democrats, 4 per cent; and the Green Party, 3.9 per cent. Proportional representation means that these first preference votes are not directly reflected in the number of seats held by each party. For example, Sinn Féin holds five Dáil seats compared with the PD's eight: although their share of the first preference vote was higher, they gained fewer second and lower preferences and ended up with only 3 per cent of the vote overall (the PDs maintained momentum and got 5 per cent overall). Proportional representation also means that coalition governments are the norm – Fianna Fáil has shared power with the PDs for the last two governments.

Politics in Ireland is very local. TDs must pay attention to their constituents or risk losing their seat and even government ministers have been known to issue statements that contradict government policy but resonate with their constituencies. This is the case even though local councils have very little power and are financed almost completely by the national government. You will notice this localism at play in everything from applications for planning permission to requests for repairs to a local school.

Major Political Parties in the Republic
Fianna Fáil

This is the country's largest political party, founded by Éamon de Valera in 1926. The politics of Fianna Fáil are right of centre and republican with a strong country base. At present Fianna Fáil is in a coalition with the Progressive Democrats. Bertie Ahern (generally known as Bertie), the party leader, is currently Taoiseach.

Fine Gael

The country's second largest political party, founded in 1933 but somewhat in decline at present. More European than Fianna Fáil and also centre-right. The current leader is Enda Kenny.

Political Terms

Dáil Éireann: seat of Irish parliament.
Oireachtas: the Irish parliament.
Seanad Éireann: upper house of parliament or Senate.
Teachta Dála (TD): member of Dáil Éireann.
Taoiseach/Taoisigh: prime minister/s.
An tUachtarán: the President.
Bunreacht na hÉireann: the Irish Constitution.

Labour Party

Founded in 1912 at a conference of the Irish Trade Union Congress in Clonmel under the inspiration of socialist leaders James Connolly, Jim Larkin and William O'Brien. Labour merged with Democratic Left in 1999 and its leader is now Pat Rabbitte.

The Progressive Democrats (PDs)

The Progressive Democrat Party was formed in 1985 by Desmond O'Malley as a breakaway party from Fianna Fáil. The PD leader is Mary Harney, the first and only female leader of a political party. Currently the PDs are in coalition with Fianna Fáil. They have progressive social policies and conservative economic policies.

Green Party

Founded in 1981 as the Ecology Party of Ireland, the party was renamed the Green Party in 1986. The party has two deputies in the Dáil. It campaigns on all issues, but has a particular interest in environmental matters.

Its leader is Trevor Sargent.

Sinn Féin

The political wing of the Provisional IRA holds one seat in Dáil Éireann. Despite overtaking the SDLP to become the main nationalist political party in the North, Sinn Féin does not have much support in the Republic. It is beginning to make inroads in inner city and working-class areas, though, with a strong anti-drug message that resonates with communities devastated by heroin addiction. It is no longer an illegal organisation.

Socialist Party

The Socialist Party was formed by Joe Higgins, following a split with the Labour Party. Higgins holds the party's single seat in Dail Éireann and raised his profile when he was jailed during the bin tax protests of 2003 (*see* box 'Bin Tax Battles', p.218).

Voting Rights

We've already reviewed your voting rights (*see* box 'Voting Rights', p.19) but, to recap, as a British citizen you have the right to vote in all local, national and European elections but not for the president or in referenda. Irish citizens can vote in all elections and referenda. You must be listed in the electoral register to exercise your right to vote. Every year a new register is complied and published in November. You can inspect the register or draft register in your local county council offices, public libraries, post offices and Garda stations. You also obtain application forms for inclusion in the register in the same places (except Garda stations).

Religion

It is hard to understate the changes that have taken place in the Republic over the last 10 years. Up until the early 1990s the Catholic Church was regarded as having an almost sacrosanct role in the life of the nation. Pronouncements from the pulpit on social issues such as divorce, contraception and abortion were common and reported widely in the press. Bishops would lobby politicians on legislation. Referenda on divorce and abortion were stridently opposed. Mass-goers would often find themselves accosted by campaigners inside the church gates. All this was to change. A sexual scandal in the early 1980s, in which a bishop was found to have had an affair and fathered a child, heralded a sea change in how the Church was regarded, although this now seems inconsequential in comparison with the child sex abuse scandals of the late 1990s. The end result has been a much chastened and far less aggressive Catholic Church. Now the Church focuses mainly on issues like poverty and drug abuse and avoids matters of sexual morality.

Losing their Religion – the Statistics

Religion is important to only 30 per cent of Irish people (the figure is 33 per cent in Britain), placing Ireland among the more secular of Western nations. The idea of sin and hell no longer hold sway. Although 87 per cent of the Irish say they believe in God, only 39 per cent believe in the devil. Only 56.2 per cent of people under 25 are satisfied with their religion or spirituality whereas 82.3 per cent of people in the 65–74 age group are satisfied. Nevertheless, 77.7 per cent of Irish people are happy with their lot, an increase on previous polls. This is despite an almost complete lack of confidence in government (only 2 per cent have confidence), the health service (5 per cent), the legal system (7 per cent) and the church (9 per cent).

(Statistics from the Diageo *Ireland Quality of Life Report* 2003 available from **www.amarach.com**.)

Today condoms are available in corner shops, births out of wedlock are common, and a substantial number of young women travel to Britain for abortions each year. However, the Church is still important in the lives of many people, particularly the elderly, and 88 per cent of the population describes themselves as Catholic. Most children are christened, most marriages take place in a church and almost all funerals do. Although the number of church-goers has plummeted, the churchgoing proportion of the population remains the highest in western Europe. The bones of Saint Thérèse of Lisieux were taken around the country in 2001 attracting huge crowds and extensive media coverage. If you live in Ireland you'll find that parish priests are still important figures in the community, although they are getting older and feebler. Priests are being recruited from Nigeria to fill the gaps left by retiring parish priests and parishes are being consolidated, with one priest saying mass in as many as three churches a day.

The 2002 Census showed that all non-Christian faiths in the Republic gained members between 1991 and 2002. The biggest increase was in the Muslim population, which rose from 3,900 in 1991 to 19,100 in 2002, a climb of 390 per cent. There are also small Buddhist and Hindu communities. In addition Anglican, Methodist, Presbyterian, Jewish and Quaker communities have existed in Ireland for many years.

Irish Food and Drink

Food

Ireland was so poor for so long that it doesn't have a great peasant repertoire like many European countries. Traditional dishes like Irish stew and coddle can be delicious but they aren't often cooked at home. Much of what is touted as indigenous cuisine is usually only trotted out for tourists, but there has been renewed interest in some traditional techniques typified by the upsurge in artisan cheese-producers around the country. Parallel with this has come an influx of new food ideas from all around the world. Whereas even 10 years ago tastes were unadventurous, now most Irish people will try anything once. To take a representative example, you still find bacon with white sauce on the menu in the National Gallery café in Dublin, but alongside it you'll find Asian

---

Traditional Irish foods
Boxty: potato griddle cakes.
Champ: mashed potato with chopped spring onions (scallions) through it.
Colcannon: mashed potato with cabbage and onions.
Irish stew: mutton, potatoes, carrots and onions.

noodle salad and marinated salmon in ginger. Ireland has also embraced European-style café culture with open arms. Many of the old Victorian pubs in the cities have been replaced with sleek, blond wood bars and cappuccino-coloured bar stools, and as soon as the sun shines every café in Dublin optimistically sets up pavement tables and umbrellas for mobile-phone- and sunglass-sporting punters.

If you want to cook at home you may find wonderful ingredients, but it depends on where you shop. You can find organic meat and vegetables in many of the main towns and cities but some foodstuffs are semi-organic anyway. Lamb, for example, is generally reared out in the fields and the mountains and the animals won't have been fed artificial feed or antibiotics. Pork, on the other hand, is often intensively and unpleasantly farmed in piggeries and you might be better off seeking out the organic version if only for the flavour. Fish is fantastic if you can get it fresh, but many inland towns don't have a fish-mongers and even on the coasts some of the best seafood is all exported to France and the continent. Some of the old tastes linger; Irish people still eat lots of butter, dairy products, bacon and the ubiquitous spud.

Eating out has become common in Ireland and in many cities you will find a little bit of everything, Dublin now boasts Filipino, Russian, Japanese, Nepalese and Korean restaurants. Two years ago it had just one Thai restaurant; their numbers are now up in the twenties and counting. Most towns boast a Chinese takeaway, supplemented more recently with an Indian restaurant. Pubs offer anything from toasted sandwiches and carvery lunches to elaborate seafood platters, although many pubs will only give you a packet of crisps with your pint in the evenings. However, you don't find good food everywhere; if you don't choose carefully you may find mediocre food at exaggerated prices. If eating out use a guide or local recommendations – the Bridgestone guide (**www.bestofbridgestone.com**) is one of the best.

Drink

What can be said about the Irish and drink that hasn't been said a thousand times before? The local pub is where you will meet your neighbours, find out what is going on in the district and generally get a feeling for the place you've

---

The Smoking Ban

The Irish attitude to smoking in public places has traditionally been lax. Pubs are characteristically full of smoke. All of this completely changed when a total ban on smoking in the workplace, which includes all pubs and restaurants, came into force at the end of March 2004. This has been a great success, although people in country areas complain that it has ruined the atmosphere in rural pubs.

Case Study: Amanda and John

Amanda and John Rogers came to their 200-year-old stone farmhouse in County Limerick by a circuitous route. 'We met in Saudi Arabia, married in Dubai and moved to South Africa,' explains Amanda, born in Lebanon and brought up in the home counties. When John, an accountant from Belfast, brought Amanda to Ireland for the first time in 1995, she 'absolutely loved it, so I always said if I settled anywhere it would be here'.

Several years later the decision was made. John applied for jobs all over Ireland and eventually decided on one in Limerick. Job secured but still homeless, they rented for six months and house-hunted in their free time. Eventually, like so many other Irish home-seekers, they found their house while driving past. 'We saw the sign and thought, that's interesting, drove up, had a chat with the farmer selling it, and that was it, we decided instantly.' Building work went on for eight months while the family (two-year-old Sophie and two boxer d ogs who travelled from South Africa) lived in a single room at the back of the farmhouse.

Asked what advice they'd give people moving to Ireland, Amanda and John immediately point out that it is easy to get a misleading perception of the country from brief visits. 'People have been extraordinarily welcoming and friendly, but in a neighbourly way rather than a close friendship kind of way. It takes a long time to establish real friendships.' Amanda thinks that this might be because the community is less transient than other places she's lived. Nonetheless, Ireland is now home to this globe-trotting couple and they 'wouldn't go anywhere else'.

moved to. The best of them marry atmosphere, friendliness and a great pint with something intangible – authenticity perhaps. You won't find a huge choice of **beers** – Guinness rules supreme, but it is quite different from Guinness anywhere else – richer, smoother and creamier. Smithwicks is like English bitter, but more full-bodied. You'll also find Breo, a white beer from the Guinness stable, a range of continental beers and the ubiquitous Bud. Recently microbreweries have started to produce a range of new beers, many of them excellent. **Whiskey** offers an even smaller choice – Bushmills from the north and Jameson from Cork are the most famous. There is growing interest in **wine** – a new wine magazine launched recently, tasting classes are packed, and specialist wine shops are opening countrywide. You'll probably even find a bottle of something or another in your local shop but prices are much higher than in the UK (*see* box 'The Cost of Booze', p.209).

Even though the pub is still the centre of most communities, statistics about the Irish and alcohol make sobering reading. Despite Ireland's boozy reputation the nation only really began to consume enormous quantities of alcohol during the Celtic Tiger years – consumption rose by 50 per cent from 1991 to 2001. Irish

Culture Shock

Culture shock is something people often associate with going far afield and getting to grips with a totally different society, language and culture. However, culture shock in a place you think is familiar, usually because you speak the language, can be just as shocking, even if it sneaks up on you in a subtler way. Many British and American people come to Ireland thinking that they understand what makes the place tick. It is generally only after a couple of months that they begin to realise that this place works to different rules and that these rules take a bit of getting used to. That said – as we saw in **Reasons for Buying** – there are more cultural similarities between the UK and Ireland than you might expect. Nonetheless you might find that your first six months have you feeling a little out of place – disgruntled at the Irish way of doing things, complaining more than usual and experiencing a general feeling of angst. This feeling does pass, and sometimes it is enough just to identify why you are feeling so out of sorts to feel much better.

people drink twice as much as the average European. They spend 10 times more on alcohol than the Greeks. Many young Irish people begin to drink at about age 12 or 13. A recent RTÉ *Prime Time* documentary showing overflowing hospital wards late at night and violence on the streets has triggered a national debate about how much the nation is drinking and what can be done about it. The only consolation is that this is nothing new – alcohol has been recognised to be a social problem in Ireland since the 18th century.

Letting Your Property

08

Many British people who buy houses in Ireland let them out at one stage or another – perhaps because they don't plan to live in the house immediately or because they want to earn extra income from the house when they are not using it. If you plan to let your house long-term, finding suitable tenants will be your main problem and there will not be an enormous amount of ongoing management work to do. Holiday lets, on the other hand, require far more input from you – or an agent. This chapter is primarily aimed at people who would like to supplement their incomes with occasional holiday rentals rather than those wishing to fund a full mortgage by letting the property or those who plan to let full-time, but there is a short section on long-term letting at the end of the chapter. If you haven't yet bought a property and are wondering how to ensure a rental income from one, the information in this chapter should help you decide what kind of property would be most suitable. Some locations are far more suitable for renting than others and some types of property are much easier to let than others.

Overview

There are lots of holiday homes in Ireland – a seaside resort renewal scheme that gave investors tax breaks on property in certain areas encouraged many people to invest in property (*see* box 'The Seaside Resort Scheme', p.264). It is estimated that up to 60 per cent of the houses in Connemara, for example, are second homes. Agencies warn that the average rental season is only 10 to 12 weeks, although the most successful can rent for up to 30 weeks including Christmas, Easter, bank holiday weekends and the summer months. These properties do tend to be in the minority. That said, many Irish families now take several short breaks throughout the year and more houses than you might expect are occupied on winter weekends. Nevertheless, it won't be easy to rent your property all year round and you shouldn't expect the return from holiday letting to fully service a mortgage. The bright side is that historically property in Ireland has been an excellent investment and over the long term the capital appreciation of your property will probably make up for any initial shortfall in income.

First Steps and Questions

It is essential to sit down and establish your financial objectives before starting to let your property, since many other decisions will depend on them – what kind of tenants to aim for, whether to use a management company or not, and so on. You should also work out what your outgoings are likely to be –

fitting out the house, general and garden maintenance, paying someone to clean the house and greet tenants may all take a chunk out of any rental income. You can employ an agent or management company to manage the lettings for you, but again this will cut into the income you can expect to get from letting the property.

Questions to Ask Yourself before Starting to Let

- What are your financial objectives?
- Do you plan just to cover your costs or do you want to maximise the income from your property?
- Do you want to use the property yourself – if so when? If you'd like to use it at Easter and in the summer – that's exactly when other people will want to be there as well.
- Do you want to be there on set dates, or can you be flexible and only go on weeks with no bookings?
- What kind of person do you want to have in your house – are children OK, what about a hen party or a group of fishermen?
- What advantages does your property have – is there anything that makes it stand out? What amenities is it near – golf courses, a good local pub within walking distance and so on.
- Will you have the time (or inclination) to manage the lettings yourself? This can entail a substantial amount of work.

Location, Choice of Property and Rental Potential

In the last few years, as more and more houses come on to the holiday home market and tenants' expectations rise, properties with extra features and facilities have become more common. For example, the traditional rent-an-Irish-cottage property generally only had one bathroom – today most have en-suite bathrooms. But if your property is particularly charming or unusual it may sell itself without requiring extra features.

If you are planning to buy to let you should also consider your target clientele – British visitors are more likely to want your property in the summer months and perhaps at Easter. Irish people may be looking for a weekend destination and so the property might rent at weekends during the year. Weekend lettings require more management since each let is only for two to three days as opposed to a couple of weeks. Or you might plan for a mixture of the two – in which case your advertising strategy might vary at different periods of the year. Remember that the British market accounts for one in five of visitors to Ireland

The Seaside Resort Scheme

From 1995 to 1999 tax breaks led to the construction of more than 5,000 holiday homes and apartments in 15 seaside towns. The scheme was estimated to cost the Exchequer an estimated €320 million plus. In many cases the numbers of houses often swamped the local village. In Enniscrone, County Sligo, 379 houses and apartments were built around a village with a population of just 692. In fact surveys showed that in some cases the scheme was actually contrary to the national tourist policy since it detracted from the unspoilt beauty of the areas. What it means for you as an investor is that many of the neighbouring properties will also be on the market and oversupply might harm your chances of finding suitable tenants. If planning to buy to let, be a little bit wary of properties in large seaside resort schemes and make sure to find out how the next-door property is renting.

so you might do very well concentrating your efforts close to home. You will also have a good understanding of what a UK visitor might want and expect from a holiday let.

Location

Location has traditionally been the most important draw for holiday properties. Lately, proximity to a large city (particularly Dublin) has become more important as short weekends away become more popular. Strangford Lough in Northern Ireland, the lakes of Cavan and the traditional spots like Wexford and Arklow are all in demand from Dublin weekenders. Clare and Connemara, along with places like Rosslare, Fethard-on-Sea and Dunmore East, are popular during Easter, the summer, at Christmas, New Year, and on bank holiday weekends. Parts of West Cork – Kinsale, Baltimore and Schull particularly – command high rents because of a shortage of good quality rental accommodation. Seaside locations that tend to be difficult to let outside the summer period include Mayo, Sligo and Donegal – mainly because they are quite a distance to travel for a weekend break. When deciding on a location, think about how your prospective tenants will get to the property. Knock airport makes Galway, Mayo and Sligo accessible from the UK, for example.

Attractions

If your property is not in one of the most popular locations it may be near another attraction. The lakes of Cavan and Fermanagh attract hundreds of fishermen; Lough Derg and the other Shannon lakes have sailing and other boating activities all year round; many houses near popular golf courses let all through the year; and attractive properties near Blue Flag beaches are in great demand during the summer. Is there a spa, health farm or leisure centre nearby? These are becoming more common in rural Ireland and attract weekend Dublin visitors. Proximity to a village is always a draw, as tenants like to be within walking distance of pubs, shops and restaurants. Award-winning restaurants or pubs are also likely to attract more tenants.

Marketing the Property

You first need to decide how much you will charge for rentals. Find out how much similar properties in the area rent for. Contact the local tourist office and ask for their brochures. Tourism Ireland should also give a good idea of rates for different types of self-catering property. If you wish to have your property listed in Tourism Ireland's websites and brochures you will have to have your property inspected and graded. Each tourist region has a self-catering supervisor. You can contact the authority in your region for more information on the grading system and how to get your property listed. Note that Tourism Ireland's listings depend solely on a checklist of facilities offered – more nebulous things like charm or character don't count. Look at the grading systems to see what the various categories require. Local auctioneers can also list your property in their holiday letting lists (generally for a proportion of the rental rather than a set fee).

Before deciding on an advertising medium you will need to decide who you are going to aim your advertising at – Irish people, British people, a more international market or a mixture? Clearly you will use different media for the different markets. However, if you want to let the property for more than the average 10 weeks or so a year, cast your net wide. For example, you might advertise on a website targeting American academics looking for a summer property, an Irish newspaper for the Easter period, and leave details of the property with the local auctioneer for longer-term lets over the winter season. Leaving an ad (laminated, if it is going to be there long-term) on the noticeboards of local pubs and shops can bring enquiries from visitors who plan to return to the area.

If you think carefully about your target market and tailor advertising to them you are likely to be more successful than if you do very general advertising. Some of the markets you could consider targeting are walkers, sailors and windsurfers and English language students (check with the nearest school if they require self-catering accommodation for their students).

Newspapers and Magazines

Newspapers are the most traditional advertising method. Cost varies depending on the circulation of the paper but this is certainly not a cheap method of marketing your property. Other disadvantages are that a newspaper only covers a specific area; you can't wax lyrical about the joys of the property since every extra word costs you money; pictures are generally not possible; and the ad only lasts for a day or so. Still, you might get good results for a particular weekend or the summer period. Irish cottages are advertised in the travel sections and the classified sections of all the main British papers. You could also try your local paper and specialist magazines – anything from sailing to literary magazines may source prospective tenants. Newspapers such as the *Sunday Times* Irish edition can be good places to advertise for bank holiday weekends and summer lets.

The Internet

The Internet has become most people's first port of call when looking for a holiday rental. Many sites have been established to help you do this (some are listed below). Advertising on the Internet is relatively cheap and gives you access to a very large audience. Most sites will charge an annual fee to list your property and give your details so that prospective tenants can contact you directly. Those that allow online booking usually cost considerably more.

Make sure that you give plenty of detail about the property and local attractions. When writing your advertisement, emphasise any special features that people may be willing to pay a little more for – open fires, antique furniture, nearby golf courses, views or a pub within walking distance. It is a good idea to spend a bit of time thinking about all the possible attractions and listing them before starting to write your ad. If a babysitter is available, for example, tell potential tenants this in your ad. When advertising on the Internet, a good photograph (preferably several) is absolutely essential. Many people select properties solely from the photograph, so if your property makes a good picture you are immediately at an advantage. Some people also create their own website with extra information, pictures and links. A website on its own is unlikely to generate traffic but including the address in your paid advertisement gives your property an extra advantage. More importantly, satisfied tenants can pass it on to friends and family. Websites don't have to be complicated; a single page with images is often enough.

Holiday Rental Websites
- **www.activeireland.ie** (for more upmarket rentals)
- **www.cottageguide.co.uk**
- **www.country-holidays.ie**
- **www.holiday-rentals.com**
- **www.irish-holiday-rentals.com**
- **www.irishlets.net**
- **www.selfcateringireland.ie**
- **www.welcomecottages.com**

Equipping the Property

You will get tenants initially through advertising and perhaps through friends if you are lucky. As your property matures you should get return business and business through recommendations and word of mouth. But you will only get return business if the property meets or exceeds your tenants' expectations in terms of facilities, furnishing and cleanliness. It is therefore very important to spend some time deciding how to furnish and manage the property to ensure that it suits your tenants. Clearly some of the equipment you'll supply will depend on the tenants you plan to attract. Sailors, for example, may appreciate an area where clothes can dry or where sails can be stored. Families with children will expect high chairs, cots and playpens.

Remember that lots of people will pass through the house, so the furniture should be robust and of good quality. Expect breakages, so don't put anything in that is particularly precious or delicate. A good rule of thumb is that everything in the house should be easy to clean, low-maintenance and hard to damage. Wooden or tiled floors with rugs are a good idea. The house shouldn't be too impersonal but don't have lots of knick-knacks around as these are easily broken and many people don't like clutter. Books can add character and atmosphere. Open fires are a big draw for most people, particularly if you plan to rent the house in the winter months – but they mustn't be the only form of heating! Irish houses can become damp if not lived in. If you won't be in the house over the winter months it is a good idea to get someone to come in and switch on the heating occasionally and it is essential to make sure that the house has been aired out before tenants arrive.

Cleanliness

It is essential that everything is spotless for your tenants – particularly the kitchen and bathroom. People's expectations of holiday lets are very high, so ensure that the person cleaning the house knows this and checks everything thoroughly. For example, tenants don't always clean pots and pans properly before leaving.

Kitchens

Equip the kitchen fully. Plates, glasses, kitchen utensils and so on don't cost that much, so be generous and supply plenty. Supply an adequate number of pots and pans and don't forget things like chopping boards, knives and corkscrews. Provide good-quality appliances, as they will get lots of use. A dishwasher is a nice addition, as people appreciate not having to wash up while on holiday. Worktops, floors and surfaces should be easy to clean. Also supply some cleaning equipment – mop and bucket, sweeping brush and so on. A vacuum cleaner is also useful (and essential if your floors are carpeted). You should also ensure that supplies like toilet rolls, soap and refuse sacks are always in stock. It is a good idea to provide kitchen essentials like salt, pepper, tea, coffee, sugar and flour, and it is also a nice extra touch to supply fresh foods like milk, fruit and bread when people arrive.

Bedrooms, Linen and Storage

Beds should be clean and comfortable. It is a good idea to try them out for a night yourself. There should be bedside tables and lamps and plenty of storage space (including clothes hangers). Provide at least one hairdryer. Maximise the amount of bed space available by supplying twin beds and pull-out sofa beds.

Try and have at least two sets of linen for each bed. Removable mattress covers can prevent soiling of the mattress. Supply bathroom towels, tea towels and tablecloths as well. Tenants generally prefer bed linen to be provided, although you can specify that the tenants should bring their own.

If you plan to use the house a lot yourself it is a good idea to have a storage area where you can put personal or high-value items away. If this area is lockable – so much the better.

Welcome Pack and Other Documents

You'll need to put together a number of documents for your tenants. First is a pre-visit pack that you post or e-mail when they make the booking. This should tell them about the area and how to get to the house, give emergency contact numbers and instructions about what to do if they are delayed en-route. You should also make up a welcome pack and a guest manual that stays in the house. The welcome pack should give information about the area. Collect leaflets and maps from your local tourist offices and keep them in a plastic folder. Include a comprehensive list of local numbers for any possible emergency. People also appreciate recommendations for local restaurants, shops and pubs. Clearly you will tailor the information for the type of tenants you expect but anything personal – local walks and maps or your family's favourite local activities and so on – are usually appreciated. The aim is to make the new arrivals feel welcome. Some people also leave a guest book where previous guests can leave comments and recommendations. The guest manual should include detailed instructions about how to work any equipment, switch on the heating and any idiosyncrasies of the house. Always include contact numbers in case of any queries. The guest manual should also include an inventory of the equipment in the house.

It is also a good idea to have a sheet of house rules pinned on a notice board in the kitchen. This should give information about rubbish disposal, the phone

> ### Case Study: Starting to Let
>
> May and Dick bought a little house in the lovely village of St Mullins in Carlow 10 years ago. They initially planned to live there after they retired, but circumstances changed and now they live only part of the time in Ireland and the rest of the year in Lancashire where Dick still works. Last year they decided to try letting the cottage while they weren't there – initially to earn some extra money to pay for a holiday for one of their daughters and her children. 'We started out advertising in newspapers – we tried the *Irish Independent* and the *Evening Herald* in Dublin and then we put another ad in our local paper here,' explains May, 'but we got absolutely no replies. Then our daughter did a website for us but that didn't really work either. Eventually we advertised it on a website guide for holiday cottages in Britain and Ireland and that triggered lots of interest.' May seems to have found ideal tenants. 'They left the place in spotless condition we had absolutely no problems with organising the letting.' In fact the whole experience was so positive that the couple plan to continue letting their cottage and wholeheartedly recommend the Internet.

number of the local contact and lists of local emergency numbers. Emergency numbers should include an electrician and a plumber and, if possible, a general repair man who is familiar with the property. It is an advantage to have someone to welcome the tenants, give them keys, show them around and explain how things work. It is also a good idea for someone to be there when the guests leave, to check that no damage has been done and to read the meters and return the deposit there and then.

Managing the Letting

Doing it Yourself

If you are planning to manage the lettings yourself you will need to set up systems to ensure that the process runs as smoothly as possible. Remember that it can be a time-consuming business and you will have to be prepared for lots of enquiries that end up leading nowhere. If you do it yourself, keep tabs on how long it is taking you and how easy you find it and assess the situation again at the end of the first year.

Bookings

Make sure you have an efficient booking calendar. It is best to decide on a changeover day and stick to this (otherwise you risk ending up with part weeks that you can't rent). Holiday rentals are generally charged by the number of nights, not the number of days, that visitors stay.

Staff

If you can't be there yourself you will need to arrange for someone local to clean the property and greet tenants. Again try to set up systems for this, with lists of what needs to be done to prepare the property for tenants and what to do in case of emergencies. It can be difficult in some areas to find someone willing to do this – especially if you won't be renting the property regularly. Enquire locally to see if there is anyone who does this for other landlords. It is wise to find out if this will be difficult to set up early on – after you've advertised the property and taken bookings is not the time to find out that no one is available to do laundry and cleaning.

Setting Up Systems

If you can, set up a series of documents on your computer that you can person-alise for each enquiry. These should include a response to queries about dates and prices, booking forms, invoices and so on. Many websites supply these free of charge (for example see **www.holiday-rentals.com**). Make sure that you respond to queries as quickly as possible. This is particularly important if you are advertising on the Internet, as Internet users will expect particularly speedy replies. You generally confirm bookings when you receive the deposit payment. If guests live in the same currency zone, cheques are often quick and conven-ient. If not then bank transfers are easier. Credit card payments are expensive and difficult to set up unless you expect a very high volume of customers. Once the booking has been made, send out standard responses for the subsequent sequence of events including receipt of booking deposit, request for balance, confirmation of booking, directions and arrival instructions, and follow-ups. Most people only send full directions to the property and a pre-visit pack only when they have received the full payment. Be clear about when you expect to receive payment.

General Administration

It is essential to keep detailed records of all your bookings and a good idea to maintain a separate folder on your computer with all the documents for each rental. This may seem complicated at first, but once you have your systems in place everything should run very smoothly.

Insurance

You must to tell your insurance company that the house is being let out. This may increase premiums, but if you need to make a claim and have not divulged this it is very likely that your insurance company will not pay out on the claim. Premiums can also be higher if a house will be empty for a large portion of the year.

Tax

It is very important to keep records of all your tenants with the dates that they have stayed in your property. You should also make sure that you keep proper records of any costs associated with the property so they can be offset against tax. You can generally deduct fixtures and fitting you've purchased, maintenance fees to agencies, insurance and an amount for general wear and tear.

Using Management Agencies

The holiday letting agency market is not as well developed in Ireland as it is in many other countries, probably because the majority of holiday homes are owned by Irish investors or individuals and there is not, as yet, much demand for a service to suit owners living abroad. There are, however, some management companies or full service agencies that will manage all aspects of letting your property, from advertising and marketing to bookings and management of the property. A service like this is expensive and some agencies will insist on having the property available all year round – so you won't be able to use it when you wish.

These are some questions to consider when considering agencies:

- Where does the agency advertise the property – nationally? internationally?
- Does the agency guarantee a minimum level of bookings?
- How much will the agency charge clients and what is their commission?
- How do they welcome tenants? Do they arrange a key pick-up or is there someone to meet and greet tenants?
- Will the agency maintain the property and do small repairs? (Ensure that they will give you receipts for any work and get your consent for larger jobs.)
- Will they inspect the property before and after each let and do an inventory inspection?
- Are agency staff available in case of emergencies? Are they available 24 hours a day, 7 days a week?
- Ask to view a property that the agency is currently managing and copies of the documentation that they send to tenants.
- Ask for references from other clients – ideally clients with property and circumstances as similar to your own as possible.

If your home will be empty for much of the year, a new organisation, Irish Home Minders (**www.irishhomeminders.com**), can arrange inspection visits to the property. It also offers a range of other services for landlords.

Formalising the Lettings

If you use an agency they will probably use a standardised agreement for your tenants. If you arrange the lettings yourself you can draw up a contract (use a solicitor to do this or base it on a standard one, but it is probably safest to use a solicitor to make absolutely sure that it is watertight) that suits your circumstances and that you can reuse for subsequent tenants. It is usual to stipulate what is covered by insurance and what is not (for example, tenants' personal property is not covered).

Long-term Lets

Immediately after the Government abolished anti-investor measures at the end of 2001, investors accounted for 40 per cent of the residential market in the Republic. Today this figure has dropped significantly and investors now make up only 20 per cent of the market. This drop is because other investments yield greater short-term returns and the rental market has softened considerably over the last couple of years. As we noted above, this means that you should analyse your situation carefully if you plan to finance a mortgage from renting.

Types of Rental Property

Many rental properties in Dublin are detached, terraced or semi-detached houses, but apartments are very commonly rented – apartment blocks are often almost exclusively populated by tenants. Apartments in Dublin divide quite neatly into three types. First there are apartment blocks built in the 1950s, 1960s and 1970s, characterised by a proportionally large square footage but rather old-fashioned design. They tend to have separate kitchens and living or dining areas in contrast with more modern apartments where open-plan layouts rule.

Then there are apartments constructed in the late 1980s and early 1990s. The blocks that line the Liffey on both sides from Heuston Station up to the beginning of Temple Bar are typical: there was generally no architect, spaces are cramped, public space almost non-existent and they look dilapidated less than 10 years on.

Towards the end of the 1990s there was a sea change, however. Developers began to realise that people would pay for good design, light and green space, and some of Dublin's most attractive and successful apartment complexes were built. For example, Custom House Square in the IFSC area of the city is a development of European quality with a wide range of apartment sizes and attractive, landscaped courtyards. If you are thinking of buying one of these, be aware that the newer apartments, despite their higher capital cost, are likely to let faster and for a higher charge than many of the older ones.

Residential Tenancies Act, 2004–08

If you decide to rent out your new property, you should familiarise yourself with and take into account new legislation which came into effect in August/September 2004 in order to give greater security of tenure to tenants. It sets out your obligations as landlord and the obligations of your tenants and provides that rent may not be greater than the open market rate and may be reviewed (upward or downward) only once a year unless there has been a substantial change in the nature of the accommodation that would warrant a review. Tenants must be given 28 days' notice of new rents.

The security of tenure is based on four-year cycles from the date that Part 4 of the act comes into force. Once a tenancy has lasted 6 months, you will only be able to terminate the tenancy during the following 3½ years if any of the following apply:

- The tenant does not comply with the obligations of the tenancy.
- The dwelling is no longer suited to the tenant's needs (e.g. overcrowded).
- You intend to sell the dwelling in the next 3 months.
- You require the dwelling for your own or a family member occupation.
- You intend to substantially refurbish the dwelling.

This 3½ year security of tenure means that tenants may opt to continue in occupation after a fixed term tenancy that has lasted 6 months or more expires, but they must notify you (the landlord) of their intention to remain.

The act provides for a system of dispute resolution through a Private Residential Tenancies Board rather than the courts.

At present landlords' yields range from about 4.5 per cent to 4.8 per cent in Dublin. Average rents are currently €1,000 for a one-bedroom apartment in south Dublin, €850 for the same in north Dublin, and €1,200 up for a two-bedroom apartment. Average rents in Belfast for one-bedroom apartments range between £450 (€642) and £480 (€685) a month, and for two-bedroom apartments between £500 (€713) and £600 (€856).

Until recently Irish law has favoured the landlord – tenants don't have very much security of tenure but legislation is being brought in to give tenants more rights (*see* box). By law tenants are entitled to a rent book or a written tenancy agreement. You can also offer a lease that binds them, and you, for a specified period – generally a year. Minimum standards apply to all rental accommodation (working appliances, heating, hot and cold water and so on). The housing agency **Threshold** (**www.threshold.ie**; **t** (01) 872 6311; 19 Mary's Abbey, Dublin 7) gives extensive information on renting for both tenants and landlords.

There can be substantial costs associated with letting a property. Almost all properties are let furnished and the fit-out costs can be high. You will need to allow for ongoing maintenance and repairs and for insurance. If you live abroad

Case Study: Feeling at Home

'I think the hardest thing is getting used to how a new place works,' says Alison Frankel, who moved from Cambridge to Dublin in 2000. 'Cambridge is relatively small, and growing up somewhere you know the bus routes, the short cuts, the free parking spaces; it is all second nature to you and you don't really think about it. Moving to Dublin meant relearning all that, and it can be a very alienating experience. I didn't even know how to pay on a bus. It took me a while to discover that if you didn't have the exact change, the driver gives you a ticket for the extra – which you take up to O'Connell Street to redeem for money. It is a crazy system, but that's what they do!' Alison and her partner Brian rented an apartment for the first six months and found that this was the best way to figure out where they wanted to live. 'We always knew we were going to buy, but we wanted to get to know the city first,' he says. 'We didn't know Darndale from Drumcondra, so we felt we couldn't really make a decent choice until we'd lived here for a while.' The strategy worked, and the couple bought an apartment in Blackrock, a coastal suburb on the southside of the city. 'It is beginning to feel more and more like home, now that I do know the shops and where the good parking is!' adds Alison.

you may decide to use a management company and there are many well-established management companies in the cities. Most of these offer a full management service (including collection of tent and maintenance of the property) as well as finding tenants for you. You can also list your property with a range of letting agents; many of these are associated with estate agents. Fees for finding tenants and arranging the lease range from one to three months' rent – depending on the agency.

Most of the larger estate agents also offer letting services and some of the more established management agents in Dublin include:

- www.accommodationlettings.ie
- www.christiesestates.com
- www.dialashortlet.com
- www.homelocators.ie
- www.masonestates.ie

References

Directory of Contacts

*To call the Republic of Ireland from Britain, dial **t** 00 353 and the drop the first zero of the local code. To call Britain from the Republic, dial **t** 00 44 and drop the first zero.*

Major Resources in Britain

Embassy of Ireland in Britain
17 Grosvenor Place
London SW1X 7HR

Passport and Visa Section
Montpelier House
106 Brompton Road
London SW3
t (020) 7235 2171/7245 9033; **f** (020) 7245 6961

British Resources in Ireland

The British Embassy, Dublin
29 Merrion Road
Ballsbridge
Dublin 4
t (01) 205 3700
www.britishembassy.ie

The British Council
Newmount House
22–24 Lower Mount Street
Dublin 2
t (01) 676 4088/676 6943; **f** (01) 676 6945
www.britishcouncil.org/ireland/

Foreign Embassies in Dublin

American Embassy
Embassy of the USA
42 Elgin Road
Dublin 4
t (01) 668 8777; **f** (01) 668 9946

Australian Embassy
2nd Floor Fitzwilton House
Wilton Terrace
Dublin 2
t (01) 676 1517; **f** (01) 662 3566
www.australianembassy.ie

Embassy of Belgium
2 Shrewsbury Road
Ballsbridge, Dublin 4
t (01) 269 1588/269 2082/283 9403; f (01) 283 8488

Embassy of Brazil
Harcourt Centre
5th Floor Europa House
41–54 Harcourt Street
Dublin 2
t (01) 475 6000; f (01) 475 1341

Embassy of Czech Republic
57 Northumberland Road
Ballsbridge, Dublin 4
t (01) 668 1135; f (01) 668 1660

Royal Danish Embassy
121 St Stephen's Green
Dublin 2
t (01) 475 6404; f (01) 478 4536
embassy@denmark.ie; www.denmark.ie

French Embassy
36 Ailesbury Road
Ballsbridge, Dublin 4
t (01) 277 5000; f (01) 277 5001
chancellerie@ambafrance.ie; www.ambafrance.ie

German Embassy
31 Trimleston Avenue
Booterstown, Blackrock
Co. Dublin
t (01) 269 3011; f (01) 269 3946
www.germanembassy.ie

Embassy of Greece
1 Upper Pembroke Street
Dublin 2
t (01) 6767 2545; f (01) 661 8892
dubgremb@eircom.net

Indian Embassy
6 Leeson Park
Dublin 6
t (01) 497 0843; f (01) 497 8074

Italian Embassy
63–65 Northumberland Road
Dublin 4
t (01) 660 1744; f (01) 668 2759
info@italianembassy.ie; www.italianembassy.ie

Embassy of Japan
Nutley Building
Merrion Centre
Nutley Lane
Dublin 4
t (01) 269 4244

Dutch Embassy
160 Merrion Road
Dublin 4
t (01) 269 3444; **f** (01) 283 9690

Embassy of Portugal
Knocksinna House
Knocksinna
Foxrock
Dublin 18
t (01) 289 4416/289 3375; **f** (01) 289 2849

Government Departments

Dept. of Education
Marlboro Street
Dublin 1
t (01) 873 4700

Dept. of Enterprise and Employment
Adelaide Road
Dublin 2
t (01) 661 4444

Dept. of Health
Hawkins Street
Dublin 2
t (01) 671 4711

Dept. of Social Welfare
Information Section
Aras Mhic Dhiarmada
Store Street
Dublin 1
t (01) 874 8444

Dept. of Social Welfare
International Operations
Floor 1
O'Connell Bridge House
D'Olier Street
Dublin 2
t (01) 874 8444

Dept. of Justice (Immigration Issues)
77 St Stephen's Green
Dublin 2
t (01) 678 9711

FAS (Head Office)
27–33 Upper Baggot Street
Dublin 4
t (01) 668 5777

National Social Service Board
Floor 7
Hume House
Ballsbridge
Dublin 4
t (01) 605 9000

National Parents' Council, Primary Schools
16–20 Cumberland St South
Dublin 2
t (01) 678 9981

National Parents' Council, Post Primary Schools
Marino Institute of Education
Griffith Avenue
Dublin 7
t (01) 857 0522

Newspapers in the Republic

Evening Echo
1–6 Academy Street
Cork
t (021) 427 2722; f (021) 427 5112

Evening Herald
Middle Abbey Street
Dublin 1
t (01) 705 5333; f (01) 872 0304

Ireland on Sunday
50 City Quay
Dublin 2
t (01) 671 8255; f (01) 671 8882

Irish Examiner
1–6 Academy Street
Cork
t (021) 427 2722; f (021) 427 3846
www.irishexaminer.ie

Irish Independent
Middle Abbey Street
Dublin 1
t (01) 705 5333; f (01) 872 0304

Irish Times
10–16 D'Olier Street
Dublin 2
t (01) 675 8000
www.ireland.com

Star
62A Terenure Road North
Dublin 6W
t (01) 490 1228; f (01) 490 2193/490 7425

Sunday Independent
Middle Abbey Street
Dublin 1
t (01) 705 5333; f (01) 705 5779

Sunday Tribune
15 Lower Baggot Street
Dublin 2
t (01) 661 5555; f (01) 661 5302
www.tribune.ie

Sunday World
18 Rathfarnham Road
Dublin 6
t (01) 490 1980; f (01) 490 1838

Newspapers in Northern Ireland

Belfast Telegraph (evening)
124–144 Royal Avenue
Belfast BT1 1EB
t (01232) 264000; f (01232) 554506
www.belfasttelegraph.co.uk

Irish News (daily)
113–117 Donegal Street
Belfast BT1 2GE
t (01232) 322226; f (01232) 337505
www.irishnews.com

Sunday Life
124–144 Royal Avenue
Belfast BT1 1EB
t (01232) 264300; f (01232) 554507

Ulster News Letter
46–56 Boucher Street
Belfast BT12 6QY
t (01232) 680000; f (01232) 664412

Health Insurance Companies

BUPA Ireland
Mill House
Fermoy
Co. Cork
t (025) 42121; customer helpline
t 1890 700890 (lo-call); **f** (01) 42122
betteroff@bupaireland.ie; www.bupaireland.ie

Health Insurance Authority
Canal House, Canal Road
Dublin 6
t (01) 406 0080; **f** (01) 406 0081
info@hia.ie; www.hia.ie

VHI Healthcare
IDA Business Park
Dublin Road
Co. Kilkenny
t (056) 775 3200; customer service **t** 1850 44 44 44 (CallSave)
info@vhi.ie; www.vhihealthcare.ie

Removal Companies

Allen Removals and Storage
Greenhills Road
Tallaght
Dublin 24
t (01) 451 3585/451 3299; **f** (01) 459 9039
sales@allenremovals.ie
enquiry@allenremovals.ie

Cronin: The Art of Moving
Damastown Industrial Park
Mulhuddart
Dublin 15
t (01) 809 7000; **f** (01) 809 7001
relo@theartofmoving.com; www.theartofmoving.com

Maguire International Moving and Storage
5 Albert Avenue Bray
Co. Wicklow
t (01) 276 1700
info@maguireinternational.ie

Oman Removals (Cork)
10 South Link Park
Frankfield, Cork
t (021) 431 0729; callsave **t** 1850 668464; **f** (021) 431 0084
sales@oman.ie

Oman Removals (Kildare)
Atlantic House
Kill
Co. Kildare
t (045) 886300; callsave
t 1850 668464; f (045) 878176
sales@oman.ie

Irish County Councils

Carlow County Council
County Offices
Athy Road
Carlow
Co. Carlow
t (059) 917 0300; f (059) 914 1503
secretar@carlowcoco.ie; www.carlow.ie

Cavan County Council
County Offices
Courthouse
Cavan
Co. Cavan
t (049) 433 1799; f (049) 436 1565
bkelly@cavancoco.ie

Clare County Council
County Offices
New Road
Ennis
Co. Clare
t (065) 682 1616; f (065) 682 8233
secretar@clarecoco.ie; www.clarecoco.ie

Cork City Council
City Hall
Cork
Co. Cork
t (021) 496 6222; f (021) 431 4238
www.corkcity.ie

Cork County Council
County Offices
County Hall
Carrigrohane Road
Cork
Co. Cork
t (021) 427 6891; f (021) 427 6321
cosec@corkcoco.ie; www.corkcoco.com

Donegal County Council
County House
Lifford
Co. Donegal
t (074) 917 2222; f (074) 914 1205
www.donegal.ie

Dublin City Council
16–19 Wellington Quay
Dublin 2
t (01) 672 2947; f (01) 672 3921
www.dublincity.ie

Galway City Council
City Hall
College Road
Galway
Co. Galway
t (091) 536400; f (091) 567493
tclerk@galwaycity.ie; www.galway.ie

Galway County Council
County Hall
Prospect Hill
Galway
Co. Galway
t (091) 509000; f (091) 509010
secretar@galwaycoco.ie; www.galway.ie

Kerry County Council
Aras An Chontae
Tralee
Co. Kerry
t (066) 712 1111; f (066) 712 2466
kcc@kerrycoco.ie; www.kerrycoco.ie

Kildare County Council
St Mary's
Naas
Co. Kildare
t (045) 873800; f (045) 876875
secretar@kildarecoco.ie; www.kildare.ie/countycouncil/

Kilkenny County Council
County Hall
John Street
Kilkenny
Co. Kilkenny
t (056) 775 2699; f (056) 776 3384
secretar@kilkennycoco.ie; www.kilkennycoco.ie

Laois County Council
County Hall
Portlaoise
Co. Laois
t (0502) 64000; f (0502) 22313
secretar@laoiscoco.ie; www.laois.ie

Leitrim County Council
Park Lane House
Carrick-On-Shannon
Co. Leitrim
t (071) 962 0005; f (071) 962 2205
secretar@leitrimcoco.ie; www.leitrimcoco.ie

Limerick City Council
City Hall
Merchant's Quay
Limerick
Co. Limerick
t (061) 415799; f (061) 418601
info@limerickcity.ie; www.limerickcity.ie

Limerick County Council
79–84 O'Connell Street
Limerick
Co. Limerick
t (061) 318477; f (061) 318478
secretary@limerickcoco.ie; www.limerickcoco.ie

Longford County Council
Aras An Chontae
Great Water Street
Longford
Co. Longford
t (043) 46231; f (043) 41233
secretar@longfordcoco.ie; www.longford.ie

Louth County Council
County Hall
Millenium Centre
St Alphonsis Road
Dundalk
Co. Louth
t (042) 933 5457; f (042) 933 4549; www.louthcoco.ie

Mayo County Council
Head Office
Aras an Chontae
The Green
Castlebar
Co. Mayo
t (094) 902 4444; f (094) 902 3937
secretar@mayococo.ie; www.mayococo.ie

Meath County Council
County Hall
Navan
Co. Meath
t (046) 902 1581; **f** (046) 902 1463
info@meathcoco.ie; www.meath.ie

Monaghan County Council
County Offices
The Glen
Monaghan
Co. Monaghan
t (047) 30500; **f** (047) 82739
secretar@monaghancoco.ie; www.monaghancoco.ie

North Tipperary County Council
The Courthouse
Nenagh
Co. Tipperary
t (067) 31771; **f** (067) 33134
secretary@tippnrcoco.ie; www.tipperarynorth.ie

Offaly County Council
The Courthouse
Tullamore
Co. Offaly
t (0506) 46800; **f** (0506) 46868
secretar@offalycoco.ie; www.offaly.ie

Roscommon County Council
The Courthouse
Roscommon
Co. Roscommon
t (090) 663 7100; **f** (090) 663 7108
secretar@roscommoncoco.ie

Sligo Borough Council
Town Hall
Sligo
Co. Sligo
t (071) 914 2141; **f** (071) 914 1056
tclerk@sligocorp.ie

Sligo County Council
Riverside
Sligo
Co. Sligo
t (071) 915 6666; **f** (071) 914 1119
secretar@sligococo.ie; www.sligococo.ie

South Dublin County Council
County Hall, Town Centre
Tallaght, Dublin 24
t (01) 414 9000; **f** (01) 414 9111
council@sdcc.ie; www.sdcc.ie

South Tipperary County Council
Head Office
Aras an Chontae
Clonmel
Co. Tipperary
t (052) 34455; f (052) 24355
secretar@southtippcoco.ie; www.southtippcoco.ie

Waterford City Council
Head Office
City Hall
The Mall
Waterford
Co. Waterford
t (051) 309900; f (051) 879124
tclerk@waterfordcity.ie; www.waterfordcity.ie

Waterford County Council
Civic Offices
Dungarvan
Co. Waterford
t (058) 22000; f (058) 42911
secretar@waterfordcoco.ie; www.waterfordcoco.ie

Westmeath County Council
County Buildings
Mullingar
Co. Westmeath
t (044) 40861; f (044) 42330
secretar@westmeathcoco.ie; www.westmeathcoco.ie

Wexford Borough Council
Municipal Buildings
Wexford
Co. Wexford
t (053) 42611; f (053) 45947
wexfordcorporation@wexfordcorp.ie; www.wexfordcorp.ie

Wexford County Council
County Hall
Spawell Road
Wexford
Co. Wexford
t (053) 65000; f (053) 43406
postmaster@wexfordcoco.ie; www.wexford.ie

Wicklow County Council
County Buildings
Wicklow
Co. Wicklow
t (0404) 20100; f (0404) 67792
cosec@wicklowcoco.ie; www.wicklow.ie

Tax Offices in Ireland

Inspector of Taxes – Dublin Area

Central Revenue Information Office
Cathedral Street off Upper O'Connell
Street, Dublin 1
(Personal callers only)
Central Telephone Information Office **t** (01) 878 0000

Taxes Central Registration Office
Arus Brugha, 9/15 Upper O'Connell
Street, Dublin 1
t (01) 865 0000
tccro@revenue.ie

Tallaght Revenue Information Office
Level 2, The Square, Tallaght, Dublin 24
(Personal callers only)

Revenue Forms and Leaflets Service
Telephone Service **t** (01) 878 0100

Dublin PAYE no.1 and PAYE No. 4,
Arus Brugha, 9/15 Upper O'Connell
Street, Dublin 1
t (01) 865 0000
paye1@revenue.ie and **paye4@revenue.ie**
(Employees)

Dublin PAYE no. 2 & PAYE No. 3,
85/93 Lower Mount Street,
Dublin 2
t (01) 647 4000
paye2@revenue.ie and **paye3@revenue.ie**
(Employees)

Dublin Tax District
1A Lower Grand Canal St, Dublin 2
t (01) 647 4000
dubittax@revenue.ie
(Self-employed individuals/trusts)

Dublin Corporation Tax District
Landsdowne House, Landsdowne Road, Dublin 4
t (01) 631 6700
dubcttax@revenue.ie
(Companies)

Dublin Directors District
Landsdowne House, Landsdowne Road, Dublin 4
t (01) 631 6700
dubdirs@revenue.ie
(Company Directors)

Inspector of Taxes Provincial Districts

Athlone Tax District
Government Offices, Pearse Street,
Athlone, Co. Westmeath
t (0902) 21800
athlntax@revenue.ie

Castlebar Tax District
Michael Davitt House, Castlebar,
Co. Mayo
t (094) 37000
mayotax@revenue.ie

Cork Tax District
Government Offices, Sullivan's Quay,
Cork
t (021) 496 6077
corkpaye@revenue.ie

Dundalk Tax District
Earl House, Earl Street,
Dundalk, Co. Louth
t (042) 935 3700
louthtax@revenue.ie

Galway Tax District
Hibernian House, Eyre Square
Galway
t (091) 536000
galwaytax@revenue.ie

Kilkenny Tax District
Government Offices, Hebron Road
Kilkenny, Co. Kilkenny
t (056) 75300
kilkentax@revenue.ie

Letterkenny Tax District
High Road, Letterkenny,
Co. Donegal
t (074) 694009
donegtax@revenue.ie

Limerick Tax District
River House, Charlotte Quay,
Limerick
t (061) 212700
limtax@revenue.ie

Thurles Tax District
Government Offices, Stradavoher,
Thurles, Co. Tipperary
t (0504) 28700
tipptax@revenue.ie

Tralee Tax District
Government Offices, Spa Road,
Tralee, Co. Kerry
t (066) 7183100
kerrytax@revenue.ie

Waterford Tax District
Government Offices, The Glen,
Waterford
t (051) 317200
tax@revenue.ie

Wexford Tax District
Government Offices, Anne Street,
Wexford
t (053) 63300
wfordtax@revenue.ie

Climate Charts

Average Temperatures

	Jan	Feb	Mar	April	May	June	July	Aug	Sept	Oct	Nov	Dec
max	46°F	46°F	51°F	55°F	60°F	65°F	68°F	67°F	63°F	57°F	51°F	46°F
	8°C	8°C	10°C	13°C	15°C	18°C	20°C	19°C	17°C	14°C	10°C	8°C
min	34°F	35°F	35°F	37°F	39°F	48°F	52°F	52°F	48°F	43°F	39°F	37°F
	1°C	2°C	2°C	3°C	4°C	9°C	11°C	11°C	9°C	6°C	4°C	3°C

Average Precipitation in Inches

	Jan	Feb	Mar	April	May	June	July	Aug	Sept	Oct	Nov	Dec
Cork	5.8	4.5	3.8	2.8	3.3	2.7	2.6	3.5	3.8	5.0	4.3	5.4
Dublin	2.7	2.0	2.1	2.0	2.2	2.2	2.0	2.8	2.6	2.8	2.5	3.0
Galway	4.8	3.3	3.8	2.4	3.0	2.8	2.5	3.8	4.1	5.0	4.7	4.8
Limerick	3.9	2.8	2.8	2.2	2.4	2.5	2.2	3.2	3.2	3.7	3.7	3.9
Waterford	3.4	2.6	2.5	2.1	2.4	2.0	2.1	2.8	2.8	3.4	2.9	3.5

Further Reading

Non-fiction

Aalen, Whelan and Stout (eds), *Atlas of the Irish Rural Landscape*. Much more than an atlas – gives insight into historical, social and other influences on the landscape.

John Ardagh, *Ireland and the Irish: Portrait of a Changing Society*

David Beresford, *Ten Men Dead*. Account of the 1980 hunger strikes in which 10 died.

Terence Brown, *Ireland: A Social and Cultural History 1922–1985*. Excellent introduction to the country.

R. F. Foster, *Modern Ireland 1600–1972*. Clearly written history.

R. F. Foster, *Paddy and Mr Punch*. Entertaining essays about the relationship between Britain and Ireland.

Eamonn Mallie and David McKittrick, *Endgame in Ireland*. The peace process.

Frank McDonald, *The Construction of Dublin*. Explains how Dublin changed in the 1990s (have a look also at *The Destruction of Dublin* if you are interested in conservation).

Sally and John McKenna, *Bridgestone Traveller's Guide*. The best food in Ireland.

Pete McCarthy, *McCarthy's Bar*. Entertaining travelogue.

Marc Mulholland, *Northern Ireland: A Very Short Introduction*. Good brief and simple introduction.

Senia Paseta, *Modern Ireland: A Very Short Introduction*. Gives a good basic summary of Irish history from the 17th century until the present.

Tim Robinson, *The Stones of Aran*. Poetic geography and mapping.

Colm Tóibín and Diarmaid Ferriter, *The Irish Famine: A Documentary*. Explains the Irish famine and its after-effect.

Fiction

Far too much to summarise but some basic recommendations include:

Peter Ackroyd, *The Last Will and Testament of Oscar Wilde*

John Banville, *The Book of Evidence*

Brendan Behan, *Borstal Boy*

Dermot Bolger, *The Journey Home*

Elizabeth Bowen, *The Death of the Heart* and *The Last September*

Seamus Deane, *Reading in the Dark*

James Joyce, *Dubliners*, *Portrait of the Artist as a Young Man* and *Ulysses*

Molly Keane, *Good Behaviour*

Mary Lavin, *In a Café: Selected Stories*

Patrick McCabe, *The Butcher Boy*

John McGahern, *Amongst Women* and *That They May Face the Rising Sun*

Brian Moore, *The Lonely Passion of Judith Hearne*

Flann O'Brien, *The Third Policeman* and *At Swim-Two-Birds*

Frank O'Connor, *Guests of the Nation*

Jonathan Swift, *Gulliver's Travels* and *The Tale of a Tub and Other Stories*

Colm Tóibín, *The South*, *The Heather Blazing* and *The Blackwater Lightship*

William Trevor, *Collected Stories*

Irish Holidays

January 1	New Year's Day
March 17	St Patrick's Day
Good Friday	
Easter Monday	
First Monday in May	May Bank Holiday
First Monday in June	June Bank Holiday
First Monday in August	August Bank Holiday
Monday closest to 31st October	October Bank Holiday
December 25	Christmas Day
December 26	St Stephen's Day
December 29	

Double Taxation Agreements Entered into by Ireland

Ireland currently has comprehensive double taxation agreements in force with 40 countries. The agreements generally cover income tax, corporation tax and capital gains tax (direct taxes). The following is a list of those agreements:

Australia	India	Poland
Austria	Italy	Portugal
Belgium	Israel	Romania
Bulgaria	Japan	Russia
Canada	Rep. of Korea	Slovak Republic
China	Latvia	South Africa
Cyprus	Lithuania	Spain
Czech Republic	Luxembourg	Sweden
Denmark	Malaysia	Switzerland
Estonia	Mexico	United Kingdom
Finland	Netherlands	United States
France	New Zealand	Zambia
Germany	Norway	
Hungary	Pakistan	

A number of new treaties are in the course of being negotiated with Croatia, Egypt, Iceland, Singapore, Slovenia, Turkey and Ukraine. Also, existing treaties are being re-negotiated with Canada and France. Copies ofexisting Double Taxation Treaties are available on the Revenue website **www.revenue.ie/fra_pubs.htm**.

Checklist – Do-it-yourself inspection of property

TASK	✔
Title	
Check that the property corresponds with its description in the title	
Number of rooms	
Plot size	
Plot	
Identify the physical boundaries of the plot	
Is there any dispute with anyone over these boundaries?	
Are there any obvious foreign elements on your plot such as pipes, cables, drainage ditches, water tanks, etc?	
Are there any signs of anyone else having rights over the property? Footpaths, access ways, cartridges from hunting, etc?	
Garden/Terrace	
Are any plants, ornaments etc on site not being sold with the property	
Walls – stand back from property and inspect from outside	
Any signs of subsidence?	
Walls vertical?	
Any obvious cracks in walls?	
Are walls well pointed?	
Any obvious damp patches?	
Any new repairs to walls or re-pointing?	
Roof – inspect from outside property	
Does roof sag?	
Are there missing/slipped tiles?	
Do all faces of roof join squarely?	
Lead present and in good order?	

Checklist – Do-it-yourself inspection of property

TASK	✔
Guttering and Downpipes – inspect from outside property	
All present?	
Securely attached?	
Fall of guttering constant?	
Any obvious leaks?	
Any recent repairs?	
Grass or vegetation growing in gutters?	
Enter Property	
Does it smell of damp?	
Does it smell 'musty'?	
Does it smell of dry rot?	
Any other strange smells?	
Doors	
Signs of rot?	
Close properly – without catching?	
Provide proper seal?	
Locks work?	
Windows	
Signs of rot?	
Close properly – without catching?	
Provide proper seal?	
Locks work?	
Excessive condensation?	
Have they been painted and maintained?	

Checklist – Do-it-yourself inspection of property

TASK	✔
Floor	
Can you see it all?	
Does it appear in good condition?	
Any sign of cracked or rotten boards?	
Does it bow in the middle?	
Do the floorboards bounce?	
Under Floor	
Can you get access under the floor?	
If so, is it ventilated?	
Is there any sign of rot?	
How close are joists?	
Are joist ends in good condition where they go into walls?	
What is maximum unsupported length of joist run?	
Is there any sign of damp or standing water?	
Roof Void	
Is it accessible?	
Is there sign of water entry?	
Can you see daylight through the roof?	
Is there an underlining between the tiles and the void?	
Is there any sign of rot in timbers	
Horizontal distance between roof timbers?	
Size of roof timbers (section)	
Maximum unsupported length of roof timbers	
Is roof insulated – if so, what depth and type of insulation?	

Checklist – Do-it-yourself inspection of property

TASK	✔
Woodwork	
Any sign of rot?	
Any sign of wood-boring insects?	
Is it dry?	
Interior Walls	
Any significant cracks?	
Any obvious damp problems?	
Any sign of recent repair/redecoration?	
Electricity	
Check electricity meter:	
How old is it?	
What is its rated capacity?	
Check all visible wiring:	
What type is it?	
Does it appear in good physical condition?	
Check all plugs:	
Is there power to plug?	
Does plug tester show good earth and show 'OK'?	
Are there enough plugs?	
Lighting:	
Do all lights work?	
Which light fittings are included in sale?	
Cold Water – Where does the water come from?	
The mains?	
A rural water scheme?	

Checklist – Do-it-yourself inspection of property

TASK	✔
A well?	
Do all hot and cold taps work?	
Is flow adequate?	
Do taps drip?	
Is there a security cut off on all taps between mains and tap?	
Do they seem in good condition?	
Is hot water 'on'? If so, does it work at all taps, showers etc?	
What type of hot water system is fitted?	
Age?	
Gas	
Is the property fitted with city (piped) gas? If so:	
Age of meter	
Does installation appear in good order?	
Is there any smell of gas?	
Is the property fitted with bottled gas? If so:	
Where are bottles stored?	
Is it ventilated to outside of premises?	
Central Heating	
Is the property fitted with central heating? If so:	
Is it 'on'?	
Will it turn on?	
What type is it?	
Is there heat at all radiators/outlets?	
Do any thermostats appear to work?	
Are there any signs of leaks?	

Checklist – Do-it-yourself inspection of property

TASK	✔
Fireplaces	
Is the property fitted with any solid fuel heaters? If so:	
Any sign of blow-back from chimneys?	
Do chimneys (outside) show stains from leakage?	
Do chimneys seem in good order?	
Phone	
Does it work?	
Number?	
Satellite TV	
Does it work?	
Is it included in the sale?	
Drainage	
What type of drainage does property have?	
If septic tank, how old?	
Who maintains it?	
When was it last maintained?	
Any smell of drainage problems in bathrooms and toilets?	
Does water drain away rapidly from all sinks, showers and toilets?	
Is there any inspection access through which you can see drainage taking place	
Is there any sign of plant ingress to drains?	
Do drains appear to be in good condition and well pointed?	
Kitchen	
Do all cupboard open/close properly?	
Any signs of rot?	

Checklist – Do-it-yourself inspection of property

TASK	✔
Tiling secure and in good order?	
Enough plugs?	
What appliances are included in sale?	
Do they work?	
Age of appliances included?	
Bathroom	
Security and condition of tiling?	
Ventilation?	
Appliances	
What appliances generally are included in sale?	
What is not included in sale?	
Furniture	
What furniture is included in sale?	
What is NOT included in sale?	
Repairs/Improvements/Additions	
What repairs have been carried out in last 2 years?	
What improvements have been carried out in last 2 years/10 years?	
What additions have been made to the property in last 2 years/10 years?	
Do they have builders receipts/guarantees?	
Do any additions or alterations comply with the building regulations?	
Defects	
Is seller aware of any defects in the property?	
NOTES	

European Standardised Information Sheet

This standardised information is an integral part of the 'Voluntary Code of Conduct on Pre-contractual Information for Home Loan', a copy of which can be obtained from your lender.

Item	Description
Up front text	'This document does not constitute a legally binding offer.
	The figures are provided in good faith and are an accurate representation of the offer that the lender would make under current market conditions based on the information that has been provided. It should be noted, however, that the figures could fluctuate with market conditions.
	The provision of this information does not oblige the lender to grant a credit.'
1. Lender	
2. Description of product	This section should provide a brief but clear description of the product.
	It should be made clear whether it is a mortgage on a property or another commonly used surety.
	It should be made clear whether the product on offer is an interest only home loan (i.e. that it involves servicing the debt with a lump sum payment at the end) or a repayment home loan (i.e. that it involves paying interest and capital over the lifetime of the home loan).
	It should be made clear whether the home loan terms are dependent on the consumer supplying a certain amount of capital (perhaps expressed as a percentage of house value).
	Where the home loan terms are dependent on a third party guarantee, this should be clearly stated.

Item	Description
3. Nominal rate (indicate type of rate and duration of fixed period)	This section should provide information on the key condition of the home loan – the interest rate. Where relevant, the description should include details of how the interest rate will vary including, for example, review periods, lock-in periods and related penalty clauses, collars and caps etc._x000D_ _x000D_ The description should include:_x000D_ – whether or not a variable rate is indexed; and_x000D_ – provide details of indexation, where appropriate.
4. Annual percentage rate of charge (APRC) based on national regulation or effective rate, where relevant	Where a national figure for APRC is not set in legislation, the equivalent effective rate should be used.
5. Amount of credit advanced and currency	
6. Duration of home loan agreement	
7. Number and frequency of payments (may vary)	
8. For repayment home loan, amount of each instalment (may vary)	
9. For interest only home loan:_x000D_ – amount of each regular interest payment;_x000D_ – amount of amount of each regular payment to the repayment vehicle	The lender should provide an indication – real or illustrative – of:_x000D_ _x000D_ a) the amount of each regular interest repayment in accordance with the frequency of the payments (see point 7);_x000D_ b) the amount of each regular payment towards the repayment vehicle, in accordance with the frequency of the payments (see point 7)._x000D_ _x000D_ Where appropriate, a warning should be given that the repayment vehicle may not cover the amount borrowed._x000D_ _x000D_ If the lender provides the repayment vehicle and has included this in part of the offer, then it should be clear whether or not the offer is tied to the consumer's agreement on that repayment vehicle.

Item	Description
10. Additional non-recurring costs, where applicable	A list of initial non-recurring costs which the consumer is expected to pay upon taking out the home loan must be provided.
	Where these costs are under the direct or indirect control of the lender, an estimate of the costs should be provided.
	Where relevant, it should be made clear if the cost is to be paid regardless of the outcome of the home loan application.
	Such costs might include, for example: – administrative costs; – legal fees; – property valuation.
	Where an offer would be dependent on the consumer's receiving these services through the lender (provided this is permitted in national legislation), it should be clearly stated.
11. Additional recurrent costs (not included in 8)	This list should include, for example: – insurance against default on payments (unemployment/death); – fire insurance; – building and contents insurance.
	Where an offer would be dependent on the consumer's receiving these services through the lender (provided this is permitted in national legislation), it should be clearly stated.
12. Early repayment	The lender should provide an indication of: – the possibility and terms of early repayment; – including an indication of any charges applicable.
	Where it is not possible to stipulate the charge at this stage, an indication should be provided that a sum sufficient to recoup the lender's costs in unwinding the transaction would be payable.
13. Internal complaint schemes	Name, address and telephone number of contact point.

Item	Description
14. Illustrative amortisation table	The lender should provide an illustrative and summarised amortisation table which includes, at least: – monthly or quarterly payments (if it is the case) for the first year; – to be followed by yearly figures over the total duration of the loan. The table should contain figures on – amount of capital reimbursed; – amount of interest; – outstanding capital; – amount of each instalment; – sum of capital and interest. It should be clearly indicated that the table is illustrative only and contain a warning if the home loan proposed has a variable interest rate.
15. Obligation to domicile bank account and salary with lender	

Index

Ireland touring atlas

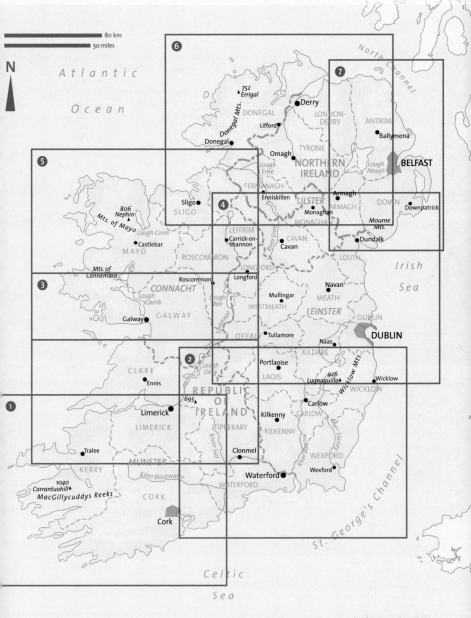

Newbridge
Kildare
nasterevin
Tully National Stud
Japanese Gardens
The Curragh
Curragh Camp
Kilcullen
Old Kilcullen
icarstown
Ardscull Motte
Ardscull
Ballitore
Athy
Moone High Cross
Ballylynan
Kilkea
Kilcullen
Crookstown
Timolin
Moone

Punchestown
Blessington
Kilbride
Glencullen
Glencree
Powerscourt Estate
Enniskerry
Kilmacanoge
Wicklow Way
Russborough House
Valleymount
Hollywood
Dunlavin
Sally Gap
L. Tay
Poulaphouca Reservoir
Wicklow Mountains
L. Dan
Glenmacnass
Roundwood
Upper Lake
Glendalough
Laragh
Lower Lake
Ashford
Glendealy

Bray
Bray Head
Kilruddery Gardens
Sugar Loaf Mountain
Greystones
Newtown Mount Kennedy
Kildare
Tomdarragh
'The Devil's Glen
Mount Usher Gardens
Rathnew
Wicklow

Wicklow Gap
Wicklow
Glen of Imaal
Cistercian Abbey
Baltinglass
Rathdangan
Rathvilly
Knockananna
Hacketstown
Askanagap
Aughrim
Avoca
Wicklow Head
Dunganstown Castle
Brittas Bay
Ardanairy

Carlow
Killeshin
Brown's Hill Dolmen
Castlemore
Tullow
Rathgall
Tinahely
Croghan Mountain
Woodenbridge
Arklow
Clogga
Kilmichael Point

Leighlinbridge
Burgage House
Muine Bheag
Ballymoon Castle
Vhitehall
Kildavin
Clonegal
Knockbrandon
Castletown
Ballymoney

Goresbridge
Mount Leinster
Bunclody
Askamore
Gorey
Courtown

Borris
Ullard
Ballymurphy
Killealy
Ferns
Ballycanew
Ballymoney

Graignamanagh
Blackstairs Mountains
Caher Roe's Den
Killann
Enniscorthy
Ballyemund

andon Hill
St Mullins
Duiske Abbey
Drummin
Clonroche
WEXFORD
Castleellis

New Ross
Ballynabola
Adamstown
Blackwater
Blackwater Harbour

Dunganstown
J.F. Kennedy Park
Newbawn
Foulksmills
Irish National Heritage Park
Ferrycarrig
Castlebridge
Curracloe
Wexford Bay

Campile
Dunbrody Abbey
Wellington Bridge
Waddingtown
Murntown
Wexford
Johnstown Castle
Wexford Harbour
Raven Point Peninsula (Nature Reserve)
Rosslare Bay
Fishguard
Pembroke
Cherbourg
Roscoff

heckpoint
Ballyhack
Arthurstown
Passage East
Duncannon
Carrick
Tintern Abbey
Bannow
Kilmore
Tacumshane
Tagoat
Kilrane
Rosslare Harbour

Fethard
Baginburn Head
Hook Head
Church Town
Kilmore Quay
Folorn Point
Saltee Islands
Lady's Island
Lady's Island Lake
Carne
Tacumshin Lake

ST GEORGE'S CHANNEL

N

20km
10miles

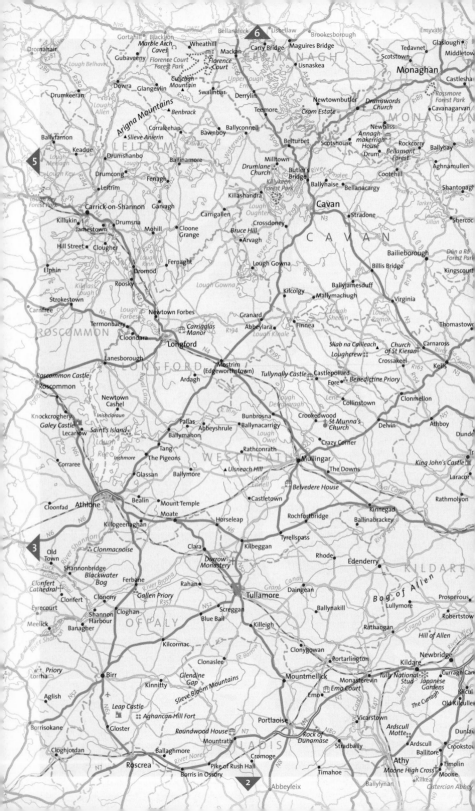

N

20km
10miles

Tory Island
West Town • East Town

Melmore Head
Fanad Head

Horn Head
Inishbofin
Tory Sound
Bloody Foreland Head
Dunfanaghy
Marblehill
Rosguill Downings Tawny Portsalor
F a n a d
Rosapenna
Carrigart Knockalla Mountain
Mulroy Bay
Carrowkee

Gweedore
Gola Island
Derrybeg
Falcarragh
Gortahork
Cloghaneely
Creeslough
Doe Castle
Muckish Mountain
Loughsalt Mountain
Millford

Owey Island
Bunbeg
Gweedore
Ards Forest Park
Altan Lough

Cruit Island
Donegal Airport
Crolly
Errigal Mountain
Barnes Gap
Kilmacrenan
Rathmelton

Aranmore Island
The Rosses
Dunlewy
Derryveagh Mountains
Glenveagh National Park
Doon Rock
Churchill

Burtonport
Dunglow
Slieve Snaght
Glendowan Mountains
Lough Beagh
Gartan Lough
Letterkenny
Manorcunningham

Doocharry
Owenea
Fintown
Lough Finn
River Swilly
Newmills
Cark Mountain

Gweebarra Bay
D O N E G A L
Drumkeen
Raphoe
Convoy
Beltan
Ballindrait

Dunmore Head
Portnoo Naran
Loughros Beg Bay
Maas
Glenties
Cloghan
Stranorlar
Ballybofey

Loughros Point
Port Maghera
Ardara
Lavagh More
Blue Stack Mountains
Croaghnageer
Ulster Way
River Finn
Castlederg

Glencolumbkille Folk Village
Glencolumbkille
Glengesh Pass
Malin Beg
Malin Bay
Tullynaha
Lough Eske
Barnesmore Gap
Lowerymore
Barnesmore
Killeter Forest
Killeter Killen

Slieve League
Teelin Kilcar
Killybegs
Bruckless
Dunkineely
Mountcharles
Donegal
Lough Mourne
Moume Beg

MacSwyne's Bay
Doorin Point
Ballintra
Carn
Lough Bradan Forest
Drumquir

St John's Point
Rossnowlagh
Pettigo
Lough Derg

Donegal Bay
Ballyshannon
Bundoran N15
Castle Caldwell
Boa Island
Kesh
White Island

Classiebawn Castle
Mullaghmore
Creevykeel
Kinlough
Belleek
Lower Lough Erne
Tully Castle
Castle Archdale
Lisnarrick
Irvinestown
Ballyard

Inishmurray
Monastery
Grange
Ballaghnatrillick
A46
Lough Navar Forest
Cliffs of Magho
A46
Derrygonnelly
Big Dog Forest
Blaney
Monea
Kilskeery
Ballinamallard

Streedagh Point
Cliffony N15
Glenniff Horseshoe loop
Truskmore Mountain
Garrison
F E R M A N A G H
Devenish Island
Monastic ruins

Ballyconnell
Lissadell House
Benbulben Mtn
Dartry Mountains
Rossinver
Kiltyclogher
Enniskillen
Castle Coole
Tamlacht

Ardtermon Castle
Raghly
Carney
Drumcliff
Glencar Lough
Glenade Lough
Manorhamilton
N16
Upper Lough Macnean
Lower Lough Erne
Culky
Lisbellaw
Maguiresbridge
Carry Bridge

Sligo Bay
Aughris Head
Aughris
Rosses Point
Coney Island
Strandhill
Knocknarea
Sligo
Carrowmore
Parke's Castle
Gortahill
Blacklion
Bellanaleck
Wheathill
Mackan
Lisnaskea

Dromore West
Skreen
Knockalongy Mountain
Ballysodare
Coolaney
Colhooney
Creevelea Abbey
Dromahair
Lough Belhavel
L E I T R I M
Marble Arch Caves
Gubaveeny
Florence Court Forest Park
Florence Court
Culleagh Mountain
Upper Lough Erne

Moss Hill
Lavagh
Mullany's Cross
Achonry
Tobercurry
Ballymote
Castlebaldwin
Keshcorran Mountain
Derry
Carrowkeel
Riverstown
Drumkeeran
Lough Allen
Dowra
Glangevlin
Swanlinbar
Derrylin
Teemore

S L I G O
Owenmore River
Temple House Lough
R287
Ballyfarnon
Slieve Anierin
Arigna Mountains
Benbrack
Bawnboy
Ballyconnell

Banada
Kesh
4
Belturbet

World Cancer Research Fund

www.wcrf-uk.org

apples

carrots

PLACES WHERE MORRISES LIVE IN Co. MAYO.

FOXFORD
BALLYCASTLE
BALLYHAUNIS

CLAREMORRIS

KNOCK CLAREMORRIS

CHARLESTOWN
BALLY GLASS

HOLLYMOUNT

CASTLEBAR

~~KILER~~

BEKAN CROSS
WESTPORT

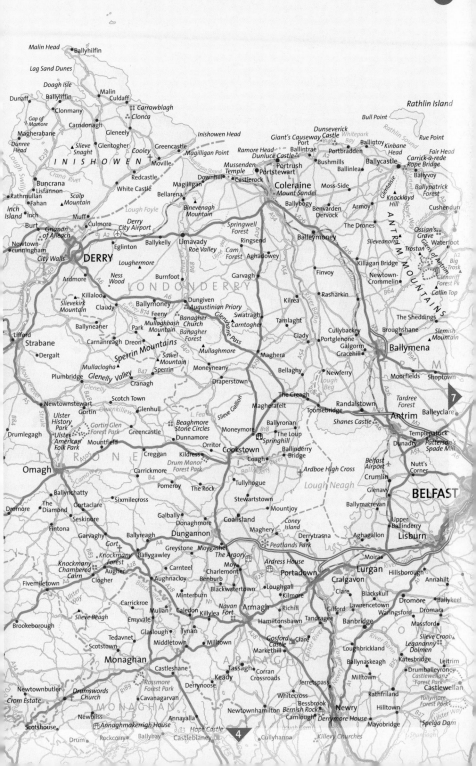

Mull of Kintyre

20km
10miles

Rathlin Island

Bull Point

Dunseverick Castle
Giant's Causeway
Port
Ramore Head
Dunluce Castle
Mussenden Temple
Downhill
Portstewart
Castlerock
Coleraine
Mount Sandel
Ballybogy
Portrush
Ballintrae
Portbradden
Bushmills
Ballinlea
Whitepark Bay
Ballintoy
Kinbane Head
Ballycastle
Carrick-a-rede Rope Bridge
Rue Point
Fair Head
Murlough Bay
Torr Head
Ballyvoy
Runabay Head
Ballypatrick Forest
Cushendun
Layde Church
Ossian's Grave
Red Bay
Waterfoot
Garron Point

Moss-Side
Armoy
Knocklayd Hill
Slieveanorra
Troston
Glens of Antrim
Big Trosk
Glenariff Forest Park
Carnlough
Carnlough Bay
Glenarm

Springwell Forest
Ringsend
Cam Forest
Aghadowey
Garvagh
Ballymoney
Benvarden
Dervock
The Drones
Killagan Bridge
Newtown-Crommelin
Collin Top

LONDONDERRY

Swatragh
Carntogher
Tamlaght
Kilrea
Rasharkin
The Sheddings
Broughshane
Slemish Mountain
Carnagee

Moneyneany
Draperstown
Maghera
Bellaghy
Clady
Portglenone
Galgorm
Gracehill
Ballymena
ANTRIM

Agnew's Hill
Ballygalley
Larne
Portmuck

The Creagh
Magherafelt
Newferry
Lough Beg
Moorfields
Shoptown
Millbrook
Glynn
Millbay
Island Magee

Ballyronan
Toomebridge
Randalstown
Tardree Forest
Ballyboley Forest
Ballynure
Glenoe
Larne Lough
The Gobbins

Moneymore
Springhill
The Loup
Ballinderry Bridge
Shanes Castle
Antrim
Ballyclare
Whitehead

Orritor
Cookstown
Coagh
Ballinderry Bridge
Templepatrick
Dunadry
Patterson's Spade Mill
Carrickfergus
Carrickfergus Castle
Liverpool
Douglas (Isle of Man)
Copeland Island

Tullyhogue
Ardboe High Cross
Lough Neagh
Belfast Airport
Crumlin
Nutt's Corner
Newtownabbey
Belfast Zoo
Cave Hill
Belfast Castle
Greenisland
Whiteabbey
Helen's Bay

Stewartstown
Mountjoy
Coney Island
Derrytrasna
Glenavy
Ballymacarrett
Upper Ballinderry
BELFAST
Belfast City Airport
Cultra
Bangor
Donaghadee
Millisle

TYRONE
Coalisland
Maghery
Peatlands Park
Aghagallon
Lisburn
Stormont Parliament House
Scrabo Hill
Movilla Abbey
Newtownards
Mount Stewart
Temple of the Winds

Dungannon
Moygashel
The Argory
Ardress House
Moiras
Giant's Ring
Ballylesson
Lagan Valley
Comber
Cunningburn
Grey Abbey
Ards Peninsula

Moy
Charlemont
Benburb
Blackwatertown
Portadown
Lurgan
Craigavon
Hillsborough
Carryduff
Ballygowan
Ardmullan
Nendrum Monastery
Balloo Crossroads
Kircubbin
Ringboy
Portavogie
Cloghy Bay

Navan Fort
Armagh
Loughgall
Kilmore
Richill
Clare
Blackskull
Annahilt
Baileysmill
Rowallane Gardens
Saintfield
Derryboye
Ardkeen
Cloghy

Killylea
Hamiltonsbawn
Tandragee
Gilford
Lawrencetown
Waringsford
Dromore
Ballykeel
Listooder
Crossgar
Delamont
Killyleagh
Audley's Castle
Portaferry
Kearney

Gosford Castle
Clare
Banbridge
Dromara
Ballynahinch
Crossgar
Loughmoney Dolmen
Quoile
Castle Ward
Strangford

Markethill
Loughbrickland
Massford
Slieve Croob
Drumaness
Inch Abbey
Saul
Struell Wells Church

Tassagh
Corran Crossroads
Ballynaskeagh
Drumballyroney
Katesbridge
Leganany Dolmen
Leitrim
Seaforde
Downpatrick
Ballynoe
Kilclief
Ballyquintin Point

Keady
Derrynoose
Jerretspass
Milltown
Rathfriland
Castlewellan Forest Park
Norman Castle
Tullymore Forest Park
Dundrum
Tyrella
Ballee
Killough
Ardglass

Newtownhamilton
Carrigatuke
Whitecross
Bessbrook
Bernish Rock
Camlough
Derrymore House
Hilltown
Castlewellan
Newcastle
Slieve Donard
Dundrum Bay

Hope Castle
Castleblaney
Cullyhanna
Slieve Gullion Forest Park
Mullaghbane
Tullymacreeve
Killevy Churches
Killevy
Newry
Mayobridge
Spelga Dam
Mourne Mountains
Silent Valley
Annalong

Broomfield
Crossmaglen
Creggan
Jonesborough
Forkhill
Warrenpoint
Narrow Water Castle
Omeath
Rostrevor
Dunmore

Cullaville
Mannan Castle
Inishkeen
Faughart
Ravensdale Forest
Slieve Foy Forest
Carlingford Mountain
Carlingford
King John's Castle
Greencastle
Kilkeel
Cranfield Point

Carrickmacross
Knockbridge
Dundalk
Cooley Peninsula
Cooley Point
Ballagan Point

LOUTH

NORTH CHANNEL
Belfast Lough
Strangford Lough
Cairnryan
Stranraer

WORKING
AND LIVING
ITALY

Kate Carlisle

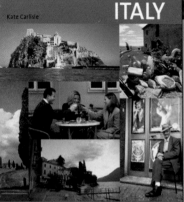

CADOGANguides

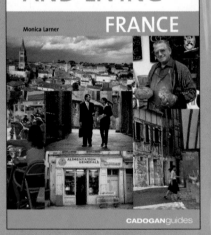

THE SUNDAY TIMES

WORKING
AND LIVING
FRANCE

Monica Larner

CADOGANguides

THE SUNDAY TIMES

WORKING
AND LIVING
SPAIN

Harvey Holtom

CADOGANguides

Also available:

WORKING AND LIVING
PORTUGAL

CADOGANguides